D1084286

A RUSSIAN ADVOCATE OF PEACE:
VASILII MALINOVSKII (1765–1814)

ARCHIVES INTERNATIONALES D'HISTOIRE DES IDÉES

INTERNATIONAL ARCHIVES OF THE HISTORY OF IDEAS

156

A RUSSIAN ADVOCATE OF PEACE: VASILII MALINOVSKII (1765–1814)

by

PAOLA FERRETTI

A RUSSIAN ADVOCATE OF PEACE: VASILII MALINOVSKII (1765–1814)

by

PAOLA FERRETTI

University of Rome, "La Sapienza"

KLUWER ACADEMIC PUBLISHERS

DORDRECHT / BOSTON / LONDON

A C.I.P. Catalogue record for this book is available from the Library of Congress.

ISBN 0-7923-4848-6

Published by Kluwer Academic Publishers,
P.O. Box 17, 3300 AA Dordrecht, The Netherlands.

Sold and distributed in the U.S.A. and Canada
by Kluwer Academic Publishers,
101 Philip Drive, Norwell, MA 02061, U.S.A.

In all other countries, sold and distributed
by Kluwer Academic Publishers,
P.O. Box 322, 3300 AH Dordrecht, The Netherlands.

Printed on acid-free paper

Printed in the Netherlands

To Daniele

CONTENTS

PREFACE

Vasilii Fedorovich Malinovskii (1765-1814) is a name which has hitherto lacked true resonance in the history of Russian culture. It is of course a name known to all students of Alexander Pushkin's biography, for Malinovskii was the first Director of the new Tsarskoe Selo Lyceum, if, sadly, for only the first three of the young poet's years at the school. For those scholars conversant with the intellectual and literary life of the "beautiful beginning" of the reign of Alexander I's reign Malinovskii has his little niche for his remarkable *Rassuzhdenie o mire i voine* (1803) and less for his *Osennie vechera* (1803), a little-known journal limited to a mere eight weekly issues and written entirely by the editor. As regards the 'eighteenth-century' Malinovskii, who lived the first thirty-five years of his life predominantly in the reign of the great Catherine, little information encumbers the memory of even specialists of the period. Indeed, his elder brother, Aleksei Fedorovich (1762-1840), is the more likely to be remembered for his literary and translating work as well for his later position as Head of the Moscow Archive of the Ministry of Foreign Affairs, which brought him into contact with Pushkin and, not unexpectedly, with Karamzin. Karamzin referred to him as "one of my few old and genuine friends", but one searches in vain for a similar accolade for Vasilii Fedorovich. Indeed, Karamzin's works, including his correspondence, would seem devoid of references to a man who, nevertheless, had so much in common with him, not least in their younger days.

Malinovskii does in fact appear in Karamzin's work, in his famous *Pis'ma russkogo puteshestvennika*, which reflects the momentous journey he made through Germany, Switzerland, France, and England in 1789-90. It is precisely in the letters from England (not published, incidentally, until the beginning of the nineteenth century) that Malinovskii is to be found, hidden under the initial M*. At that period of his life Malinovskii was at the Russian Embassy in London and met many visiting Russians, including Karamzin. It was with Karamzin that he spent time in the summer of 1790, sharings outings and ideas. That summer Malinovskii finished the writing of the first part of his treatise on peace and war at Richmond, the country home of the Russian Ambassador, Count Semen Vorontsov, and it was also that summer that Karamzin at a dinner in the home of Alexander Baxter, the Russian Consul, proposed a toast to "eternal peace and thriving trade".

Unlike Karamzin's *Pis'ma*, which began to appear in his *Moskovskii zhurnal* already in 1791 and brought him instant fame, Malinovskii's writings from these and subsequent years were, even when published, unrecognized as his and thus brought him no literary reputation. Only in recent years has Malinovskii, for instance, been recognized as the author of the travel letters from England and Scotland which were published under the title 'Rossiianin v Anglii' in the journal *Priiatnoe i poleznoe preprovozhdenie vremeni* (1796) and of the 'Zapiski o Moldavii', appearing there the following year and reflecting his first isit to Moldavia soon after his return from England. The observations of the 'Rossiianin' about England have long been recognized as among the most acute penned by Russian visitors in the eighteenth century and affording interesting parallels with Karamzin's letters, but they take on new stature and significance within the canon of Malinovskii's writings.

Only in 1958 was the first serious attempt made by the Soviet scholar E.A. Arab-Ogly to provide both a selection of Malinovskii's work, published and unpublished, and a detailed account of his life and career. It was a notable event but it was only a beginning, only a glance, however informed and valuable, into the events of Malinovskii's life and into the world of his ideas. It was a 'zakuska', a prelude to the main dish, for which, however, so many ingredients were still lacking. Paola Ferretti has changed all this and has produced the study that was needed of this most attractive and in so many ways most modern thinker.

It was my good fortune that Ms Ferretti chose to come to Cambridge to study for her doctorate under my supervision in the autumn of 1990. It was the "English element" in my researches that had first brought me to

Malinovskii and it now brought Ms Ferretti to me, exactly two hundred years after the meeting of Karamzin and Malinovskii on English soil. She was a pleasure to supervise. Her research was thorough and the discoveries she made were many and important. It is also a tribute to her talents as a linguist as well as a scholar that she has written her book in English, which will perhaps bring both its author and Malinovskii the wide recognition they undoubtedly deserve.

Anthony Cross
Professor of Slavonic Studies at the University of Cambridge and
Fellow of the British Academy

ACKNOWLEDGEMENTS

This book is a revised version of my Ph.D. thesis, which I completed at the University of Cambridge under the supervision of Anthony Cross.

I was first introduced to the figure of Vasilii Malinovskii by E.A. Arab-Ogly, during a conversation which took place in Moscow in March 1988. Arab-Ogly, who was the editor of a selection of Malinovskii's works published in 1958, drew my attention to the relevance of his legacy to the history of Russian thought. My idea of introducing to the Italian public his most significant work, the *Dissertation on Peace and War*, resulted from this conversation. I had the opportunity to present an Italian translation of Malinovskii's work, which included the integral edition of his major opus, at an international conference on peace studies held in Naples in 1990. During the conference the significance of Malinovskii and his work were discussed by Arab-Ogly, invited for the occasion, and by Riccardo Picchio, who was to give me important advice regarding the direction in which it would be useful to point my future research. Luigi Cortesi, who organized the conference and supported the preparation of the Italian edition of Malinovskii's work, also encouraged me to pursue my research on this thinker and his ideas on peace in particular.

During my Ph.D. research I had the opportunity to work with Anthony Cross, who from the very beginning showed a genuine interest and enthusiasm in the subject of my thesis. He generously provided much-needed encouragement, valued counsel and scholarly information, which it is my pleasure to acknowledge here. Working with him was an enriching and challenging experience.

I also wish to express my gratitude to Simon Franklin for his constructive remarks after my first year of research. A paper I presented on Malinovskii at a research seminar in the Department of Slavonic Studies of the University of Cambridge brought very helpful comments and suggestions. In Cambridge I could also rely on the efficiency and courtesy of the staff of the University Library and of the Library of the Faculty of Modern and Medieval Languages.

In his letters from Berlin Michael Schippan provided a number of suggestions for the analysis of Malinovskii's ideas on peace. I am also grateful to William Butler and to Jerzy Skowronek, who gave me some advice on relevant matters. My conversations with Roger Bartlett proved particularly fruitful for the establishment of Malinovskii's contribution to the debate on serf emancipation. In Italy I benefitted from the help and advice of Michele Colucci.

A turning point in the process of writing this work was represented by my meeting with a direct descendant of the Russian thinker, Nataliia Borisovna Meshkova-Malinovskaia. From her I received valuable concrete help in obtaining materials relevant to my work and an illuminating insight into the world of the Malinovskii's family through their various generations. The restoration of her ancestor's importance had become the main direction in which Nataliia Borisovna channelled her inexhaustible energies before her premature death. I regret that she cannot read the fruits of my research.

Liudmila Borisovna Mikhailova, of the Muzei-Litsei of Tsarskoe Selo, was also indispensable for my work on Malinovskii. Her familiarity with the life of the Director of the first Russian Lycée and with his manuscripts, which she developed over a number of years of research, represented an important point of reference for me.

My thanks are also due to the staffs of the Saltykov-Shchedrin Public Library in St Petersburg and of RGADA and RGALI in Moscow. Svetlana Romanovna Dolgova provided important assistance on a subject in which she was personally interested. I am grateful to the assistants in the Archive of the Institute of Russian Literature (Pushkinskii dom) in general and to Natal'ia Dmitrievna Kochetkova in particular for their kindness and help. I also had much assistance from Leonid Matveevich Arinshtein and from Irina Iur'eva.

In Kiev I benefitted from the friendly welcome of the Ukrainian Academy of Science, particularly in the person of Aleksei Sidorenko, and from the kindness of the staff working in the Central History Archive of Ukraina.

My English prose immensely benefitted from the patient and careful revision of Anthony Cross. Translating Malinovskii's quotations from

Russian into English would have been impossible for me without the help of Nicola Murphy, which it is my pleasure to acknowledge.

For intellectual assistance on perpetual peace projects, logistic support and first aid with word processing, I have to thank Daniele Archibugi.

My Ph.D. work was financed by annual grants awarded by the Italian Ministry for University and Scientific Research. During the course of my research in Russia I benefitted from financial support from the Worts Travelling Scholars Fund, the Finley Bursary Scheme, the Research Awards for Overseas Students in the Humanities and Social Sciences, and the BUAS-NASEES Joint Research and Development Committee.

Versions of parts of individual chapters of this book have appeared separately: 'V.F. Malinovskii and his «Rassuzhdenie o mire i voine»' was published on the *Study Group on Eighteenth-Century Russia Newsletter*, no. 21 (1993) as a synopsis of the paper presented in January 1993 at the annual meeting of the Study Group; a paper entitled '«Razdelenie zemel'»: a Proposal Against the Servile System by V.F. Malinovskii', was presented at the Fifth International Conference of the Study Group on Eighteenth-Century Russia and published in M. di Salvo, L. Hughes (eds.), *A Window on Russia: Papers from the V International Conference of the Study Group on Eighteenth-Century Russia. Gargnano 1994* (Rome, 1996), pp. 107-113; the article 'A «Rossijanin v Anglii» in 1789-1791: V.F. Malinovskij', appeared in *Russica Romana*, no. 2 (1995), pp. 83-109.

A RUSSIAN ADVOCATE OF PEACE:

VASILII MALINOVSKII (1765-1814)

INTRODUCTION

Vasilii Fedorovich Malinovskii represents one of the most significant voices on the Russian cultural scene between the end of the eighteenth and the beginning of the nineteenth centuries. His passionate concern for political and social questions was constantly inspired by a belief in the primacy of reason and morality in the conduct of individuals and societies and by the rejection of a number of cultural conventions characteristic of his age. He left posterity a rich and original body of thought, condensed in a few hundred pages, many of them still unpublished. His published work appeared in those crucial years between the French Revolution and the defeat of Napoleon, and exerted an influence on the successive development of Russian thought which is yet to be recognized in its true proportions.

Despite his undoubted importance, Malinovskii has been long neglected. The history of his fate is the history of the three separate identities in which he, as it were, has been frequently divided: the first Director of the Tsarskoe Selo Lycée, the author of proposals for social and administrative reforms in Russia, and the creator of a plan for the establishment of perpetual peace in Europe. Very rarely communicating with each other, these three identities were inevitably outlined with a high degree of partiality and lacked the necessary integration. The fact that the majority of Malinovskii's works remained until very recent years in manuscript form did not favour an overall consideration of his opus.

The name of Malinovskii acquired an undoubted popularity in the histories of the celebrated «first Russian Lycée», one of the most important institutions for the development of Russian liberal thought. At Tsarskoe Selo Pushkin and some of the Decembrists were to achieve their education. Official historiography of nineteenth century has given posterity, however, a deliberately misleading portrayal of the first Director as a timid, dreamy and somewhat opportunistic figure, substantially leaving no trace in the education of the young *litseisty*, especially when compared with the more influential role attributed to the subsequent Director, E.A. Engel'gardt[1]. Only in contemporary works on the Lycée an attempt to reverse this view can be observed, without a significant effort, nevertheless, to corroborate the different evaluation of the Director's activity with solid references to the works of the thinker and the reformer.

The fortune of the author of projects of social reforms was chronologically and ideologically limited to a very short moment: at the end of the nineteenth century the historian V. Semevskii inserted Malinovskii's proposal on land property in the context of the debate on serf emancipation; not familiar with his remaining works, however, he dismissed Malinovskii's real importance and the wider impact for the future of the country of the policies suggested by him. Ignorance of the proposals elaborated by the Russian thinker concerning the solution of the Jewish question, universal education and other aspects of contemporary society also influenced Semevskii's consideration of the constitutional reforms contained in Malinovskii's diary of 1803, first published by him in 1915. After Semevskii, Malinovskii's plans were more or less consigned to oblivion.

As the author of the *Dissertation on Peace and War*, Malinovskii received attention characterized above all by the attempt to regard his work on a European level, neglecting the implications of his thought for the transformation of Russian society and overevaluating his debt to the West in the elaboration of the plan at the expenses of its original features. The first European echo of Malinovskii's treatise appeared in the *Herald of Peace* in 1858, when Professor D.I. Kachenovskii introduced to the public of the London Peace Society «this curious work», pointing out nevertheless that «Mr. Mahnofsky's (*sic*) views deserve the attention of this Society and of all the Christian world. His name can be mentioned with the names of St. Pierre, Kant, Bentham, and of others, enemies of war»[2]. The first West European consideration of his contribution to the international debate on

---

[1] It should be noted however that there were more interesting developments in the field of fiction inspired by Pushkin. Initially attracted by the figure of Malinovskii as Director of the Lycée, Tynianov was probably the first author to give a general projection of his figure in the light he deserved (Iu. Tynianov, *Pushkin* (Moskva, 1937)).

[2] D.I. Kachenovskii, 'Dissertation on War and Peace by Basil Mahnofsky (*sic*), St. Petersburgh, 1803', *The Herald of Peace* (1 June 1858), pp. 71-72.

war and peace came nevertheless only in 1988, with a study by W. Butler devoted to his treatise[3].

The European context was also considered the most congenial for Malinovskii's treatise in a few recent Russian works: the first two parts of his *Dissertation* were re-published in 1963 alongside the major European plans for perpetual peace[4] and studied in 1987 in the widest context of speculation on peace and war in Europe[5]. In 1978 Part III of the treatise was first published by J. Skowronek[6]. Consideration of Malinovskii's parallel contribution to the development of Russian social thought received, on the other hand, a very marginal treatment in these works.

There are two valuable exceptions to this picture of Malinovskii's fortune: the work of B. Meilakh and that of E.A. Arab-Ogly, both appearing in 1958. In the few pages devoted to Malinovskii in his *Pushkin i ego epokha* Meilakh provided the first recognition of him in his true perspective, concluding however that «the interesting question of Malinovskii's world outlook waits for its researcher: when that has been done another page of the history of social life at the end of eighteenth and the beginning of the nineteenth centuries will be written»[7].

The invitation issued by Meilakh was to coincide with Arab-Ogly's work[8], which appeared in the same year, following a previous study on the Russian thinker[9]. In the introduction to the first re-publication of Malinovskii's treatise and other articles, consideration of the main features of his *Dissertation on Peace and War* was integrated with evaluation of his concrete attempts to reform existing institutions in Russian society and completed with references to his activity as organizer of life at the Tsarskoe Selo Lycée.

---

[3] W.E. Butler, 'Law and Peace in Prerevolutionary Russia: the Case of V.F. Malinovskii', in J. Witte, F.S. Alexander (eds.), *The Weightier Matters of the Law* (Atlanta, 1988), pp. 163-175.

[4] I.S. Andreeva, A.V. Gulyga (eds.), *Traktaty o vechnom mire* (Moskva, 1963).

[5] A.O. Chubar'ian, *Evropeiskaia ideia v istorii. Problemy voiny i mira* (Moskva, 1987).

[6] J. Skowronek,'"Rozwazania o pokoju i wojnie" Wasyla F. Malinowskiego', *Teki archiwalne*, no. 17 (1978), pp. 30-57.

[7] B. Meilakh, *Pushkin i ego epokha* (Moskva, 1958) p. 31.

[8] E.A. Arab-Ogly, 'Vydaiushchiisia russkii prosvetitel'', in V.F. Malinovskii, *Izbrannye obshchestvenno-politicheskie sochineniia*, ed. E.A. Arab-Ogly (Moskva, 1958), pp. 3-38.

[9] E.A. Arab-Ogly, 'Vydaiushchiisia russkii prosvetitel'-demokrat' (K 150-letiiu vykhoda v svet "Rassuzhdeniia o mire i voine"), *Voprosy filosofii*, no. 2 (1954), pp. 181-197.

In an attempt to reverse the previous vague definitions of Malinovskii as a «*chudak-patsifist*» (an eccentric pacifist) or a «*kabinetnyi mechtatel'*» (a dreamer closed in his study), both authors radicalized nevertheless Malinovskii's views, applying with a certain rigidity the scheme of Marxist-Leninist interpretation to a figure who was in fact more rich and complex. The orientation towards proclaiming Malinovskii a potential revolutionary reflected a more general interest in the period between Radishchev and the Decembrists as an unexplored and rewarding field in the search for revolutionary ancestry which absorbed Soviet criticism in those years[10].

The present book is aimed at offering a detailed analysis of Malinovskii's activity in the three different fields mentioned above. Showing the deep interdependence and reciprocal influence of these different sides, it also attempts to propose an understanding of his figure based on their reintegration. The importance of Malinovskii's social philosophy in the elaboration of his plan for perpetual peace is in fact immense. It is the fusion of a passionate desire for peace with concrete proposals for its attainment and a reasoned programme of necessary social reforms that distinguishes Malinovskii's contribution to the history of Russian progressive thinking. He conceived his peaceful states within the context of a reformed Europe, and proposed a number of changes for its institutions. The Russian domestic situation needed a no less radical re-organization, which was drafted by Malinovskii in different works. Considering the importance he attached to education in modelling a better society, it is understandable that he came to consider his appointment as Lycée Director as the moment in which he was closest to the realization of a part of his programme.

This book is also aimed at redefining Malinovskii's ideological profile from a more balanced perspective. His figure shows in fact many features of a typical enlightened liberal. He attached an unquestionable importance to problems of a spiritual and religious nature, a fact which was virtually ignored in Soviet works. Far from being a defender of absolutist ideology, Malinovskii believed in constitutional monarchy; he embodied nevertheless the most progressive developments of Russian moderate liberalism, placing an important stress on the welfare of all strata of Russian population and being constantly inspired by a genuine love for freedom and progress.

---

[10] See M. Raeff, 'Filling the Gap between Radishchev and the Decembrists', *Slavic Review*, XXVI, no. 3 (1967), pp. 395-413.

Malinovskii relied on the fundamental role of a sovereign to establish a political life governed by just rules respectful of the rights of the people in all fields of the social life. In all his works he described nevertheless a quite ideal model of the political ruler. On Peter the Great he implicitly recognized the objective merit of having introduced Russia to the path of progress and modernity. While personally he experienced only the growing conservatism characterizing the reign of Catherine II after the French Revolution, in subsequent years he pointed out that the process of reform was to continue along the lines indicated by the Empress. As regards Alexander I, Malinovskii certainly shared the optimistic expectations of freedom and prosperity following the accession to the throne of the young Emperor, and indeed took advantage of that atmosphere, but he never praised him with any particular enthusiasm (even before his reactionary change after 1815).

In fact, none of these monarchs corresponded to his ideal of the tsar of a peaceful and well-ordered Russia and was never the object of a panegyric on Malinovskii's side. The ideal ruler imagined by the thinker, moved by a desire to acquire glory as a just legislator and determined impartially to promote the general welfare, never appeared on the political scene of Russia. During his lifetime Malinovskii witnessed the regular disappointment of promises of major changes made by the Russian rulers. This did not lead, nevertheless, to a weakening of his views on political and social problems. The transition from the ideals of the eighteenth century to the struggle for reforms by the Decembrists and its subsequent developments was embodied in Malinovskii's personal life and activity more significantly than in any other figure of his time.

This book represents the first monograph on Malinovskii. It will be structured in two parts. The first will be focused on a study of Malinovskii's life, while the second will be divided into three chapters devoted to the different aspects of his activity: the work of the peace thinker, of the social reformer and of the pedagogue will be examined in each of them.

The appearance of a number of new primary sources, anonymously published or unpublished, made it essential to devote a prominent place in the book to retracing his biography in the light of the information they contained. This choice reflects the need to achieve a more complete picture of the events and moments characterizing the life of the Russian thinker. The extant information about Malinovskii was in fact fragmentary and offered highly unequal coverage of the different periods of his life. On the basis of an examination of archival materials of a private and official nature, on the one hand, and of works only recently attributed to him, on the other, an attempt will be made to offer a picture of Malinovskii's life without any significant lacuna.

An important contribution came in this respect particularly from the establishment of Malinovskii's authorship of two travel accounts appearing on the pages of a Moscow journal in 1796 and 1797: the series of letters entitled 'Rossianin v Anglii' and 'Zapiski iz Moldavii'. The presence of Malinovskii at the Russian Embassy in London in 1789-1791 did not escape the attention of A.G. Cross, who placed him in the context of Anglo-Russian relations at the end of the eighteenth century on the one hand and provided evidence of his personal contacts with Karamzin in London on the other[11]. The attribution to Malinovskii of the report from England adds important elements to the picture of his sojourn in that country and sheds new light on the works elaborated during that period.

Reconstruction of factual events will be accompanied by an interpretation of their significance in Malinovskii's intellectual and spiritual evolution and in the context of contemporary Russia. The peculiarities of his figure will however be illuminated also in the course of the investigation of the three sides of his activity.

In the second chapter I will explore Malinovskii's treatment of the themes of war and peace. He was not the only thinker of the Napoleonic era to address this theme, neither was he the most important one, on a European level. But his reflections are significant in that they are the most broadly and articulately ever expressed by a Russian. His *Dissertation* will be analyzed in the context of the Russian tradition of speculation on peace and compared with the European models of perpetual peace projects.

In the third chapter I will examine Malinovskii's programme of social reforms. His preoccupation to serve «human happiness» particularly reflected in his proposals to solve one the crucial problems affecting contemporary Russia, that of serfdom. His ideas on serf emancipation will be analyzed on the basis of the four works he devoted to this question.

The fourth chapter will be an investigation of Malinovskii's role in the birth and organization of the Tsarskoe Selo Lycée, the school which was to

---

[11] See A.G. Cross, *"By the Banks of the Thames": Russians in Eighteenth-Century Britain* (Newtonville, Mass., 1980), pp. 32-33, and 'Whose Initials? Unidentified Persons in Karamzin's Letters from England', *Study Group on Eighteenth-Century Russia Newsletter*, no. 6 (1978), pp. 26-36.

gain the reputation of the most «revolutionary» educational institution in nineteenth-century Russia. It will be aimed at restoring the real contribution given by its first Director to the establishment of the «spirit of the Lycée» on the basis of an analysis of his ideas on education and an examination of how they were embodied in the life of the Lycée. A section will be devoted to a particular subject: Malinovskii's influence on the Lycée's most famous pupil, Aleksandr Pushkin.

Malinovskii's statements will be abundantly quoted in the course of the research, partly because of the necessity to give space to new documentary and literary materials illuminating his life and work, and partly for the obvious reason that Malinovskii's ideas are better expressed in his own voice.

CHAPTER 1: AN INTELLECTUAL BIOGRAPHY

Malinovskii's contemporaries knew very little about him. Few were aware of his constant and untiring search for ways to implement his projects for social and political reform. An examination of the development of Malinovskii's professional career leaves the impression that he was just one more among the innumerable, zealous bureaucrats in the service of the Russian empire of the late 18th and early 19th centuries: he was transferred from one state office to the next, and although his professional capabilities were appreciated, they did not lead to any significant promotion.

Recognition of Malinovskii and his significance as a thinker came not in his lifetime but only in the twentieth century, when the first substantial studies on him and his work were published, fulfilling the prophecy contained in one of the letters he wrote towards the end of his life:

> It is a great consolation to me, that books commemorating me have been selected: they alone can sometimes justify my character and present in the best light the life-style and qualities of a person, whose misfortune it is not to have the means to realise his good desires nor to demonstrate in practice the truth of his convictions, that the aspirations of the whole of one's life should be to benefit not only one's contemporaries, but also one's descendants[1].

In tracing his biography, we will observe how Malinovskii's experience, although limited, informed his thinking on many social and philosophical problems. We will follow him from his service in the

---

[1] Letter to A.A. Samborskii, published in V.F. Malinovskii, *Izbrannye obshchestvenno-politicheskie sochineniia*, ed. E.A. Arab-Ogly (Moskva, 1958), pp. 154-155.

Kollegiia inostrannykh del (College of Foreign Affairs), in the very heart
of the Russian empire and of administrative St Petersburg, to his service in
the diplomatic mission in London, where his perception of the problems is
broadened, becomes universal and acquires the utopian features
characterizing his major work, the *Rassuzhdenie o mire i voine*
(Dissertation on Peace and War). During the period spent in Jassy, beyond
the extreme periphery of the empire, Malinovskii had the opportunity to
concentrate on more immediate social problems affecting Russia, which
were to be reflected later in his work as a journalist. After long years of
faithful, unrewarded service, he moved from the antechambers of great
foreign politics to the corridors of the most promising Lycée in Russia in
the first quarter of the nineteenth century, and thereby acquired a unique
opportunity to influence a group of intelligent young men with his vision of
the world. He became an important point of reference for these pupils who
came from different social backgrounds and were groomed to be the future
leaders of Russian society. He served as Director for only two years, dying
at the age of forty nine, with so much still to accomplish. Among the papers
and materials unpublished at his death, we find an article about the removal
of Jews to a new land, entitled 'Uteshenie dshcheri iudeiskoi', an 'Istoriia
Rossii dlia prostykh i malykh', articles of an historical, religious and
political nature, translations from French, German and English
philosophers, and various other materials.

1.1. Spiritual and Intellectual Formation (1765-1789)

1.1.1. Family history

The family into which Vasilii Fedorovich was born, on 18 July 1765,
was of noble and ancient lineage[2]. As witnessed in an eighteenth-century

---

[2] Personal documents record how as early as 1041 the family name of Malinovskii,
thanks to exemplary Christian virtues, was adorned with the title of «Pobozh'» (A.A.
Rubets, «*Nastavnikam, khranivshim iunost' nashu*». *Pamiatnaia knizhka chinov
imperatorskogo Aleksandrovskogo, byvshego tsarskosel'skogo, litseia. S 1811 po 1911
god* (Spb., 1911), p. 194). A confirmation of this origin is found in a recent extensive
biographical study devoted to the figure of Aleksei Fedorovich and based mainly on archival
materials, where we find valuable information about Malinovskii's family: S. Dolgova,
'Aleksei Fedorovich Malinovskii', in A.F. Malinovskii, *Obozrenie Moskvy*, ed. S.
Dolgova (Moskva, 1992); see particularly p. 183.

document, from the Polish and Lithuanian areas their forbears had spread in different directions[3]. Vasilii Fedorovich's direct ancestors came from the stock which had settled down in the principality of Smolensk.

According to a custom which was not unusual among the Little Russian gentry, the noble origin of the Malinovskii did not prevent the male members of the family from embracing, in the eighteenth century, an ecclesiastic career, as a decorous escape from an economic condition which could not have been too prosperous.

The name of Vasilii Fedorovich's grandfather and that of his father were linked to the history of the religious institution where they served in Moscow, the Trinity Church (Troitskaia tserkov'), an ancient church situated on the left hand of the Samotechnyi Pond (now disappeared), and re-built in stone in 1688[4]. In 1722 Malinovskii's grandfather, Avksentii Filippovich (1698-1765) became the priest of that church; there he served, as its respected and caring «*nastoiatel'*» (Dean), for the rest of his life. When he died, he left his son as the head of the church. Vasilii Fedorovich's father, Fedor Avksent'evich (1738-1811), had received his education in the Slavonic-Greek-Latin Academy. In 1765 he became «*nastoiatel'*» of the Trinity Church, and in 1766 was appointed its archpriest by Archbishop Platon. His wife, Anna Nikolaevna Arsen'eva (1744-1778), was the mother of six children: Aleksei, Vasilii, Pavel, Paraskeva, Elizaveta and Natal'ia[5]. Beloved by his parishioners for his personal qualities[6], Fedor Avksent'evich was a man of a strong and peculiar personality, whose interests were not strictly circumscribed by the spiritual life, and who enjoyed friendly relations with some of the most interesting figures of Catherinian Russia. He was very close to the Pushkin family, who lived next to the Trinity Church: for the children of Lev Aleksandrovich Pushkin (grandfather of the famous poet) he became very soon the spiritual father[7]; when Count

---

Other secondary sources used for the biography are: V. Semevskii, 'Razmyshlenie V.F. Malinovskogo o preobrazovanii gosudarstvennogo ustroistva Rossii', *Golos minuvshego*, no. 10 (1915), pp. 239-264; D. Kobeko, 'Pervyi direktor tsarskosel'skogo litseia', *Zhurnal Ministerstva narodnogo prosveshchenia*, no. 7 (1915), pp. 3-17.

[3] See Dolgova, *op.cit.*, p. 183.

[4] For more detailed information on this church, see I. Orlov, *Istoricheskoe opisanie Moskovskoi Troitskoi tserkvi* (Moskva, 1844).

[5] Elizaveta was to marry the Reverend of Orenburg Ivan Andreevich Polianskii, Natal'ia Pavel Afanas'evich Sokhatskii.

[6] He was described as characterized by «blagorazumnaia sniskhoditel'nost', krotost', terpenie, iskrenniaia dobrozhelatel'nost'», see I. Orlov, *op.cit.*, p. 93.

[7] The connections between the two families were to last for decades: Aleksei Fedorovich's daughter, Ekaterina, was a close friend of Natal'ia Goncharova; one of Pushkin's best friends in the Lycée was Ivan Vasil'evich, son of Vasilii Fedorovich, and

N.P. Sheremetev was given a son by the peasant he had married, Fedor
Avksent'evich was one of the first Russians to have knowledge of this
unusual event in the strict society of the eighteenth century, and to provide
spiritual assistance to the count when his wife died; he was also intimate
with other eminent Muscovites close to the Trinity Church, like the Vice-
Chancellor I.A. Osterman and Professor M.M. Snegirev. He was to be in
charge of the Trinity Church until the time when «the dark calumny of base
people found its way to the Archbishop»[8]; he was obliged to leave that
church and was transferred, in 1798, to the Tatianinskaia tserkov'[9], which
served Moscow University.

   The «calumny» that cost him his post was connected with a
controversial aspect of his life: Fedor Avksent'evich's supposed
involvement with Novikov's activity. His name figured in fact among
Novikov's possible «*edinomyshlenniki*» (sympathizers) at his interrogation
in Schlüsselburg in 1792[10], and thanks to this evidence he has often been
considered one of the few mason «*sviashchenniki*» (priests) of eighteenth-
century Russia. If in general we are able to refer to Fedor Avksent'evich as
to one of the central figures in Vasilii's early formation, it seems difficult
to evaluate to what extent the inclination towards Freemasonry of the father
might have fostered a similar attitude in him.

   Son and grandson of archpriests, Vasilii Fedorovich did not embrace
an ecclesiastical career, but in his attempts to pursue, with varied success,
different vocations (those of political and social reformer, philanthropist,
pedagogue), he was always influenced by the strong ethical background
provided by his father's teaching. Malinovskii seems particularly indebted
to him for certain ideas that were echoed several times in his subsequent
writings: the commitment to the need for education, the idea of individual
responsibility in the improvement of society, the impulse towards the search
for eternity.

---

after the Director's death Pushkin's historical interests brought him to visit frequently the
house of Aleksei Fedorovich. For a detailed picture of these connections, see Dolgova,
op.cit., pp. 199-207.

   [8] Orlov, *op.cit.*, p. 93.

   [9] See N. Rozanov, *O Tatianinskoi tserkvi imperatorskogo Moskovskogo
universiteta*, I (Moskva, 1869).

   [10] See M.N. Longinov, *Novikov i moskovskie martinisty* (Moskva, 1867). In the
account of Novikov's answers when interrogated about the masonic membership of certain
persons, we find: «He also pleads ignorance regarding A.A. Rzhevskii and the priest
Malinovskii's membership of the Masons» (p. 327). Fedor Avksent'evich is recorded as a
possible Freemason in G.V. Vernadskii, *Russkoe Masonstvo v tsarstvovanie Ekateriny II*
(Petrograd, 1917), pp. 11-12.

In 1813, two years after Fedor Avksent'evich's death, the sermons delivered by him on various occasions as *«nastoiatel'»* of the University church were gathered and published in Moscow[11]. Reading them we gain a comprehensive picture of his spiritual and intellectual personality, in which the religious principles of Russian Orthodoxy fuse quite harmoniously with the values of the philosophy of the Enlightenment. In his capacity as religious educator of the University alumni, he did not fail to stress the concept that in the process of knowledge the achievements of reason must be accompanied and justified by faith. By constantly using expressions like *«pomoshch' razuma»* (the help of reason), *«uspekhi razuma chelovecheskogo»* (the achievement of reason), *«prosveshchenie razuma»* (the enlightenment of reason), however, he emphasized the role of reason in the formation of pupils. If «true enlightenment springs from God»[12], his concern was to instill in the young minds whose spiritual welfare he was called to look after the idea of establishing the appropriate equilibrium between the two elements: «And as soon as the thirst for knowledge dares to overstep the limit set by God's law, the lamp of reason invariably goes out»[13]. He warned the students about the negative consequences of their failure to reach that fruitful combination of *«premudrost'»* (wisdom) and *«blagochestie»* (piety): «Friends of true Christian enlightenment, sons of the Fatherland will reproach you with a vain waste of time and effort, which you have spent on acquiring knowledge which has not brought either you or society the least benefit»[14]. The idea of an *«obshchestvennaia sviaz'»* (link with society) as a necessary duty for the authentic Christian is one of the recurrent features in his teaching[15].

It is in Vasilii Fedorovich's family, therefore, that the first, fruitful seeds for the elaboration of his own vision of the world are to be found, especially concerning the ethical nature of his social commitment.

---

[11] *Izbrannye poucheniia iunosham, v Imperatorskom Moskovskom Universitete vospityvaiushchimsia, govorennye (...) Fedorom Malinovskim* (Moskva, 1813). The first of the sermons published there, *Slovo o nerazryvnoi sviazi istinnogo ...* had been published separately in 1798; in 1799 was published his *Slovo pri pogrebenii tainogo sovetnika, senatora... Pavla Mikhailova Kozlova.*

[12] *Izbrannye poucheniia iunosham...*, p. 2.

[13] *Ibid.*, pp. 4-5.

[14] *Ibid.*, p. 10.

[15] It is particularly apparent in a sermon permeated by civic virtue and entitled 'Ob otnosheniiakh pravoslaviia Khristianskago k obshchestvennomu blagopoluchiiu', where the effort to conceive the faith as deeply rooted in the commitment to the welfare of the entire society carries important implications also for political life: «Christian teaching perfectly favours and promotes the benefits of good government among all peoples» (*ibid.*, p. 39).

1.1.2. Early years and University

Vasilii's early years were characterized by a pronounced inclination for reading; his own description of his first reading experiences shows an interesting combination of religious books and texts of the literature of the Enlightenment:

> When I had learnt the Kiev primer and the Psalter from cover to cover, I began to write: a man stands in water up to his throat and asks for drink and cannot slake his thirst; and soon after I found myself in a glorious school. Then I thought, I am a pupil. I began to read books, and the first book which I came upon after the Psalter was Candide or the Optimist. Voltaire[16] is the reason why I, absolutely contrary to the intention of this book of his, think to this very day, that everything in the world is for the best. After the Optimist I remember I read the Russian chronicler, called the Sinopsis[17]. Thanks to this book I came to love the Great Prince Dmitrii Ivanovich Donskoi, who liberated Russia from the Tatars (...) Among the books I had as a pupil was a book called «Kratkoe poniatie o vsekh naukakh»[18]; in this book I found that man is a literary animal (...) I read assiduously (...) Books taught me also that man is not only highly reasonable, but also highly sensible[19].

Rousseau must also have had a place among his favourite authors, as he refers later to his *Emile and Sophie* [20] as to the book that he used to read «always with exceptional pleasure»[21].

Vasilii, the «*razumnoi mal'chik*» (the reasonable boy)[22], had also discovered very soon that his passion for reading was illuminated by an unusual ethical pathos, which was to remain unaltered for the rest of his life:

---

[16] The first Russian translation of Voltaire's *Candide*, on the initiative of Catherine II, was published in St Petersburg in 1769, translated by S. Bashilov.

[17] *Sinopsis, ili Kratkoe opisanie ot razlichnykh letopistsev o nachale Slaviano-Rossiiskogo naroda, i pervonachal'nykh Kniazei bogosposaemogo grada Kieva.* Sochinenie Arkhimandrita Inokentiia Gizelia (Moskva, 1714).

[18] Published in Moscow in 1764, translated from a German work by J.A.S. Formey (1711-1797).

[19] 'Rossiianin v Anglii', in *Priiatnoe i poleznoe preprovozhdenie vremeni*, XI (1796), pp. 213-214.

[20] Malinovskii refers to book Five of *Emile* ('Emile and Sophie').

[21] RGALI (former TSGALI), Fond 312, op.1, no. 7, f.3.

[22] 'Rossiianin v Anglii', *Priiatnoe i poleznoe preprovozhdenie vremeni*, XI (1796), p. 214.

> I felt that man should be happy and choose the object of his happiness: I found no better object than to be useful. It seemed to me that there is no man happier than the one who can make others happy[23].

Vasilii Fedorovich was enrolled on 13 November 1774 in Moscow University, the «*slavnoe uchilishche*» (glorious school) mentioned above, in the faculty of philosophy. We learn from his «*attestat*» that he attended courses in the French, German, Russian, English and Italian[24] languages and in History and Geography, and that he was a student «of sufficient diligence, who also behaved honourably and decently»[25].

The teaching of Turkish, in addition to the most important modern European languages, was introduced in Moscow University at that time thanks to a special disposition of Catherine II[26]. Despite the fact that there is no mention of this language in any of the official documents referring to Malinovskii, we may date from his university years his learning of Turkish, the mastery of which was to prove to be of great importance in his subsequent career.

Among the scholars dominating Moscow University at the time when Malinovskii attended it we find some of the most significant names of the second half of eighteenth century. One of them was S.E. Desnitskii, Professor of Law, who was also appointed to teach English. Together with I.A. Tret'iakov, Desnitskii had been educated at the University of Glasgow and had assimilated and disseminated in Russia the ideas of Lord Kames, John Millar and above all, Adam Smith[27]. Malinovskii also attended the

---

[23] *Ibid.*, p. 215.

[24] Among the books which belonged to the «pupil Vasilii Malinovskii» we found an Italian translation of German tales: *Favole e racconti del celeberrimo Gellert*. Tradotti in prosa poetica toscana da G.I.G. di Fraporta, P. lettore della lingua italiana nell'Università di Lipsia (Lipsia, 1770), in TSDIAU (Tsentral'nii Derzhavnii Istorichnii Arkhiv Ukraini), Fond 2039, op. 1, no. 77. Gellert's *Moralische Vorlesungen*, were translated into Russian in 1787 under the title *O nravstvennom vospitanii detei*.

[25] IRLI, R.III, op. 2, no. 2179.

[26] See S.P. Shevyrev, *Istoriia Imperatorskogo Moskovskogo universiteta* (Moskva, 1855), p. 190.

[27] To this figure are devoted several works; among them, see particularly M.P. Alekseev, 'Adam Smith and His Russian Admirers of the Eighteenth Century', in W.R. Scott (ed.), *Adam Smith as Student and Professor* (New York, 1965), pp. 424-431; M.T. Beliavskii, 'Semen Desnitskii i novye dokumenty o ego deiatel'nosti', *Vestnik Moskovskogo universiteta*, Istoriia, no. 4 (1969), pp. 61-74; A. Brown, 'S.E. Desnitskii i I.A. Tret'iakov v Glazgovskom universitete (1761-1767)', *ibid.*, pp. 75-88; A. Brown, 'S.E. Desnitskii, Adam Smith, and the Nakaz of Catherine II', *Oxford Slavonic Papers*, VII (1974), pp. 42-59; F. Venturi, 'From Scotland to Russia: An Eighteenth-Century Debate on Feudalism', in A.G. Cross (ed.), *Great Britain and Russia in the Eighteenth Century: Contacts and Comparison* (Newtonville, Mass., 1979), pp. 2-24; A.G. Cross, 'The High

lectures of J.G. Schwarts (d. 1784)[28], Professor of German in that University and a leading figure in the masonic Moscow of the time, especially among the Rosicrucians, the movement to which he belonged. The question of Schwarts' influence on Malinovskii introduces us to the problem of his hypothetical involvement with the mystical brotherhoods of his time. In this respect, there are a number of elements which cannot be ignored, when considering the possible impact of Freemasonry on his outlook.

In one of his earliest unpublished works, entitled *Materialy po istorii germanskoi religioznoi filosofii* [29], apparently a translation of excerpts from the novel *Theobald oder die Schwärmer* [30], by Johann Heinrich Jung-Stilling (1740-1817), Malinovskii shows an easy familiarity with the thought of the German and French mystical thinkers who influenced the Russian Rosicrucians, among them particularly Jakob Böhme and Mme de Guyon.

Also illuminating in identifying the persistence of this interest in Malinovskii's life is a much later reference to Freemasonry made by somebody else. «*Martinizm*» is in fact a key word used by A.S. Pushkin to characterize the cultural atmosphere in the first years of the Tsarskoe Selo Lycée[31]. *Martinisty* was the name given to the followers of the masonic movement inspired by the doctrine of the French theosophist Louise-Claude de Saint Martin, a pupil of the Swedish philosopher and mystic Emanuel Swedenborg. In an undated letter Malinovskii sent a «respected friend» a new book, «explaining all the teaching of the well-known Swedenborg», commenting that «inspite of many errors, it does contain pure truths»[32]. He seems to allude here to a translation which appeared in St Petersburg in 1785, published by Novikov: *Issledovanie o zabluzhdeniiakh i istine*.

Road and the Low: Russian Students and Travellers in Eighteenth-Century Scotland', *Coexistence*, no. 29 (1992), pp. 113-124.

[28] He was appointed professor of German on 26 August 1779. See M. Longinov, *Novikov i Shvarts* (Moskva, 1857), p. 6.

[29] IRLI, Fond 244, op. 25, no. 317.

[30] I am grateful to Michael Schippan for this information. A first complete translation of this German novel appeared in Russia only in 1819.

[31] See B.L. Modzalevskii, *Pushkin pod tainym nadzorom*, p. 37. According to B. Meilakh, this reference by Pushkin must be considered a relevant factor in a discussion about Freemasonry in Malinovskii. He relates it primarily to an influence exerted by Novikov, and mentions in this respect two other facts: the affinity between Malinovskii's project of founding a «free» community in the steppes of the region of Ufa, in the early 90s, and the utopian plan about a republic in Siberia developed by Novikov's followers; the distinctly «Novikovskian» character of his journal *Osennie vechera*. See B. Meilakh, *Pushkin i ego epokha* (Moskva, 1958), pp. 32-33.

[32] IRLI, Fond 244, op. 25, no. 350, f.1.

There are also a few autobiographical moments in Malinovskii's work where he used a distinctly masonic imagery: his «awakening» to a new vision allegorized by the representation of society as a building to climb employing different sorts of stairs[33], for example, or the way in which the intense struggle between flesh and soul experienced by him is described in his last *Dnevnik* [34].

In general, it seems difficult to exclude the influence on this thinker of a doctrine that offered several ideas that he might have found congenial to his own vision and that attracted so many among his relatives, friends and educators. Apart from his father, his elder brother Aleksei (1762-1841) is mentioned as a member of the Rosicrucian circles, at least during his time at university[35]. Aleksei had entered Moscow University three years before Vasilii, and was deeply involved with Novikov's editorial activity. He was in fact one of the alumni of Moscow University recruited by Novikov to work on his periodicals: he contributed several translations to *Moskovskie vedomosti* [36], *Vecherniaia zaria*, *Utrennii svet*, *Moskovskoe ezhemesiachnoe izdanie*, and *Gorodskaia i derevenskaia biblioteka*. For Novikov's University Press he translated in 1783 *Dukh Biuffona*[37], a pamphlet devoted to the work of the French naturalist. He also translated, in 1787, a work representative of a particular development in French Enlightenment thought: *Rassuzhdenie o nachale i osnovanii grazhdanskikh obshchezhitii, zakliuchaiushchee v sebe ubeditel'nye issledovaniia vopreki Zhan Zhaku Russo* (1787), in which the radicalism of the French philosopher was openly criticized. In an original work published in 1788 under the title *Otrada v skuke...* Aleksei Fedorovich compiled an anthology of extracts from Voltaire, Fontenelle, Malesherbes, Leibniz and other prominent European authors.

A correct evaluation of the relationship between the two brothers (important also to illuminate their sharing of masonic views) is, however, made difficult by the apparent absence of any correspondence between them in any of the succeeding years, a fact that could hardly be interpreted as a sign of intimacy. Especially if compared with the number of letters of various character sent by Vasilii to his younger brother Pavel (1766-1832),

---

[33] 'Rossiianin v Anglii', XI, pp. 216-219.

[34] RGALI, Fond 312, op. 1, no. 3, ff.12, 33.

[35] See Vernadskii, *op.cit.*, p. 208.

[36] See on this also A.N. Neustroev, *Istoricheskoe rozyskanie o russkikh povremennikh izdaniiakh i zbornikakh za 1703-1803* (Spb., 1874), p. 69.

[37] Translated from G.L. Ferri, *Génie de M. de Buffon* (Paris, 1778). Note Vasilii Fedorovich's appraisal of Buffon in a later work ('Rossiianin v Anglii', XI, pp. 145).

always addressed as his «*liubeznyi brat*»[38]. Pavel Fedorovich Malinovskii was employed during his youth in the service of Field Marshal P.S. Saltykov, took part in the capture of the fort of Ochakov and was later given the rank of «*statskii sovetnik*» (counsellor of State) and appointed Director of the Gosudarstvennyi Assignatsionnyi Bank (State Assignat Bank). Count N.P. Sheremetev appointed him to supervise the education of his only son Dmitrii Nikolaevich[39].

1.1.3. The first official appointment

In 1781, the year he completed his studies, Vasilii Fedorovich was recruited by Gerhard Friedrich Müller (G.F. Miller, 1705-1783)[40] to work in the Moscow Archive of the College of Foreign Affairs[41]. In a letter signed by him (and accompaning Malinovskii's petition for the post), Müller wrote that during his university years the young applicant «studied at his own expense» and «made rather good progress»[42], and recommended his engagement as extremely desirable for the College. To demonstrate his linguistic skills, Malinovskii submitted, enclosed with his «*chelobitnaia*», samples of his own translations from several languages[43].

In another official document, a «*skazka*» dated 2 December 1782, Malinovskii gave further information about himself, pointing out his being

> the son of an archpriest, of the male sex, who does not own souls or peasants (...), who has not been on any military campaign, nor under legal investigation and has not been fined or been under any suspicion, who has never taken leave or been given leave for any time and who has not received any rank on retirement[44].

---

[38] See the letters in IRLI, Fond 244, op.25, no. 334.

[39] On his life, see A.E. Rozen, *Zapiski dekabrista* (Moskva, 1984), pp. 103-105. Note that after Vasilii Fedorovich's death it was Pavel who took care of his six children, together with Anna Andreevna Samborskaia, sister of Malinovskii's wife.

[40] For an extensive biography of Müller and a discussion of his place in Russian historiography, see J.L. Black, *G.-F. Müller and the Imperial Russian Academy* (Kingston, 1986).

[41] See Malinovskii's letter to A.R. Vorontsov republished in V.F. Malinovskii, *op.cit.*, p. 151: «I was selected for the service from the students of Moscow University by the late counsellor Müller in 1781».

[42] RGADA (former TSGADA), Fond 180, op.1, no. 57, f. 215.

[43] RGADA, Fond 180, op.1, no. 57, ff. 217-219.

[44] RGADA, Fond 180, op.1, no. 58, f. 388.

The circumstance that the Archive was headed at that time by Müller must have been important in Vasilii's choice. Academician, historian and publisher, Müller had arrived in Russia in 1725 from one of the most prestigious intellectual centres of the German Enlightenment, Leipzig, and after years of research and expeditions in Siberia was involved in advanced editorial initiatives like the periodical *Ezhemesiachnye sochineniia* (1755). Under his direction (he was appointed to the post in 1766) and that of N.N. Bantysh-Kamenskii, the Moscow Archive had become an important centre in the cultural life of Russia; its systematic activity in translating and editing ancient and contemporary documents was to become indispensable for generations of historians, philologists and writers. Müller shared with Novikov the idea that historical and literary documents of the past had to be made accessible in Russia to a larger public and consistently with this belief he contributed to his periodical *Drevniaia rossiiskaia Vivliofika* and involved Novikov in a project for the creation of a special press devoted to the Archive's activity.

After Müller's death Vasilii Fedorovich was moved to St Petersburg, where he worked for seven years in the service of the Vice-Chancellor I.A. Osterman (1722-1804), in the College of Foreign Affairs, with the particular responsibility for following the daily registration of secret affairs. In 1784 he had been transferred from the position of «*arkhivarius*» to that of «*perevodchik*»(translator)[45].

Another circumstance of relevance when considering the reasons for Vasilii's choice of a career in the College must have been the presence of his elder brother in the Moscow Archive since 1788. The two «archpriest's children» had followed the same initial path, which had brought them from Moscow University very nearly in the same years (Aleksei was enrolled in 1771, Vasilii in 1774) to an appointment in the College of Foreign Affairs. The meaning of the «*kantseliarskaia obiazannost'*» (chancellery duty) in the life of the two brothers was however to diverge very soon. The post that Vasilii occupied in the College was to become for him a sterile bureaucratic commitment from which he would repeatedly look for an escape. Being averse to the practice of ingratiating himself with the most powerful in

---

[45] It is not without interest to note that in the official acts of the College referring to his promotion, the name of Malinovskii is associated with that of the other *aktuarius* Ivan Merzliukin, a serf who had been freed thanks to the service of his father (RGADA, Fond 180, op.1, no. 60, ff.124-125).

order to achieve promotion in the service, Vasilii was to come to consider his years as public servant as just a useless and distressing waste of time[46].

The appointment in the College was crucial, on the other hand, for Aleksei. Thanks to it he acquired a prominent position in Russian society of the time. In 1793 a career advancement was denied to him apparently because he originated «not from the nobility»[47], possibly as a consequence of his previous work for Novikov. That circumstance obliged Aleksei Fedorovich to produce a document, obtained from Mogilev province, confirming his noble origin[48]. Maybe as a consequence of that episode, he chose to devote himself entirely to a life of quiet archival work and erudition, withdrawing from the contemporary political debate and pursuing a service career that lasted for sixty two years and was accompanied by honorific recognition of his achievement as an historian. Apparently, the political ideals of his university years were laid aside in an effort to become reconciled with his position as impartial observer of events of the past that he brought to new life with his work on the ancient documents. He became a highly appreciated first «pomoshchnik» (assistant) for Bantysh-Kamenskii and later was particularly concerned with the formation of the younger archivists[49].

In 1826, in the turbulent climate following the repression of the Decembrist revolt, an accusation was made against Aleksei Fedorovich, but thanks to a letter of explanation addressed by him to Nicholas I, it did not have any real consequence for his career and he could continue his work in the Archive until his death.

Better known for his contribution to the first edition, in 1800, of the *Slovo o polku Igoreve*[50], his name must also be associated with a number of works and projects of an historical character undertaken by the Archive, especially in the first two decades of the nineteenth century[51]. He was also

[46] See particularly the work *Sluzhba*, IRLI, Fond 244, op. 25, no. 311.

[47] See Dolgova, *op.cit.*, p. 183.

[48] This document represents now an important additional source for the knowledge of the historical roots of the family. The noble origin of the Russian Malinovskiis was then officially confirmed in 1860 by the Russian Heraldry (*ibid.*).

[49] For a detailed account of Moscow Archive and of «*arkhivnye iunoshi*» (the young people of the archive) in the years when A. Malinovskii was there, see Dolgova, *op.cit.*, pp. 178-196.

[50] About his primary role in the first edition of the *Slovo*, see M.N. Speranskii, 'Perevod «Slova o polku Igoreve» v bumagakh A.F. Malinovskogo', in O. Derzhavina (ed.), *Drevnerusskaia literatura i ee sviazi s novym vremenem* (Moskva, 1967).

[51] In 1807 was published his *Istoricheskoe opisanie drevnego rossiiskogo muzeia, pod nazvaniem Masterskoi i Oruzheinoi palaty v Moskve obretaiushchegosia*. Important were his *Biograficheskie svedeniia o kniaze Dmitrii Mikhailoviche Pozharskom* (1814), his

very active in the world of literature: he translated several works, among them A.F. Kotzebue's *Menschenhass und Reue*, C.H. Spiess's *Das Ehrenwort*[52], works for the theatre by L.S. Mercier and J.M. Boutet de Monvel. He also wrote essays on the history of Russian theatre and was the author of original works, including the comedy *Razdrazhennyi muzh, ili Priezzhie iz Ukrainy*, published in 1799, and the libretto *Starinnye sviatki*.

For a correct understanding of the differing attitudes of the Malinovskii brothers towards their service in the College, it can be relevant to consider the autobiographical remarks in Vasilii Fedorovich's later work. The reasons for his deep contempt for his career as public servant are perhaps to be found in the fact that his expectations when deciding on service in the College were completely unfulfilled. Looking retrospectively at his choice of profession, Malinovskii saw in fact clearly that he had imagined work in the College to be the most congenial to his commitment to reason and «social usefulness» and opposed to a career merely devoted to «*uchenie i nauki*» (studies and sciences) and the pursuit of personal glory:

> But in the ardent years of youth I favoured the path of service, thinking that there are many writers as it is, but vice and misfortune multiply among people with each new day, and all their teachings remain vain; a person in service, though, can to a higher degree carry out in a practical way everything that he deems to be useful[53].

As we shall see, Vasilii Malinovskii was radically to change his mind on this point.

1.1.4. The question of peace: a first discovery

Malinovskii's first years after leaving the university, which he spent working in the archives of the College of Foreign Affairs, might have played, anyhow, an important role in his intellectual development, especially with respect to his thinking on the question of peace. From those years dates in fact the first expression of his critique of war. In a fragment, written in 1782, on the occasion of «rumours about a war for the Crimea», we find an early «declaration of intent» which anticipates the already

---

Istoricheskii vzgliad na mezhevanie v Rossii do 1765 (1844) and the essay *Obozrenie Moskvy*, first published by S. Dolgova.

[52] *Nenavist' k liudiam i raskaianie* (Moskva, 1796); *Chestnoe slovo* (Moskva, 1793).

[53] 'Rossiianin v Anglii', XI (1796), p. 215.

mature treatment in his *Rassuzhdenie o mire i voine* and explains the ethical vision behind it. In his formulation the eighteen-year-old author is moved by emotional considerations regarding the disastrous effects of conscription on the life of the Russian peasants:

> They are already preparing to spill rivers of blood, the weapons of hatred are being sharpened and the thunderous machines are now ready to smite people. The father dispirited by old age and the mother burdened by sickness are deprived of support in their decrepitude. Their children are abducted. There the tender wife bids her spouse farewell. The air is filled with the wails of innocent infants, deprived of their fathers[54].

Malinovskii's portrayal of the *«rekrutshchina»* has striking similarities with Radishchev's description of the same event in his *Puteshestvie iz Peterburga v Moskvu* [55]. In Malinovskii's mind the view of the cruel spectacle gives rise to a strong attack against war and to the first appearance of the idea of a personal responsibility in the elimination of this problem:

> O war, cruel war! For how long will the human race sacrifice itself to you? For as long as it remains in this condition. Every person attempts to save only himself from misfortune and also his loved ones, who are very few in number, and afterward he gazes on this misfortune with equanimity and the ardent desire to avert it is extinguished in him. But will I be so base? Can I be so calm, when others will be spilling blood? The man pierced by the death-dealing weapon is like you, he is a person, your brother.

It is worthy of note that another peace project had been translated a few years before by a Russian man of letters working in the College of Foreign Affairs. The poet I.F. Bogdanovich, who had worked as a translator in the College from 1764 to 1776, published in St Petersburg in 1771 a translation entitled *Sokrashchenie, sdelannoe Zhan-Zhakom Russo, zhenevskim grazhdaninom, iz proekta o vechnom mire, sochinennogo g. abbatom de Sen-P'erom*[56].

Among Malinovskii's colleagues in the College of Foreign Affairs at that time we find R.M. Tsebrikov (1763-1817), although there is no evidence of personal contacts between the two men. Born in Kharkov, he attended University in Leipzig, and on his return to Russia was employed as

---

[54] RGALI, Fond 312, op. 1, no. 1, f. 1.

[55] A.N. Radishchev, *Izbrannye filosofskie i obshchestvenno-politicheskie proizvedeniia*, ed. I. Shchipanov (Moskva, 1952), p. 185. A similarity in the representation of this scene was first pointed out by Meilakh, *op.cit.*, p. 34.

[56] From Rousseau's *Extrait du Projet de Paix Perpétuelle de Monsieur l'Abbé de Saint-Pierre* (1758-59).

perevodchik in the College up to 1788, when he was sent to Turkey to work in Potemkin's chancellery during the Second Russo-Turkish war. Tsebrikov, who personally witnessed the horrors of a real war, recorded it in a *Dnevnik*[57], based on his experience during the years 1788-89. Alongside the day-by-day portrayal of the tragic events accompanying the capture of the Turkish fort of Ochakov, Tsebrikov expressed his radical political views and an unusually harsh condemnation of war in general[58]. He was also the author of several translations, including one of the peace project written by the Frenchman Ange Goudar (1720-1791) in 1757[59]. It appeared in 1789 in St Petersburg with the title *Mir Evropy ili proekt vseobshchego zamireniia*[60] and was something between an original composition and a compilation of the ideas expressed by Goudar.

The picture of Malinovskii's intellectual activity before his departure for England can now be integrated by consideration of another early work: a sort of pamphlet devoted to the Emperor Joseph II and entitled 'Pochemu narod dolzhen liubit' imperatora Iosifa i chego zhelaet blagomysliashchii ego narod'[61]. The manuscript, which was presented as a translation from German, bears the inscription: «Izdano v Vene na nemetskom iazyke. 1787 godu» (published in Vienna in German), and is signed «V...M....». It contains a passionate description of Joseph II as a just legislator whose initiatives of reform were undertaken in the true spirit of Enlightenment. His reforms in favour of freedom of thinking and civic and religious rights are enthusiastically praised by the author, who also considers, on the other

---

[57] His diary has been published with the title 'R.M. Tsebrikov. Vokrug Ochakova. 1788 (Dnevnik ochevidtsa)', ed. A.F. Bychkov, *Russkaia starina*, IX, no. 84 (1895), pp. 147-212. On him see A.I. Kuz'min, 'R.M. Tsebrikov - literator XVIII veka', in *Problemy teorii i istorii literatury* (Moskva, 1971), pp. 106-111.

[58] «And is not war itself, whose causes are covered by faith, just demands, and the defence of the fatherland and of its rights, more often the source of pride, vainglory, envy of a particular individual, and for the most part personal into the bargain?» (Tsebrikov, *op.cit.*, pp. 152-153); «I looked at the Ochakovskaia fortress (...) and the great heaps of dead bodies thrown into the moats aroused horror in me, the ruined houses of the former inhabitants struck me as a loathsome disgrace and the thought of the pernicious invention of cannons, bombs, mortars, shot... artillery... of so glorious a science, vividly portrayed to me the complete vileness of its activities (...) Here, mankind, you beings endowed with reason, a fact you so pride yourselves upon, is your ghastly fate!» (*ibid.*, p. 210).

[59] *La paix d'Europe ne peut s'établir qu'à la suite d'une longue trève, ou Projet de pacification générale, combiné par une suspension d'armes de vingt ans, entre toutes les puissances politiques* (Amsterdam, 1757).

[60] It was published with a dedication to A.A. Bezborodko, who took part in the Turkish war and was rewarded for it.

[61] TSDIAU, Fond 2039, op. 1, no. 68, ff. 1-12. The work was found in Kiev by N.B. Meshkova-Malinovskaia and illustrated by her in an unpublished article entitled *O novoi rabote V.F. Malinovskogo*.

hand, the reasons behind the hostility to Joseph II of a part of the population, and proposes his suggestions to perfect his conduct as a ruler.

It is difficult to ascertain to what extent the work, which was undoubtedly largely inspired by contemporary literature on the subject[62], can be considered an original work of Malinovskii. It shows a deep knowledge of the politics of Joseph II and of the situation in his Empire which was perhaps difficult to achieve for the young Malinovskii. Among the features emerging from the text we can note on the other hand a distinct anti-war feeling[63] which is particularly consistent with the subsequent development of the Russian thinker.

1.2. The English Experience (1789-1791)

1.2.1. Malinovskii at the Russian Embassy in London

After a few years of work in the College of Foreign Affairs, the young Malinovskii had lost any interest in it, and expressed his intention to spend a period of time away from the service and from Russia. Quite naturally, he turned his eyes to England, the enlightened country he had admired from his early years[64]. It was in the autumn of 1789, at a time when his superior was receiving more and more alarmed despatches from the Russian ambassador in Paris, I.M. Simolin[65], that Malinovskii managed to obtain the appointment he himself requested, «wishing to get to know a state, famed for the wisdom and happiness of its government and

---

[62] During her research on its possible models N.B. Meshkova-Malinovskaia located an anonymous work published in Vienna in 1787 and entitled *Kaiser Joseph wird doch geliebt. Eine kleine Antwort auf die kürzlich erschienene Schrift: Warum wird Kaiser Joseph von seinem Volke nicht geliebt?* This work presents nevertheless a number of substantial differences with Malinovskii's one.

[63] «Right-thinking men of the people want Emperor Joseph to love civil servants no less than the military (...) Right-thinking people wish children of officials and residents of capital cities again to be exempt from recruitment to military service (...) The spirit of citizenship has become debased, the number of bachelors increases daily, they state clearly that they do not wish to marry because they do not want to bring a soldier into the world» (TSDIAU, Fond 2039, op. 1, no. 68, f. 8).

[64] «Of all the enlightened European peoples the English appealed to me most» ('Rossiianin v Anglii', XI, p. 215).

[65] 'Frantsuzskaia revoliutsiia 1789 v doneseniiakh russkogo posla v Parizhe I.M. Simolina', *Literaturnoe nasledstvo*, XXIX-XXX (1937), pp. 343-358.

inhabitants, without concern for the profits of service»[66]. He was to work as a *perevodchik* in the Russian Embassy in London, under the service of Count Semen Vorontsov, ambassador in England from 1785 to 1806.

Thus, he was given the opportunity to visit the country that would always act as an ideal point of reference for him, a few important reservations notwithstanding. Such an admiring attitude was a fairly widespread phenomenon in some Russian intellectual circles of the time, particularly among the masons, who looked upon England as the country in which the Enlightenment had reached its apotheosis, both in public institutions and in the private life of every citizen. Anglophilia[67] flourished in Russia, replacing enthusiasms for other European cultures which succeeded one another throughout the course of the century.

At the time of his arrival in Britain Malinovskii was a promising young philosopher, filled with reforming spirit and fervour for the Enlightenment. When he returned to St Petersburg, almost two years later, he took back with him the first part of what remains his most significant work, the *Dissertation on Peace and War*, which he wrote at Richmond in 1790. Its sequel was composed later, in 1798, near St Petersburg, and the two parts were not published in Russia until 1803. The coherent plan of universal peace elaborated by Malinovskii had its origin, therefore, in England. The importance of his brief stay in London cannot be overestimated: he found himself in a completely different world, in the «civilized» world he had dreamt about when in his «barbaric» fatherland, and in the privileged position of having a window on major European political events. The observation of the Russian foreign affairs, on the other hand, acquired a particular character, wisely distanced from immediate involvement in the internal situation. On 19 August 1789 Malinovskii wrote, in one of his most lucid and effective pleas against warfare:

> Twelve o'clock can be heard striking in turns in different places in the vicinity. The stillness and silence reigning everywhere are broken only by the barking of dogs, those ever vigilant guards who offer us an example of loyalty.

---

66 See the letter to Vorontsov republished in V.F. Malinovskii, *op.cit.*, p. 151.

67 On Anglophilia in Russia see E.J. Simmons, *English literature and culture in Russia (1553-1840)* (Cambridge, Mass., 1935), pp. 73-99. On the cultural relations between the two countries see A.G. Cross (ed.), *Great Britain and Russia in the Eighteenth Century: Contacts and Comparison* (Newtonville, Mass., 1979); A.G. Cross, *Anglo-Russica. Aspects of Cultural Relations between Great Britain and Russia in the Eighteenth and Early Nineteenth Centuries* (Oxford/Providence 1993). Among Soviet works, see in particular M.P. Alekseev, *Russko-angliiskie literaturnye sviazi* (Moskva, 1982).

All city dwellers settle to rest - the darkness of approaching autumn spreads
around. No candles are to be seen in the windows, no human voice can be
heard anywhere. Besides the houses sunk in darkness (...) there is no sign
of occupation. This emptiness, this cheerless silence brings to mind a town
laid to waste by an enemy. I also recall that my fatherland is at war with two
neighbours. The treacherous Gustav[68] broke the agreements of peace,
hoping to gain glory thus! What ignorance in an enlightened century - to
think of achieving glory by destruction and death. Not until the veil of this
barbaric delusion is drawn back will we learn to value war correctly and to
consider it the first sign (...) which the human race voluntarily turns upon
itself.
Deluded mortals, open your eyes! Do not blind yourselves any longer! Why
do you wage war on each other? Arm yourself against the evils of nature,
perfect those blessings she has favoured you with.
Nationalities are not all composed of like peoples. Each of them has their
particular accomplishments which, with general accord, could serve to
further the general felicity of the human race[69].

In England Malinovskii developed his activity in the close-knit society
of the Russian Embassy[70], itself practically constituting an island within the
British island, on which all the Russians living in England in those years
inevitably converged and where prestigious Russian guests travelling
around Europe were met with warmth and ceremony. The community of
Russians was dominated by the personality of the ambassador Vorontsov,
extremely hospitable and anglophile (although he had a poor command of
the English language), as his predecessors Antiokh Kantemir, Ivan
Chernyshev and A. Musin-Pushkin had been. After a brilliant military
career, voluntarily interrupted, and after a brief appointment in Venice,
Vorontsov had won in England a reputation as a skilful and clever «political
head», thanks to successful interventions in moments of tension between the
two countries[71], and had obtained remarkable prestige in social life. The
ambassador highly appreciated Malinovskii's work for the Embassy[72], as we

---

[68] The reference is to the King of Sweden Gustav III, engaged in an offensive against
Russia. The other war front mentioned by Malinovskii is the Turkish one.

[69] The fragment figures among Samborskii's papers as *Razmyshleniia neizvestnogo
litsa po povodu ob'iavleniia voiny Shvetsiei Rossii, o nagubnosti voiny i prekrashchenii
vrazhdy mezhdu narodami*. It is dated «19 Avgusta. Bez svechi (without a candle). 1789»
(TSDIAU, Fond 2053, op.1, no. 982). Because of the darkness in which he wrote,
Malinovskii's letters are large and wavering.

[70] On the Russian Embassy in London, see V.N. Aleksandrenko, *Russkie
diplomaticheskie agenty v Londone v XVIII v.*, 2 vols. (Warsaw, 1897); A.G. Cross, *«By
the Banks of the Thames»: Russians in Eighteenth-Century Britain* (Newtonville, Mass.,
1980).

[71] The most detailed study of the figure of Vorontsov is J.W. Marcum, *Semen R.
Vorontsov: Minister to the Court of St James for Catherine II, 1785-1796* (Ph.D. thesis,
University of North Carolina at Chapel Hill, 1970).

[72] Malinovskii was not, however, among the five Russians mentioned by Vorontsov
as those who had benefitted most from their sojourn abroad to be useful to Russia.

know from what Vasilii Fedorovich wrote in 1803 to his brother Aleksandr Romanovich Vorontsov: he returned in fact to Russia «with a glowing recommendation from his Excellency the Ambassador Count Semen Romanovich Vorontsov in respect of conduct and work»[73].

Another central figure in the «Russian» London of that time was Iakov Smirnov (1754-1840), chaplain to the church serving the Russian Embassy. This man had many interests and did not limit himself to tending the souls assigned to his care, but rather played an active part in the cultural and political life of the community[74].

His predecessor had been A.A. Samborskii (1732-1815), one of whose daughters Malinovskii was to marry after his return to Russia. The intellectual debt incurred by Malinovskii towards this man was first pointed out at the beginning of the twentieth century[75]. After having attended the Kievan Spiritual Academy, Samborskii had been sent to England by Catherine II in 1765 to be the chaplain to the Embassy and also to learn the principles of agronomy elaborated in that country. Samborskii had spent seventeen years in England and had even married an Englishwoman. He had returned to Russia in 1780 and in 1784 he had been appointed religious tutor to the Grand Dukes Aleksandr and Konstantin Pavlovich. He was the compiler of the *Opisanie prakticheskogo aglinskogo zemledeliia, sobrannoe iz raznykh aglinskikh pisatelei*, edited under the supervision of Desnitskii and published in Moscow in 1781, through which he tried to bring the ideas of English agronomy to bear on Russian society, and of the *Polozhenie prakticheskoi shkoly zemledeliia i sel'skogo khoziaistva*, published in St Petersburg in 1792. It is primarily to Samborskii that Malinovskii owed the important role he ascribed to agriculture: at the estate of Belozerka, situated between Pavlovsk and Tsarskoe Selo, Samborskii had had the opportunity to bring into realization his ideas on agronomy. And it was at that estate that Malinovskii was to write the second part of his *Rassuzhdenie*.

Also affiliated to the Russian Embassy in London from 1789 to 1791 was Viktor Pavlovich Kochubei (1768-1834), a young Russian aristocrat

---

According to him, they were G.A. Seniavin, F.V. Rostopchin, G.A. Demidov, V.N. Zinov'ev and V.P. Kochubei (see *Arkhiv kniazia Vorontsova* (Spb., 1870-1875), IX, pp. 416-417).

[73] Letter to A.R. Vorontsov, p. 151.

[74] See A.G. Cross, 'Yakov Smirnov: a Russian Priest of Many Parts', *Oxford Slavonic Papers*, NS VIII (1975), pp. 37-52. See also W.E. Butler, 'Yakov Smirnov and the Law of Nations', *Oxford Slavonic Papers*, NS XII (1979), pp. 40-45.

[75] V. Semevskii has analyzed the relationship of Samborskii and Malinovskii in his 'Razmyshlenie V.F. Malinovskogo o preobrazovanii gosudarstvennogo ustroistva Rossii', *Golos minuvshego*, no. 10 (1915).

who was to hold several important ministerial offices after his return to Russia. Future member of Alexander I's Neglasnyi Komitet (1801-1803) and Minister of Home Affairs from 1802 to 1807, he was to play an important role as official channel for Malinovskii's reforming ideas. In his letters to him, he was to call Kochubei «friend of mankind»[76]. The two Russians shared a deep admiration for the English institutional model and enlightened views on the reform of Russian society, especially on such question as the abolition of serfdom. In 1802 Kochubei received from him a copy of his 'Zapiska o osvobozhdenii rabov', one of Malinovskii's most radical writings on that problem.

Another young Russian close to the London embassy at that time was S.S. Dzhunkovskii (1762-1839). He arrived in England in 1784 to become tutor of Samborskii's son Aleksandr[77], and was virtually adopted by him, after the death of that son in 1792. He remained in England for seven years. After his return to Russia he wrote a poem entitled 'Aleksandrova' (1793) to celebrate the «English garden» laid out by Samborskii in the estate given by Catherine II to her grandson Alexander[78]. Dzhunkovskii was to become «korrespondent» of the Free Economic Society in 1794 (incidentally, the same year when Malinovskii was appointed a member[79]) and its Secretary in 1803, thanks to his studies in agronomy.

Despite being rather closed in itself, the community of Russians did not, of course, avoid contact with English and foreign citizens in London. One of the personalities whose connections with the Russian Embassy are better documented is John Paradise (1743-1795), who was very close to Vorontsov and well known to Karamzin[80]. A man of «cosmopolitan faith»

---

[76] See Malinovskii's letter to him published in *Izbrannye obshchestvenno-politicheskie sochineniia*, p. 149.

[77] About his progress and Dzhunkovskii's ability, see a letter sent on 16 April 1785 from Hertford (where Samborskii's son was studying, see Cross, *«By the Banks of the Thames»*, p. 42): «Sir, Mr D'junkovsky will inform you of the progress made by your son and Mr Balabin in English, which is much to my satisfaction (...) Mr D'junkovsky speaks and writes the language of this country surprisingly well. I need not to observe to you, that he professes an uncommon degree of general knowledge, accompanied with the greatest candour and good humour» (TSDIAU, Fond 2053, op.1, no. 1154).

[78] The garden was planned to illustrate Catherine II's tale *Skazka o tsareviche Khlore*. On Dzhunkovskii and this episode, see A.G. Cross, *'Anglofiliia u trona'. Britantsy i russkie v vek Ekateriny II. Katalog vystavki* (London, 1992), p. 94, and 'Dzhunkovskii's «Aleksandrova»: Putting Samborskii in the Picture', in *Study Group on Eighteenth Century Russia*, no. 3 (1975), pp. 22-29.

[79] See the official act referring to his membership, RGALI, Fond 312, op. 2, no. 3.

[80] *Ibid.*, pp. 27-28. On the figure of Paradise, see A. Shepperson, *John Paradise and Lucy Ludwell of London and Williamsburg* (Richmond, Virginia, 1942); G. Struve, 'John Paradise - Friend of Doctor Johnson, American Citizen and Russian «Agent»', *Virginia*

who described himself as a «friend of freedom», Paradise put himself at the service of the Russian government and received a significant pension from Catherine II. The possibility of a personal contact between Malinovskii and the author of the *Plan for an Universal and Perpetual Peace*, Jeremy Bentham, has frequently been considered[81]. Although this work was not published until 1843, its composition dates back to the years 1786-1789, and any possible manuscript circulation may have attracted the attention of Malinovskii. The possibility that the two men met in England is far from being excluded, considering the contacts between Bentham and Malinovskii's various predecessors in the Russian mission, and also taking into account the close relations of his brother Samuel with Malinovskii's fatherland[82]. Sadly, it was nevertheless impossible to find any direct evidence of this contact[83].

1.2.2. The English period through a «new» source: 'Rossiianin v Anglii'

The idea of a thorough investigation of Malinovskii's «English» period has, at first sight, considerable appeal, considering how fruitful this short stay was to be for the young Russian thinker. Interest in his English experience could, however, only lead, until recently, to the disappointing conclusion that it was impossible to find any evidence of his encounters and personal experiences. During the twenty months that he spent in Britain Malinovskii was engaged in an obscure and anonymous role of «translator», one such as not to leave traces of any relevance in the history of Russian diplomacy of the eighteenth century. In the absence of any documentation concerning the work really done by him for the Russian Embassy or illuminating his possible contacts with the prominent Englishmen close to it, the country really seen by Malinovskii seemed destined to remain an enigma.

Magazine of History and Biography, LVII (1949), pp. 355-375; A.G. Cross, 'Vasilii Petrov v Anglii', *XVIII vek*, XI (1976), pp. 240-241.

[81] See in particular Cross, «*By the Banks of the Thames*», p. 32, and V.F. Malinovskii, *Izbrannye obshchestvenno-politicheskie sochineniia*, p. 27.

[82] M.S. Anderson, 'Samuel Bentham in Russia, 1779-1791', *The American Slavonic and East European Review*, XV, 2 (1956), pp. 157-172; I.R. Christie, 'Jeremy Bentham and Prince Potemkin', *The Bentham Newsletter*, no.10 (June 1986), pp.17-21.

[83] On this point see in particular A.T. Milne (ed.), *The Correspondence of Jeremy Bentham*, IV (London, 1981), and the recent study by I.R. Christie, *The Benthams in Russia. 1780-1791* (Oxford, 1993).

In point of fact, an autobiographical, detailed account of his English period was available, and even in a published form, as early as two centuries ago. Since the very first day when he set foot in London, 31 October 1789, and until the end of March 1791, Malinovskii wrote a series of letters illuminating his short sojourn in England. They were published anonymously in a Russian journal in 1796, under the title 'Rossiianin v Anglii. Otryvki iz pisem odnogo puteshestvennika'[84]. Introducing the text, the editor of the journal *Priiatnoe i poleznoe preprovozhdenie vremeni* explained how the secret about the author's name was kept «by his own will and modesty» (IX, p. 56)[85].

The text itself, one of the not too numerous written accounts left by Russian travellers in eighteenth-century England, has not been completely ignored, particularly in recent times[86]. The reflections it contains suggested its author was a young Muscovite, well-educated but not of noble origin.

In 1987 Lotman proposed hypothetically the name of Malinovskii[87]. The idea circulated and consolidated itself[88]. In 1991, in a brief paper which was almost entirely ignored, a young Russian scholar set it down in black and white, accumulating biographical and textual evidences in favour

---

[84] *Priiatnoe i poleznoe preprovozhdenie vremeni*, IX (1796), pp. 56-63, pp. 65-71, pp. 97-107; XI (1796), pp. 11-14, pp. 61-75, pp. 97-109, pp. 145-155, pp. 209-219, pp. 257-264, pp. 321-332, XII (1796), pp. 356-367, pp. 381-395, pp. 403-410. Subsequent references will be made in the text by page number.

[85] From 1796 the editor was P.A. Sokhatskii, replacing V.S. Podshivalov. The editorial note was signed nevertheless with a «I». For a discussion about the identity of the author contributing to the journal and signing with that letter, see N.D. Kochetkova, 'Problema «lozhnoi chuvstvitel'nosti» v literature russkogo sentimentalizma', in A.M. Panchenko (ed.), *XVIII vek*, XVII (1991), pp. 61-73.

[86] See A.G. Cross, «*By the Banks of the Thames*», *op.cit.*, pp. 245-251, his 'The High Road and the Low: Russian Students and Travellers in Eighteenth-Century Scotland', pp. 121-122; 'Russian Perceptions of England, and Russian National Awareness at the End of the Eighteenth and the Beginning of the Nineteenth Centuries', *Slavonic and East European Review*, LXI (1983), pp. 96-106; E. Waegemans, 'Ein Reisender aus Russland in England. Zur Englandkenntnis im Russland des 18. Jahrhunderts', in H. Grasshoff (ed.), *Literaturbeziehungen im 18. Jahrhundert. Studien und Quellen zur Deutsch-russischen und russisch-westeuropäischen Kommunikation* (Berlin, 1986), pp. 261-270.

[87] Iu. Lotman, *Sotvorenie Karamzina* (Moskva, 1987), pp. 190. Lotman attributed to Malinovskii an important role in Vorontsov's circle and to the 'Rossiianin v Anglii' a certain impact on the contemporary literature («In certain places the sketches strikingly recall pages of Karamzin's 'Pis'ma'»), but about its authorship he did not go further than saying «he may be Malinovskii».

[88] See A.G. Cross, '*Anglofiliia u trona'. Britantsy i russkie v vek Ekateriny II. Katalog vystavki*, p. 102. The text is referred to as «as regards content, the most interesting of all the accounts by Russians of their sojourns in England published in the XVIII century».

of this hypothesis[89]. She pointed out the exact coincidence between Malinovskii's stay in England and the period covered by the journey of the 'Rossiianin v Anglii'; the circumstance that the editor of *Priiatnoe i poleznoe preprovozhdenie vremeni*, published in Moscow from 1794 to 1798, was Pavel Sokhatskii[90], a professor of Moscow University, who had married a younger sister of Malinovskii, Natal'ia Fedorovna; the fact that the author of the correspondence chose the day on which Malinovskii was born, the 18th July, to recollect memories of his childhood and education; the recurrence in the text of certain typical «Malinovskian» features: his admiration for British institutions and condemnation of the aspects of depravity associated with London's life, his longing for a «rural life», his enthusiasm for English women.

Further confirmation of Malinovskii's authorship came from a brief article published in 1992 by V. Besprozvannyi[91]. His previous studies on *Priiatnoe i poleznoe preprovozhdenie vremeni* led him to suggest that the letters from England and another article published in the same journal, 'Zapiski o Moldavii'[92], belonged to the same pen, that of Malinovskii. He noted the coincidence of these publications with the beginning of Sokhatskii's editorship, which marked a more anglophile orientation of the journal, and highlighted the same external circumstances pointed out by Mikhailova to demonstrate Malinovskii's authorship of the 'Rossiianin v Anglii'.

The following analysis of the text will provide a few elements for a discussion of the thematic and lexical evidences which can reinforce this attribution, showing the continuity of Malinovskii's thought and the recurrence of certain notions and terminology.

Presented as a series of letters from England, 'Rossiianin v Anglii' represents more than a mere account of travel impressions, it constitutes a sort of *summa* of Malinovskii's philosophical conceptions, the place where

---

[89] Liudmila Borisovna Mikhailova read her paper (still unpublished) at the conference 'Tsarskosel'skii Litsei i traditsii evropeiskogo prosveshcheniia', held in Pushkin 16-18 October 1991.

[90] Pavel Afanas'evich Sokhatskii (1765-1809), Professor of Aesthetics and Philology, was the author of a *Slovo o glavnoi tseli vospitaniia* and various odes (to Shuvalov, Paul, Alexander I). Besides *Priiatnoe i poleznoe preprovozhdenie vremeni* he was the editor of *Ipokrena ili utekhi liuboslaviia* (1799-1801) and *Novosti russkoi literatury*.

[91] V. Besprozvannyi, 'Kto byl avtorom «Rossiianina v Anglii»?', *V chest' 70-letiiu professora Iu.M. Lotmana* (Tartu, 1992), pp. 49-56.

[92] Attribution to Malinovskii of the *Notes on Moldavia* is seemingly done in ignorance of the previous literature on this subject (see the present work, 1.3.1., footnote no. 6).

are to be found the criteria which had informed his life until the moment when he wrote and the first draft of his projects for the future.

Although it is the only available source on his English period, the strictly «biographical» use that can be made of this literary account is complicated by Malinovskii's attitude to anonymity and discretion about the people with whom he had contacts, a feature that goes much beyond the degree of secrecy commonly practiced by Russian eighteenth-century writers. Only in a few cases do we have a precise account of his movements, while the names of his English acquaintances are hidden behind vague national or social identifications[93].

The series of letters opens with a statement absolutely unjustified as a stylistical invention: «I am already in London. My first stay here last year was so fleeting, it is as if I had not been in England at all» (IX, pp. 56-57). We are not aware of other travels in Europe previously accomplished by Malinovskii. The only autobiographical reference we have been able to find to sustain the hypothesis of a previous journey to England is a mention in the diary of his last years, where referring to 1788 he wrote: «At the same time I was in a state of great indecision, after visiting England as a courier. I did not know what to do with myself»[94]. The idea that Malinovskii went for the first time to England as «diplomatic courier» is certainly entirely plausible. At that time it was not unusual, for a young member of the College of Foreign Affairs, to act simultaneously as a courier abroad. Such was the case with Nikolai L'vov, who in 1776-1777 was sent by the College to London, Madrid and Paris with this specific task, and of Count Evgraf Komarovskii, who went to London in 1787. In Malinovskii's case, this first contact with England was to give rise to the intention of finding an opportunity to deepen his knowledge of this country.

---

[93] An interesting example occurs in his letters from Scotland, where he has a meeting with a person who, we are brought to believe from the text, deeply impressed Malinovskii, and about whose identity we would have been tempted to speculate if Malinovskii had said something more than simply referring to him as to a «Russkii Anglichanin» (XII, p. 363). It must not be forgotten that he chose to characterize himself only as a «Rossiianin v Anglii». Elsewhere in the Scottish letters he mentions a «Russkaia Shotlandka» (XII, p. 388): from the previous description we know that the Scottish girl is defined as such because of her having spent a few years in St Petersburg, so it seems natural to assume a similar characteristic for the «Russkii Anglichanin».

[94] RGALI, Fond 312, op. 1, no. 3, f. 82. It is worth noting that the Decembrist Andrei Evgenevich Rozen (1799-1884), who married Malinovskii's daughter Anna, wrote in his memoirs that his father-in-law «travelled in Germany, France and England with advantage and with scientific purpose» (A.E. Rozen, *op.cit.*, p. 101).

*1.2.3. Malinovskii's «philosophical» journey and the 'English vogue'
in Russian memoirs*

Malinovskii was not the only Russian visitor, nor the first, who left a
written account of his travel in England. In the second half of the eighteenth
century an increasing interest in England brought to this country a
considerable number of Russian travellers[95]. From the 1770s, the Russian
visitors who recorded their impressions on life and society in that country
touched almost unanimously upon a certain number of themes, partly
suggested by the English novel of the eighteenth century. The
Enlightenment of English people and the legendary beauty of English
women, the excellence of the institutions and the immaculate condition of
streets are easy to find in the accounts left by Ekaterina Romanovna
Dashkova, Aleksandr Borisovich Kurakin, Grigorii Aleksandrovich
Demidov, Vladimir Orlov.

By the end of the 1780s, Russian visitors to England could count on a
certain corpus of consolidated ideas on English society and habits. In the
travel accounts written by Count Evgraf Fedorovich Komarovskii, Vasilii
Nikolaevich Zinov'ev, Petr Ivanovich Makarov[96] in the years nearer to
Malinovskii's stay, we observe the different ways in which these ideas meet
with the experiences of the travellers in the actual country[97]. Each of these
Russians expressed his opinion on this body of ideas, ranging from harsh
criticism to blind acceptance, and modelling it according to the more or less
«literary» orientation of the account[98]. Even in the sort of philosophical-

---

[95] For a discussion of this phenomenon, see particularly A.G. Cross, 'Russians on
the Grand Tour', in *«By the Banks of the Thames»: Russians in Eighteenth-Century
Britain, op.cit.*, pp. 230-251. On Russian travellers in eighteenth century see K.V. Sivkov,
Puteshestviia russkikh liudei za granitsu v XVIII veke (Spb., 1914).

[96] *Zapiski grafa E.F. Komarovskogo* (Moscow, 1914); 'Zhurnal puteshestviia V.N.
Zinov'eva po Germanii, Italii, Frantsii i Anglii v 1784-1788', *Russkaia starina*, XXXIII
(1878), pp. 421-440, 593-598; *Sochineniia i perevody Petra Makarova*, II (2nd edition,
Moskva, 1817), pp. 5-50.

[97] These accounts did not merely reflect the contemporary image of England, they
also influenced it. In this respect a distinction must be nevertheless made about the
obviously different impact on the Russian perception of England of published and
unpublished reports. On problems related to manuscript circulation of unpublished Russian
memoirs, see A.G. Tartakovskii, *Russkaia memuaristika XVIII-pervoi poloviny XIX v. Ot
rukopisi k knige* (Moskva, 1991).

[98] In the Western European literature the travel genre could boast a mature and
elaborate tradition, which was not entirely ignored by the Russian travellers. See T. Roboli,
'Literatura puteshestvii', in *Russkaia proza* (Leningrad, 1926); R.K. Wilson, *The Literary
Travelogue. A Comparative Study with Special Relevance to Russian Literature from
Fonvizin to Pushkin* (The Hague, 1973); E.S. Ivashina, '«Puteshestvie» kak zhanr russkoi

touristic guide to England left by Makarov for the use of his less wealthy fellow-countrymen[99], the factual information about the country could hardly be considered the main purpose of the account. In 1795 the topos of England in the Russian travelogue was already mature and consolidated enough to allow Makarov to refer parodically to it (as well as to the «sentimental» vogue so closely connected to it):

> Of course it will seem strange to you that at this time I am not strolling through some fine and spacious country park, not sitting on soft, green grass (...), not entrusting zephyrs to bear my feelings, my sighs, to the goddess of this paradise, a young, delightful English girl, fair-haired, tender, languorous, sensitive (...), not describing the buildings, the statues, the pictures (...), not discoursing on the government, the Ministry, the Politics, the trade and the laws of England[100].

Any purely «documentary» intention is also absent from Malinovskii's report. He is obviously concerned with a broadening of the Russian knowledge of England, and he employs realistic details when describing monuments, landscapes and cultural events. His descriptions and information about local customs serve nevertheless to advance the arguments proposed by him.

To understand better the nature of Malinovskii's work, it would be useful to compare it to the most celebrated contribution made by an eighteenth-century Russian writer to the travel genre, Karamzin's *Pis'ma russkogo puteshestvennika*[101]. The parallel is inevitable and illuminating: the English section of the *Letters* refers to a period, from July to September 1790, when Malinovskii was there; the two travellers visited substantially the same places, they even met, in the pages of Karamzin's text, companions on a pleasant and instructive excursion on the Thames during which they had the opportunity to discuss issues like the concept of «salus publica» in England (and probably, the corresponding notion of «obshchestvennoe blago» in Russia)[102]. Karamzin's interest in the question of peace[103], during

literatury kontsa XVIII-pervoi treti XIX veka', in L.A. Kolobaeva (ed.), *Kul'turologicheskie aspekty teorii i istorii russkoi literatury* (Moskva, 1978).

[99] See especially the calculations on the incredibly small amount of money with which a Russian could live honourably in that fabulous country (*op.cit.*, pp. 40-41).

[100] The first part of Makarov's letters appeared in *Moskovskii Merkurii* (1803), I, no. 1, under the title 'Rossiianin v Londone; ili pis'ma k druz'iam moim' (passage quoted: pp. 34-35).

[101] On Karamzin's attitude toward England, see particularly A.G. Cross, 'Karamzin and England', *The Slavonic and East European Review*, XLIII, no. 100 (1964).

[102] M. Karamzin, *Pis'ma russkogo puteshestvennika*, eds. Iu. Lotman, N. Marchenko, B. Uspenskii (Leningrad, 1984), pp. 355-357. Karamzin alludes there to a mysterious figure, designated only by the initial M., together with whom (along with

his stay in London, is also documented, incidentally, by a precise episode mentioned in his «English» *Letters*: during dinner with the Russian consul Alexander Baxter, when he is invited to propose a toast, he does so to «eternal peace and thriving trade»[104].

On a stylistic level Malinovskii's account suffers by comparison with Karamzin's text[105]. However, if we bear in mind that Karamzin's English *Letters* were written in the early 1790s but published entirely only in 1801[106], it is legitimate to speculate on the extent to which the Russian writer might have been indebted to Malinovskii's vision[107]. The similarities in their statements about several aspects of British life stand out quite distinctly even against the background of commonplaces shown by other Russian travellers in contemporary memoirs. Moreover, a few peculiarities of the English section, if compared with the rest of Karamzin's *Letters*, might serve also to reinforce arguments in this direction: not too immediate

---

another Russian, G.A. Demidov) he enjoys this journey. Some years ago it was suggested that the man in question was indeed V.F. Malinovskii (See A.G. Cross, 'Whose Initials? Unidentified Persons in Karamzin's Letters from England', *Study Group on Eighteenth Century Russia*, no. 6 (1978), pp. 26-36).

[103] Karamzin also translated Schiller's *Lied an die Freude*. Under the title 'Pesn' mira' ir appeared in *Moskovskii zhurnal*, V (1792) no. 2.

[104] Karamzin, *op.cit.*, p. 338. For a specific discussion of his position on peace, see J.L. Black, 'N.M. Karamzin, Napoleon and the Notion of Defensive War in Russian History', *Canadian Slavonic Papers*, XII, no. 1 (1970), pp. 30-46.

[105] Unlike Karamzin, Malinovskii makes very few concessions to any sort of «entertainment», in his epistolary journey. One of them is the section entitled 'Komary', where, in the hope of placating the mosquitos tormenting his nights, Malinovskii outlines a treatise on them, a «Short Dissertation on Matters Astrological, Natural and Philosophical», where he cannnot avoid, however, didacticism, although humorous, comparing the mosquitos to the sanguinary conquerors and heroes of history (XI, pp. 145-148).

[106] The publishing history of this text is particularly complex. On it see V.V. Sipovskii, *N.M. Karamzin, avtor 'Pisem russkogo puteshestvennika'* (Spb., 1899) and N.A. Marchenko, 'Istoriia teksta «Pisem russkogo puteshestvennika»', in M. Karamzin, *Pis'ma russkogo puteshestvennika, op. cit.*.

The first part of the text appeared in *Moskovskii zhurnal* in 1791-1792 and ended with the chapter entitled 'Parizh, 27 marta' (before Karamzin's arrival in London). In the first volume of the almanac *Aglaia* (1794) Karamzin published the excerpt 'Puteshestvie v London', which included nevertheless only the description of his voyage towards London. Its last fragment, entitled 'London', ends with the statement: «We entered London». The second volume of *Aglaia* does not follow the chronological order, it refers to the period preceding the English stay.

[107] The possibility of an exchange of ideas between the two writers was first pointed out by Lotman, who wrote: «In certain places the sketches strikingly recall pages of Karamzin's 'Pis'ma', which allows one to speak of some sort of common circle of sources and of a unity of mood» (Iu. Lotman, *Sotvorenie Karamzina*, p. 191). Quite significantly, before him M.A. Arzumanova, in a discussion about eighteenth-century literature, raised the idea that 'Rossiianin v Anglii' could be an early draft of Karamzin's English *Letters*. Her hypothesis, which did not appear in any article, was mentioned to me by Prof. A.Cross in a conversation.

and vivid, they seem to have a derivative character[108], and as in the case of Malinovskii's account, some of them are given proper titles, instead of mere geographical indications of the places visited.

Very much in the fashion of the time, of a correspondence-miscellany about virtually every possible subject, Malinovskii's account alternates its picture of England with openly biographical passages and serious reflections on general philosophical themes, such as happiness or the interdependence of body and mind. But they are far from being «incidental reasoning», for whose intrusion into the account indulgence is asked by the editor of *Priiatnoe i poleznoe preprovozhdenie vremeni* (IX, p. 65). Malinovskii's reflections on «melancholia», or «indecision», for instance, represent psychological studies inescapable in contact with a specific cultural climate, the English pre-romantic one, and are used by Malinovskii to warn against the temptations of mental attitudes that can obscure reason. His narrative manner is thus very sober and plain, sometimes archaically rhetorical.

Malinovskii as traveller demonstrates an approach to his task which is no less recognizable than in his other literary incarnations: he conceives the idea of writing only for purposes of universal utility, his prose is much more didactic than entertaining, and he wants to convince by the strength of his arguments, rather than to please his public. It would be more appropriate to see his travel diary within the tradition of the philosophical journey through which a critical picture of reality can be offered, in the spirit of Radishchev's work, rather than within that of the sentimental journey in the Karamzinian sense.

The meaning that Malinovskii intends to give to his stay in England emerges clearly in the first lines of this series of letters, and is part of a more general and ambitious plan:

> I have postulated the happiness of man as the subject of my research throughout my life[109], and that is why I want to see English manners and customs, which are praised so highly, in reality, and to you, as to a friend, I will communicate my observations, applying them to the benefit of our fellow countrymen; without this they could have no appeal, for England itself has been described by so many (IX, p. 57).

---

[108] See A.G. Cross, 'Karamzin and England', p. 96, and *N.M. Karamzin. A Study of his Literary Career. 1783-1803* (London and Amsterdam, 1971), pp. 65-95.

[109] In a letter from Jassy to his future wife, Malinovskii was to write, similarly: «I have postulated that the object of my life is to do something useful» (RGALI, Fond 312, op. 1, no. 7, f. 1).

This position makes an important difference between him and his contemporaries in describing their impressions from England. The stylistic device of the Muscovite addressee, in keeping with the Russian adaptation of the Western travelogue, represents then something more than a mere narrative convention: it offers to Malinovskii the opportunity to personalize and give flesh to his constant references to Russian reality.

1.2.4. Comparing England and Russia

European and National History. In 'Rossiianin v Anglii' the relationship between Russia and England is part of the general one between Russians and Europeans, to be seen, in turn, in the frame of a sort of history of the peoples of the world. In the letter entitled 'Inostrantsy i Rossiiane', Malinovskii outlines a taxonomy of the peoples of the world, based on a tripartite division which is offered, synchronically and diachronically, by the geography and history of various civilizations: the wild peoples («*dikie*»), living in a state of natural simplicity and absence of laws; the barbaric peoples («*varvarskie*»), in the unhappy condition of having left the state of nature without replacing it with correct and true knowledge but with false prejudices; finally, the third stage, the one in which Europe is to be considered: «The whole of Europe was for a long time sunk in barbarity, now it is a most enlightened part of the world. The knowledge necessary to man's prosperity is steadily approaching perfection» (IX, p. 59). The author can focus at this point on an account of the position of Russia in this picture:

> Russians are for Europe a new people, who are approaching enlightenment
> at an excellent pace. Just as we have already matched the whole of Europe in
> military arts, thus we will match them in other sciences too (...) We have
> become famous for our strength, now it behoves us to achieve equal fame
> for our character and enlightenment (IX, p. 60).

The idea that the era in which Russia had considered her main purpose to be catching up with Europe in the art of war was over, and that it was now time to measure the forces on a different ground, is full of implications. We are offered already in the first pages some of the notions that will be systematically organized in *Rassuzhdenie o mire i voine* and variously developed in the subsequent writings. Particularly important here is the presence of one of the main conceptual points on which the treatise on peace was to be organized: the opposition between the civilizations based on war and those based on *«prosveshchenie»* (enlightenment). The recurrent presence of certain themes (the concern for *«chelovecheskoe blagodenstvie»* (prosperity of mankind), the notion of *«liubov' otechestva»* (love for the fatherland), the considerations on the *«nastoiashchaia slava»* (genuine glory) as opposed to the ephemeral one, and the appraisal of the authentic *«velikie liudi»* (great men), for example), if certainly not typical of this writer only, can be detected as a recognizably «Malinovskian» feature of this text when associated with a peculiar ideological context like this.

A prominent place is given in his letters to the theme of a Russian historiography. Its discussion is introduced in very clear terms in the letter dated 20 September 1790 and entitled 'Istoriia': «Living among English people, I think all the more about Russians. We, gentle brother[110], do not have a genuine History of our fatherland» (XI, p. 257).

At the time when Malinovskii wrote, the quest for a «national» history, one of the issues most familiar to Russian writers inspired by the Enlightenment, could only count on a few remarkable attempts in this direction. Malinovskii expresses his disapproval on the fact that in order to acquire knowledge of the past of their own country Russians still had to content themselves with the historical descriptions written by foreign writers; several European historians had in fact published works on Russia over the last few decades; among them Malinovskii cites only Pierre-Charles Levesque (XI, p. 262)[111]. If we are able to find decisive appraisals of other European historians elsewhere in the correspondence (he mentions favourably Gibbon, IX, p. 101), in the case of Levesque his criticism seems to be addressed not as much to the ideological orientation of his work, as to his not being a Russian. Karamzin, who personally met Levesque in France, expressed substantially the same opinion, in the same year, in his *Letters*, where his polemical attack on foreign historians concentrated on the person of Levesque, whose work «although it has many shortcomings, is nevertheless better than all the others (...) until now we have no good Russian History, that is one written with philosophic insight, with a critical

---

[110] In 'Rossiianin v Anglii' the author uses alternatively the words *brat* and *drug*. Malinovskii's addressee could simply be a fictitious one. In this respect, however, it is interesting to consider that a great number of the letters sent by Malinovskii to his real brother Pavel Fedorovich begin with the formula *liubeznoi brat*, as in this case. It should also be remembered that the editor of the journal, Sokhatskii, was his brother-in-law. Additionally, the word *brat* was widely used among Masons.

[111] The work by Levesque, *Histoire de Russie tirée des chroniques originales, de pièces authentiques et des meilleurs historiens de la nation* (Paris, 1782), had a strong impact as the first general history of Russia and of its empire.

edge, with noble eloquence. Tacitus, Hume, Robertson, Gibbon, these are the models!»[112]. Also for Karamzin, Levesque's main defect is therefore his being alien to that real knowledge of Russia that only comes from being born there[113]. Malinovskii strengthens his view about the absence of a national history by resorting to an allegorical comparison:

> In the judgement of a Russian any European is like the man who, having quarrelled with a lion about the superiority of people over beasts such as himself, showed him a statue of Hercules rending the jaws of a lion in an engraver's shop. We can answer foreigners (...) in the same way as this lion answered: if we had Writers, we would show Europeans that we are no worse than they are (XI, p. 261).

The historical vision outlined in this letter is elaborate and rich enough to let us suppose that the young Malinovskii intended to put historical work among his future tasks: he advocates an understanding of Russian history in which the less glorious moments (like the period under the Tatar yoke) are to be judged with more condescension when compared with similar situations of subjection in other European countries; without idealizing the Russian past, he thinks that it is necessary to highlight the importance of rulers like Dmitrii Donskoi, for example, or of historical experiences like the one of Novgorod, «which flourished at a time when almost all Europe was still sunk in barbarity» (XI, p. 257). Talking about the level of civilization reached by Novgorod, Malinovskii mentions its «*narodnaia gordost'*» (people's pride) (XI, p. 257), emphasizing thereby the rule of the people as a determining force in the country's past[114].

At the end of the letter devoted to this subject Malinovskii makes the suggestion that the task of writing a Russian history should be made more attractive to Russian writers by promising a suitable remuneration for it. But before that, showing an unusual lack of modesty, Malinovskii proposes himself, if not as a proper historical writer, as a self appointed «*sadovnik*»

---

[112] Karamzin, *op.cit.*, p. 252.

[113] «In addition Russia is not his motherland» (*op.cit.*, XI, p. 253). The similarity of views on Levesque between the two authors has been remarked also by Waegemans, *op.cit.*, p. 267.

[114] In this respect it is important to note that especially in Radishchev's work the reference to Novgorod as to a moment of remarkable freedom and democracy in the history of Russia had evident critical implications for the Russia of Catherine (see particularly the section 'Novgorod' in *Puteshestvie iz Peterburga v Moskvu*). Particularly interesting is the circumstance that in order to prove the position of power reached by Novgorod both Malinovskii (XI, p. 257) and Radishchev (*op.cit.*, p. 87) quote the proverb «Kto protiv Boga i Novgoroda?».

A famous work emphasizing Novgorodian liberty was Ia. Kniazhnin's tragedy *Vadim Novgorodskii*, written in 1789 and published in 1793.

(gardener) (XI, p. 260) with the mission of disseminating a correct knowledge of the past among the Russians.

In point of fact, the only proper major work of purely historical nature in his literary career was to be his 'Istoriia Rossii dlia prostykh i malykh', written in 1803[115]; judging from the manuscript left by him, he apparently did not go, however, beyond the stage of a first draft. In 'Istoriia Rossii', a work published in his periodical *Osennie vechera*, where several articles have a distinctive historical character, he still complained about the lack of comprehensive historical works, and suggested that «as there is not one good complete history of the fatherland», the only reasonable thing to do was to look back to the *«starye letopisi»* (old chronicles)[116].

In this letter Malinovskii starts from denouncing the absence of an adequate historical knowledge of the past in his country to show what appears to be its most deplorable consequence: the absence of patriotic feelings among the Russian people. The necessity of *«liubov' otechestva»* [117], a notion to which he was to return in several writings, is not seen here in an anticosmopolitan sense; on the contrary, Malinovskii sees it as a virtue shared by the most educated and advanced part of the European population of that time: «people of generous disposition with delicate feelings of honour and with enlightened minds are always distinguished by love for their fatherland» (XI, p. 259).

The link between the idea that Russia had its own peculiar history, still to be recognized and adequately described, and the quest for love for the fatherland, was not new, having been developed already by Lomonosov in his historical writings of the 1750s and then not rarely used in an anti-state and anti-autocratic sense by the enlightened writers of the 1770s and 1780s. After the French Revolution, its use could on the other hand sound like a conservative warning for the Russian rulers, to whom the consequences of neglecting the national feelings of their people had to appear extremely clearly[118]. In the case of Malinovskii, there is a statement which is

---

115 IRLI, Fond 244, op. 25, no. 307.

116 'Istoriia Rossii', *Osennie vechera* no. 6 (1803), pp. 41. Here he transcribes a passage of the *Stepennaia kniga* to parallel the French menace and the Tatar one. Note that the *Stepennaia kniga* was edited by Müller in 1775.

117 In elaborating this notion in the context of his English letters, Malinovskii was probably influenced by the contemporary English debate. It should be mentioned, in this respect, *A Discourse on the Love of our Country*, delivered by Richard Price on 4 November 1789.

118 On this, see W. Gleason, 'State and Nationality in Late-Eighteenth-Century Russian Thought, in *Moral Idealists, Bureaucracy, and Catherine the Great* (New

particularly illuminating in understanding his interpretation of the problem: «The chief and only means to arouse and preserve love for the fatherland consists in *the people's respect for themselves*» (XI, p. 260) (underlined by the author). Emphasizing the notion of the respect of the Russian people for themselves, Malinovskii introduces an important element into the discussion on the national awareness, rich in political implications as to the nature of this awareness. The quest for a history more conscious of the worth of Russia's past appears to be not only a quest for a stronger sense of national identity, but also the only way seen by Malinovskii to educate the Russian people to a higher degree of «civic» awareness, comparable to the one observed among the English people[119].

Malinovskii's England. The constant comparison with his fatherland explains the large space devoted in Malinovskii's letters from England to considerations on Russian history or other «domestic» themes. But Malinovskii's tour of England was also a voyage of discovery, during which he had the opportunity to create for himself an image of England based on first-hand impressions. Before undertaking it, he wants to make clear a preliminary point: his determination not to pay uncritical tribute to that country. His love for England does not feed itself on that unconditional exterophilia which characterized his homeland at that time and had as a counterpart an endless contempt for everything which was Russian. In this respect Malinovskii, echoing other commentators, deplores the fact that the Russians deprive themselves even of the pleasure of speaking their own language (IX, pp. 62-63).

How does the young Malinovskii proceed to build his picture of England as it emerges from *Rossiianin v Anglii*? He visits trials and churches, the theatres and the Stock Exchange, is received in private houses

---

Brunswick, 1981); on the national self-awareness, see I. Serman, 'Russian National Consciousness and its Development in the Eighteenth Century', in R. Bartlett, J. M. Hartley (eds.), *Russia in the Age of the Enlightenment* (Basingstoke, 1990), pp. 41-56. A particularly relevant contribution to the discussion on the subject is A.G. Cross, 'Russian Perceptions of England, and Russian National Awareness at the End of the Eighteenth and the Beginning of the Nineteenth Centuries', *Slavonic and East European Review*, LXI (1983), pp. 89-106, where space is also given to the position of the author of 'Rossiianin v Anglii'.

[119] It is interesting to see how just a few years later another Russian traveller in England, N.N. Murav'ev, will relate to the love for the fatherland typical of the English people the main source of anything good that is to be found in England, with the important difference that the Malinovskian moderate idea of «*liubov' otechestva*» (love for the fatherland) becomes in Murav'ev's observations «*strast' k otechestvu*» (passion for the fatherland), denoted by a much stronger patriotic zeal ('Opyt o Velikobritanii i posledstvennye rassuzhdeniia', *Severnyi vestnik*, V (Spb., 1805), pp. 250-251).

and in jails, sees the famed streets of London, and above all, he travels extensively around Britain. He was one of the very few Russians travellers of the eighteenth century to reach Edinburgh[120].

His final evaluation is overwhelmingly in favour of England, but not without critical comments. He admires the remarkable interest in public affairs among the common English people[121] and their «natural» good qualities. He ponders other national psychological features, first of all the melancholia, which arises from the unfavourable weather and becomes a characteristic feature spreading over all the arts practiced by the English.

Paying his homage to the commonplace that expected English women to be extraordinarily attractive, he enumerates all the reasons why he finds them not only beautiful creatures, but also ideal intellectual companions (not surprisingly, on his return to Russia he was to chose a half-English wife for himself):

> English women are wonderful! Fair, rosy, and they have good features and pleasant figures. In this they resemble our Russian girls. They love reading and can reason! While among us this can be considered a rarity. (...) They are not so much lively as sensitive, tender, and are great devotees of music and dance. I was very surprised that they talk more of politics, the ministry, and the condition of the state, than they do of apparel (IX, p. 66).

He is surprised to see English women at trials and compares them with their Russian counterparts, sharing the same surprise and using almost the same words as Karamzin[122]: «Our women for the most part sit at their toilette, or make the rounds of the French shops, while English women are present at the law court and listen to fine speeches» (IX, p. 103).

Analyzing the position of English women in society as it is reflected in the legislation concerning such problems as divorce and infidelity, he finds that they are given a certain number of rights[123]. The contrast with his

---

[120] See A.G. Cross, 'The High Road and the Low: Russian Students and Travellers in Eighteenth-Century Scotland', *op. cit.*.

[121] Referring to a merchant, Malinovskii writes «he debated like a Minister about affairs of state» (XII, p. 359).

[122] Complaining about the Russian woman, Karamzin writes in his *Letters*: «while at home she only sits at her toilette» (*op.cit.*, p. 365). A parallel between the two writers should however take into account Karamzin's inclination to admire in English women above all their qualities as wives.

[123] «Although the local laws give the husband power over his wife, if he behaves cruelly, then the wife can make a complaint about him (...). In the event of divorce, if the wife does not want to remarry, the husband may be obliged to give her an annual sum for her keep, in proportion to his income» (XI, pp. 327-328).

«barbaric» homeland[124] is even more apparent when Malinovskii is asked by English people about the current situation in Russia: «Men with laughter and women with horror ask if it is true, that our husbands beat their wives» (XI, p. 328)[125].

For most of the Russian travellers to England, this country was first of all perceived through the image that they received in London. In this respect, Malinovskii's impression is far from being positive. He describes the English capital as an example of architectural development absolutely not to be followed, a sort of urban nightmare where

> The houses all stand one alongside the other, as if joined, and they are so tall that they shut off the sunlight, while the lower storeys, where the kitchens are, are completely underground: light reaches them through a grill, over which people walk, for the windows are lower than the street (IX, p. 67).

London seems to have everything to lose from a comparison with Moscow, recalled as a sort of Paradise on Earth when depicted as its natural antithesis:

> In big European towns poor people live in the attics, where they are barely protected from bad weather, or in the lower storeys, where even air cannot reach them; but in Moscow every poor fellow is his own proprietor and master of his own house (IX, p. 68).

The socio-architectural polarization up-down, observed by Malinovskii in the European capitals, also strikes Karamzin, who records:

> It is important to know that all London houses are built with an underground section, where generally are the kitchen, the cellar, and also some sort of very poorly lit rooms for the servants, serving girls or poor people. In Paris want climbs up to the attic under the clouds, here it descends into the earth[126].

To Malinovskii's eyes, London presents a huge number of social problems:

> There is an awful multitude of poor people (...), luxury is excessive here (...) in the evening it is dangerous to walk or to travel around London (...) there are many dissolute girls (...) suicides occur very frequently (...)

---

[124] On the state of female education in Russia, see J.L. Black, 'Educating Women in Eighteenth-Century Russia', in *Citizens for the Fatherland. Education, Educators, and Pedagogical Ideals in Eighteenth-Century Russia* (New York, 1979).

[125] The habit of Russian men to beat their wives was also echoed in the *Domostroi*.

[126] Karamzin, *op.cit.*, pp. 336-337.

madness is also not at all rare here (...) drunkness is not unusual (IX, pp. 68-70).

The letter entitled *Anglichane*, which had opened with the statement that the English had become a «modnyi narod» (fashionable people), thus concludes with a warning to his countrymen not to imitate them in their more dubious pursuits.

One of the institutional aspects of English life to which Malinovskii gives a prominent place, in his letters, is the legal system. In other works he will depict the English parliamentary system, or eulogize the freedom of the English press[127]. Here he seems interested in emphasizing the excellence of a system based on a notion still particularly alien to Russian culture of the time: the primacy of law. One of the obligatory stops for a Russian visitor in England at that period was the trial of the ex-governor of the East India Company, Warren Hastings, lasting from 1788 to 1795[128]. Attending one of its sessions at Westminster Hall, Malinovskii comments on the eloquence of his prosecutors, Edmund Burke, Richard Sheridan and Charles Fox; he is fascinated by its external aspects (the people elegantly dressed in the law courts, the gravity of the judges) no less than by the institution as such. 31 January 1790 is spent by him observing a trial, described meticulously (and without comment) in its procedures, rituals, and in the different roles played by the participants.

After having scrutinized the English legal system, Malinovskii gives a general evaluation of the administration of justice in that country in the section entitled 'Angliiskii sud' (XI, pp. 321-332). The two main aspects stressed by him are that English people do not interpret the laws but follow the letter of them, and that they do not consider it a humiliation to submit themselves to law. This judgment will be echoed particularly by another visitor after him, Murav'ev, who will state that in England «the law is equal for all»[129], implying with that that it is not conceived to serve primarily the rich.

---

[127] In his unpublished article 'Bespristrastnyi sovet velikobritanskomu narodu', Malinovskii wrote: «Free book printing, this valuable support of your blessed constitution, gives you the means to direct the opinion of an enlightened public, to point out in good time all the mistakes and abuses of the government» (IRLI, Fond 244, op. 25, no. 321, f.1).

[128] Karamzin gives a vivid description of the same event, *op.cit.*, pp. 371-373. On it see also Komarovskii, *op.cit.,* pp. 16-17.

[129] Murav'ev, *op.cit.*, p. 155.

   Scotland. On 3rd November 1790 the Russian visitor reaches Scotland, after a journey during which he has had the opportunity to taste all the delights of travelling in England, the country where «you have not had time to go into the chamber, when the horses are already ready» (XI, p. 356) and where all the routes are «such, as is the road from Petersburg to Tsarskoe Selo» (XI, p. 357). He will spend four months in Edinburgh, before moving back to London at the end of February 1791; proceeding on the way back he will visit Newcastle upon Tyne (8 March), York (16 March) and Manchester. The reasons for this midwinter excursion to Edinburgh, characterized by Malinovskii as *«uchenyi gorod»* (a learned city), could hardly have been merely touristic. Apart from a mysterious hint about the «usefulness» of his stay in Scotland[130], the text itself, however, offers little evidence to support the assumption of a possible unofficial, secret mission.

   For Edinburgh and the events that happened to him there Malinovskii reserves the most enthusiastic words in the entire account. He finds the New Town architecturally remarkable, visits and appreciates above all its *«arkhiv vsekh publichnikh del»* (archive of all public matters) and converses with a prominent *«Russkii Anglichanin»* (Russian Englishman). Visiting the Scottish churches, he listens to the sermons of two of the most famous preachers of his time, Dr. Blair and Dr. Greenfield, and finds remarkable the way they can «leave an impression in a man, and sow good principles in his heart, which will further not only the eternal but also the temporal felicity of a man» (XI, p. 364).

   A Quaker dream. Finally, it is in Scotland that the young philosopher has a personal experience destined to have far-reaching consequences in his further development. In the account entitled 'Shotlandskoe voskresenie' we find Malinovskii attending a service in a Quaker church. Thanks to the extremely quiet setting, he very soon falls asleep, and has an illuminating dream. The real traveller turns into his imaginary alter-ego, and explores a city inhabited by a peaceful and happy community; he attends another, imaginary service, during which a sermon about the *«liubov' blizhnego»* (love of your neighbour) is delivered, beautiful voices sing psalms and twelve young couples are married. After the service, the foreign visitor is given by the preacher full explanation of their community:

---

   [130] «The affectionate treatment of my acquaintances and confirmation of the usefulness of the time I spend here keep me in a cheerful frame of mind» (XI, p. 388).

> In conversation with him I found out that in his parish there were no
> disobedient sons, no fathers who cursed their children, no husband who
> hated his wife, no wife who betrayed her husband, no master nasty to his
> servants. I enquired what arrangements he made for the poor. We have no
> poor, he said, for laziness and idleness are considered sins; and every one
> who wants to work is provided with sufficient employment. The elderly,
> the sick and the orphaned, if they cannot support themselves, are
> supported by the parishioners (...). When I showed astonishment at all I
> had heard, the priest said to me: surely you are a Christian? How can you
> be surprised? Have you not read what example was left us by the
> Christians of the Apostolic era? Surely you know that Christ said that the
> whole of his law consists in loving God and loving your neighbour? (XI,
> pp. 381-382).

It is not difficult to see how this short passage acquires the features of
a utopian dream, in the tradition of the literary *«son»* (dream) so
characteristic of eighteenth-century Russian literature of the
Enlightenment[131]. To identify it as such, it is sufficient to underline aspects
like the quest for a return to the purity of original Christianity; the absence
of indigence and social conflicts; the reference to paradisal motifs in the
description of uncontaminated nature adorned by beautiful creations of
human work[132]; the necessity of a peaceful condition and attitude of mind
before access to the church could be gained[133].

The «visionary» fragment is inserted without breaking the continuity
of the texture of the travel account[134], framed with particular care for
narrative verisimilitude, and the shift between the two services in the
Quaker churches, the real one and the imagined, is worked out in masterly
fashion.

---

[131] Quite typically, the utopian passage assumes the form of a fragment located in a
work written in a different genre. After Sumarokov's *Shchastlivoe obshchestvo: son'*
(1759), we find descriptions of ideal lands contained in dreams in M. Chulkov's
Peresmeshnik, ili Slavenskie skazki (1789) ('Son Kidala'), in Radishchev's *Puteshestvie iz
Peterburga v Moskvu* (1790) ('Spasskaia polest''). After the French Revolution the utopian
dream becomes however quite rare.

On utopian literature in XVIII century, see particularly S. Baehr, 'The Rise of the
Russian Utopia', in *The Paradise Myth in Eighteenth-Century Russia* (Stanford, 1991),
providing an up-to-date bibliography on the subject. See also a reference to utopian dreams
in V. Shestakov, 'The Evolution of Russian Literary Utopias', in *Utopia and Antiutopia in
Russia*, forthcoming.

[132] See before: «I suddenly saw a vast square, spread with turf and planted with
flowers and trees, among which stood a huge and wonderful building» (XI, p.366).

[133] «Approaching it respectfully I saw over the doors the following inscription (...)
Before stepping into the temple, make peace with your enemy» (XI, p. 366).

[134] «It must be acknowledged that Quaker churches are so quiet that you can even
sleep in them. And thus I fell asleep and saw the following dream (...)» (XI, p. 365).

The literary form more consistently taken by Malinovskii's rational thought is certainly the project rather than the utopia, but it should be considered that a contradiction between reformistic and utopian thinking was shared by a considerable part of eighteenth-century literature inspired by the Enlightenment.

In point of fact, this literary «son» could more fruitfully be seen as a revealing vision of a present and real situation rather than as a hopeful anticipation of an ideal future. It is a sort of initiatory experience that introduces Malinovskii into the reality of a particular community, the Quakers. The use of the dream device[135] allows him to depict in enthusiastic terms (without incurring Russian censorship) a community modelled on a genuine Christian ethic where his two major concerns, peace and social justice, were given an ideal solution.

Malinovskii's enthusiasm over the contact with the Quakers is not paralleled by any similar reaction among Russian visitors to England at that time. Despite the almost identical external circumstances, Karamzin's sleeping in a Quaker Church is not illuminated by any dream, and the writer, disappointed by his long and unfulfilled wait for a sermon, leaves the church with the irritated exclamation: «Gentlemen Quakers! You will not lure me further!»[136]. For another Russian traveller, Zinov'ev, the encounter with a Quaker community is equally very far from making the same impact: he simply concludes that «they deprive themselves (...) of many of the innocent pleasures of this world»[137].

Among Malinovskii's contemporaries, Radishchev was an exception when eulogizing, in his *Journey from Petersburg to Moscow*, the generous soul of the Quakers[138], because the knowledge of their experience was certainly far from being widespread in eighteenth-century Russia[139]. The

---

[135] Another literary dream in Malinovskii's work is apparently to be found in the final, unpublished chapter of *Pustynnik* entitled 'Son', but is to be considered rather as a political anti-utopia: in it a conqueror, in whom it is not difficult to recognize Napoleon, makes the European peoples blindly follow him until they are precipitated into an abyss.

[136] Karamzin, *op.cit.*, p. 344.

[137] Zinov'ev, *op.cit.*, p. 440.

[138] Radishchev, *op.cit.*, p. 173. In the work 'O zakonopolozhenii', one of his memoranda drawn up for legislative reforms, Radishchev makes the suggestion that it would be instructive to investigate the system introduced by the Quakers in Pennsylvania, based on the abolition of capital and corporal punishment (*op.cit.*, p. 473).

[139] For an analysis of the presence of Quakers in Russia, see A. Pypin, 'Imperator Aleksander I i kvakery', *Vestnik Evropy*, no.10 (1869), pp. 751-769, J. Benson, *Quakers Pioneers in Russia* (London, 1902), R.C. Scott, *Quakers in Russia* (London, 1964), A.B. McMillin, 'Quakers in Early Nineteenth-Century Russia', *Slavonic and East European Studies*, no. 125 (1973), pp. 567-579.

contacts with the «Society of Friends» had been limited, over the past century, to a few, sporadic episodes, mostly of a personal character: in 1698 Peter I had had an encounter with a Quaker delegation[140]; in 1768 Catherine the Great and her grandchildren Alexander and Constantine had been inoculated by Thomas Dimsdale, known as «the Quaker doctor»; Alexander I was to attend a Quaker meeting in England only in 1813 (showing a great interest in them).

Malinovskii's first-hand acquaintance with the Quakers can be supposed to have therefore acquired, in his eyes, the features of an authentic revelation. It is difficult to assert to what extent the young Russian philosopher was influenced by the Quaker experience in the formation of his thinking on peace[141]. The relevance of this model can however be detected by a direct reference to the Quakers in his *Rassuzhdenie o mire i voine*[142].

Industrial towns. In his search for aspects of the British life which are *«dostoiny podrazhaniia»* (worthy of imitation) (XI, p. 408), Malinovskii cannot avoid being struck by the industrial towns. He gives a full description of a factory in Manchester, where he observes the new manufacturing process used in a wool mill (XI, pp. 406-408). Before him, two other Russians had gone on a tour of inspection of English manufactures: Kurakin and Zinov'ev. It is particularly interesting to compare Malinovskii's observations with those left by the latter. In Leeds Zinov'ev visited several of them and in the report left by him in the form of letters to the Russian ambassador Vorontsov he gave a detailed account of them; his approach however seems quite detached, and the possibility of individual enrichment that the manufactures can provide seems one of the

---

[140] Among others, he had a conversation with William Penn (see R. C. Scott, *Quakers in Russia*, p. 38), the author of *An Essay towards the Present and Future Peace of Europe* (1693).

[141] The issue of peace was historically considerably relevant in the Quaker communities. On the subject see particularly M.E. Hirst, *The Quakers in Peace and War* (London, 1923), and G.W. Knowles (ed.), *Quakers and Peace* (London, 1927).

[142] In part III of the *Rassuzhdenie* Malinovskii wrote: «Only the simple, little known Quakers judged that a Christian is not permitted to make war, and some of their followers never take up arms or even defend themselves in a besieged city» (See the text published in J. Skowronek, '«Rozwazania o pokoju i wojnie» Wasyla F. Malinowskiego', *Teki archiwalne*, no. 17 (1978), p. 44). In a manuscript of 1804 Malinovskii mentions the impact on sixteenth-century German culture of the «English sects of Quakers, Methodists and others» ('Materialy po istorii germanskoi religioznoi filosofii», IRLI, Fond 244, op. 25, no. 317, f. 9).

most remarkable things to him[143]. An explanation for this can be found in the excerpts not included in the nineteenth century publication of his 'Zhurnal puteshestvii', from which it is clear that Zinov'ev sees differently the priorities of the economic development of Russia: «In this respect I suggest that the first object of our government should be to strive with all its might to encourage and increase cultivation of the land»[144].

Malinovskii's position is in favour of the introduction of the new manufacturing processes in Russia, but according to him much more than a description is necessary to attain this purpose, so he refrains from a more detailed account. As for English trade, about which he says in another passage that Russian merchants should be encouraged to go abroad to learn new and more efficient trading methods (XI, p. 393), for the advance of manufactures his suggestion is that a massive transference of people and competence is the only way to bring Russia to a new economic stage.

> I am not going to describe the other manufactures to you, for such description is tedious, and cannot be sufficient to introduce them into Russia. For that machines and the people used to controlling them are necessary; export of the former from here is forbidden, but it is possible to summon people to Russia and they could easily start up factories like the ones here (XI, p. 4O8).

Malinovskii's position was certainly in keeping with a persistent policy on the part of the Russian government of recruiting British entrepreneurs and British craftsmen in order to give a decisive impulse to industrial development in Russia[145]. Moreover, Malinovskii was to contribute substantially to the theoretical debate on industrialization with his translation into Russian of Alexander Hamilton's *Report on the Subject of Manufactures* (written in 1791). According to what he says in the short preface that he added, it was the Minister of Finance, Dmitrii A. Gur'ev, who arranged for the publication in Russia of Hamilton's book. The Russian

---

[143] He gives the amount of the fortune accumulated by the manufactory run by the «Tudor et Comp.», 'Zhurnal puteshestviia V.N. Zinov'eva po Germanii, Italii, Frantsii i Anglii v 1784-1788 gg.', *Russkaia starina*, XXIII (1878), p. 423. To Vorontsov he promised a more detailed account to be given on his return in London (p. 424).

[144] Quoted in Iu. Lotman, 'Cherty real'noi politiki v pozitsii Karamzina 1790-kh gg.', *XVIII vek*, XIII (1981), p. 115. The statement brought the author, on the other hand, to important conclusions concerning the elimination of serfdom in Russia (see the discussion *ibid.*, pp. 114-115).

[145] On the subject, see particularly E. Robinson, 'The Transference of British Technology to Russia 1760-1820: A Preliminary Enquiry', in Barrie M. Ratcliffe (ed.), *Great Britain and Her World, 1750-1914: Essays in Honour of W.O. Henderson* (Manchester, 1975), pp. 1-26.

translation did not appear in St Petersburg until 1807. We are also
informed by Malinovskii that a copy of the book was at that time available
in England only in manuscript[146].

The prisons. On the way back from Manchester to London,
Malinovskii is also impressed by his visit to a prison, «built according to the
plan of the glorious Howard» (XI, p. 408), where he finds that the
conditions in terms of hygiene and humanity are ideal. Before entering into
his description of the English prisons, Karamzin gives a similar comment:
«I spent today like Howard - I inspected prisons - I praised the
solicitousness of the English governing body, deplored the people, and felt
abhorrence at the people»[147]. The common enthusiastic reference to John
Howard (1726-1790) might have mirrored the recent popularity given to
the English philanthropist, author of the book *The State of Prisons in
England and Wales* (1777), by his inspection of the Russian prisons in
1789[148].

Considered in its entirety, Malinovskii's account from England is a
rich and intriguing document illuminating his intellectual evolution. Apart
from the fruitful and far-reaching influence of the political considerations
here developed, Malinovskii's letters contain the seeds of all his future
activity as social and political thinker, philanthropist and pedagogue.

---

[146] «The minister of crown affairs, Dmitrii Aleksandrovich Gur'ev, inspired by an
indefatigable concern to bring Russian manufacture to a flourishing condition, for which
our glass factories give us obvious experience (...), ordered this essay from England; it is
so rare that we were obliged to be content with the manuscript; it is the translation prepared
from the latter which is now being published for an enlightened public, in a precise
testimony to the usefulness of the practical comments made, and their absolute relevance to
Russia's condition», *Otchet general-kaznacheia Aleksandra Gamil'tona, uchinennyi
Amerikanskim shtatam 1791 g. o pol'ze manufaktur i otnoshenii onykh k torgovle i
zemledeliiu* (Spb., 1807), p. II. According to another source, it was originally Count
Vorontsov who in 1792 expressed the wish to be sent Hamilton's reports to Congress, with
the intention to transmit them to his brother Aleksandr, then Minister of Commerce, in order
to spread in Russia important information on this country (See a letter to Hamilton from
Governor Morris in London, in H.C.Syrett, J.E.Cook (eds.), *The Papers of Alexander
Hamilton* (New York and London, 1966), XI, pp. 260-261).
[147] Karamzin, *op. cit.* p. 339. This is not the only place where Karamzin refers
favourably to the work of the English philanthropist (see A.G. Cross, 'Karamzin and
England', p. 98).
[148] On the subject see in particular A.G. Cross, 'The Philanthropist, the Travelling
Tutor and the Empress: British Visitors and Catherine II's Plans for Penal and Medical
Reform', in R.P. Bartlett (ed.), *Russia and the World of the Eighteenth Century*
(Columbus, Ohio, 1988), pp. 214-228.

These letters reveal a philosophical foundation not present to the same extent in any other contemporary Russian account. In them Malinovskii provided his own, personal image of England and a durable system of cultural and political references on which he drew for the rest of his life. One of the most synthetic judgements on this country is contained in an article written in 1803 for his journal *Osennie vechera*, where his wish to deplore the worse aspects of English life reaches a complex and paradigmatical equilibrium with his interest in the sane and good principles of that society:

> England contains everything that is corrupt in the world, especially in herheart, London. England is a proud Babylon, a Tyre, a Sidon, a Sodom, a Gomorrah! Will the righteous Judge of the world not call to account all lawlessness, all evil doing and inhumanity? Do they not trade there in everything that is holy and pure? Do they not even sell votes here? Liverpool, Liverpool! You send dungeons to Africa and transport the people you steal there to America!
> But where are there people of such gentle humanity, that they have renounced the use of sugar, because it is mixed not with the blood of oxen, as the simple Russians think, but with *human* blood, as the English know well. Where do truth and justice sit firmly on their throne, untainted by hypocrisy and bribery? In England. Where has wisdom disseminated the most of its teaching? There again; there too family prosperity dwells; (...) there philanthropy opens prisons, builds hospitals, seeks out the poor (...). Where will you find kind, diligent, sincere executors of the Gospel teaching? In England. There also you will find love of the fatherland and a social spirit reigning supreme[149].

1.3. The years in Jassy, work in the College of Foreign Affairs and publicist activity (1791-1811)

1.3.1. 1791-1792: First journey to Moldavia

Soon after his return from England in 1791, the young Malinovskii expressed the desire to be sent to the theatre of war in Turkey, as he was to record later in a letter to V.P. Kochubei: «I went there for the first time from England to see the war in reality and to supplement my book about it with all possible attestations of its evils»[150]. When he arrived in Jassy, the

---

[149] *Osennie vechera* (Spb., 1803), pp. 21-23.

war between Russia and Turkey, which began in 1787, was already
concluded; his knowledge of the Turkish language, however, allowed him
to take part, as secretary, in the peace negotiations, led for Russia by Count
F.V. Rostopchin[151].

One of the conditions of the treaty provided for the return of the
Danubian principalities to the Turkish empire, and this was condemned by
Malinovskii. He witnessed the disappointment of the Moldavian and
Wallachian patriots, whose desire for independence was ignored. In the
same letter to Kochubei quoted above he wrote:

> While I was there the last resolution was completed, which decided the fate
> of Moldavia and Wallachia. I witnessed the insulting of their fatherland by
> the former enemies; close acquaintances, with friendly intent, revealed their
> indignation and resentments when the given word on liberation was not
> kept. You will believe this, judging from your own experiences; the extent
> to which love of the fatherland and a sense of the people's honour enliven a
> noble heart does not depend on rank and grade of service; I took these
> rebukes, these reproaches to heart, as if made personally to me, and
> remembered these lands, bore them always in my heart.

He did not have the opportunity to exercise any influence on the course
of diplomatic events, but the sense of a personal responsibility was not to
leave him and was to lie behind his decision, a few years later, to return to
Jassy and accomplish the duty he felt towards the Danubian peoples.

Apart from the reasons mentioned above to explain Malinovskii's
original decision to go to Jassy, we can presume that he looked on this move
as a possible way to secure a position in Russian society, which became
particularly important at a time when he was determined to marry the
woman he loved, Sof'ia Andreevna Samborskaia (1772-1812), the second
daughter of A.A. Samborskii. In a letter to her, dated 4 September 1791,
Malinovskii communicates the sense he had intended to give to his stay in
Jassy in the context of his private happiness and the way these expectations
were frustrated:

> My fortune is not secure, and for that reason I parted from you, and came
> here (...) For you rank and riches are nothing, if you love me (...). But
> you know Russia - there, without them, a man is not considered a man. I

---

150 See Malinovskii's letter to V.P. Kochubei, *Chteniia v imperatorskom
Obshchestve istorii i drevnostei rossiiskikh pri Moskovskom universitete*, V, no. 1 (1863),
pp. 172-175, also republished in V.F. Malinovskii, *Izbrannye obshchestvenno-
politicheskie sochineniia*, pp. 149-151.

151 «Peace caught up with me on the threshold, and instead of amid battles and
sieges, I found myself at the Congress as a colleague of the former minister, Count
Rostopchin» (*ibid.*, p. 149).

have made it the purpose of my life, to do something useful (...) you know my disposition, my intolerance of obliging influential people, here for the present time I do nothing but roam among the crowds of those seeking favours and must count it good fortune if anyone's gaze should fall on me[152].

Malinovskii stayed in Jassy until February or March 1792[153]. At the end of the congress he was given the rank of *kollezhskii asessor* and returned to St Petersburg, where he continued to serve in the College of Foreign Affairs.

Malinovskii's short stay in Jassy did not prevent him from showing a particular interest in Moldavian culture and institutions. He recorded his observations on that country in a series of notes, and on his return to St Petersburg he looked for a way to submit them to the attention of Russian readers without exposing himself to excessive publicity.

Malinovskii's 'Zapiski o Moldavii' appeared in 1797 on the pages of *Priiatnoe i poleznoe preprovozhdenie vremeni*[154], the periodical edited by his brother-in-law Pavel Sokhatskii; they were introduced by the editor as coming «from a person who has been there during the last Turkish war», and his authorship was concealed under the initials «V.M.»[155]. These notes are the most important source of information on Malinovskii's views about Moldavia.

It should be recalled that the previous year Malinovskii's work 'Rossiianin v Anglii' was published in the same journal. In point of fact, the 'Notes on Moldavia' may be seen as a sort of sequel to those letters, transferred into a virtually antithetical cultural context. The fields of investigation on which the traveller focuses his attention are in many ways the same: here, as in England, he is interested in analyzing the degree of civilization of the country, the sense of patriotism in the population, the

---

[152] RGALI, Fond 312, op. 1, n. 7, f. 1.

[153] On 4 January 1792 he wrote: «I think you have heard that peace has been concluded, but I must wait here until it has been ratified, as we say. In brief, I must stay here another two months or so» RGALI, Fond 312, op.1, no. 7, f. 2.

[154] *Priiatnoe i poleznoe preprovozhdenie vremeni*, XIII (1797), pp. 417-425; XIV (1797), pp. 10-15, pp. 26-37. Subsequent references will be made in the text by page number.

[155] Malinovskii was first proposed as the author of these notes by I.S. Dostian, 'Dunaiskie kniazhestva v russkoi publitsistike kontsa XVIII i nachala XIX veka', *Revue Roumaine d'Histoire*, XX, no. 1 (1981), p. 33. His authorship is confirmed in G. Bogach, *Alte pazhin' de istoriografie literare* (Kishinev, 1984), pp. 87-106. We have found an allusion to Malinovskii's authorship also in the unpublished article by Liudmila Mikhailova quoted above and in V. Besprozvannyi, 'Kto byl avtorom «Rossiianina v Anglii»?', *V chest' 70-letiiu professora Iu.M. Lotmana* (Tartu, 1992), pp. 49-56.

position of women in society. The perceptible change is in the perspective
of the observer: if in England Malinovskii was in the position of an
admiring witness of the progress of the most enlightened nation in the
world, here he can feel himself much more civilized and advanced than the
natives[156].

The notes are structured as a series of entries on specific issues,
illustrating Malinovskii's response to different aspects of local culture. Each
of the notes bears a title: 'Moldaviia', 'Zhidy', 'Moldavane i Turki',
'Turetskoe igo', 'Strannoe obyknovenie', 'Prosveshchennyi Moldavan',
'Pozhar', 'Divan', 'Svad'ba', 'Vstrecha', 'Avantiur'e'.

In the first note, he ascribes to Moldavia a particular place in the
history of civilization: «This land is midway between wildness and
enlightenment: while the natural state is lost, it has not been endowed with
the good institutions of human intellect» (XIII, p. 417). A subsequent
remark, however, counterbalances this seemingly unsympathetic position:
the state of semi-barbarity is entirely ascribed to the effects of the Turkish
yoke and not to an intrinsic, permanent quality, for the oppressors «want to
prolong the servitude of this land through ignorance» (XIII, p. 417). This
interpretation is coherently developed by Malinovskii, who hereby assumes
a position significantly different from that of other European
contemporaries. The descriptions of Moldavia and Wallachia written
principally by German and French travellers during the eighteenth century
were in fact full of contempt for the semi-barbarous peoples and
condescending derision for their habits[157]. As Soviet historians in

---

[156] This is explicitly stated in one case, when he writes about his acquaintance with a
local «*prosveshchennyi*» young man. Malinovskii underlines the affinities in their position:
«His conversations surprised me, and I recalled at this point an observation long familiar to
me, that it is a great misfortune for a man to be more enlightened than others of his nation
and his era; such a man will be in torment all through his life (...) In intercourse with him I
sense my national superiority over him, and it is flattering to see that he ackowledges this»
(XIV, pp. 28-30).

[157] See particularly F.I. Sulzer, *Geschichte der Transalpinischen Daciens* (Wien,
1781-1782) and J.L. Carra, *Histoire de la Moldavie et de la Valachie* (Jassy, 1777). A
similar attitude was continued by Prince De Ligne, Langeron and others. See also I.
Raicevich, *Osservazioni storiche, naturali e politiche intorno la Valachia e la Moldavia*
(Napoli, 1788). During the last quarter of the XVIII century the increasing interest in Russia
for Moldavian affairs was witnessed by numerous translations from other languages:
Descriptio Moldaviae, by Dmitrii Kantemir, appeared in Russian in 1789, Carra's work was
translated with the title *Istoriia Moldavii i Valakhii s rassuzhdeniem o nastoiashchem
sostoianii sikh oboikh kniazhestv* (Spb., 1791). Among the original writings on Moldavia,
see particularly F.V. Baur, *Zapiski povestvovatel'nye, zemleopisatel'nye i politicheskie o
kniazhestve Volosskom* (Spb., 1791). A few years after Malinovskii's notes D. Bantysh-
Kamenskii published his *Puteshestvie v Moldaviiu, Valakhiiu i Serbiiu* (Moskva, 1810). On

particular have emphasized, the inhabitants of these countries were able to rid themselves of the negative aspects of the influence of the Turkish oppression in a relatively short time and to draw close to European culture. The presence of Russians in these countries, beginning with the Russo-Turkish war of 1789-1791, had an important role in helping this process[158].

Moldavia is seen by Malinovskii as a land of paradoxes and missed opportunities rather than as a barbaric land. It is not with contempt, but with a sort of amused curiosity that he approaches the Divan, the local representative organ, comically compared to the English Parliament. Remarks of an ethnographic character are here given more space than in 'Rossiianin v Anglii', for he is concerned with an obviously more «exotic» region. Climate particularly commands his attention, being here «very close to the Italian» (XIII, p. 419), as well as the most folkloristic aspects of this land.

He looks at Moldavia, well disposed to trace its affinities with Russia, as in the case of faith, which is described as: «identical with ours, except that ignorance and barbarity conjoin to it many absurdities» (XIII, p. 419)[159]. Certainly the particular backwardness of the position of Moldavian women is perceived as a sign of barbarity: «Those who dislike learned women should come here, and when they have seen the comely statuettes, will confess that it is as bad for women to know nothing as to know a lot» (XIII, pp. 421-422)[160]. Malinovskii does not conceal, on the other hand, his

---

the general subject see G. Bezviconi, *Contributii la istoria relatiilor româno-ruse* (Bucuresti, 1962).

[158] On this theme see above all A. Vianu, *Quelques aspects de l'influence exercée par la pensée progressiste russe sur la société roumaine de la fin du XVIII siècle* (Bucarest, 1955); I.S. Dostian, *Russkaia obshchestvennaia mysl' i balkanskie narody. Ot Radisheva do dekabristov* (Moskva, 1980). On the penetration of a specific aspect of the Russian culture of the time, see K.V. Sivkov, 'Chitateli i rasprostraniteli «Puteshestvie iz Peterburga v Moskvu» A.N. Radishcheva v kontse XVIII v.', *Istoricheskie zapiski* no. 40 (1952), pp. 279-282. In this article we are informed that as early as four years after its publication in Russia Radishchev's book could circulate in manuscript also in Moldavia. On the implications of the presence of the Russian army in Moldavia see G. Haupt, 'La Russie et le Principautés Danubiennes en 1790. Le Prince Potemkin-Tavricheskij et le *Courrier de Moldavie*', *Cahiers du monde russe et soviétique*, VII (1966), pp. 58-62; see also V.S. Kiriiak, *Bratstva zhivye rodniki. Kniga v Moldavii XVII - nachalo XIX v.* (Kishinev, 1986).

See also, on the other hand, the recent studies devoted to analyzing the development of Moldavian thought in connection with European cultural history, for instance G.E. Bobyne, *Gumanizm v filosofskoi i obshchestvennoi mysli Moldavii v XVII-nachale XVIII v.* (Kishinev, 1988).

[159] Malinovskii censures on the other hand the Moldavian habit of exhuming corpses and judging from their degree of decomposition their fate in the other world.

[160] Malinovskii echoes in this case similar remarks by foreign observers, see for instance Carra: «Je ne crois pas qu'aucune femme, pas même les princesses regnantes

admiration for certain aspects of the Moldavian social organization. For instance, he considers that the local system of distribution of land might provide a model for Russia:

> Land here either belongs fully to the peasants, or is rented from landowners. They can leave it when they want to, and thus the boyars take care of them and are afraid to persecute them, because otherwise the land would be left without workers and they would be without income. The peasants, being free, do not loaf idly about and are not too lazy to work (XIII, p. 423).

In general, Malinovskii regards this region as exemplifying the view that history repeats itself: the Danubian principalities are now in a condition not too different from that typical of the Russian state under the Tatar yoke, as he was to outline in an article written a few years later[161], and Moldavian people have to emancipate themselves to enter the concert of European nations[162].

1.3.2. 1792-1798: Return to the College of Foreign Affairs and «Ufa project»

The years Malinovskii spent in Russia between his return from Jassy in 1792 and his next departure for Moldavia in 1800 have presented hitherto a certain lacuna in his biography. It was only known that he returned to St Petersburg and continued to serve in the College of Foreign Affairs for another eight years, working in obscurity and proving particularly reticent in taking advantage of his numerous connections in order to get significant personal benefits.

---

aujourd'hui en Moldavie & en Valachie, sachent lire & écrire (...) ne reconnoissent d'autre loi, d'autre volonté suprême, que celle des hommes» (op.cit., p.193). The perception of the travellers of those days corresponded to an apparent backwardness in women's education, see the data on the subject in A.I. Eshanu, *Shkola i prosveshchenie v Moldavii (XV - nachalo XVIII v.)* (Kishinev, 1983).

161 «Our princes and archbishops went to the horde to be installed on their thrones, and by the infidels' will were hampered by the intrigues of their rivals, little better the Moldavian and Wallachian lords today», *Osennie vechera*, p. 51.

162 In this respect, we do not entirely agree with Dostian's interpretation of Malinovskii's ideas on the emancipation of Moldavia: «Antique reminiscences, appeals to the historical right of the people, recollections of great and powerful forbears are extremely characteristic phenomena in pre-Romantic social thought, particularly in Russia. Malinovskii employed precisely arguments of this sort to demonstrate the population's right to national freedom and the inevitability to struggle for it» (Dostian, *op.cit.*, p. 34). Malinovskii's position comes from a different background, as witnessed by the way he was to return to this theme in part III of his *Rassuzhdenie*.

The rank of *kollezhskii asessor* he was given at the end of the peace congress did not bring any significant change in his life. Constrained as he was by a bureaucratic post that was far from being his ideal, he felt the precious experience and knowledge he had gained visiting Europe and Moldavia could have been better employed in the service of Russian society. His deep dissatisfaction, which lasted for almost a decade, is reflected in a number of private documents which have now been discovered in the archives. These documents show a man frustrated and tired, but also psychologically and intellectually involved in a particular project which could completely change his life.

After his return from Jassy in 1792, he married Sof'ia Samborskaia[163]. The difficulties in contracting this marriage intensified his frustration. We do not know its exact date, but in a letter to his future wife, written on 17 July, the day before his 28th birthday, Vasilii Fedorovich said: «this day could have been joyful for me if your father had said to you that you were free to love me and had given me your hand»[164].

Sof'ia Andreevna was to prove his ideal companion, an intelligent and tender woman with a strain of melancholy which attracted Malinovskii[165] and a strong inclination for philosophy which also fascinated him. To her he wrote several letters, both during their life together and especially during their forced separations. Written in Russian and English[166] and addressed to his *«liubeznaia uchenitsa»* (gentle pupil) or «charming philosopher», they reveal the family dimension of this thinker and his qualities as affectionate husband and caring father.

In these letters Malinovskii did not fail to record his dissatisfaction with his work in the College and his moral yearning for a more interesting and rewarding activity. He was also particularly obsessed with the wish to gain recognition from his contemporaries:

---

[163] As recorded by A.A. Samborskii (TSDIAU, Fond 2053, op.1, no. 134, f. 28).

[164] IRLI, Fond 312, op. 1, n. 7, f. 4. This is the only occasion in which we found a critical reference to Samborskii in Malinovskii's papers. Sof'ia's father, on the other hand, neutrally recorded elsewhere to have married her to the «asessor inostrannykh del V.F. Malinovskii» (TSDIAU, Fond 2053, op.1, no. 134, f. 28). The only letters sent by Samborskii to Vasilii Fedorovich seem to be congratulatory letters on the birth of his children (*ibid.*, ff. 31-32, 33-34, 35-36).

[165] He writes: «I should have chosen a cheerful friend, however I chose you, although I knew that you are a 'reflective, sad maiden'» , IRLI, Fond 312, op. 1, n. 7, f. 4.

[166] Particularly interesting are two groups of letters, held in IRLI, Fond RIII, op. 2, no. 2182-2184 (4 letters), and no. 2185-2194 (10 letters).

Fame is my deity - she is my tyrant, for it is only because I may serve her
that I am wretched - she is the cause of the gloomy days of my life,
however I love her, - although she reminds me that I have achieved nothing
and appals me with the idea that I will do nothing in the future[167].

As early as the middle of 1792 Malinovskii was firmly resolved to
look for an escape from the bureaucratic life he was leading in the College.
He was to elaborate a project to abandon forever St Petersburg society and
to settle down in a village somewhere in the Ufa steppes. The most
important document revealing his plans is a long and elaborate letter sent on
17 August 1792 from Belozerka[168] to an unknown addressee (the
establishing of whose identity would undoubtedly help to clarify aspects of
the project). Malinovskii describes him as «companion of my glory», but
we do not know whether he is referring to the «glory» he shared with him
in his previous engagements in Jassy[169] or London or to a fame still to
come. At all events, the letter reveals Malinovskii's appreciation of his
friendship with this particularly clever man (he writes «you have a divine
intellect»), even though he is well aware that it could be compromising for
him. The letter takes the form of a detailed programme, a concrete
proposal to his friend to join him:

cursing wordly life, I vowed to choose another, (...) I thought of distant
lands and consequently of you, companion of my glory! (...) When I have
chosen my life, I will consider it a crime if you refuse to come to me.

Given the impossibility, at the time when he was writing, of being
useful to Russian society[170], Malinovskii considered the necessity of
rejecting it for something entirely different. The project is not presented as
having only a strictly private dimension, it seems to be also a *conditio sine
qua non* for the proper development of a mysterious «society»[171]:
Malinovskii proposes the inclusion of his future wife in this secret society,

---

[167] IRLI, Fond 312, op. 1, n. 7, f. 5.

[168] *Ibid.*, n. 8, ff. 1-2.

[169] In this respect it may be worthy mentioning a letter to Samborskii written in
November 1799 by a Luka Sechkarev in which Malinovskii is mentioned by him as «my
sweet-spoken interlocutor of Jassy on ancient learning, Vasilii Fedorovich» (TSDIAU,
Fond 2053, op. 1, no. 540).

[170] In the letter Malinovskii explicitly writes: «I regard my present condition as a
living death, however I console myself with patience and the choice of my female
companion, and the fact that I can always reason and prepare myself to be useful».

[171] The interest in this sort of societies at the time when Malinovskii conceived his
plan was not exclusively of masonic origin, see Herder's 'Gespräch über eine unsichtbar-
sichtbare Gesellschaft' (1793). On Karamzin's translation of Herder's work, see A. Cross,
N.M. Karamzin: a Study of His Literary Career 1783-1803 (1971), p. 201.

to which the unidentified friend and Malinovskii himself belong or plan to belong:

> it seems I have already taken a big step having you and Sofia as my life companions, the inclusion of her friend in our society is a great gain, she will enliven it, she will give it a new charm, will soften its gloom and the dryness of the conversations (...) but eveything depends on independence (...) I have already written about the village, I would favour the Ufa region.

The designated place was to be located in a precise region: «Only 1.200 versts from Moscow, in five days we can be there». The plan goes far beyond Malinovskii's own individual need for freedom and peace of mind: it is apparently conceived as a starting point for a re-shaping of Russian society on the basis of different social and economic criteria. One of the most interesting aspects of the plan is, for instance, the intention to establish a new and non-oppressive variant of the relationship between landowners and peasants. In this respect Malinovskii imagines that:

> the proximity of Tatar peoples will give us greater resources for our activities, they will take the place of peasants for us, and all the better because they are not our property, they are free and we will be fathers for them, not lords

In this relationship a primary role is ascribed to women: «our wives will instruct their wives and daughters (...), fortunately we have or will have such wives that scorn nothing which serves to benefit other people».

A typical feature of Malinovskii's way of thinking, also reflected in his lifestyle, was his firm rejection of the excesses of luxury and his demand for a return to modesty and simplicity. He shared this position with a good number of contemporaries, not exclusively Russian, in the *querelle* on luxury typical of the century[172]. The sober and essential life Malinovskii prefigured for his community in the Ufa steppes was definitely to meet this need:

> we do not need carriages, we will travel by *drozhki* and ride the best horses. Any sort of dress is good, what one is ashamed of here will seem rich there; our houses will not be huge palaces, but of excellent taste, and healthy, surrounded by gardens, small but comfortable, cleanliness replacing rich furnishings.

---

[172] Among the vast literature on the subject, see in particular C. Borghero (ed.), *La polemica sul lusso nel Settecento francese* (Torino, 1974), J.L. Black, 'N.M. Karamzin and the Dilemma of Luxury in Eighteenth-Century Russia', *Studies on Voltaire and the Eighteenth Century* CLI-CLV (1976), pp. 313-322.

The dream assumes therefore the features of a return to primitive, paradisical purity and beauty[173], whose delights are fused in Malinovskii's imagination with the joys of his imminent married life. The advantages of a rural life as opposed to the unnatural urban life would compensate for the sense of isolation:

> not one of us will be downcast from anxiety or gloomy from unpleasant fears, which urban life brings with it, like a noisy sea troubling everyone (...) reading and music will be pleasant pastimes for us all together; we can have guests too, who will not be influential or richer than us (...) we will not have boring city visitors, who come to the house like spies (...) our gaze will not be darkened by the sight of a proud master (...) Hidden in the hills from the world and all its finery we will breathe the pure air of freedom and independence. Our days will flow by like a quiet river, and death itself will do nothing to us, only put an end to our labours for the benefit of others.

Malinovskii draws the attention of his interlocutor to the fact that their way of life would soon be able to attract other people («Believe me, people will run to us to find peace and happiness»), so that the small society consisting of those four persons would soon acquire the size of a proper community, with particular features:

> There is enough land there, we will call in artists and settle unfortunates without great expense, we will distribute others among the Tatar inhabitants, whose behaviour we will manage to improve, we will bring in English people too, agriculture will flourish there as well.

Malinovskii is also anxious not to incur the suspicion of the Russian government:

> The Court cannot look on us suspiciously, we will not introduce sects or form parties, but will foster good behaviour and happiness. We will also instil respect towards the government, which guarantees security and property.

Even though radical in its essence, the project was therefore not conceived as providing a form of revolutionary opposition to Russian government. The utopian idea of founding free communities and escaping the unjust society they lived in appeared several times in Russian culture of the second half of the eighteenth century, being particularly widespread

---

[173] See S. Baehr, *The Paradise Myth in Eighteenth-Century Russia* (Stanford, 1991), in particular the chapter 'The «Language» of Paradise: A Typological Introduction'.

among the Novikovian groups. As highlighted for the first time by Meilakh, Malinovskii's Ufa project has undoubtedly much in common with their plan of founding an autonomous republic in Siberia[174]. It also shares a few features with the utopian legends on fantastic lands elaborated by the Russian popular culture since the seventeenth century[175].

Considered from a strictly biographical point of view, the Ufa project can be seen as the main variation on a theme particularly dear to Malinovskii, the building of an ideal community ruled by just social and political rules and kept apart from the rest of the world. This idea reappeared periodically during his life: we find it in his fascination with the community of Quakers, in the sort of life evoked in *Pustynnik*, in the organization he planned for the Tsarskoe Selo Lycée.

To illustrate the «Ufa dream» a second letter, dated 21 November 1792[176] and also sent to a mysterious friend[177] is even more relevant. In his attempt to persuade him to join the new life, Malinovskii finds poetical comparisons:

> This condition of life may be likened to a ship in which one can safely sail over life's sea, it is the real fulfillment of all the rules of wisdom in every minute of our existence (...) Monasteries arose from the banding together of people escaping vice. And all the rules which they undertook to fulfill have been turned into habits, into a way of life. This institution can serve us not as a model, but as an example for the arrangement of our state of life.

Here the reference to the activity of a secret society is even more accentuated than in the first letter:

> I tell you personally, kind friend, for apart from the walls there is not and must not be any audience. But it will not be like that when we resolve to turn the principles of the friends of men into a way of life, and a set of habits, then in the peasant and in a neighbour and in a guest we will find an interlocutor and companion, or a fellow member and assistant, for then all our talks will be like the gatherings we have now and the whole of life will be a realization of the principles of our society.

---

[174] See B.S. Meilakh, *Pushkin i ego epokha* (Moskva, 1958), p. 32.

[175] See M. Schippan, 'Die Französische Revolution von 1789 und Friedenvorstellungen in Russland bis 1825', *Zeitschrift für Slawistik*, no. 34 (1989), p. 356.

[176] RGALI, Fond 312, op. 1, n.1, f. 3.

[177] This friend, probably the same as in the other letter, could only be identified on the basis of a biographical fact mentioned by Malinovskii: «Choosing himself a poor wife, for which many condemned you».

The years passed without bringing Malinovskii any real opportunity to realize his project.

One of the few traceable events occurred on 15 June 1794, when Vasilii Feodorovich became a member of the Free Economic Society[178], a fact having apparent implications for his theoretical and practical involvement in the solution of the problem of peasant property in Russia.

The following years were particularly unhappy ones in the life of the Russian thinker, as his diaries reveal. Malinovskii felt a compulsion to record all the events of his intellectual and spiritual life, and many of his notebooks have been preserved in the Russian and Ukrainian archives. The one referring, in its initial part, to 1794[179] is particularly interesting, showing him very much taken by reflections on the most basic problems of a psychological, scientific and linguistic nature[180].

The project of the «Ufa paradise» did not remain, however, merely a dream, as witnessed by the correspondence with his wife in the following years. We have to assume that it reappeared only three years after the date of its first elaboration. These letters mark the progression in the realization of the project and provide information about the stops made by Malinovskii during his journey in search of the ideal village.

He apparently set off at the very beginning of February 1796: on 8 February 1796 he laconically communicated to his wife from Kursk: «I am half the way»[181]. On 10 February Malinovskii was at a place called Sirovorotka, from where he wrote:

> I have four hundred versts still to cover, that is not many now, God willing
> I will arrive quickly and now that I have got to know the road I will be able
> to make better progress and do without stops on the return journey, for

---

[178] See the official act, IRLI, Fond 312, op. 2, no. 3, f. 1.

[179] TSDIAU, Fond 2039, op. 1, no. 83. The diary continues up to 1812.

[180] The first page of the diary, introduced by a gloomy statement («When hatred takes the place of love, then gloomy darkness so deepens, that a man does not know what is going on»), is divided vertically in two parts, each of them containing a series of words associated by category and in total opposition. The mental exercise on the very essential principles of human life leads him to incursions in the field of linguistic typologies, where he attempts to trace language universals, and to an identification of the role of time and space: «Everything we feel or understand is existence shaped by time and place. To understand with the soul and to feel with the body is to know existence (...) in proportion to the strength of our perceptions signs of revulsion or desire appear in us through body movements and voice. And thus languages arise, the first and common one is children's language, in which several vowels, a-e-i-o-u, can be made out and by means of these vowels they convey everything, for this everything is extremely limited: hunger and pain» (f. 2).

[181] IRLI, Fond RIII, op. 2, no. 2182-2184, f. 2 (In English in the original).

much has been the result of a change in the weather; there are no dangers[182].

On 12 February he wrote from Trostenez:

> I am feasting at Mr Nadarjinsky, I was here all day and slept tonight, as he asked me to stay for dinner today, it is being his nameday - do you remember as we have been at his house at Petersbourg, when A.F. was there - it is three years since - now the time changes the scenes - Now we are separated (...) and I am going to purchase an estate. He praises very much the country of Ekaterinoslaw and the Lady likewise. They have a village there and stayed there a year or more. He says I should by no means neglect the opportunity (...) The place here is not indifferent to me - you stayed here when a young girl[183].

In this letter Malinovskii also wrote that he planned to be home by the end of February. He seemingly found a suitable village and was about to buy it, as he wrote to his wife in a letter sent from Saltykovka, on 18 February 1796:

> I have arrived, kind mistress, when I am here with you, then things will be more cheerful; I fear, my sweet Sofiia, that you will say I have led you into the steppe, but I will remind you of our agreement, which we made in the old days when we were still lovers, I will call you a deceiver. I drink tea and joke with you - the village is neglected but could even be a principality. You will live as a mistress of the steppe, then later you will be a princess (...) the heart and soul require nourishment - the best is graciousness, friendship and love - I will love you and Liza, with N.I.[184] if he comes I will enjoy friendship, and I will keep graciousness for the peasants[185].

On 1 March 1796 he was still in Ekaterinoslav, from where he wrote to Sof'ia Andreevna:

> The governor promises me a good place, only he asked me to stay here three days and then I set off for Moscou and if it pleases God to see you well and happy - all is for the best. The village is good enough, yet it is not worth 10000 r. as there is no more but 10 men[186].

---

[182] *Ibid.*

[183] *Ibid.*, f. 3 (In English in the original).

[184] The person indicated with these initials could be tentatively identified in Prince Nikolai Ivanovich Saltykov (1736-1816). Malinovskii declared in fact that he was writing from Saltykovka. In a letter dated 1797 Samborskii informed him of his difficult financial position and gave positive evaluation of Pavel Fedorovich Malinovskii, who was employed in the service of Field Marshal P.S. Saltykov (TSDIAU, Fond 2053, op.1, no. 447, ff. 1-2).

[185] IRLI, Fond 312, op. 1, n. 7, f. 6.

[186] IRLI, Fond RIII, op. 2, no. 2182-2184, f.1 (In English in the original).

The project, so close to being realized, nevertheless failed. There is no record of the reasons for the failure, which were in all probability of a financial nature[187]. Malinovskii returned to St Petersburg and his work at the College of Foreign Affairs absorbed him entirely again. It brought him to Moscow for a short period during the first half of 1797. In a letter from Moscow dated 20 April 1797 Vasilii Fedorovich took the opportunity to complain about his being «exceedingly busy in the Colledge every day»[188]. Four days later he reiterated his dissatisfaction and his readiness to leave Moscow:

> I am in the Colledge, the weather is dull, I have no garden to walk, no nightingale to hear, yet I am happy, as I hear the Emperor will set off the 8 of May and we will be (...) to go the next day and even the same, which I believe will be the case with your husband impatient to embrace you my beloved wife and our angels[189].

On 10 May 1797 he communicated to Sof'ia Andreevna his imminent return from Moscow in the most passionate strain: «Let it be like my coming from Jassy, I will look upon you as my bride. The first day of my arrival will be like our wedding day»[190]. The Ufa dream was definitively abandoned. Malinovskii started, instead, looking forward to living on the country estate of Belozerka, the beloved spot where in 1798 he wrote the second part of his *Rassuzhdenie o mire i voine*. He perceived Belozerka as his ideal *locus amoenus*, partially replacing the Ufa village he dreamt about, and representing a particularly inspiring place for his intellectual activity, as a letter to his wife, written from St Petersburg, clearly shows:

> I imagine I am like Cicero in exile, if my letter is not as flowing as he wrote to his Terentia, I feel the sorrow of being separated is as lively: indeed I was many times as wise and as happy at Belozerka as he was at his Tusculanum, and all ways as studious[191].

---

[187] In Samborskii's Fond in Kiev there are a few letters dated 1800 in which the Reverend asks Pavel Fedorovich Malinovskii to act as intermediary between him and his daughter Sofia, to whom he intended to donate certain sums of money (Fond 2053, op.1, nos 594, 603, 605). In one of them Samborskii mentioned 1000 *chervontsy* to be destined specifically «for the purchase of a village» (no. 603).

[188] IRLI, Fond RIII, op. 2, no. 2185-2194, f.1 (In English in the original).

[189] *Ibid.*, f. 2 (In English in the original).

[190] *Ibid.*, f. 4 (In English in the original).

[191] IRLI, Fond RIII, op. 2, no. 2182-2184, f. 5. The letter, written in October, is without indication of the year (In English in the original).

1.3.3. 1799-1802: Malinovskii Consul General in Moldavia

The experience in Jassy in 1791-92 had been important in the life of Malinovskii. A few years later, when the position of consul general in Moldavia and Wallachia fell vacant, he asked his former colleague Fedor Vasil'evich Rostopchin to be appointed to that office:

> When my colleague became first minister and the post of Consul General long remained vacant, I made up my mind and wrote to him, that I wished to take advantage of it to further the prosperity of these lands and, making use of the present union of Russia and Turkey, to secure and, if possible, extend the articles agreed in the treaty for their benefit[192].

He was appointed Consul General by a special *ukaz* issued by the Emperor Paul I on 30 July 1800, and he arrived in Jassy after a difficult journey in December of the same year, together with his two children and his wife, who was again pregnant. This time Malinovskii was to spend almost two years in Jassy, from 1801 to the end of 1802.

Malinovskii's second stay in Jassy should be seen within the context of the extreme attention paid by the Russian government in those years to the situation in the Danubian principalities, since they were alarmed by the possibility that those regions would present England or France with an excuse to attack. One of the tasks of the Russian consuls was, therefore, to consolidate the influence of their country in those regions, a task made difficult by the frustration of the two principalities' autonomist aspirations brought about by the peace of Jassy. The attitude towards Turkey had to be one of extreme friendliness, but on the other hand the consuls had to take care that the Ottoman empire did not violate the few privileges left to the principalities. Such was the delicate situation when the new Russian Consul arrived in Jassy.

Malinovskii's diplomatic activity in Jassy proved to be crucial in the establishment of good and correct relations between Russia and Moldavia and Wallachia, as documented by a series of official reports and letters; studies of Malinovskii's role have already been made on the evidence they provide[193].

---

[192] *Izbrannye obshchestvenno-politicheskie sochineniia*, p. 149.

[193] Three letters sent by Malinovskii have been published in *Vneshniaia politika Rossii XIX i nachala XX veka. Dokumenty rossiiskogo Ministerstva inostrannykh del* (Moskva, 1960), pp. 144-145, p. 172, pp. 237-238. The years spent by Malinovskii in Moldavia are analyzed in A. Vianu, 'Iluministul rus V.F. Malinovski in principatele Dunarene', *Studii. Revista de istorie*, no. 2 (1960), pp. 165-181; G.S. Grosul, 'Rol' V.F.

He pursued two main objectives, the defence of Danubian autonomous status and the improvement of the conditions of the local peasantry. Consistent with the policy of the Russian government, Consul Malinovskii was particularly concerned with violations of the conditions established by the treaty of 1791. He was quick to become an active mediator on behalf of the local patriots in their appeals to Russia to intervene in their favour. The Moldavian sovereign himself, Constantin Ipsilanti, made use of his courageous complicity to suggest to Paul I that he help his country without violating the peace agreements with Turkey: the intervention of Russian armies was requested, alleging as a pretext the ruinous incursions of the Pasvantoglu's bands into Moldavia[194]. Malinovskii sent similar petitions to Alexander I, enclosing statements by local aristocrats[195].

The diplomatic action led by the consul general in Jassy was taken up by the Russian ambassador in Constantinople, V. Tamara, who on the basis of the missives sent to him by Malinovskii, took decisive diplomatic steps against the Porte[196].

The agreement between Russia and Turkey about the status of the Danubian principalities, signed in September 1802, has frequently been heralded as a personal success of the Russian consul general[197].

In his reports to the Ministry, Malinovskii acted not only in the realm of diplomatic relations between the countries in question, he also affirmed the necessity to bring into effect some reforms in the principalities, above all in internal administration, in order to deprive the Phanariot Greeks of the right to take up government offices. An extension of power to local aristocrats seemed to him one of the best measures to favour political stability and welfare:

Malinovskogo v razvitii druzhestvennykh russko-moldavskikh politicheskikh sviazei', *Materialy nauchnoi konferentsii profes.-prepod. sostava KGU, posviashchennoi 300-letiiu D. Kantemira*, (Kishinev, 1974). See also G.S. Grosul, *Dunaiskie kniazhestva v politike Rossii. 1774-1806* (Kishinev, 1975), where the reconstruction of Malinovskii's activity is based on materials held mainly in the AVPR archives, and I.F. Iovva, *Peredovaia Rossiia i obshchestvenno-politicheskoe dvizhenie v Moldavii* (Kishinev, 1986), pp. 53-55, where Malinovskii's stay in Jassy is linked, though briefly, with the development of his position on the law of peoples.

[194] *Ibid.*, p. 151. Grosul justly underlines that there is no reason to believe that the intervention of Russia invoked by Ipsilanti was conceived also by the Russian theorist of peace as preparing a new war (*ibid.*, p. 152).

[195] See the letter sent to Alexander I and published in *Vneshniaia politika Rossii XIX i nachala XX veka, op.cit.*, p. 172.

[196] See particularly the secret missive sent by Malinovskii on 22 June 1802, published in *Vneshniaia politika Rossii XIX i nachala XX veka*, pp. 237-238.

[197] Grosul, pp. 157-164, G.N. Seliakh, 'Russko-turetskoe soglashenie 1802 g. o Dunaiskikh kniazhestvakh', *Voprosy istorii*, no. 12 (1961), pp. 195-202.

> There is one way to guarantee to both principalities those benefits and advantages they have been endowed with by Russia's beneficial action, to forestall all the evils that result from frequent and unjustified changes of princes, and that is to empower the boyars and to share with them the power of the sovereign[198].

Expressing his views about the reorganization of political life in the principalities, the consul general took the opportunity to submit a few proposals:

> the sovereign's revenues must be separated from the land's. The Divan should be authorized to collect these and use them for the land's requirements, giving the Divan in general more power and importance in the government of the principality and including in it not only the leading boyars, but also the other lesser ones[199].

The Russian consul was well aware of the poor condition of Moldavian «representative» institutions, particularly the Divan, which he had the opportunity to visit in 1791 and continued to observe now, as recorded in a letter to his wife, witnessing the spirit in which he perceived his involvement in local life[200].

The official documents which survive to elucidate Malinovskii's diplomatic activity show him also involved, far beyond his duties, in attempts to improve the fate of Moldavian and Wallachian peasants, trying to induce the Russian government to help them. In one of his reports to the Ministry of Foreign Affairs, written in 1801, he underlined for instance that «Since the last peace the people's taxes and burdens have immeasurably increased and become intolerable»[201] and that it was impossible to ignore that the people «have never been so oppressed as regards heavy duties and burdens»[202]. Explaining the great hardship of the local population under the fiscal pressure imposed by the Turko-Phanariot oppressors, Malinovskii found touching strains:

> One *okolash* does not have time to leave the house, before three others go in behind him in pursuit of the same object, and when a person

---

[198] Quoted in Grosul, *op.cit.*, p. 162.

[199] *Ibid.*, p. 163.

[200] In the letter to his wife (elsewhere addressed, from Jassy, as «Madame la Consulesse»), dated 17 August 1802, he wrote: «send me my *moondir*, sword, hat, shirt, *vse*. Do not forget the consular stick, as I am going tomorrow to Divan in hope of a happy meeting» (IRLI, Fond RIII, op. 2, no. 2185-2194, f. 7).

[201] See Grosul, *op.cit.*, p. 46.

[202] *Ibid.*

> unfortunately does not have the ready money to give satisfaction, then they
> tear the last item of clothing from him and take away everything they find
> in the house[203].

One of the less strictly political of Malinovskii's duties in Jassy was the
gathering of information on the state and size of local businesses, in the
framework of Russia's increasing interest in trade in the Danubian
principalities. In 1802 he drew the attention of the Russian government to
the fact that the Moldavian sovereign wanted to increase the customs-duties
on certain goods (such as vodka, horses and oxen) pertaining to the transit
trade between Russia and European states.

Malinovskii was also active in favouring the return to their homeland
of several Russians who were oppressed by the difficult conditions in the
principalities and had appealed to him for help. In a subsequent survey of
his experience in Jassy, Malinovskii will not hide his satisfaction with his
contribution, giving some of the figures by which it could be judged:

> And in this way I managed to resettle 3.600 souls, who had been lost to
> their fatherland. My two successors did not achieve half of that in the
> course of ten years, and spent 30.000 roubles where I spent 4.000. The
> court received my successes favourably; reliable people have said this: a
> report was ordered to be written (and was written) about rewarding me
> with the order of St.Anna[204].

If with the Moldavian sovereign Constantin Ipsilanti Malinovskii found
a way to accomplish his duties without incurring too many obstacles, it was
not so with his successor Alexandru Sutu, a Greek from Constantinople.
Malinovskii records the attempts of the latter to gain the favour of the
Russian consul:

> He allocated me a pension twice that paid me by my sovereign the Emperor
> in a year; they brought it during the first month, left the purse, not daring to
> disobey their tsar by taking it back; I appeared and asked in person, what
> he had in mind? The condition of my friendship was the fulfillment of the
> conditions of the treaty to the benefit of the land: when he upheld them
> reliably, then he could rely on my service (...) Judge me (...), can I change
> and betray my obligation of service, honour and humanity?[205]

Not accepting the munificent gratitude of the sovereign of Moldavia
for his «cooperation», Malinovskii gave another example of his

---

[203] *Ibid.*, p. 49.
[204] Letter to Kochubei published in *Izbrannye obshchestvenno-politicheskie sochineniia*, p. 150.
[205] *Ibid.*, pp. 150-151.

disinterested way of conceiving his consular duties. He was certainly an exception in his time. Russian consuls in these regions were generally presented with the opportunity to accumulate fortunes. The only present he accepted during his stay in Jassy[206] was a curious souvenir we can still see today. In 1800 the Moldavian people presented him with a *kubok* in metal, a goblet on a pedestal representing on its oval faces scenes from Moldavian life and standing on three legs (one human, one equine, one of an ox). The small goblet (18 cm high) has been carefully preserved by Malinovskii's descendants, and is now kept in the Muzei Pushkina in Tsarskoe Selo.

Because of Sutu's intrigues, the «*neugomonnyi konsul*» (indefatigable consul)[207] was nevertheless recalled to St Petersburg in December 1802, though not without a certain personal satisfaction[208].

The Moldavian chapter in Malinovskii's life did not end completely with his return to Russia. He continued to be regarded as a respected specialist on Moldavian affairs, to whom the local authorities would turn for opinions and suggestions. The Moldavian Metropolitan Veniamin Kostaki, worried by the peasants' agitations in his country, wrote to him, for instance, in the years 1803-1804. Malinovskii's answer was in keeping with the position he elaborated in those years about peasants' property in Russia:

> investigate, looking around without prejudice (...) the position of the peasants and boyars (...) Take a sip from the chalice of each of them. I propose that there are other reasons for the decline of agriculture. The first is that the peasants do not have their own land, consequently they are not concerned about the land of others (...) the boyars must think about what should be done (...) If they do not want to give the inhabitants a piece of land each (...) from their estates (...) then they should at least follow the German example and give them land to rent[209].

---

[206] See references to this fact in A.E. Rozen, *Zapiski dekabrista* (Irkutsk, 1984, 2 ed.), p. 101, and M. Rudenskaia, S. Rudenskaia, *'Nastavnikam ... za blago vozdadim'* (Leningrad, 1986), pp. 289-293.

[207] As Malinovskii depicted himself, see *Izbrannye obshchestvenno-politicheskie sochineniia*, p. 151.

[208] See a letter dated 9 December 1802, sent to Samborskii by E. Volkov from Jassy («I will only say that Vasilii Fedorovich left Moldavia, but not before the overthrow of the crafty oppressor Prince Sutso (...) Vasilii Fedorovich, as far as I observed and as he confessed to me himself on the first night's stop from here, to which I had the honour of accompanying him, was very cheerful») TSDIAU, Fond 2053, op.1, no. 626, ff. 1-2.

[209] Grosul, *op.cit.,* p. 203. Grosul quotes from V. Urechia, *Istoria rominilor* (Bucuresti, 1900), XI, pp. 24-27. It is interesting to note that in that work the fragments, reproduced in translation, are erroneously attributed by the historian to a certain Moldavian aristocrat named 'Melinesku' and living in St Petersburg (as noted also by Rudenskaia, *op.cit.*, p. 292).

Malinovskii's 'Zapiska o osvobozhdenii rabov', an article containing one of the most progressive proposals of his time on the problem of serf emancipation in Russia, had been written precisely in Jassy, in November 1802.

Equally in Jassy the Russian thinker started writing Part III of his *Rassuzhdenie o mire i voine*. In this respect, it should be pointed out that his observation of the political situation in Moldavia proved to be particularly important in elaborating his notion of the rights of peoples. In chapter III of the third section of his major work, entitled 'Osvobozhdenie narodov', Malinovskii anticipated the complete autonomy of the Danubian regions:

> Moldavia and Wallachia also are subject by force alone to the Turks, who
> oppress them without pity or mercy. They are a distinct people and can
> govern themselves better by their own leaders, unifying their ancient
> properties in Bessarabia and Transylvania and forming three independent
> united regions and one power[210].

1.3.4. 1803-1811: Publicist and philanthropic activity

On his return to Petersburg, Malinovskii resigned himself to a further significant period of obscure «*kabinetnaia zhizn'*»[211], while continuing his intense intellectual activity.

Among the initiatives of this period it is important to mention those which were publicistic in nature: in 1803 his idea of creating a periodical in which progressive ideas could be expressed took concrete form in the publication of *Osennie vechera* [212]. In the course of the previous years, Malinovskii had been developing a personal idea of the importance of the press in shaping and reflecting, at the same time, the values and ideas of a country[213]. The project of founding a Russian periodical dated back to at least 1799, the year in which he wrote the *povest' Pustynnik*, as in the first page of its manuscript the subtitle was precisely 'ezhenedel'noe izdanie'[214].

---

[210] See the text of *Rassuzhdenie* part III published in J. Skowronek, '«Rozwazania o pokoju i wojnie» Wasyla F. Malinowskiego', *Teki archiwalne*, no. 17 (1978), pp. 34-35.

[211] Life spent in a study.

[212] *Osennie vechera. Ezhenedel'noe izdanie 1803 goda* (Spb., 1803), pri Gubernskom Pravlenii. Subsequent references will be made in the text by page number to this edition.

[213] See for instance in 'Rossiianin v Anglii': «I advise everyone to read the newspapers of the country in which he is travelling», *Priiatnoe i poleznoe preprovozhdenie vremeni*, XII (1796), p. 360.

[214] IRLI, Fond 244, op. 25, no. 307, f. 5. The manuscript of *Pustynnik* is contained in a «*zapisnaia kniga*» (notebook) alongside the article 'Glas sovesti', later published in

Only after the turn of the century, however, did Malinovskii make his first attempts in this area of activity, taking advantage of the new freedom allowed by the censorship after the accession of Alexander I. The initiative coincided with Malinovskii's first public appearence as a political publicist, a role for which the Russian philosopher had long been preparing himself. An important article entitled 'Primechanie o aziatskikh narodakh', which remained in manuscript until the Soviet era, also seems to date from 1803.

Osennie vechera appeared on Saturdays and the editor planned the publication of twelve issues in the three months of autumn, according to his idea that «the autumn evenings, curtailing the concerns of day, give sufficient time to reflect about oneself before sleep» (p. 3). Of the twelve projected, only eight issues appeared, all filled with articles written exclusively by the editor himself[215], although the periodical was not initially conceived as a personal tribune for Malinovskii the publicist but as an organ through which to involve other intellectuals in a public discussion of the state of Russian society and European politics.

The first issue came out on 26 September. *Osennie vechera* was printed in a very limited number of copies[216]. No issue exceeds eight pages, and all contain one or two short articles and a prayer or a song. With the only exceptions of one article in the first issue and of one in the first part of the second issue, all the articles bear a title: 'O voine' (nos. 2-3), 'Liubov' Rossii' (no. 5), 'Istoriia Rossii', 'Glas sovesti' (no. 6), 'Voskresenie' (no. 7), 'Svoia storona' (no. 8)[217].

No. 1 announces the programme of the journal, aimed to make its readers «think about the soul». The invitation to give priority to spiritual needs is expressed in archaic language, where the allusions to the imminent punishment of sinners resemble very closely the tone and contents of the *povest' Pustynnik*.

In the second issue considerations «of the inevitability of death and eternal life» bring the editor to ask himself, for the benefit of his readers, which are the most reasonable and wise ways of life to be pursued:

Osennie vechera, and *Istoriia dlia prostykh i malykh*, that he apparently planned to include in one of the subsequent numbers.

[215] As already suggested in the only article dealing with this publication, A.G. Maksimov, '«Osennie vechera» 1803 goda. Ezhenedel'noe izdanie V.F. Malinovskogo', *Literaturnyi vestnik*, V, no. 4 (1903), pp. 445-450.

[216] The only available copy today is an edition of 1803 in which all the issues were gathered, and where number four is unfortunately missing.

[217] In Arab-Ogly's edition of 1958 four were re-published: 'O voine', 'Liubov' Rossii', 'Istoriia Rossii', 'Svoia storona' .

> to withdraw from the world, to abandon everything and run into the
> wilderness! (...) such settlements, where people would work the land, tend
> gardens, pray to God and save their souls, where no person would tempt
> another, no-one would argue or quarrel, but live together like brothers,
> content with little, not desiring wealth and not enticing one another with
> luxury (p. 9).

Malinovskii does not reject in principle the idea of abandoning society,
but having recently experienced how difficult it can be, he suggests to his
readers a different path, which may be seen as the ultimate rejection of his
«Ufa project» and as a declaration of intent for his journal: «But while
there is nowhere to withdraw to, it is essential to know how to live in the
world and protect oneself from vice! (...) so that by one's actions and
treatment of people one attains blessed eternity» (p. 10).

As early as in the second part of this issue the periodical takes a
definitely less spiritual orientation. The article entitled 'O voine', which
continues in no. 3, is devoted to an analysis of contemporary politics and
shows a close thematic relationship with his major work *Rassuzhdenie o
mire i voine*, also published in 1803. Here Malinovskii illustrates his ideas
on the current opposition between England and France. He blames England
for its violation of the Peace of Amiens but not for its being in an isolated
and courageous opposition to France. He makes an important distinction
between the English court, which caused the violation of the peace, and the
English people, ready to defend themselves at a time when «French troops
have spread from Italy to Holstein» (p. 17). During the Napoleonic era
France gave a new actuality, according to Malinovskii, to the aggressive
wars of the past by conquering territories in Europe. Behind the false idea
of spreading republicanism, it attacked the security and freedom of the
independent peoples of Europe and menaced the stability of the world. In
Malinovskii's words, the fear of a French attack on English freedom had
the positive effect that «the spirit of the people awakened» (p. 24). The
article, written in a very direct and vehement style, is an invitation to
Russia to forget the recent conflict with England over the fort of Ochakov
and to support its position.

The article in the fifth issue, entitled 'Liubov' Rossii', is a strong call
to unity for all the peoples, classes and religious confessions of Russia[218],
which is an indispensible measure with which to face the menace France

---

[218] Here Malinovskii cites «veroterpenie» as a quality of the Russian people and
insists importantly on the toleration that should be shown towards the «staroobriadtsy».

presents to Europe. Resorting, as examples, to the glorious deeds of Suvorov in the Italian campaign of 1798-99 and the expansionistic power of Russia in Africa and America, Malinovskii aims to awaken in his readers (addressed as «*liubeznye sograzhdane*»: gentle fellow-citizens) a vigorous nationalism. The fifth issue is completed by 'Pesn'', a prayer in which he asks God to intervene for him personally:

> Evildoers have arisen against me,
> They oppress and rend my breast.
> They have slandered an innocent,
> Their vicious jowls howl[219].

Apart from 'Glas sovesti', an invitation to listen to the voice of conscience, this «personal guard of every person» (p. 47), the sixth issue includes an article entitled 'Istoriia Rossii', where in his call for unity Malinovskii quotes directly from the *Stepennaia kniga*. The passage refers to the ruinous attack of the barbarous Batyi on the Russian land, when the «gnev bozhii» (divine wrath) punished the ambition and corruption of the Russian princes, and is quoted by him because «similar causes produce similar events».

'Voskresenie' is the title of the article in the seventh issue. This day should be left only «for the spirit». He attacks the current Russian habit: «the general failure to observe Sunday, defiled by markets, dances and drunkenness, or agricultural work» (p. 52); «Sunday is a commercial day throughout Russia!» (p. 50), pointing out its negative consequences:

> how can the people educate themselves, if they do not have even one free day! (...) On Sunday the children of the poor in villages and towns could learn to read and write, as has been successfully introduced in many lands (pp. 53-54).

The allusion is above all to the English example, already praised on the pages of 'Rossiianin v Anglii'[220]. The last issue is filled with 'Svoia

---

[219] (Zlodei na menia vozstali / Stesniaiut grud' moiu i rvut/ Nevinnogo oklevetali, / Ikh zlobny cheliusti revut). The verses are evidently occasioned by a personal offence suffered by Malinovskii in his capacity as editor of the journal. We are not able nevertheless to clarify from whom and in what circumstances he was the object of the calumny. This is also the only poem he is known to have written.

[220] The description of the English Sunday in 'Rossiianin v Anglii' is precisely antithetic to that of the Russians: «Sunday is spent in a thoroughly Christian way. They neither play cards, nor dance, nor sing songs, nor work. There are no theatrical entertainments on this day, and no shows, and all the shops are closed», *Priiatnoe i poleznoe preprovozhdenie vremeni*, XI (1796), pp. 97-98. He also praises the English Sundays schools: «Throughout England schools have recently been set up where the

storona', where Malinovskii expresses his hope that the *«liubov' svoei storony»* (the love of one's own side), a legitimate feeling, does not degenerate into a blind Great Russian nationalism, a *«vrednoe pristrastie»* (harmful partiality), but flows into a more general *«liubov' otechestva»* involving all the other nationalities on the vast territory under the influence of Russia. In this respect he outlines the importance of creating national universities in order to inculcate a *«dukh obshchestvennyi»* (social spirit) and of founding national newspapers. Two other contributions are 'Nakazanie', an article recalling the old chroniclers' idea that wars and conflicts, disease and death are God's punishment and that «the punishment is God's voice awakening our conscience», and 'Pravda', an essay looking forward to seeing the advent of justice in Europe as a time when «golden peace and joyful abundance accompany the truth».

The publication of *Osennie vechera* was interrupted after the eighth issue. In the first number the editor had launched an invitation to other intellectuals who shared his views:

> At the end of each week new comments and considerations will be published (...) those well disposed to the general usefulness of teaching and enlightenment are invited graciously to communicate true instances of human life known to them, so that the teaching can be solidly confirmed by examples (p. 8).

The editor's optimistic expectations went entirely unanswered and he remained the only contributor to the journal. The periodical itself was virtually ignored by other journalists[221]. The reasons for its failure are certainly not to be found in the range of the themes. If we compare *Osennie vechera* with its more popular and prestigious journalistic counterpart, Karamzin's *Vestnik Evropy*[222], appearing in 1802-1803, we find a striking similarity in matter: a strong interest in history, the need for Russia to be more advanced in education, the nationalistic turn of the ideals of enlightenment, the debate on Russia's internal reforms, the blame and concern about French aggression. But the approach could not be more different. In Malinovskii's journal we do not find any concessions to

---

children of the poor, boys and girls, learn to read and write on Sundays», *ibid.*, XII (1796), pp. 389-390.

[221] A short notice of the foundation of the weekly periodical was given in the *S-Peterburgskie Vedomosti* (1803), nos. 77, 78, 83.

[222] See A.G. Cross, 'N.M. Karamzin's «Messenger of Europe» (*Vestnik Evropy*), 1802-3', *Forum for Modern Language Studies*, V, no. 1 (1969), pp. 1-25, and the chapter 'The Messenger of Europe. 1802-1803', in *N.M. Karamzin: a Study of His Literary Career 1783-1803*.

«modernity» in language or approach to these subjects. The rigorous position of the editor, especially on social issues, is advanced in a moralistic, prophetic tone. The initially strongly spiritual and moralizing orientation modified itself in the course of the weeks under the impact of European political events, to become a call for political, religious, social, and cultural unity. But the language remained the same, and it did not impress his contemporaries.

In the following years, Malinovskii did not cease to express his opinion about the most important political events of his time, particularly in foreign policy; his articles remained, however, unpublished. His undated 'Mnenie o mire s Velikobritaniei', written apparently after 1807, is an attempt to persuade the Russian government to abandon the alliance with Napoleon, called «*novyi syn Filippa Makedonskogo*» (the new son of Philip of Macedonia):

> Friendship with the emperor Napoleon is generally unpleasant, and to many also suspect, even repulsive and dangerous. As moderate, philanthropic and charitable as are the intentions of the Russian emperor, just so limited and vainly ambitious are the motives of the French. The only peace which Europe might expect from him is her submission to his influence, and dependency (...) it would be advisable to open new direct dealings with Great Britain and conclude a peace which observed the strictest neutrality[223].

In another unpublished article, also presumably written after 1807, and entitled 'Bespristrastnyi sovet velikobritanskomu narodu', Malinovskii's attitude towards England is marked by a relevant change: he cannot refrain from accusing this «narod vol'nyi, prosveshchennyi i razmyshliaiushchii» of being involved in an aggressive policy:

> You are rich and scatter gold throughout Europe (...) but will all powers, all peoples sacrifice their blood for gold? Reliance on your own wealth is to blame for a careless and unjust treatment of allies. You do not behave with the proper respect towards them and you do not know how to preserve loyalty toward yourself, you are cold, indifferent and slow to assist your allies[224].

Showing no gratitude for the help previously received from Russia, which prevented Napoleon attacking England, this country is now leading an anti-Russian and generally belligerent policy:

---

[223] IRLI, Fond 244, op. 25, no. 320.
[224] *Ibid.*, no. 321, f. 1.

more active in hostility than in friendship, you have concluded an alliance
with Turkey, the main advantage of which is not only trade and its
benefits, but the desire to harm Russia. The first fruit of this union was the
severance of peaceable negotiations, for which reciprocal plenipotentiaries
had already travelled to the appointed place. Thus, the British government
has provided new grounds for blame, that it spreads the flame of war
everywhere, and fans it where it was ready to go out.

In April 1809 Malinovskii wrote his 'Mysli o sredstvakh skoreishego
obshchego primireniia Evropy'[225], in which he proposed the division of the
Turkish Empire as the only solution to the state of war and dangerous
instability which characterized Europe in those years. Concentrating all
their forces against their real, common enemy, European states would be
able to reach a new order, which would include the liberation of Greece,
the independence for Belgrade and Russia's annexation of Moldavia and
Wallachia.

The publicist activity of these years was accompanied by significant
philanthropic fervour on Malinovskii's part: in 1802 he took part in the
foundation of the «Bibleiskoe obshchestvo»[226], modelled on similar English
institutions, and became one of its most active members. This society
undertook, among other projects, the completion of a plan which
Malinovskii considered too ambitious to be carried out by one man: the
translation of the scriptures from Hebrew into Russian. Malinovskii, a man
of wide and varied education, versed in many European languages, Turkish,
Latin and ancient Greek, dedicated himself during this period to the study
of Hebrew and managed to complete the translation of several works,
including Exodus, Ecclesiastes, Job and the Psalms.

An important part of his charity work was his collaboration with the
«Filantropicheskii Komitet», of which he was one of the founders and one
of the most assiduous members. His activity within this organization led to
his appointment as Director of the «Dom Trudoliubiia», founded in
November 1808, which aimed, *inter alia*, to support young girls in need[227].

These activities did not prevent Malinovskii from pursuing official
channels in seeking to attain the realization of the ideas of reform set out in
his major work, the *Rassuzhdenie*. The very real importance which

---

[225] *Ibid.*, no. 318.

[226] In 1813 the institution could count on the work, in their capacity as Vice-
presidents, of V.P. Kochubei, A.K. Razumovskii, M.I. Donaurov, R.A. Koshelev. See *O
bibleiskikh obshchestvakh, i uchrezhdenii takovogo zhe v Sanktpeterburge* (Spb., 1813),
p. 47. On the involvement of the Bible Society in educational reforms, see J.T. Flynn, *The
University Reform of Tsar Alexander I. 1802-1835* (Washington, D.C., 1988).

[227] See the *Ustav Sanktpeterburgskogo Doma Trudoliubiia* (Spb., 1830).

Malinovskii ascribed to this project is emphasised by his attempt to associate it with other plans emerging in Europe at that time: in April 1804 he sent a revised copy of it to the Minister of Foreign Affairs, A.A. Czartoryski, who had drawn up an ambitious programme for reorganizing relations among European states[228].

In 1805 Malinovskii obtained the rank of *statskii sovetnik* and the following year he received the order of St Vladimir of the fourth degree. In December 1806, just before receiving the latter honour, he wrote a note entitled 'Sluzhba', probably a speech he intended to deliver in front of his colleagues in the College, as it is addressed to his «kind and honourable colleagues»[229], and alludes to a different sort of cross, «that cross, which promises us a better meeting there (...), the sole witness of our sincerely zealous service to our Sovereign and Fatherland». In this respect, Malinovskii stresses his intention to amend, for the future, his negative attitude toward the service «which until now I have regarded as a distraction and a vain waste of time»; in this *mea culpa* in front of God, he makes a profession of humility and patience, and promises to exercise himself in the difficult art of being a good servant of the state:

> Forgive me the futile years spent in this, all the temptations of my colleagues, the insults to my superiors, the fervour and envy and the various misdemeanours of arrogant self-love, everything I have neglected as regards my subordinates and those in my charge, forgive and do not call to account and blot out the evil that has been done...

These formal acknowledgements did not correspond, in point of fact, to any improvement in his personal financial position: the years from 1802 to 1812 brought financial difficulties for Malinovskii and his family, while in the same period he devoted himself to the mitigation of the material conditions of the most derelict in Russian society[230].

Malinovskii did, however, take the opportunity to complain about the injustice of the semi-obscure service in which he had spent almost thirty years of his life: in June 1810 he resolved to send a letter to the Minister of

---

[228] See on this subject P.K. Grimsted, 'Czartoryski's System for Russian Foreign Policy, 1803', *California Slavic Studies*, no. 5 (1970), p. 19-91, and also J. Skowronek, 'Le programme européen du prince Adam Jerzy Czartoryski en 1801-1805', *Acta Poloniae Historica*, no. 10 (1967), pp. 137-159, and, by the same author, *Antynapoleonskie koncepcje Czartoryskiego* (Warszawa, 1969). The episode involving Malinovskii is also mentioned in W.H. Zawadski, 'Adam Czartoryski: an Advocate of Slavonic Solidarity at the Congress of Vienna', in *Oxford Slavonic Papers*, NS X (1977), pp. 73-97.

[229] *Sluzhba*, IRLI, Fond 244, op. 25, no. 311.

[230] See Rubets, *op.cit.*, p. 199.

Foreign Affairs, N.P. Rumiantsev, asking for a sum of money to be allocated to him. Such a measure would serve as a partial compensation for the wrong which he felt he had been done: «This favour would serve as assistance towards living expenses and as a sign of approval of long service which has remained unnoticed»[231].

1.4. Appointment as First Director of the Tsarskoe Selo Lycée (1811-1814)

1.4.1. A Director for a new institution

On 19 October 1811 the Tsarskoe Selo Lycée was opened. On 12 June of that year Malinovskii had been appointed its first Director.

The importance of this institution[232] in the history of Russian liberal thought is generally recognized: here the Decembrists achieved their education, here Pushkin's poetic genius first encountered the ideas of freedom and egalitarianism. The name of the first Director of the Tsarskoe Selo Lycée can be found in any study on Pushkin. What had earned Malinovskii the office which was to ensure his posthumous fame more than the intellectual work of his entire life? A correct understanding of the circumstances in which Malinovskii achieved this appointment allows this episode to be integrated harmoniously into the context of his life. We are faced in fact, in this case, with a particular interpretation of this event, well-established in the historiography on the first Director and seemingly legitimated by the reminiscences of the students of the first course.

One of the students less affected by the liberal atmosphere of the Lycée, Baron M.A. Korf, a future supporter of Tsar Nicholas I, wrote, not without a certain acrimony, that Malinovskii owed his appointment to the fact that he had married the Archpriest Samborskii's daughter. In establishing the reasons for the appointment of Malinovskii, Baron Korf did not exclude also the possible role of the State Secretary M.M. Speranskii, a

---

231 Quoted in D. Kobeko, 'Pervyi direktor tsarskosel'skogo litseia', *Zhurnal Ministerstva narodnogo prosveshchenia*, no. 7 (1915), p. 4.
232 The origin and functioning of the Tsarskoe Selo Lycée will be examined in detail in chapter 4.

long-time close friend of Samborskii[233]. In 1784 Samborskii had become the spiritual mentor of the future Emperor Alexander and of his brother Konstantin, and he later had the opportunity to support Speranskii actively, making use of the influence he had over Alexander I.

This interpretation of the reasons behind Malinovskii's appointment is difficult to reconcile with his well-known rejection of the system of «protection» and corruption widespread in the Russian society of his time. It is based on certain facts, which can, nevertheless, be read in a different way. Analyzing Malinovskii's private documents, we become aware of the fact that he did make several efforts to gain this prestigious appointment. The personal channels he attempted to make use of emerge quite clearly from the letters he sent to his younger brother Pavel. That correspondence is particularly illuminating about the preparatory phase in the creation of the first Russian lycée.

In one of those letters, undated, he referred to the interview he had had with Count A.K. Razumovskii, Minister of Education, during which practical details of the appointment had been defined: the possibility that his son Ivan might be admitted to the school, despite being older than other students; the dream that the beloved estate of Belozerka, where he had finished the second part of his *Dissertation*, once assigned to his father-in-law Samborskii, might be assigned to the *litseisty* and, therefore, that he, as a pedagogue, might be able to walk around it[234].

More generally, the letters to his brother reveal that certain family connections must have been instrumental in his being preferred as Director, though not in the way suggested by Korf: the contribution of his brother Pavel himself seems to have been much more influential. Without dismissing the possible role of Samborskii and even of Speranskii, it should be remembered that Pavel, who had the rank of *statskii sovetnik* and had been appointed Director of the State Assignation Bank[235], had won the favour of Count N.P. Sheremetev[236], and had even been nominated by him as his executor. Count Razumovskii was married to a sister of Sheremetev, and he was certainly influenced as to who to put at the head of the new Lycée by the intercession of Pavel Malinovskii, who was, in addition,

---

[233] See Ia. Grot, *Pushkin, ego litseiskie tovarishchi i nastavniki* (Spb., 1899), p. 223.

[234] V.F. Malinovskii, *Izbrannye obshchestvenno-politicheskie sochineniia*, p. 153.

[235] See Kobeko, *op.cit.*, p. 4.

[236] See O. Zakharova, 'Graf A.R. Vorontsov i graf N.P. Sheremetev', in V.N. Alekseev (ed.), *Vorontsovy - dva veka v istorii Rossii* (Vladimir, 1992) p. 67.

supported by the friendship of M.I. Donaurov (1758-1817), tutor of Sheremetev's son, as well as by his acquaintance with R.A. Koshelev.

The person repeatedly indicated by Malinovskii as his «*blagodetel'*» in the Lycée appointment is Donaurov. He must have been explicitly requested by Malinovskii to intercede in his favour, if on 16 June 1811 Vasilii Fedorovich wrote to his brother Pavel: «A decree has now been sent to the Senate about my appointment as director of the Lycée: it has remained in the hands of the board with the salary. Congratulate me! Thank Mikhail Ivanovich». It is also interesting to take into account the opposite view: what made Donaurov decide in favour of Malinovskii? In a letter sent on 23 January to Samborskii he wrote, referring to his «*sodeistvie*» (assistance) in favour of the Reverend's son-in-law: «I consider that this will be no less useful to society»[237]. We can therefore assume that the considerations on the upright intellectual life Malinovskii had led since then entitled him to that post, in the eyes of his «protectors».

We cannot exclude the possible help of Speranskii, but we have to add a further consideration: the friendship between Malinovskii and him, initially mediated by Samborskii, had acquired a strictly personal character, and dated back to earlier years, as shown in a letter sent by Malinovskii to his wife on 24 April 1797, in which he refers to their intimate friendship with Elizabeth Stephens, Speranskii's wife[238].

Three letters sent by Malinovskii to his brother referring to his appointment at Tsarskoe Selo were first published in 1915 by one of the «biographers of the first Director», D.I. Kobeko, with the aim of demonstrating his hypothesis: Malinovskii's adherence to secret societies. Razumovskii, Koshelev and Donaurov had in fact an important feature in common: they were *martinisty* [239].

Our opinion is that a certain network of connections worked in obtaining the appointment which meant so much to Malinovskii at that

---

[237] TSDIAU, Fond 2053, op.1, no. 808, f. 1. In the Ustav of the Lycée the Director was required to be «a man of exceptionally broad knowledge in sciences and languages, of an exemplary life» (paragraph 78, quoted by Pavlova, p. 16).

[238] He wrote: «How pleasant it will be to enjoy the spring at Belozerka (...) if our dear friend Eliza will be there she will add to our joy and her ingenious conversation will add a great charm to ours (...) Pray lot dear Mrs Stephens wait for my arrival and to amend for her absence at our wedding, tell her I intend to celebrate it the day of my arrival from here to Belozerka, she must be a sitting mother and bring you to my bedroom and bless both you and me. I will love her as much as you praise her for her kindness and friendship to you (...) give new charms to our married life», IRLI, Fond RIII, op.2, no. 2185-2194, f.2. Speranskii and his future wife had met at Samborskii's house in St Petersburg (see A.G.Cross, «*By the Banks of the Thames*»: *Russians in Eighteenth-Century Britain*, p.43).

[239] See Kobeko, *op. cit.*, p. 7.

moment in his life. That network included persons who represented the most advanced part of the Russian society of the time, who were deeply concerned for the welfare of their homeland and fully convinced that they were choosing the most appropriate person to head the Tsarskoe Selo Lycée. Certainly Malinovskii's appointment came at a moment of great expectations about the renewal of Russia, to which the Masons were not, possibly, indifferent.

Analysis of Malinovskii's papers helps us to a correct understanding of the historical context in which his appointment took place. Such a reading of the evidence tends to be more in harmony with the image that we find in a number of biographical events.

1.4.2. The opening of the Lycée

The new important official engagement changed Malinovskii's life. As shown in a letter to his brother Pavel, he got into debt to meet the initial expenses that the new lifestyle inevitably involved:

> Do me a favour, gentle brother, rescue me from my present straits, later things are bound to be easier (...) even if I find 1.000 roubles, I have to pay interest (...) I need a carriage for travelling and like it or not three or so horses, for the minister said that rooms will be prepared for my arrival, but my drozhky is worn out, completely broken down; so many debts have piled up until my new salary is paid; even without the carriage - there is the new uniform![240].

Although being officially still employed in the College of Foreign Affairs, Malinovskii started quite soon to devote all his energies to the organization of the first Russian Lycée. During the summer of 1811 the eyes of all progressive Russia were turned to Tsarskoe Selo, where the new initiative proceeded actively. The Director was deeply involved in the preliminary work for the imminent opening in the autumn: he selected the teaching staff, undertook the adaptation of the four-storey wing of the court palace destined to host the Lycée in Tsarskoe Selo[241] and solved a number of practical and bureaucratic problems connected with its arrangement.

---

[240] See the letter of 16 June 1811 to his brother Pavel, published in *Izbrannye obshchestvenno-politicheskie sochineniia*, p. 153. The letters to Pavel Malinovskii were published for the first time by Kobeko, *op.cit.* pp. 5-7.

[241] The adaptation of the four-storey wing of Catherine's palace was carried out by Vasilii Petrovich Stasov according to architectural principles in keeping with the Enlightenment spirit (see on this O.A. Iatsenko, '«Sviashchennyi khram nauk».

In August and September Malinovskii presided over the exams for admission to the school[242]. He accepted a limited number of students, who were selected strictly on the basis of their individual aptitudes, excluding social criteria[243], which were frequently paramount at that time in Russia. On that occasion the Director also had to give his judgment about the future students; there is a record of Malinovskii's first impressions of Pushkin, to whom he gave «*ochen' khorosho*» (very good) in Russian grammar; among the others, he classified the young Anton Del'vig as «*preslabyi*» (very weak) in French[244].

The inauguration of the Lycée, on 19 October 1811, was expected to be the occasion when important indications about the future policy of the institution would be publicly given to the country. For the occasion a representative selection of St Petersburg society was to come to Tsarskoe Selo. In his capacity as Director, Malinovskii was called to deliver a speech in the presence of all the future *litseisty*, the Minister of Narodnoe Prosveshchenie Razumovskii, the Emperor Alexander I and other official personalities. The occasion was momentous: the principles and positions expressed by the educators on that occasion were to gain official approval and have a lasting influence on the education of the new Russia.

Malinovskii's contribution to the first public presentation of the Lycée was not particularly brilliant. From a report written by a *litseist* of the first course, we get a picture of a weak speech delivered by the Director and of the disappointed reactions of some of the people present:

> Our director V.F.Malinovskii came timidly out onto the stage with a package in his hand. As pale as death, he began to read something: he read

---

Pedagogicheskie motivy v litseiskoi arkhitekture', in S.M. Nekrasov (ed.), '...*I v prosveshchenii stat' s vekom naravne'*. Sbornik nauchnykh trudov (Spb., 1992), pp. 27-34.

[242] The first exams took place in Razumovskii's house on 12 August. On 22 September thirty students (out of the thirty-eight selected for the exams) were officially admitted to attend the Lycée (see M. Rudenskaia, S. Rudenskaia, '*Nastavnikam ... za blago vozdadim*' (Leningrad, 1986), pp. 28-32).

[243] Only five pupils had noble titles. Malinovskii personally supported the admission of a brilliant student, although he was not of noble origin: V. Vol'khovskii. On 15 December he wrote to his mother: «Gracious Madam Aleksandra Matveevna! (...) I can now tell you still more about your son. His gentleness, diligence and success picked him out among many who have powerful and exalted parents. Here is proof that we reward only true worth with distinction (...) allow me to congratulate you on having so worthy a son, whose name is written in golden letters in the hall of our Lycée» (TSDIAU, Fond 2039, op. 1, no. 54, f. 11).

[244] A.A. Rubets, '*Nastavnikam, khranivshim iunost' nashu'. Pamiatnaia knizhka chinov imperatorskogo Aleksandrovskogo, byvshego tsarskosel'skogo, litseia. S 1811 po 1911 god* (Spb., 1911), p. 201.

for rather a long while, but his voice was so feeble and halting, it was unlikely many people could hear him. It was noticeable that those sitting in the back rows of the hall began to whisper and lean back in their chairs. It was not a very encouraging appearance for an orator...[245]

The report, written several years later (it was published in 1859[246]), lastingly affected historians' opinion about Malinovskii[247], leaving a negative shadow on his otherwise transparent personality.

Examining Malinovskii's documents, we find quite a different version of that day, one of the most important in his life. He expressed his opinion on that episode on various occasions[248]. The day after the inauguration he wrote a letter to his brother Pavel in which he described the event:

> Gentle brother, yesterday my first feat, the opening of the Lycée, was accomplished. My heart's desire was that the Sovereign should be satisfied and I saw this satisfaction on the face of his majesty and of all the imperial family. They liked everything, and everything we had set up met with approval, as they assured me in turns. The order of the ceremony came off without the slightest hitch: I gave my speech with the permission of the minister: loudly, with my voice sometimes breaking from anxiety, but without stopping. All the guests and the members of the council greeted me, saying that the establishment of the school was in good hands. Judge for yourself, even Arakcheev, who does not go in for flattery, declared his confidence in me, and the minister of justice. Due to his eloquence he expressed himself even more favourably, and mentioned you. Thank God everything is fine (...) the Sovereign, at the end of the assembly, approached the rows of children, arranged according to height, and spoke to them. Be true to your word, show you understand the promises to be exemplary young people with which you have entered the Lycée. I send the speech[249].

As we see, Malinovskii could not hide a certain satisfaction with the way he had been able to get out of a difficult and delicate situation. Instead of concluding that Pushchin's report was simply not true, or too altered by

[245] I.I. Pushchin, *Zapiski o Pushkine. Pis'ma*, eds. M.P. Mironenko, S.V. Mironenko (Moskva, 1988), p. 36.

[246] In *Atenei*, II (1859), no. 8.

[247] N.L. Brodskii, *A.S. Pushkin* (Moskva, 1937), p. 30; G. Chulkov, *Zhizn' Pushkina* (Moskva, 1938), p. 38; L.P. Grossman *Pushkin* (Moskva, 1939), pp. 70-72.

[248] See Malinovskii's note the day after: «20 October. Yesterday was the celebrated occasion of the Lycée's opening. All the children gathered the evening before and I withdrew to prepare for my speech. I rehearsed it in the assembly hall before the minister and received permission to deliver it (...) everything happened as planned. The Sovereign, both the empresses and all the visitors, who were leading figures, were satisfied and saluted me. The Sovereign, at the end of the assembly, said to the children 'keep to your word to be such as the decree demands and as our speeches have proclaimed'» ('Pamiatnaia kniga Litseia', IRLI, Fond 244, op. 25, no. 290, f. 5). The document was published in P.G. Tichini, O.I. Bilets'kii (eds.), *O.S. Pushkin (statti ta materiali)* (Kiev, 1938), p. 181.

[249] IRLI, Fond 244, op. 25, no. 334/2.

the years, it is now possible to state that the reason behind Malinovskii's embarassment when he delivered his speech was not his personal weakness or fear of the authorities, but the circumstance that he was delivering someone else's words. As has recently been pointed out, the text officially known as Malinovskii's discourse is not the one he had written for the event, but that commissioned for him by Razumovskii[250].

Two documents are now available which restore the ideas he originally wished to express on this occasion: a draft and a revised version of the same speech[251]. The rough draft[252] contains presumably the text of the speech Malinovskii submitted to Razumovskii in order to get his permission (as suggested also by an indication written on the draft by his son Ivan). This version was probably revised after indications by Razumovskii. The revised version available repeats substantially the same notions in a more embellished form and with concessions to the official tone of the event. Instead of the approval he expected[253], Malinovskii got back a completely different version, probably written by I.I. Martynov, which had to replace his own[254].

The draft of Malinovskii's discourse is particularly valuable for us, so we will concentrate on it, trying to analyze it and point out the ideas which could have attracted the censorial attention of Razumovskii. Its text, which we traced recently, is the following:

---

[250] The official speech is published in *Rechi, proiznesennye pri torzhestvennom otkrytii Imperatorskogo Tsarsko-sel'skogo Litseia, v prisutstvii ego Imperatorskogo Velichestva i avgusteishei familii, i stikhi na sei sluchai sochinennye* (Spb., 1811), pp. 1-2.

[251] The revised version, written in a copyist's handwriting, contains substantially the same ideas (TSDIAU, Fond 2039, op. 1, no. 84, f. 1).

[252] Two articles were recently devoted to this episode: L.B. Mikhailova, 'Neproiznesennaia rech' direktora litseia', *Vechernii Leningrad,* no. 68 (1989), p. 3, and L.B. Mikhailova, E.S. Lebedeva, 'V nachale zhizni pomniu ia', in S.M. Nekrasov (ed.), *'...I v prosveshchenii stat' s vekom naravne'*, pp. 35-45.

[253] In the draft of a letter to the Minister, Malinovskii wrote: «I have the honour of presenting for your Excellency's perusal the outlines of a short speech, which I should read at the opening of the Lycée. Everything that you are pleased to point out or add to it I will accept with the devotion I sincerely hold for your person» (IRLI, Fond 244, op. 25, no. 351).

[254] «The examinations are followed by the opening of the Lycée. On this occasion Malinovskii had to deliver a speech. He forwarded his plan to the minister; the Count returned it and together with it sent a different draft of the speech. In the official sources (...) we do not find Malinovskii's composition; the Count's draft is preserved, and the speech which Malinovskii gave at the opening is reliably known to conform closely to the minister's outline; and from Martynov's acknowledgements (in his notes) it is clear that this speech was written by Ivan Ivanovich», A.A. Rubets, *'Nastavnikam, khranivshim iunost' nashu'. Pamiatnaia knizhka chinov imperatorskogo Aleksandrovskogo, byvshego tsarskosel'skogo, litseia. S 1811 po 1911 god* (Spb., 1911), pp. 194-204. See also 'Vospominaniia I.I. Martynova', *Sovremennik*, nos. 3,4 (1856).

Through the beneficial care and munificence of the Imperial majesty a small select number of well brought up, capable and noble children, destined for the most important areas of state service, has been gathered together. Having spent thirty years in my own fatherland and partly also in foreign lands I am entrusted with preparing them for this important goal. On this triumphant day of the opening of the Imperial Lycée I bear witness before my conscience of the sincere desire to fulfill the high intentions of this new and renowned school, and to be governed in everything by the will and directions of my superior.

My assistants, the tutors and other officials, who have been selected from many with great care and impartiality, are also enlivened by an equal spirit of enthusiasm to achieve a single goal, the best moral and intellectual education of these children. Prospects of personal gain on their account, harmful theorising and rules, reprehensible behaviour, all this will be banished from among us. We will expect the improvement of our condition through the charity and munificence of His Imperial Majesty, through the petitions of our fair-minded superior. Our intelligence, our diligence will be applied to the good fundamental customs and decrees of our fatherland and through our lives we will give an example of good conduct to the youth. May God help us in this; I undertake to strive for this myself and I vouch for you, my respected colleagues: may this solemn obligation, before the Imperial Sovereign himself, not be blotted from the memory of any of us, either leaders or subordinates.

And you, dear children, vow in your hearts, with the sincerity proper to your age, to justify your selection and to respond to your superiors' and teachers' sincere care for you by firmly imprinting in your memory this solemn assembly and your vows; contemplate your great privileges and the importance of your appointment, which oblige you in return to excellent behaviour, to application and the observance of strict order and to obedience. Let us try through a new education to inculcate the old rules and customs of our fatherland; attachment to the faith, submission to the sovereign, honour of parents and love of kin, loyalty to one's word, following conscience and honour in everything[255].

We can draw a few conclusions about this important document. First of all, Malinovskii's sense of dignity is apparent when he considers his previous personal and professional history as a sort of necessary and appropriate requirement for that office: his own spotless thirty-years experience of service entitles him to be the Director of students destined to become high-level servants of the Russian state.

The speech that Malinovskii never managed to deliver contains *in nuce* the principles which were to inform his future activity as a pedagogue. Malinovskii highlights the deeply innovative character of this initiative by frequently using the adjective «new»: «this new and renowned school», «through a new education».

---

[255] TSDIAU, Fond 2039, op. 1, no. 103. I am greatly indebted to L.B. Mikhailova for her help in restoring the original text from the draft.

As in all his other works, he also stresses the notion of reason. In the part addressed to his «respectable assistants», most of them were personally selected by him on the basis of identity of sentiments and thinking, Malinovskii points out that they are called to give the children «the best education of their morality and reason». The students, in turn, are invited to be aware of their privileged position in Russian society, and to be worthy of it. All his appeal to his «amiable children», is imbued with the sense of fatherhood which will be a recognizable feature of his task as a pedagogue at Tsarskoe Selo; particularly relevant is his orientation towards a non-repressive education.

On the whole, this speech does not sound particularly audacious, but it certainly shows a different position from that of the author of the discourse Malinovskii was finally obliged to deliver on that solemn day. Most of the short text of the official speech is devoted to adulatory formulas and panegyrics. The heavily archaic intonation is alien to Malinovskii's style: the Lycée is for example indicated as a *vertograd* (an image not found in his writings).

The intonation, in the tradition of early eighteenth-century panegyrical odes, is also striking. Catherine II is recalled as the inspirer of Tsarskoe Selo's residence and named «Velikaia v Zhenakh». Expressing his faith in the premises which predisposed the brilliant future of this institution, the author of the speech refers to the «blagorastvorennyi vozdukh», and hopes to educate in the young students the «vernye sluzhiteli Prestola Monarshego», and he is certain that «the small number of children (...) is not inconvenient for the complete supervision of their education and behaviour».

Nothing could have been more distant from Malinovskii's style and beliefs. The only way he probably had to disown this declaration was by delivering the most high-sounding speech in a humble tone which would sound in itself as a contradiction.

1.4.3. The last two years

The years 1811-1813 saw Malinovskii absorbed by the life of the Lycée. On 9 February 1812 his wife Sof'ia Andreevna died. He was profoundly struck by this loss. In his diary of the last years[256] the event

---

[256] RGALI, Fond 312, op. 1, n. 3, ff. 1-92.

coincides with an increase in his mystical preoccupations. The pages of the spiritual diary are populated by a number of religious presences and by the figure of a mysterious lover[257]. We face an endless alternation of desire and rejection, surrender to physical temptation and contrition, which exhausted Malinovskii's intellectual energies.

In his public life, Malinovskii was squeezed between the accomplishment of his practical duties as Director and his diminishing responsibilities for the education of the pupils of Tsarskoe Selo. The conflict with Razumovskii over the speech had inaugurated in fact an entire series of tense moments in his compulsory relationship with the Minister about the direction of the Lycée.

In March 1812 Alexander I unexpectedly deprived his Minister Speranskii of all the power he had been given before. Accused of being philo-Napoleonic at a time when Russia was entering the war against France, and opposed because of his internal reforms against the nobility, he was sent into exile. The fall of Speranskii, who had supported the nomination of the Director of Tsarskoe Selo, exercized a negative influence on the position of Malinovskii in the Lycée. We can assume that rumours started to circulate about his imminent replacement[258], as Tynianov suggests in his novel *Pushkin* [259], where the decline of Malinovskii's energies and hopes is vividly described. Tynianov adds a further element, not supported by evidence, as far as we know: Malinovskii's systematic yielding to alcoholism[260].

In point of fact, Malinovskii did not cease to look for a wider audience for his ideas on European politics: in 1813 his work 'Obshchii mir' appeared in the periodical *Syn otechestva* [261], marking the last stage in the evolution of his political thought. The article was published anonymously, but there is no doubt that it belongs to the pen of Malinovskii[262].

---

[257] We do not know anything about the young lady he mentions in the diary, but can assume that she was not noble (*ibid.*, ff. 39, 52, 79).

[258] In a letter to his brother Pavel we find an allusion to Professor Koshanskii as a possible candidate. About him Malinovskii wrote: «it seems he would really have liked this position, but he is not straightforward», published in D. Kobeko, 'Pervyi direktor tsarskosel'skogo litseia', *Zhurnal Ministerstva narodnogo prosveshchenia*, no. 7 (1915), pp. 15-16.

[259] Iu. Tynianov, *Pushkin* (Moskva, 1981), p. 312.

[260] *Ibid.*, p. 338.

[261] 'Obshchii mir', *Syn otechestva*, LI (1813), no. 10, pp. 235-244.

[262] A contemporary confirmation of his authorship came with the article that N.F. Koshanskii, one of the teachers of Tsarskoe Selo, wrote to commemorate his death: 'Izvestie o zhizni Malinovskogo', *Syn otechestva*, no. 13, XVIII (1814).

Considering the experience of Napoleon's campaign in Russia, and the European scenario of those years, Malinovskii could elaborate a suggestion about a solution that European states should adopt in order to reach a stable peace. At the beginning of his essay he seemed to ascribe a utopian character to the project of perpetual peace he had elaborated in 1803. He wrote: «a general peace is no more than a chimera». Malinovskii's suggestion for the present moment is very clear: «the ratification of a peaceful decree between the allies based on the equilibrium and security of all Europe, before peace is concluded with France»[263]. As the Russians revealed themselves invincible, as Russia «has made itself the focal point, which has attracted all the powers of Europe to itself and determined world opinion», to the Russians belongs at that stage also a specific task: «to ensure the liberty of peoples by their general union among themselves, turning all their partial treaties into a single one». Although writing from the position of an «isolated philosopher», as he defined himself, Malinovskii was certain that his recommendation would have a certain echo[264].

On 4 March 1814 Vasilii Fedorovich acted as the chairman at a conference of the Lycée to examine the new rules which would involve the Director, the *nadzirateli* (inspectors) of the students' rooms, and the ones to which the students themselves would have to submit, according to the prescription of the minister. This event, which marked a more reactionary development in the life of the Lycée, was also to be the last official function of Vasilii Fedorovich as Director of Tsarskoe Selo. He died very soon after, on 23 March 1814, after a brief and unexpected illness[265].

The day after his death, at 18.00 in the evening, the entire Lycée gathered for his funeral. The burial ceremony[266] was solemn, as witnessed by a contemporary description. Vasilii Fedorovich was buried in St Petersburg, in the Georgievskvoe cemetery[267]. He left six children, three sons, Ivan, Andrei and Osip, and three daughters, Elizaveta, Anna and

---

263 *Izbrannye obshchestvenno-politicheskie sochineniia*, p. 96.

264 The editor of *Syn otechestva*, in a footnote, pointed out that the article was written before the Frankfurt Declaration of 1 December 1813 (when the European sovereigns decided to continue war against Napoleon), commenting: «It is pleasant and comforting that these desires have not remained empty desires!» (*ibid.*, p. 98).

265 Official sources recorded it as «nervnaia goriachka», see M.A. Tsiavlovskii, *Letopis' zhizni i tvorchestva A.S. Pushkina* (Moskva, 1951), p. 55.

266 IRLI, Fond 25, no. 335. A description is also to be found in Rubets, *op. cit.*, pp. 203-204. See also Dolgova, *op. cit.*, p. 206.

267 His grave and that of Samborskii were long believed lost. Only in 1961, on the 150th anniversary of the Lycée, were they discovered by M.P. Rudenskaia, as a result of whose initiative a memorial plaque was attached to it.

Mariia. They were assigned to the care of Pavel Fedorovich and of Anna Andreevna Samborskaia, their mother's sister[268]. Two of his daughters later married two students of the Lycée and future Decembrists, and their fates were bound to them after the repression of the failed attempt of 1825[269].

---

[268] Malinovskii's family received financial help from the Russian state: «his family received, over and above an extraordinary payment from the Lycée's funds of the annual salary, the same amount (2.600 r.) from the state treasury as a pension« (I.Ia. Seleznev, *Istoricheskii ocherk Imperatorskogo byvshego Tsarskosel'skogo, nyne Aleksandrovskogo Litseia za pervoe ego piatidesiatiletie, s 1811 po 1861 god* (Spb., 1861) p. 46). According to Seleznev, that was due to Razumovskii's intercession in favour of Malinovskii's children (p. 44).

[269] Anna Vasil'evna married the Decembrist A.E. Rozen, and followed him to Siberia; Mariia Vasil'evna became the wife of V.D. Vol'khovskii. Their brother Ivan married I.I. Pushchin's sister Mariia.

CHAPTER 2: THE PEACE THINKER

This chapter is devoted to an analysis of Malinovskii's contribution to the history of thinking on peace. The first section will be based on the views he expressed in the work he specifically devoted to this subject, his *Dissertation on Peace and War*. This is also the only book he wrote and published in his career and has a central place in his intellectual life. Analysis of the main aspects of this work will be integrated with a consideration of his other articles on the same theme.

The appearance of Malinovskii's treatise was a unique phenomenon in Russian history. The second section will nevertheless offer a review of the Russian tradition on peace, aimed at investigating the persistence of a few particular themes which were to be fruitfully integrated in the *Dissertation*: the development of anti-war rhetoric in Russian culture, the establishment of an idea of «narodnoe pravo», the critique of the concept of heroism, the interpretation of «just war».

Western sources were undoubtedly more relevant for Malinovskii's ideas. The second half of the eighteenth century saw a proliferation of schemes aimed at establishing a universal and perpetual peace in Europe. Some of the most significant thinkers of that time, including Jean-Jacques Rousseau, Jeremy Bentham and Immanuel Kant, devoted their works to this subject. Far from being a simple imitator of the European models, Malinovskii interacted with this tradition in developing his own original approach to the theme of war and peace. The third section will explore affinities and differences between the Russian thinker and the European authors.

2.1. Malinovskii's major work: 'Dissertation on Peace and War'

Malinovskii's political views on the problems related to peace and war
find their most significant expression in his *Dissertation on Peace and War*.
Although the treatise is one of his earliest works, the theme of peace receives
a mature and thorough treatment. That theme will continue to engage the
Russian thinker for the rest of his life, being addressed in a number of articles
and notes. The systematic approach characterizing the *Dissertation* and the
radical stance of the young author emerging from it were to remain
nevertheless exclusive features of this work.

The publication history of the treatise plays an important role in the
understanding of the project contained in it. Malinovskii conceived the work
as consisting of three parts. The first was completed at Richmond in 1790,
while the second was written at Belozerka in 1798. Signed with initials, only
these two parts were published in the St Petersburg edition of 1803. In the
postscript to a letter to G. Derzhavin of 4 August 1812, Malinovskii was to
mention the third, final part he had written. Presenting his admired poet with
a copy of the printed work, he wrote:

> After nine years of silence[1], this is the first thing I have written for the
> public: allow me, around an Author so famous in our fatherland, to be
> like the ivy twining itself around the oak (...)
> P.S. I myself wrote the book about peace and war in England and in these
> parts: there is also a continuation, but now is a quarrelsome time, and one
> can say in short: go and make war, fight away etc.[2].

This letter thus contains Malinovskii's acknowledgment of his
authorship of the treatise[3], a fact which was not always recognized during the
nineteenth century. It also provides an explanation why he chose to postpone
the publication of the third part to a more propitious moment: the delicate
political moment did not favour acceptance of the radical proposals contained

---

[1] Before the attribution to Malinovskii of 'Rossiianin v Anglii' and 'Zapiski o
Moldavii' this reference sounded quite mysterious, as *Rassuzhdenie o mire i voine* was
believed to be his first published work. As regards the «nine years of silence», they
coincide with the «unproductive» period in Malinovskii's life which was comprised
between his two journeys to Moldavia.

[2] *Sochineniia Derzhavina s ob"iasnitel'nymi primechaniami Ia. Grota*, VI (Spb.,
1871), p. 239.

[3] Previously Malinovskii had mentioned his authorship also in a letter to A.R.
Vorontsov of 16 August 1803 (when he presented his work to him): «I myself wrote the
book about peace and war in England and in these parts: there is also a continuation»
(*Arkhiv kniazia Vorontsova*, XXX (1884), p. 394). Another confirmation came from
Malinovskii's son Ivan, who described the book as written by his father (see V.F.
Malinovskii, *Izbrannye obshchestvenno-politicheskie sochineniia*, p.156).

in it. This part, without which the overall plan cannnot be understood, was rediscovered and published only recently[4]. It was dated Jassy 1801 - St Peterburg 1803 and signed only with the initials 'V.M.'

Despite the coherence and ideological continuity characterizing the three parts, the thirteen years which elapsed during their elaboration were too crucial in European history not to have affected Malinovskii's plan. Each of the three parts shows distinctive features and seems inspired by a different attitude. Malinovskii's critique of war in Part I is a piece of rhetoric based on a moral and intellectual condemnation of war. It is divided into seven sections, which are mostly focused on a highly critical depiction of war. In the introductory section, the 'Privychka k voine i mnenie o neobkhodimosti onoi', Malinovskii attacks the prevailing opinion in favour of war. The following four sections, entitled 'Mnimye pol'zy voiny', 'Predubezhdeniia narodov', 'Pochtenie k voine, geroistvo i velikost' dukha' and 'Bedstviia voiny', are devoted to a reformulation of the general causes of war from a new standpoint. In the sixth and seventh sections are examined the 'Vygody mira' on the one hand and the 'Prichiny voiny i politika' on the other, analyzing the connections between war and the commonly established practice of politics.

Part II is characterized by a specifically juridical approach, aimed at providing the basis for the establishment of a perpetual peace in Europe. It is divided into eight sections. In the first two, 'Obshchenarodnye zakony' and 'Obshchii soiuz i sovet', Malinovskii outlines his plan, which is based on the creation of a «General Union» of European peoples. In the third and the fourth sections, 'Oblegchenie zol voiny' and 'Vooruzheniia' are given further rules which are to be observed among the states. The fifth and the sixth

---

[4] There are two manuscript copies of Part III: the first was sent by Malinovskii to Vorontsov in 1803 and is held in RGADA, Fond 1261, op. 2822; the second copy, with a few corrections, was sent to the Minister of Foreign Affairs, A.A. Czartoryski, on April 1804, and is held in AVPR, Fond Kantseliariia, op. 7869, ff. 3-32. The Polish scholar J. Skowronek was the first to draw attention to the third part of Malinovskii's treatise. He has published it, separately from the rest of the work, in '«Rozwazania o pokoju i wojnie» Wasyla F. Malinowskiego', *Teki archiwalne*, no. 17 (1978), pp. 23-57. Skowronek used the second version of Part III, comparing it with the first. He also published a translation in Polish of the third part, entitled 'Memorial Wasilija Fiodorowicza Malinowskiego o narodowym samokresleniu, jako podstawie niezawislego bytu politicznego narodow, pod tytulem 'Rozwazania o pokoju i wojnie', czesc III Jassy 1801- S.Peterburg 1803', in Adam Jerzy Czartoryski, *Pamietniki i memorialy polityczne 1776-1809*, ed. J. Skowronek (Warszawa, 1986), pp. 567-597.

Among Soviet scholars, I.S. Dostian analyzed its contents in '«Evropeiskaia utopiia» V.F. Malinovskogo', *Voprosy istorii*, no. 6 (1979). This notwithstanding, a complete publication of the *Dissertation* is still not available in Russian. An edition of Malinovskii's full treatise was the Italian translation, V.F. Malinovskij, *Ragionamento sulla pace e sulla guerra*, ed. P. Ferretti (Napoli, 1990).

sections, 'Vozrazheniia samovlastiia i nezavisimosti' and 'Pravo estestvennoe i pravo grazhdanskoe', provide a theoretical basis for Malinovskii's proposal. In the seventh section, 'Soedinenie po soglasiiu', the author indicates the necessity of a pacific way of achieving the «General Union» of European peoples. In the last section of the first part, 'Posledstviia predydushchego', all the points covered before are recapitulated in a more assertive way.

Part III is oriented towards a definition of the global changes necessary to transform radically European societies in order to introduce the situation of peace proposed by Malinovskii. It consists of nine sections. In 'Pravo narodov' a new regulation for the relations among peoples is suggested. In the second section, 'Nyneshnee sostoianie Evropy', Malinovskii discusses the state of Europe and the position of Russia within it. The third and the fourth sections, 'Osvobozhdenie narodov' and 'Ravnovesie i razdelenie iazykov' basically develop his theory of the identity between language and state, which should lead to a re-definition of the European balance of powers. In 'Razdelenie zemel'' we find a radical proposal for land reform. In 'Vospitanie i vera' Malinovskii shows how a correct interpretation of the Christian doctrine is essential for a pacific coexistence of European peoples. Two more sections, 'Nauka narodnogo prava' and 'Uslovnoe pravo narodov' are a criticism of the conventional law of nations. The last section, 'Ob"iavlenie voiny', claims for the peoples themselves the right to declare war.

2.1.1. Part I: a moral plea against war

Rarely in European history did an event have an impact on the conscience and mind of all contemporaries comparable to that effected by the French revolution. In Russia it represented a significant change in the perceptions of politics and society of many intellectuals[5]. In establishing Malinovskii's attitude towards the French revolution we are faced with contradictory elements: in his first published work, 'Rossiianin v Anglii', there is a certain ambiguity which allows to interpret it as a work in favour of

---

[5] Among the vast literature on this subject, see in particular Iu.M. Lotman, 'Politicheskoe myshlenie Radishcheva i Karamzina i opyt frantsuzskoi revoliutsii'; Iu.V. Stennik, 'Tema Velikoi frantsuzskoi revoliutsii v konservativnoi literature i publitsistike 1790-kh godov', both in G.M. Fridlender (ed.), *Velikaia frantsuzskaia revoliutsiia i russkaia literatura* (Leningrad, 1990), pp. 55-68; 69-90; M.M. Shtrange, *Russkoe obshchestvo i frantsuzskaia revoliutsiia 1789-1794* (Moskva, 1956).

revolution[6]; it contrasts nevertheless with his subsequent openly critical statements[7] and with the development of his stance as the typical figure of a Russian liberal thinker opposing disruptive means of achieving a better society[8].

Written a few months after the French revolution, the first part of the *Dissertation on Peace and War* can certainly be seen, however, as reflecting a quite widespread fear: that European powers would not hesitate to resort to war in order to restore the *ancien régime* in France. The harsh critique of war in Part I may be seen as representing Malinovskii's response to this possibility. Using a rhetorical style which was never to be equally effective in the two other parts of his treatise, Malinovskii appeals to the moral and intellectual values of his contemporaries to eradicate current opinions in favour of war. One of the key arguments used by Malinovskii, to which all further considerations can be more or less directly related, is his stress on the discrepancy between Reason, governing the progress of human societies, and war, having disruptive effects. The advocacy of the primacy of Reason in ruling society was typical of many enlightened writers of eighteenth-century Russia. The unusual significance of Malinovskii's discourse lies in the important discovery made by him of the utter irreconciliability of the two systems of thought represented by War on one side and Enlightenment on the other.

The constant sense of being on the threshold of a new era, of a unique historical occasion, distinguished by the rule of Reason, atrophied and decayed in the prevailing warmongering climate, is everywhere apparent in the first part. As a pioneer of this new era, Malinovskii was to set himself, in Part I and II, the task of facilitating its advent by issuing the invitation to

---

[6] A number of indirect allusions might suggest a pro-revolutionary interpretation of the 'Rossiianin v Anglii'. Using devices well known to the eighteenth-century Russian writer dealing with so delicate an issue, Malinovskii probably managed to be understood in his time. An attack on the French *ancien régime* can be seen, for example, in his sarcastic treatment of a theme like 'Frantsuzhenki, mody i rumiany'. In the section entitled 'Razvaliny' (dated December 1790), containing reflections on the ephemeral character of glory, power and honours, an echo could be seen of the text by C. Volney *Ruines, ou Méditations sur les révolutions des empires*, appeared in 1791.

[7] In a letter he wrote: «for any revolution weaves itself a nest in the hearts of those deprived of a lawful way to demonstrate their sorrows and griefs, like a spark hiding in the ashes» (quoted in G.S. Grosul, *Dunaiskie kniazhestva v politike Rossii. 1774-1806* (Kishinev, 1975), p. 203).

[8] Arab-Ogly believed that revolutionary ideas were not alien to Malinovskii. To substantiate his interpretation he quoted an excerpt from his diary in which Malinovskii emphasised the use of reference to the French revolution in justifying reactionary policies: «The example of France is a bugbear, which is used by malevolent forces to turn man away from all good initiatives» (V.F. Malinovskii, *Izbrannye obshchestvenno-politicheskie sochineniia*, pp. 21-22).

embrace the way of peace and by outlining the features of new institutions, which would shelter people from the always incumbent menace of generalized conflicts. Already in the opening chapter of Part I he states that the interference of one system of thought in the other can only be ruinous:

> We think to unite enlightenment and the quietness of our ways with the barbarity of war, preserving in the latter the philanthropy and moderation, uncharacteristic of coarse peoples, but this philanthropy and moderation no more assist the cruelties of war than the philanthropy and mercy of an executioner, which make him ease some of the sufferings of those punished, but do not hinder him from torturing and killing them[9].

The opposition between the two systems of thought finds its justification in the fact that the ideal referent of Malinovskii's discourse is always Europe, a community already highly defined, made by the presence of the Enlightenment as equidistant from the barbarity of past times as from the uncivilized peoples of the epoch in which Malinovskii wrote:

> Enlightenment should disseminate our views and show us that the prosperity of each state is inseparable from the general prosperity of Europe (...) Europe is already sufficiently prepared for peace. The law, customs, sciences and trade[10] unite its inhabitants and already make of her some type of special community. even languages, separating one people from another, do not make an important obstacle in the intercourse of its inhabitants: for the most part they are similar to each other, and some would serve as common languages for Europeans (p. 45).

In this first part a prominent place is given to criticism of the arguments generally used by the defenders of war. One of Malinovskii's primary intents is thus to do away with evident distortions that favour war: «Some say that if there was no war, then people would multiply to such an extent, that the earth could not house or support them» (p. 46). Malinovskii attacks this opinion as an unacceptable imposture. Once again, the rules governing a system, that of the Enlightenment, tending towards the progressive improvement of the human condition, seem to him not to be valid within the system of war: here it is in fact acceptable that conflicts are seen as a salutary restraint to an

---

[9] V.F. Malinovskii, *Izbrannye obshchestvenno-politicheskie sochineniia*, p. 42. References are made in the text by page number to this edition.

[10] The stress on the historical role of commerce in the establishment of relations among peoples was frequently met in European thinking, particularly in those of an economic nature. It was highlighted by Novikov in his work entitled 'O torgovle voobshche' (in N.I. Novikov, *Izbrannye sochineniia*, ed. G.P. Makogonenko (Moskva, Leningrad, 1951), p. 505.

excessive population growth[11], according to a criterion sharply in contrast with the one orienting the medical sciences towards the discovery and the application of new medicines[12].

Another argument in favour of war is the idea that a state of peace would enfeeble Europe, which would end up by succumbing to its enemies. The image of Europe as an enlightened unit which may require defence from the barbaric peoples surrounding it is not alien, in fact, to Malinovskii's thought. This image had important implications for his thinking on peace, leading him to accept the notion of aggressive wars in the case of conflicts against Turkey[13], which he considered as a sort of Russian «holy war». This notwithstanding, external attacks on Europe are better prevented than met with arms: «Europe, being in peace and concord within itself, can, by its combined powers, restrain at the start and forestall any attempts against it» (pp. 46-47). The building of a European organization and the aims it has to set itself begin thus to take shape already in this first part.

One of the effects of war more commonly displayed as one of its advantages is the territorial expansion obtained thereby by states. According to the Russian thinker, the greatness based upon such conquests is in reality ephemeral and fallacious, it does not lead in fact to effective power for a

[11] This thesis was commonly sustained and was to achieve a particular popularity in Thomas Malthus's *Essay on Population*, which was based on observation of the English context. The work appeared, however, only in 1798.

[12] In this respect Malinovskii mentions the case of small-pox: «According to this opinion the introduction of the small-pox inoculation in our time has also been misguided» (p. 46). In 1767 Catherine II and her family had been inoculated by Dr Dimsdale. The Empress had invited the nobility to follow her example, highlighting the progressive meaning of that procedure (see R.P. Bartlett, 'Russia and the Eighteenth-Century Adoption of Inoculation for Smallpox', in R. Bartlett, A. Cross, K. Rasmussen (eds.), *Russia and the World of the Eighteenth Century* (Columbus, Ohio, 1988); A. Lentin, 'Shcherbatov, Inoculation and Dr Dimsdale', *Study Group on Eighteenth-Century Russia Newsletter*, no. 17 (1989), pp. 8-11). She also encouraged the publication in Russia of Dimsdale's work *The Present Method of Inoculating for the Small-Pox* (which was translated in 1770 under the title *Nyneshnii sposob privivat' ospu* and printed in the unusually large number of 1200 copies) (see A.G. Cross, 'Anglofiliia u trona'. *Britantsy i russkie v vek Ekateriny II. Katalog vystavki* (London, 1992), p. 57).

[13] In an article apparently written in 1803, 'Primechanie o aziatskikh narodakh', Malinovskii warned against the threat to Europe represented by Tatar peoples, pointing out «the wildness of these peoples and their particular way of life (...) they are all warlike». He also repeatedly highlighted the role of Russia in the defence of Europe: «Russia alone protects Europe from these enemies, ready to swallow her up with all her enlightenment» (*Izbrannye obshchestvenno-politicheskie sochineniia*, p. 133). Malinovskii explicitly admitted that the cases in which European civilization was under attack required resort to war: in his note 'Mysli o sredstvakh skoreishego obshchego primireniia Evropy' (on it see the present work, p. 92) he wrote: «If it is really essential to make war, then at least we should apply our arms to the defence and protection of suffering and oppressed humanity and show our common enemies at the gates of enlightenment and civil improvement and Christianity» (IRLI, Fond 244, op. 25, no. 318).

state, but exposes it, on the contrary, to an imminent ruin. He answers this argument by opposing to it a different idea of the greatness of a people, based on a different vision of state identity:

> The most dependable strength of a state is the strength of the people, which it comprises. One people is formed not only by a unified authority, but by the neighbourhood of the land, one faith, one language, one set of interests, one set of identical or similar habits and customs (p. 48).

It is not surprising that the lands and the people acquired by means of war join like foreign elements to the state body so identified, and are destined sooner or later to reveal themselves as fatally harmful, as shown in a number of historical examples. The case of France under Louis XIV is chosen to illustrate how the glory obtained with war and the greatness of the court do not correspond to true glory.

The system of thought based upon the acceptance of war leads to a series of other breakdowns of reason, like the generalizations concerning defects and virtues of peoples, unacceptable for the learned man of the Europe of the Enlightenment. In the field of morality one sees therefore the loss of the notion of the individual within a people, and the taking shape of a double moral standard: positive values like love, gratitude, friendship, are not universally valid, they are limited only to individuals within the same people. Peoples themselves, then, are not exempt from developing harmful prejudices towards other peoples:

> Superstition, ignorance and hatred overcome the humane impulses of one people to another: they make peoples, fighting between themselves, not consider each other any longer as human beings (p. 51).

The first prejudice, superstition, in which the various religious beliefs are taken to excess, leads to a disavowal of the Christian law, whose greatest merit is the exhortation to love each other. The authentic Christian law (in its panconfessional variant, and expunged, as Malinovskii will indicate in the third part of the *Dissertation*, of any misinterpretation added to it) is then considered as the religious corollary of the system of thought of the Enlightenment, in a relationship of undeniable identity with ethics itself. The second prejudice, ignorance, the unfulfilled mutual knowledge of peoples, «produces among peoples the most stupid and harmful concepts about each other. It attributes strange and ridiculous habits to them» (p. 51). The third one, hate, in its turn:

is a consequence of war; the disasters occasioned at various times by one
people to another in its name are forever in the memory. This hate is
nourished from generation to generation, and infants suck it in with their
mother's milk. It attributes horrific vices to the enemy, which they do not
have (p. 52).

It is paradoxical that the peoples themselves nourish this hate,
originated by the effects of war wanted not by them but by those who govern
them.

Malinovskii does not exclude an analysis of the psychological factors
influencing man's inclination towards war. The emotional elements often
accompanying war are admiration for exploits and acts of heroism and the
power exerted by the accoutrements of war. Besides that, war attracts men
because it seems to them a legitimate way to achieve fame and greatness.
«They regard war as a certain path to glory and think that they cannot be
great, otherwise than through war, because great people have achieved glory
through it» (p. 53). The Russian thinker invites the reader nevertheless to
consider what real greatness consists of, by underlining first of all the
extreme historical variability of the concept of greatness in a conqueror:

Every people considers itself to have great men, but not all these are such,
for they may be endowed with greatness by poets or historians, or they
appeared great in comparison with their fellow countrymen or
contemporaries. But there have been men, considered great by all peoples
and all centuries. They are very few in number and decrease or increase
as time passes, depending on how people think and in what they perceive
glory and greatness.(p. 53).

Malinovskii attempts to undermine strongly rooted opinions, to which
he ascribes an enormous impact, and tries to increase the effectiveness of his
arguments by resorting to harsh irony. He spares no scorn for the most
celebrated leaders of the past, beginning with Alexander the Great (as regards
whom he makes a distinction between historical truth and the creation of
legend around his feats[14]) and Caesar and finishing with their pale epigones,
more or less contemporary to the epoch in which Malinovskii wrote: Charles
XII, with his pathological inclination to imitate Alexander the Great and
destined to be tragically frustrated; Louis XIV, great disturber of Europe's
peace; Frederick II, whose qualities have been cancelled by his desire to
obtain glory by means of conquests. On the basis of the unacceptable

---

[14] Malinovskii considers Q. Curtius Rufus responsible for the creation of this
legend. An excerpt from his history of Alexander the Great was later translated by A.P.
Kunitsyn and published in *Syn otechestva*, II (1812).

opposition established between the systems of thought of War and of Enlightenment, Malinovskii makes an effective comparison between the conqueror and the marauder: they share the same custom of bringing ruin among men in order to achieve their designs, the same sporadic, incidental and superfluous acts of nobility, and only the scale of their actions makes possible a distinction between them, and, sometimes, the end of their days: «the brigand dies on the scaffold renowned as a great evil-doer, the conqueror dies a natural death renowned as a great hero» (p. 55).

The conquerors are historical calamities, «they sell glory at the price of blood» (p. 56). Real greatness lies, on the contrary, in the capacity to make good use of virtue, making it serve mankind's welfare. As only by means of just laws is it possible «to pour out wisdom and blessings on man» (p. 56), Malinovskii stressed the fact that:

> No-one is as worthy to be called great as the legislator (...) the fame of the legislators will never be subject to doubt, their names will remain honoured and loved, when the names of all the others will be consigned to oblivion or hatred (pp. 56-57).

The Russian thinker continues his discourse by comparing the effects of war and those of peace on the people's welfare, its increase being considered the primary aim of an enlightened society. The absolute incompatibility of war with the search for the common weal is quite clear: «war gives a quite different direction to our ideas about the wisdom of the government of the state» (p. 60). The state of suffering and exploitation resulting from being the citizens of a state submitted to severe impositions, made heavier by war, is, for example, in clear contradiction to the pursuit of people's welfare.

The real prosperity of a state must be, according to Malinovskii, estimated on the basis of the general welfare of the population and in all the regions it inhabits: «the prosperity of states lies in the general plenty of its people, but not in the wealth of certain towns or of private individuals»[15] (pp. 62-63).

The meaning of *«obshchenarodnoe blagodenstvie»* (general prosperity of the peoples) has not only a social, but also a geographical dimension. During «modern» atrocities, ironically juxtaposed by Malinovskii to the

---

[15] There is no doubt that using the adjective «chastnyi» the Russian thinker meant the private interests of privileged classes. Note that in his translation of Hamilton's *Report* Malinovskii used two different versions for the same expression, «particular classes»: «chastnye liudi» and «nekotoroe soslovie» (*Otchet general-kaznacheia Aleksandra Gamil'tona, uchinennyi Amerikanskim shtatam 1791 g. o pol'ze manufaktur i otnoshenii onykh k torgovle i zemledeliiu* (Spb., 1807), p. 5, p. 60).

«barbaric» conflicts of the past, it happens that capital cities are exempt from the destruction and become happy islands of citizens who can rejoice at the war and be curious about it from a reasonably safe distance. Misleading in the same way are the low «visibility» of the catastrophical effects of war, their being often limited to the poorest strata of the population, who end up by bearing the entire weight of the rise in the cost of living, and the different system of conscription, diversified according to the regions.

Again on the theme of people's welfare, Malinovskii underlines the deep conflict of views which separates him from the politicians ruling the states. They often rejoice at the statistics of population increase, but this can not be considered as an aim in itself; as an absolute datum it is an unreliable indicator of the level of prosperity of a people.

Talking about the economic activities from which a people's prosperity can arise, Malinovskii registers a further divergence between the customs of peace time and those of war time: «trade and craftsmanship, receiving little encouragement, decline because of war» (p. 59). Malinovskii is, however, the defender of a substantially agrarian vision of economic life, he has words of reproof for the excessive encouragement of trade at the expense of agriculture[16], which provides authentic richness, preferable to the apparent one given by trade and craftsmanship:

> The richest states have more than once suffered hunger. Neither the fertility of France nor the perfection of England's agriculture have always saved them from enduring the direst deficiencies (p. 62).

On addition, everybody will realize that it does not make economic sense to keep big armies, mainly constituted of peasants who do not gain any advantage by being soldiers, and who can not contribute to the population increase by being away from their wives. He concludes:

> war destroys the first foundations of society, the security of life and property. Laws punish many unfortunate murderers and thieves with death, but the guardians of these laws, the governors of peoples, not knowing how to forestall war, subject the entire state to murder and robbery (p. 59).

Malinovskii illustrates on the other hand the decisive change that the elimination of conflicts and the turning of attention exclusively to the

---

[16] He wrote: «In all lands craftsmanship and trade (...) are encouraged too much and without discrimination at the expense of agriculture» (p. 61). About the conflicting roles of trade and agriculture in Malinovskii's works, see chapter 3.4..

people's welfare would bring. Whereas in a state whose main concern is security any other consideration must inevitably recede, Malinovskii paints a glowing vision of a Europe free from wars, rich with a wealth otherwise restrained by a situation of war, and therefore also honourable because the states would no longer need to rely on the proceeds of maintaining, in fact, if not officially, vices like drunkenness, gambling and so on. Europe would also be advanced in sciences, being capable of financing «laudable undertakings». These would be endowed with good laws, that is to say simple and universally intelligible laws, neither cruel and unjust, nor so obscure and intricate as to result in ambiguous and variable interpretations, according to the particular case and the good or bad faith of the legislators. In a state of peace the rulers' love of glory would find its more suitable application and fulfilment: they would try to outdo each other in making their subjects happy, and «instead of glorious politicians and warriors they will make themselves fathers of the people and glorious legislators» (p. 66).

Malinovskii ends Part I of the *Dissertation* with a chapter entitled 'Prichiny voiny i politika'. In his work there is a constant association of «political» with an art understood in an exclusively negative sense, characterized by a detrimental secretiveness and absolutely diverging from any idea of authentic popular welfare[17]. In Malinovskii's thought, then, there emerges the necessity for a deep revision of politics and its aims. Politics has always played a decisive role in provoking many conflicts:

> Politics, complicating affairs by its subtle ruses, provides them with the particular opportunity to resolve them by force (...). Politics disposes of the fate of Europe, it has an important and secret aspect, so that no-one dares to draw near it and few can make it out in its entirety. Like the ancient mysteries of the Egyptians, it conceals itself from common folk (p. 68).

Malinovskii then comes down from the level of general formulations to present a brief historical review exemplifying this notion of politics. None of the European courts escaped the practice of such politics: certainly not Italy,

---

[17] In his article entitled 'Mnenie o mire s Velikobritaniei', written after 1807 and aimed at persuading the Russian rulers to abandon the alliance with France following the treaties of Tilsit (see the present work, p. 77), Malinovskii introduced his own, positive definition of politics: «The art of politics lies in knowing how to use propitious times and circumstances and, avoiding all extremes, to preserve moderation. This latter is not to be understood as harmful inconstancy and variability of partialities, but as respect for the vital interests of state which could suffer from failure to consider circumstances and timing» (IRLI, Fond 244, op. 25, no. 320). The same notion is repeated with substantially the same words in his 'Mysli o sredstvakh skoreishego obshchego primireniia Evropy' (IRLI, Fond 244, op. 25, no. 318).

native land of the men who introduced into European cabinets a political practice permeated by the three fatal maxims of «simulation, injustice and secrecy». This latter

> bears sufficient testimony against politics, for it is most necessary where schemes are bad, and can be useful and proper in the actions of dishonest people, who are trying to deceive each other, but not in the behaviour of peoples. Its preservation would never have been considered so important, if politics had not had something to hide (p. 69).

The court of France never «spared any means to magnify itself and to cause harm to others» (p. 69). With exponents such as Richelieu, Mazarin, Fleury, Vergennes, it gave Europe undoubtedly the most dishonourable examples of politics. About Prussia and its sovereign Frederick II Malinovskii remembers that this monarch «placed his politics in the force of arms, and to demonstrate his wit called cannons the reasons of the sovereigns» (p. 71). If the secrecy of the politics put into practice in the courts prevents peoples from having any influence on the ruling of the states they belong to, the publicity that the «political writers» give to it certainly does not promote the cause of the peoples. Among them, the fomenters of war are Malinovskii's worst enemies and he gives a biting taxonomy of this category[18].

2.1.2. Part II: regulations for a peace project

Eight years after the elaboration of Part I Malinovskii completed its sequel. There are countless elements which show ideological continuity with the discourse he developed in the previous part of his *Dissertation*. Part II reflects nevertheless an entirely different historical phase: the aggressive entity on the international scene was now France, a country whose political profile had changed deeply from that of 1790. Revolutionary wars led to a massive restructuring of nations across Europe, disintegrating a large number of states based upon dynasty[19]. French expansionist politics needed to be

---

[18] He divides the political writers who foment war into three groups: those inspired exclusively by a blind love for the fatherland, whose welfare they believe is attainable at the expense of other peoples; writers moved by the wish to flatter their court and justify its conduct; journalists, who are only concerned with filling paper with news, rumours, conjectures and lies (pp. 71-73).

[19] Although Malinovskii became a sharp critic of the expansionist foreign policy of France, he never advocated a return to a pre-revolutionary Europe, based on a dynastic view of the states. In Part III he will illustrate the changes he considered necessary in the

faced with a solid network of laws which could provide an antidote to further conflicts in Europe. In this respect, the field of international relations was characterized by an undoubted legislative void. Malinovskii thus focused his effort on providing the juridical way to the establishment of a perpetual peace: the creation of a representative, supranational organ for all European peoples. The «General Union» (*Obshchii soiuz*) he proposed to create was to be empowered with control over European welfare and security[20].

In Part I Malinovskii had asserted the high degree of integration among the European peoples and their state of «preparedness» for peace. Here he notices that in the European states, which are so close to each other and characterized by a number of common features, a certain degree of reciprocal influence is inevitable. It is better, therefore, to establish international laws (*obshchenarodnye zakony*) which would avoid abuses of power and violations of the independence of some states by other states. The peoples, at the height of a process of inevitable improvement, will decide to join their interests thanks to a common agreement. This point deserves particular attention. Malinovskii believed that a procedure based on consent could ensure that the full sovereignty of the states was guaranteed:

> the establishment of international rules or laws and their observance are not interference in international affairs, nor violation of independence, for these cannot be confirmed except by consent (p. 74).

This notion of voluntary agreement as opposed to the use of force is repeatedly emphasized by Malinovskii. In chapter seven, entitled 'Soedinenie po soglasiiu', he wrote:

> the dignity and independence of European powers will not suffer in the least when, having prescribed their laws themselves, they observe their fulfillment: each power will keep its own laws and at the same time will gain the advantage of others, and will deliver itself from harm not only through arms but through the strength of laws (p. 87).

---

organization of the European states after the Revolution had shown the weakness of the previous equilibrium.

[20] Malinovskii's scheme for European peace is analyzed in W.E. Butler, 'Law and Peace in Prerevolutionary Russia: the Case of V.F. Malinovskii', in J. Witte, F.S. Alexander (eds.), *The Weightier Matters of the Law* (Atlanta, 1988), pp. 163-175. It was judged as an «independent» work in V.E. Grabar, *Materialy k istorii literatury mezhdunarodnogo prava v Rossii (1647-1917)*, Moskva, 1958. (Translated in V.E. Grabar, *The History of International Law in Russia, 1647-1917*, ed. W. Butler (Oxford, 1990)).

The institution of regulations, even if imperfect, provides an escape from the arbitrary use of power, exactly as it historically happened within each state. It is thus necessary to repeat the same modalities which occurred in the creation of the state's institutions: the comparison constantly drawn by Malinovskii, in keeping with the theory of the social contract, is between the yielding of the natural power to the civic one by individuals and the abandoning of arbitrary power by the states. War is in fact a form of violence, and for its prevention it is necessary to adopt measures similar to those adopted in the life of society. A legal order is as necessary for states forming a general alliance as it was in the union of individuals in civic society.

Malinovskii shows the inefficiency of the current system of mediation, where under the appearence of general justice are often pursued, in reality, only the interests of the intermediary, and where the casual and personal disposition of the rulers plays an excessive role. He observes how neither the temporary peace agreements nor the alliance agreements can act as rules, being dictated by changeable conditions, and therefore variable themselves. It is necessary, instead, to have permanent laws in order to regulate the mutual conduct of the states; they should be effective even when they are violated, because the transgression would be perceived as such, thanks to the comparison with a just rule.

Independence, territorial sovereignty and sovereignty of the peoples can be protected only by a General Union, where a special General Council, formed by plenipotentiaries of the European states, would make laws respected, in order to avert any violation of the peace and to solve any conflict in a better way. The principle of election for plenipotentiaries is clearly stated:

> Their selection both the first time and on all subsequent occasions must meet with general approval, and can be revoked by a majority of votes: as this affair is important and foremost for all Europe, so these people should necessarily be foremost in talents and virtues. Their persons will be honoured in all lands (pp. 76-77).

The choice of plenipotentiaries for this institution is shown as an alternative to recourse to diplomats and envoys, whose activity is condemned by Malinovskii as particularly negative in the relations between states and often directly responsible for provoking war (p. 77).

Malinovskii did not exclude the use of force on the part of the members of the General Union:

> In the event of failure to follow the decisions of the General Council, the
> recalcitrant power is excluded from all the general privileges and all
> dealings, and in the event of persistent obstinacy the common force is
> used to effect observance of the law (p. 77).

He proposed that each case of aggression should be settled within the
General Union. In this respect he believed it necessary to proceed first to a
definition of the notion of aggression, and suggested that it should be
interpreted as a violation of national frontiers[21]:

> it is necessary to define precisely the event of attack overland and by sea.
> Attack defines itself by its very name as alien troops entering frontiers (p.
> 78).

Aggression of this sort could justify, according to Malinovskii, the
beginning of a just war[22].

The mutual respect among states should not be dictated by
considerations concerning greatness and power, but exclusively based upon
the observance of the law by each state. The task of the General Union will
be to get rid permanently of one of the most recurrent causes of war, the
prospect of territorial acquisition:

> All European powers, having precisely defined their frontiers, will
> acknowledge them mutually inalterable and guarantee their inviolability:
> so that they cannot be broken by any war or any conquests (p. 79).

The General Union should also regulate other aspects involving military
security in Europe. Often the act itself of mobilizing armies was sufficient to
lead to a war: the law will then limit it to the cases of real necessity and
urgency, considering the benefits of some states inseparable from those of the
others. Regulation of international trade should also be competence of the
common government. The genuine 'general good' pursued by the General
Union will always be achieved, anyhow, not by coercion but by agreement.

One of the most remarkable aspects of the proposals contained in Part II
is the advocacy of the monitoring of a ruler's conduct through the publication

---

[21] The definition of aggression as the crossing by a foreign army of the frontiers of a
state was highlighted as particularly original by A.O. Chubar'ian, *Evropeiskaia ideia v
istorii. Problemy voiny i mira* (Moskva, 1987), pp. 138-139.

[22] It should be noted that Malinovskii does not use here the word «*spravedlivaia*»
(just), well established in the Russian political literature, but the word «*zakonnaia*» (legal)
(p. 79).

of «faithful and impartial bulletins of every political event», which could act as an antidote to the practice of secrecy. In this respect he wrote that:

> In England the people make representations about war and peace to the king. In this fortunate land, the people are permitted to judge their government in its quarrels with other powers, on the basis that the government, through partiality, cannot itself judge, and that the people will suffer from war, while the government will endure nothing because of it (p. 88).

In Malinovskii's project a new form of «balance» takes shape, which has little in common with the old notion of *ravnovesie* (equilibrium) criticized in Part I of his *Dissertation*. It is based upon the observance of the just law established among the European states. In Malinovskii's thought it is evident that every unjust act, partial resolution or violence by one state inevitably reflects on the balance of the whole system of states who are members of the General Union. It also brings disadvantages to the people of that state: «One who breaks the rulers of the people's oath to society subjects that people to the danger of revenge and is guilty before the people» (p. 88).

No less evident for Malinovskii is the external-internal relation in the non-observance of just law. The government of a state is appointed to ensure that its internal laws are observed. It cannot, therefore, contradict itself in conflicts with foreign peoples. It is necessary that the law observed is always the same:

> Every power tries to prove the fairness of its war, but who decides fairness without laws? Where are the laws, where is the authority that judges fairness? When so much caution and labour are devoted to investigating a private crime before a single culprit is condemned to death, surely war, which causes thousands of deaths, cannot be decided upon by partiality alone? (p. 82).

2.1.3. Part III: redefining European societies

In an article published in *Osennie vechera* in 1803, entitled 'O voine', Malinovskii noted that France was effecting its expansionist ambitions in Europe «by means of restoring small republics», with the result that «French troops have spread from Italy to Holstein» and «not only is equilibrium lost, but the independence of peoples is also destroyed»[23]. Malinovskii's response

---

[23] V.F. Malinovskii, *Izbrannye obshchestvenno-politicheskie sochineniia*, pp. 99-100.

to this dramatic loss of the previous *status quo* and balance is not limited to registering the trauma for European peoples. Part III contains a powerful prospect for their liberation, from Napoleon as well as from any other future despotic conqueror. In fact, it would be a mistake to interpret it exclusively in an anti-Napoleonic sense. It arises instead from the attempt to get to the root of the ethnic problems characterizing European conflicts of a national nature and to provide a correct solution for them[24].

After the radical changes occurring in Europe, the «juridical» approach, characterizing Part II of his *Dissertation* and the plan of perpetual peace behind it, is shown to be insufficient. It needs to be integrated into a more radical and global set of proposals involving social, economic and religious aspects of political stability. Part III is thus informed by the idea of a re-shaping of European frontiers on the basis of a correct ethno-linguistic regrouping and of a radical reform of land ownership, education and religion, aimed at giving more social and political justice to every citizen[25]. The constant attention given here to the establishment of a «just» domestic order in the states, considered as an indispensable basis for the security of the international peace, represents perhaps the most interesting and original aspect of the entire treatise. It must also be seen as a direct result of the desire for reform typical of the first years of Alexandrinian Russia.

Legal theory has a prominent place in the final part of the *Dissertation*. In Part II a chapter was devoted to 'Pravo estestvennoe i pravo grazhdanskoe'[26]. In Part III Malinovskii introduces his considerations on two concepts used to refer to international law. The first is *«pravo narodov»*, illustrated in chapter one. Apparently Malinovskii meant by it the most basic rights of peoples. The notion of *«pravo narodov»* is based on an identity between the rights of the individual and the rights of the people. In its context the welfare of peoples is pursued in keeping with the love that each people nourishes for itself. According to Malinovskii it should be considered as applying also to non-European peoples:

---

[24] It should be noted that while peace projects flourished during the last decade of the eighteenth century, the first fifteen years of the nineteenth century saw their decrease, certainly as an effect of Napoleonic wars. The appearance of pamphlets on war was more typical of this period (see for example G. Pokrovskii (Medynskii), *Rassuzhdenie o voine i svoistvakh, voine nuzhnykh* (Moskva, 1810)).

[25] In this respect it is quite curious to read Chubar'ian's judgment, written in ignorance of Part III of the *Dissertation*, about the fact that the Russian thinker «avoided posing the social problems of European peace», a defect obviously attributed to Malinovskii's «aristocratic» origin (*op. cit.*, p. 140).

[26] It was in fact focused on two points: the identity of objects between the two notions and the importance for the European states of respecting the same law.

> The rights of peoples belong just as properly to Africans and Asiatic peoples as to Europeans, with the one difference, that the latter, due to their enlightenment, can elucidate them more precisely and bring them into operation through constant communication among themselves and for that reason European peoples form one community[27].

The right of peoples to independence and freedom is violated by war, which introduces slavery in their existence:

> But also war through its terror retains the chain of enslavement of peoples: peoples liberated by a general peace will find essential in their weakness to preserve it and strengthen it by their mutual forces (p. 31).

Malinovskii's attention to the peoples' rights leads him to a radical critique of despotism and of the great empires:

> These vast domains are concerned only to keep foreign peoples under their might, and to deprive them of the means and powers to strive for their own good, according to peoples' rights: this state of submission is oppression of the people, the murder of its prosperity and a prolongation of the evils of war (...) In vast domains despotism is inevitable because they are governed by force, law and community of interest lose their effectiveness, like the peal of a bell that does not carry far enough and must be replaced by a stick (p. 31).

The second concept Malinovskii uses in his discourse is «*narodnoe pravo*» [28], developed in chapter seven. He seems to refer by it to the current law of nations. He criticizes it as a science equating natural law with the law of nations and points out that it is supposed to be based on a state of nature and independence which has long been lost. Malinovskii blames the fact that while natural right is absorbed into the law governing civic society, in the field of international relations peoples are left to the mere natural law («peoples are left to rule themselves by natural laws», p. 45). The current law of nations is also criticized by Malinovskii as being substantially a legitimization of the *status quo*, instead of an attempt to prescribe just rules:

---

[27] Skowronek, '«Rozwazania o pokoju i wojnie» Wasyla F. Malinowskiego', p. 30. References will be made in the text by page number to this edition.

[28] The «narodnoe pravo» was to be codified in Russia by A.P. Kunitsyn, one of the young intellectuals recruited by Malinovskii to teach at the Tsarskoe Selo Lycée. His two-volume book *Pravo estestvennoe* (1818) was written under the influence of Bentham (see B. Hollingsworth, 'A.P. Kunitsyn and the Social Movement under Alexander I', *Slavonic and East European Review*, XLIII (1964), p. 117). In his work Kunitsyn elaborated a particularly progressive interpretation of the «narodnoe pravo», highlighting the notions of the welfare and self-determination of peoples (*Pravo estestvennoe* is published in I.Ia Shchipanov (ed.), *Russkie prosvetiteli ot Radishcheva do Dekabristov*, I (Moskva, 1966)).

> The writers of the law of nations have copied it from customs and usage:
> what they saw, that they said, adding some morals and exortations. They
> have justified abuse by demonstrating the principles of what occurs
> through chance, ignorance and misfortune, and not of what should occur
> according to reason and enlightenment for the common weal. They have
> accomodated themselves to the present state of affairs. And instead of
> condemning it they have derived rules from it and based their science of
> the law of nations upon them (p. 45).

Of theoreticians of the law of nations Malinovskii mentions only the
Swiss Emmerich de Vattel (1714-1767), who was the author of the treatise
*Les droits des gens ou Principes de la loi naturelle appliqués à la conduite et
aux affaires des nations et des souverains* (Neuchâtel, 1758). To the writers
of the law of nations Malinovskii attributes an important responsibility: they
have shaped the law of nations as a codex of war.

> They saw how powers made agreements about peace and union, and laid
> down rules for these conditions; they saw the latter not being fulfilled and
> the resolution of all quarrels by war, and they laid down rules for war.
> And so up to now the codified law of nations is the law of war and short-
> lived peace (p. 45).

Malinovskii's opposition to the current law of nations is also based on
the fact that it gives priority to the needs of states instead of those of peoples:
«in addition it is not the law of peoples but the the law of powers, for in it
people are divided up according to power blocks, and not according to their
nationality» (p. 45). It is seen as fundamentally inadequate and supporting
autocratic power, in conflict with the interests of peoples:

> the codified law of nations is the law of an autocratic power and is
> relevant only to such. A people subject to another's power cannot use it,
> for it is the law of autocrats and demands that a people stops being a
> people and has no distinguishing traits or particular love for itself (p.45).

As we see, this critique of the law of nations also gives Malinovskii an
opportunity to state clearly his political preferences. He envisages the advent
of a time when the establishment of an «uslovnoe pravo» would facilitate the
affirmation of a just domestic and international order:

> But when an agreed law has become established, and has made itself part
> of public life, as a supplement to the civic law (...) then the internal
> government of peoples and the external management of their affairs will
> take on a different aspect. Wars will not be so common and peace will be
> general and prolonged through the refinement of the agreed law of
> independent powers (p. 48).

In chapter eight Malinovskii's original notion of *«uslovnoe pravo narodov»* (agreed rights of peoples) is given detailed treatment. The elaboration of such a law should be achieved by subordinating the natural law of a people to a common codex respectful of the freedom, peace and security of all peoples. It should represent a guarantee against the use of force and violations of justice in international relations. It should also regulate questions like frontiers and the property of states, resorting to the use of a common military force if necessary (p. 52). The representative principle which should operate within this law is again emphasized in an attempt to contrast it with autocratic power:

> This empowerment of rulers does not absolve them from any mutual obligations and does not give them any new rights, except the one right to set agreements with another on behalf of the people and through their power to bring to realization everything agreed upon (p. 49). It is necessary for the peoples to assemble through their agents and generally to deliberate over all their affairs (p. 50).

Malinovskii's idea of a General Union is advanced as the most suitable alternative in the relations among European peoples. In this respect chapter three ('Osvobozhdenie narodov') provides a number of interesting proposals aimed at transforming the state of contemporary Europe and creating a new order. This order should be based on the idea of self-government for each people: «every people has the right to govern itself, submitting only in its external relations to international laws» (p. 34). Eliminating the obstacles coming from Turkish[29] and Austrian empires, and the hegemonic aspirations of Napoleonic France, Malinovskii's scheme foresees autonomy for Moldavia and Wallachia, Greece, Hungary. Venice should constitute an independent region (*«oblast'»*) within the union (*«soiuz»*) of Italian republics. The same should happen to Switzerland, the Netherlands and Holland, free to choose the union most suitable to their linguistic origin (possibly Germany, certainly not France). Bulgaria, Bohemia, Bosnia, Serbia, Croatia, Dalmatia and other peoples of Slavic origin should constitute autonomous regions within a state (*«derzhava»*) of the *«slavianorusskie»* peoples. Poland, re-united in its three parts, including that belonging to Russia, should constitute a special

---

[29] The partition of the Turkish Empire was proposed as a necessary measure leading to the liberation of a number of European peoples also in his 'Mysli o sredstvakh skoreishego obshchego primireniia Evropy' (IRLI, Fond 244, op. 25, no. 318).

«slavenorossiiskoi iazyk»[30]. Given the emphasis placed upon the peoples' independence and freedom, Malinovskii's idea of a sort of pan-Slavic union does not seem to have any imperialistic or Great Russian connotation[31].

Each union should create an organ concerned with issues of common interest:

> All peoples who share one language, while governing themselves in their departments based on geographical position in the best fashion, will form, for each separate language, one general assembly for external affairs, and there these will be arranged and decided, like the united Netherlands of the Dutch Republic or the American states, sending a plenipotentiary from each region to a general assembly of its own language (p. 36).

The General Union should be empowered to deliberate on internal conflicts within these unions (p. 36).

Malinovskii's idea of the *«oblasti»* (regions) does not necessarily coincide with the conventional notion of state, in some cases it corresponds to a new political community. His proposal of European re-grouping on an ethno-linguistic basis is developed in detail in the chapter entitled 'Ravnovesie i razdelenie iazykov'. Malinovskii believes that European balance, unlike the old concept, based on *«vzaimnoe protivopolozhenie sil»* (mutual opposition of forces) as a means of security, would enormously benefit from a new partition of Europe into particular languages. The partition proposed by him should restore the peoples' «natural» condition, historically sacrificed to the ambition of expanding empires or to abstract notions of a geo-political nature:

> The inhabitants of lands cannot be divided other than by their language. In future frontiers should be designated according to this principle. The residence of one or another people is its right to ownership, extending to those places which it genuinely occupies (p. 39).

Malinovskii enumerates the *«iazyki»* (languages) (including «Velikobritanskii», an example of unity of English with Scottish and Irish)

---

[30] The term *«iazyk»* (language) is frequently used by Malinovskii in the meaning of *«narod»* (people), in keeping with a quite common eighteenth-century usage. In the context of his scheme for a new European order it indicates a union gathering peoples of the same language.

[31] Certainly in Malinovskii's subsequent works there are elements indicating an evolution towards a stronger nationalistic position. In this respect his article 'Liubov' Rossii', published in *Osennie vechera*, is quite significant: here patriotic feelings lead him to advocate the creation of an enlarged Russian state, based on «odno plemia slaveno-rusov» (V.F. Malinovskii, *Izbrannye obshchestvenno-politicheskie sochineniia*, pp. 104-105).

and the corresponding unions populating his picture of Europe. He does not ignore the difficulties of bringing into being his ideas in the cases in which the peoples «through prolonged enslavement have intermingled with the dominant nation and have become divided among themselves, and decreased, and demeaned themselves» (p. 39). The new partition of Europe would represent a guarantee against warfare, being based on the peoples' expectations and needs, instead of those of the courts:

> Up to the present time, peoples have acted on their own account, only the dynasties governing them have disposed of their fate and often were themselves not of their people. They mixed strangers together and divided their own people, and until now each language has defined itself not according to its people but according to its ruling dynasty, and has taken up arms against itself and has affirmed its generality by the subjugation of particular parts (p. 40).

There is no doubt that Malinovskii's attempt to re-design the geo-political map of Europe was extremely ambitious. It was an ambition which was not unknown to the perpetual peace projects tradition. After Napoleonic disintegration of the previous unsatisfactory political equilibrium, the elaboration of more radical plans was implicitly encouraged. To propose a repartitioning of Europe based upon a rational criterion - such as ethno-linguistic communities - was certainly unrealistic, but it was plainly consistent, on the other hand, with the intellectual climate of the Enlightenment.

Malinovskii was perfectly aware of the fact that an unjust domestic order could have negative repercussions on the stability of the General Union. Chapter five is thus devoted to illustrate his proposal of reform concerning one of the crucial questions for the welfare of peoples: land property. Although each region is free to choose the best government, the author suggests that every citizen should be assigned a tract of land. This would be an effective measure for the reinforcement of national feelings and the correction of other evils affecting European societies[32]. The size of land properties should also be regulated, in order to avoid accumulation. These measures are dictated first of all by a need for social justice. They are also aimed, nevertheless, at preventing revolutionary attempts at reestablishing economic and social balance (p. 42).

---

[32] He wrote: «In order to attach each person to his society, to arouse his love towards it, everyone must be made a participant in its domains. In order to improve morals and promote conjugal life, the upkeep of the family must be secured by inheritance. In order to halt this burgeoning luxury, voluptuousness and dissipation, which is weakening the rich, their lands must be decreased and allotted to the poor» (p. 42).

In Malinovskii's ideal Europe religious tolerance and widespread education have a prominent place: in the chapter entitled 'Vospitanie i vera' he illustrates his proposals in that sense[33]. One of the most interesting aspects of the educational changes advocated by Malinovskii is the necessity to have local universities in each state; they are regarded in fact as a measure reinforcing national identity (p. 43).

Malinovskii's concept of General Union underwent a radical change over the years and was deeply affected by historical events. His article 'Obshchii mir' (1813)[34], which was long believed to be the third part of the *Dissertation* mentioned by Malinovskii in his letter to Derzhavin[35], contains the final variant of the General Union. Napoleon's invasion of Russia had had a catastrophic impact on the conscience of every Russian[36]. In 'Obshchii mir' the Russian thinker illustrated his belief that the times were now mature for a general peace and proposed the transformation of the previous treaties of alliance against Napoleon into a General Union. Emphasizing the role of his fatherland in this process, Malinovskii produced, nevertheless, a significant shift in the orientation of his ideas: his defence of the right of peoples to self-government and social justice, which was one of the most valuable features of his treatise, was destined to be lost in the politics of tsarist Russia. Quite significantly, the Congress of Vienna was to bring to bear an idea of peace and balance in which the aspirations of the peoples were considered much less important than the interests of the monarchs.

---

[33] On Malinovskii's views on religious reform, see chapter 3.1.. His ideas on education are treated in detail in chapter 4.2.2..

[34] See the present work, pp. 89-90.

[35] Curiously enough, Malinovskii was on the other hand erroneously identified as the author of an anonymous work on the theme of war entitled *Rassuzhdenie ob uchastii, priemlemom Rossieiu v nyneshnei voine, sochinennoe drugom politicheskoi svobody i vzaimnoi nezavisimosti vsekh narodov* (Köln, 1807). The Soviet writer G. Shtorm wrote in his «historical chronicle» *Deti dobroi nadezhdy*, devoted to the figures of Radishchev and F. Ushakov: «A comparison of the style and content of the named 'Rassuzhdenie' and 'Rassuzhdenie o mire i voine' (...) gives grounds to think that the same person was the author of both books» (G.P. Shtorm, *Izbrannye proizvedeniia* (Moskva, 1985), I, p. 551). Shtorm's reference was brought to my attention by Nataliia Borisovna Meshkova-Malinovskaia.

[36] Only a few years before, Malinovskii himself had not considered the possibility of an armed attack on Russia realistic. In a previous article entitled 'Mnenie o mire s Velikobritaniei' he had written: «Russia is quite secure against any aggressive attack, being protected by her remoteness, the severity of her climate and even more by the courage and fervour of her sons» (IRLI Fond 244, op. 25, no. 320).

2.2. The national context: speculation on peace in the Russian tradition

The *Dissertation on Peace and War* has no Russian precedent in its commitment to the subject. It would nevertheless be a mistake to imagine it as emerging from a cultural void in national terms. Over the centuries a number of voices were raised in Russia in favour of peace and contributed in varying degrees to the building of a culture far from war-mongering values. The context in which these calls appeared and the modalities of their expression reveal, almost inevitably, a certain uniformity. On the one hand, we find the general attitude towards peace expressed by figures from ecclesiastical circles, in whose sermons this concept is contemplated in the spirit of a broader and undifferentiated religious *pax* [37]. On the other hand, pleas in favour of the elimination of war came from the men of letters of the Russian court, for whom love of peace can often be translated as nothing more than a gracious invitation to the sovereigns to end a particular conflict or as the desire to ratify a *status quo* which is only casually and temporarily pacific[38].

It is also necessary to distinguish between two phenomena of a different nature: the presence of a strongly rooted anti-war feeling in the Russian people, recurring in its oral cultural patrimony and persisting over the centuries, and the emergence of a concern for peace in works of literature, which stand as marginal expressions of a culture historically oriented more towards war than peace. «Pacifism» as a widespread feeling in the Russian people, distinct from the theory and practice of wars led by sovereigns, and coupled with the general perception of war as a global tragedy having disastrous repercussions on every-day life, has been highlighted in recent times, above all by Soviet scholars[39].

---

[37] It is important to bear in mind that in Russian culture the word «peace» is used both in the religious meaning of harmony among men and in the one pertaining more to the field of international relations, meaning the absence of armed conflicts among sovereign powers, and in this conjunction it presents itself in almost all the authors we will consider.

[38] The connections between pacifist feelings and Russian court politics have been analized by R.E. Jones, 'Opposition to War and Expansion in Late Eighteenth Century Russia', *Jahrbücher fur Geschichte Osteuropas*, no. 32 (1984), pp. 34-51.

[39] See L.N. Pushkarev, 'Voinskaia tematika v narodnom tvorchestve', in *Obshchestvenno-politicheskaia mysl' Rossii. Vtoraia polovina XVII veka* (Moskva, 1982), and also his introductory considerations in 'Problemy mira i voiny v tvorchestve russkikh prosvetitelei XVIII v.', in *Russkaia kul'tura v usloviiakh inozemnykh nashestvii i voin* (Moskva, 1990). Another work of Pushkarev is devoted to the study of Russian soldiers' song: *Soldatskaia pesnia - istochnik po istorii voennogo byta russkoi reguliarnoi armii XVIII - pervoi poloviny XIX vekov* (Moskva, 1969). A certain emphasis was placed upon

The following pages will outline the evolution of the ideal of peace, from its earliest acquisition of dignity as a literary-publicistic theme, and establishment within a substantially belligerent tradition, to the time, as early as the mid-eighteenth century, when it came to the attention of writers who question the causes of war and start to call into doubt its inevitability[40].

As this review will show, the idea of peace never became a project for reform. It lived a fragmentary and weak life, restricted to the voices of minor figures, or to neglected pages in the works of authors of more established reputation, or owed an evident debt to Western Europe, as part of the recurring process of intellectual appropriation.

2.2.1. The genesis of the ideal of peace

The origins of Russian thinking on peace may be traced back to the very first literary expressions in Russia. In the descriptions of the chroniclers of ancient Rus war is the event most frequently covered. The continuous aggressions by the peoples of the steppes as well as the unceasing fratricidal struggles among the Russian princes are usually seen as ineluctable phenomena, occuring as implacable divine punishment for the sins of mankind.

After the invasion of the Mongols and the Golden Horde into the Russian land, the theme of battles, so often elaborated by the literary civilization of Rus, led to the establishment of a distinct genre, the *voinskie povesti*, the tales of war, where love for the Russian land finds expression in the exaltation of heroism shown on the field of battle against the impious Tartar invader. The narrations of this cycle, although differing in origin, epoch of composition and literary value, are characterized by the recurring presence of certain formulas and stylistic techniques[41].

---

the development of a particularly successful theme, that of the forced separation of the *muzhik-voin* from his loved ones.

[40] Regrettably, an exhaustive history of the origins and development of Russian thought on peace has never been written. M.N. Stoliarov is the author of a brief work, *Russkie pisateli i voina* (Moskva, 1915) (published under the pseudonym of S. Ashevskii), in which Russian writers of the eighteenth and nineteenth centuries are seen in their relation to war. M. Schippan gives important suggestions for a history of Russian pacifism in 'Die Französische Revolution von 1789 und Friedensvorstellungen in Russland bis 1825', *Zeitschrift für Slawistik*, no. 34 (1989), pp. 353-361.

[41] For example the portrayal of the enemies of Rus disguised as wild beasts, or the description of the battles as masses of arrows darkening the sun and thick scuffles which prevent the fighters from seeing each other is typical. Also typical is the stylistic device according to which the intervention by celestial forces at the Russian heroes' side is

Whereas a spirit of enthusiastic admiration for the feats of the princes, who venture in arms beyond the frontiers of the Russian land, thus increasing its greatness, is still perceptible in the *letopisi* of the XI and XII centuries, the attention gradually shifts to defensive wars, leaving the aggressive ones in the background[42]. History as described in the literary documents seems to acquire a moral connotation which no longer permits the celebration of a warlike spirit and the blood shed in battles. As early as the XIII century in the *voinskie povesti* the scheme of a sort of moral war codex is elaborated, according to which the defender of the fatherland, who has moral justice on his side, will triumph over the brute force of the invader. One of the highest products of the literary civilization of Rus, the *Slovo o polku Igoreve*, seems to mark the transition, in the XII century, between these two phases, and the birth of a certain sensibility to the problem of peace.

It is only in the second half of the XVII century that the emergence of anti-warmongering feeling in Russia reached a remarkable degree of elaboration. It took above all the state of foreign policy in the years of Alexis Mikhailovich's reign[43], with Russia involved in extensive military conflicts with Poland and Turkey, and wrestling with the unification process of Ukrainian and Belorussian territories, to give numerous impulses to the intellectuals of the time to undertake a theoretical revision of all the problems associated with war and for a first systematic approach to the theme of peace. This process also occured thanks to the mediation of Western culture, since Ukrainian and Belorussian lands experienced the strong influence of Humanism flourishing in Poland particularly in the second half of the XVI century.

One of the first theoretical treatments of the theme of peace and war can be found in the writings of Simeon Polotskii (1629-1680)[44]. In the work of

---

always followed by the flight of the enemies in terror. See A.S. Orlov, 'Ob osobennostiakh stilia formy russkikh voinskikh povestei, konchaia XVII v.', *Chteniia v Imperatorskom obshchestve Istorii i drevnostei rossiiskikh pri Moskovskom universitete*, no. 4 (1902), pp. 1-50. On the general subject see V. Borisov, *Drevnerusskie voennye povesti* (Kiev, 1906) and V.P. Adrianova-Perets (ed.), *Voinskie povesti drevnei Rusi* (Moskva-Leningrad, 1949).

[42] According to D.S. Likhachev, the birth of a sort of moral shame about the exaltation of war was a more likely source of this new focus than the historical reality of an actual decrease in attacks on distant lands. See D.S. Likhachev, *Literatura - real'nost' - literatura* (Leningrad, 1981), pp. 133-135.

[43] P. Longworth, *Alexis, Tsar of All the Russias* (London, 1984).

[44] A detailed account of the theme of peace in Polotskii and its connections with the Russian foreign politics is given by L. Pushkarev in 'Problemy voiny i mira v tvorchestve pridvornykh obshchestvenno-politicheskikh deiatelei Rossii vtoroi poloviny XVII v.', in *Obshchestvenno-politicheskaia mysl' Rossii. Vtoraia polovina XVII veka* (Moskva, 1982).

this Belorussian monk who found his fortune as a poet in the Muscovy of
Tsar Aleksei Mikhailovich we find, probably for the first time in the history
of Russian political thought, the formulation of criteria governing the
sovereigns' conduct in undertaking war, with a precise distinction being
drawn between just and unjust war. Polotskii, engaging in a polemic with
Erasmus' teachings[45], consisting in a generalized condemnation of every kind
of war as contrary to Christian doctrine, defines a different theory, which
marks a step forward in comparison with the official Church view on war.
Polotskii does not completely deny that war is a sort of divine punishment for
the sins of men. Indeed, in some of his lines he inclines to consider the Devil,
«vrag mira» (enemy of the world), responsible for promoting wars. But on
the whole he gives a more modern and pragmatic vision of the causes of war,
focused on man and his very earthly desire to appropriate the goods of others.

The theme of peace and war is referred to in many of Polotskii's
writings, both in poetry (in the Vertograd mnogotsvetnyi, in the Metry, in Orel
rossiiskii) and prose (in the sermons Slovo k pravoslavnomu voinstvu and
Slovo k pravoslavnomu i khristoimenitomu zaporozhskomu voinstvu,
contained in Vecheria dushevnaia)[46]. It is in his Beseda o brani, in particular,
that Polotskii expounds his theory in an accomplished way. He maintains
here that only the conjunction of four conditions makes a war «pravednaia»,
whereas the lack of even one of them makes the war «nepravednaia».
Polotskii seems here to take up again, a few years after their original
formulation in Europe, the criteria of just war already sanctioned by the law
of nations, particularly by Grotius[47]. The first condition is that the supreme
power declaring war must be legitimate. The second condition concerns the
justness of the causes of war: a war can be undertaken in order to punish

---

For Polotskii's editions, see Izbrannye sochineniia (Moskva-Leningrad, 1953), ed. I.
Eremin, and, more recently, Virshi, eds. V. Bylinin and L. Zvonareva (Minsk, 1990).

[45] On the connections between seventeenth-century Russian culture and Erasmus'
teaching, see M.P. Alekseev, 'Erazm Rotterdamskii v russkom perevode XVII veka', in
Slavianskaia filologiia. Sbornik statei. IV Mezhdunarodnyi s'ezd slavistov (Moskva,
1958), pp. 275-336.

[46] A. Eleonskaia worked on these themes in '«Obed dushevnyi» i «Vecheria
dushevnaia» Simeona Polotskogo v istoriko-literaturnom protsesse', in A. Robinson (ed.),
Razvitie barokko i zarozhdenie klassitsizma v Rossii. XVII - nachala XVIII v., (Moskva,
1989). See also her Russkaia oratorskaia proza v literaturnom protsesse XVII veka
(Moskva, 1990), pp. 92-99. An analysis of Polotskii's style can be found in A. Hippisley,
The Poetic Style of Simeon Polotsky, Birmingham Slavonic Monographs, no. 16
(Birmingham, 1985).

[47] The first Russian translation of De Jure Belli ac Pacis (1625) by Grotius
appeared in 1712. The penetration of Grotius's ideas in Russia has been studied by W.
Butler in 'Grotius' Influence in Russia', in H. Bull, B. Kingsbury, A. Roberts (eds.), Hugo
Grotius and International Relations, (Oxford, 1990).

offences given to a state in its entirety, for instance. The third condition
prescribes good intentions: a war is just if it is aimed at establishing a lasting
peace, and not at causing harm, for instance to increase the state or to
conquer new lands. And recourse to war must only follow after all other
peaceful means have been tried. The fourth condition is that war must be
conducted in an honourable way: peaceful civilians must not be offended,
children, women, elders, monks, merchants or peasants must not be killed or
robbed, and so forth. In *Beseda o brani* Polotskii proposes a distinction
between good and bad for peace too; a distinction closely related to the one
concerning war: a bad peace is in fact nothing other than the consequence of
an unjust war, whereas a good peace is attained by means of a just war[48].

Polotskii's teaching did not go unheard. Karion Istomin, one of his
followers, composed in 1687 the *slovo Egda zhe uslyshite brani i nestroeniia,
- ne uboitesia*. In this appeal to Russian warriors to be worthy defenders of
the Orthodox faith against the infidels, Istomin also expounded, however, his
considerations on the destructive nature of war, which he condemned with
inspired rhetoric[49]. In 1692 he translated into Russian the *Strategematon libri
IV*, composed between 88 and 96 AD by Sextus Iulius Frontinus and
dedicated to the military art. In his preface he argued that once war is
inevitable, the state must carefully prepare itself for war. The 33 rules of the
«voinaia khitrost'» (astuteness in war), which Istomin put at the end of the
book, are an original addition to his otherwise faithful translation[50].

In the period immediately preceeding Polotskii's writings the theme of
peace as opposed to war also significantly appears in Polish and Ukrainian
oratorical prose. Mention should be made of sermons of the Polish Jesuit Petr
Skarga such as *O pokhvale miru*, in which peace is praised as the condition
for the flourishing of virtues and all the arts, and *K voinam*, a passionate call
for the defence of the fatherland in a just war such as one against infidels[51].
He has much in common with Polotskii: he shares, for instance, the same
feeling of intolerance for the abnormal social disparities characterizing

---

[48] Quoted in Eleonskaia, *Russkaia oratorskaia proza v literaturnom protsesse XVII
veka*, p. 97.

[49] He wrote: «For it is never so much famine and plague, flames and wild beasts,
rivers and seas that cause people to perish, as the sword of war and execution by firearms»
(*Ibid.,* p. 99). The *slovo* is published in V.I. Buganov (ed.), *Pamiatniki obshchestvenno-
politicheskoi mysli v Rossii kontsa XVII veka. Literaturnye panegiriki* (Moskva, 1983),
vyp. 1.

[50] The text was translated in Russian as *Knigi o khitrostiiakh*. The 33 rules are
published in Pushkarev, *Obshchestvenno-politicheskaia mysl' Rossii. Vtoraia polovina
XVII veka*, pp. 277-278.

[51] Eleonoskaia, *op. cit.,* p. 96.

Russian society. Indeed, in another work by the same author we find
particularly tragic strains in the description of the state of the Russian
peasants[52]. The Ukrainian writer Antonii Radivilovskii was the author of the
Slova chasu voiny; the first of them contains considerations on just and unjust
wars, and just wars naturally included wars in defence of the fatherland
against infidel invaders.

2.2.2. Peace at the court of Peter the Great

During the second half of the seventeenth century the writers of the
«Raskol» continued to associate in a unique, undifferentiated whole
misfortunes of every kind, famines together with internal and external wars,
natural disasters and armed conflicts[53]. Only in the age of Peter the Great the
elaboration of the idea of peace reached its next stage. The Russian monarch
surrounded himself with advisers for state matters and stimulated the
production of a considerable number of documents related to the theme of
war[54].

In his *Politikolepnaia apofeozis* (1709) Iosif Turoboiskii, prefect of the
Moscow's Slavonic-Greek-Latin Academy, defended peace and its power in
creating the authentic *«blagopoluchie»* of peoples[55]. An interesting position
on peace was held by Feofan Prokopovich. «Western» in cultural formation,
professor in the Kiev Mogila Academy, declared enemy of ignorance and of
any kind of superstition, which in his *Dukhovnyi reglament* are set against
the development of sciences and instruction, within the *«uchenaia druzhina»*
he was one of the most important advisers of Peter the Great.

Prokopovich was the theorist of an enlightened absolutism based upon
social differences, which were considered «natural», but having decreed that,
he recommended clemency to the landowners and patience to the peasants. It
was from this viewpoint that he worked on state problems and took part in
the compilation of several legislative acts. In his approach to the problem of
war as it appears in the *Pravda voli monarshei*, for instance, he ascribed an
important role to the maintenance of peace within the state, but also to the

[52] *Ibid.*, p. 93.
[53] See A.N. Robinson, *Bor'ba idei v russkoi literature XVII veka* (Moskva, 1974), p. 217.
[54] See particularly A.I. Kuz'min, 'Voennaia tema v literature petrovskogo vremeni', *XVIII vek*, IX (1974), pp. 168-183.
[55] See S.V. Paparigopulo, 'Progressivnye russkie mysliteli XVIII veka o mire i voine', *Voprosy filosofii*, no. 2 (1960), pp. 132-142.

state's capacity to face militarily the aggressions from outside. He also related to this vision the concept of *«vsenarodnaia pol'za»,* or *«obshchee blago»* (general weal) intended as a duty of the monarch towards his subjects[56].

A similar approach to the problems of peace and war can be found in another active supporter of Peter's reforms, the archimandrite G. Buzhinskii. For him wars conducted to defend or restore the territorial integrity were just, and the defence of the fatherland was indeed the highest duty of every citizen[57]. Among the vast systematic publicistic material on the theme of war, directly or indirectly inspired by Peter the Great, one of the most interesting works is P.P. Shafirov's *Rassuzhdenie, kakie zakonnye prichiny Petr Velikii k nachatiiu voiny protiv korolia Karla Shvedskogo imel,* written in 1717. Shafirov's work is one of the first examples of a Russian pamphlet dealing with questions of international law[58].

The idea of a Russia rightly included in the European juridical community constantly emerges in Shafirov's *Rassuzhdenie*[59]; at a philological level it shows a gradual replacement of medieval Russia's «diplomatic lexicon» by the current European terminology. Rather than proceeding to a theorization of the distinctions between just and unjust wars, or to an indiscriminate defence of peace, Shafirov is concerned only to show how, once a war has begun, principles of legality and justice must be observed in the relations among states. The pamphlet is a typical product of the beginning of the XVIII century. There is no doubt that Peter the Great not only commissioned, but also encouraged Shafirov in every way to write it, personally put his hand to the compilation of some sections and arranged to have it printed in large print runs.

---

[56] On the concept of *«obshchee blago»* in Prokopovich, see the detailed study by G. Gurvich, *«Pravda voli monarshei» Feofana Prokopovicha i ee zapadnoevropeiskie istochniki* (Iur'ev, 1915), particularly pp. 14-15 and pp. 77-85.

[57] See N.F. Utkina, V.M. Nichik, P.S. Shkurinov, *Russkaia mysl' v vek prosveshcheniia* (Moskva, 1990), p. 50.

[58] See V.E. Grabar, 'Pervaia russkaia kniga po mezhdunarodnomu pravu («Rassuzhdenie» P.P. Shafirova)', *Vestnik Moskovskogo universiteta,* no. 7 (1950) pp. 101-110.

[59] The first part of the book is dedicated to the enumeration of the ancient and modern causes for which Russia was «rightly» obliged to start the Northern War against the kingdom of Sweden. Shafirov draws the reader's attention above all to the modern causes of the recently finished war (P.P. Shafirov, *A Discourse concerning the Just Causes of the War between Sweden and Russia* (ed. W. Butler) (Dobbs Ferry, N.Y., 1973).

2.2.3. Eighteenth-century poets on peace

The ideals of peace re-echoed not only in the religious publicists and in the court *traktatistika*, but also in the pages of the major poets of the eighteenth century. In their work declamations in favour of peace are present in different proportions and tones, never imposing themselves, however, as central literary themes or developing into a theoretical treatment. It is impossible to forget that throughout Classicism war continues to be considered a «high» subject and it is endlessly represented in epic poems, tragedies, odes and so forth, so that the role reserved for perorations in favour of peace can only be minor and often confined to a few hints.

A selection from the pages on peace of A. Kantemir could not avoid to take into account the footnote written with his own hand to verse 224 of his second *Satira*, composed around 1743. It shows a critical attitude not towards war in general, but towards the conduct of war contrary to certain moral principles, and contains an invitation to assign greater preference to the «blago otechestva»[60].

In the work of A.P. Sumarokov one of the most effective declarations in favour of peace is that in which he ascribes to the eponymous hero of his tragedy *Khorev* (1747), set in ancient Kiev, both a passionate defence of peace as the means by which men are differentiated from wild beasts, and a deep disillusionment with the concept of heroism as manifest in feats of war[61].

---

[60] He wrote: «War is conducted against an armed enemy, that is why any animosity against an unarmed, innocent people, such as the peasants in villages and the bourgeoisie in towns, does not accord with the rules of war and is repugnant to philanthropic feeling. Many military leaders oppress such people, rob them, torture them, to enrich themselves with their poor belongings. Such leaders do not care for the good of their fatherland, for it is well-known that the hearts of people who have been protected will be the more easily won over to their conquerors. He who behaves gently towards the population will be more likely to conquer a land than he who destroys and burns indiscriminately and mercilessly: severity is not wont to produce loyal subjects» (A.D. Kantemir, *Sobranie stikhotvorenii* (Leningrad, 1956), p. 85).

[61] See particularly the following passage:
«Or should we in our martial actions be like
The wild beasts howling in the wilderness
Who have no mercy?
It is not their examples it behoves us to follow on the battlefield
Enough of drinking our own blood in barbarity
When we beat each other in the name of duty
And mingle defence with revenge
Under the guise of courage we elevate brutality
What name have you given to evil, trumpet of flattery?
You have called murder and plunder heroism!».

The figure of M.V. Lomonosov deserves particular attention. In his vast literary production the theme of peace and war is met several times. He celebrates nevertheless much more often the pomp of victories than the advantages of a state of peace. In the historical works, in the tragedy *Tamira i Selim*, in the unfinished «heroic» poem *Petr Velikii* and in the odes, beginning from the one on Khotin (1739), notes of enthusiasm are often associated with the clamour of battles, the capacity to lead victorious wars is part of the greatness of a state, and the efforts of Peter the Great to create and maintain the Russian fleet and army are an important part of his greatness as a monarch[62]. Peace seems to be no more than a state of temporary stoppage of these activities. In this regard it is useful to remember that in his work entitled *O sokhranenii i razmnozhenii rossiiskogo naroda*, one of the most studied among his publicistic works[63], the plan of a subject that Lomonosov intended to develop can be found, entitled *O sokhranenii voennogo iskusstva vo vremia dolgovremennogo mira*[64]. In the only published part[65] Lomonosov supports the concept of «*narodnoe pravo*» (law of the nations), or «*estestvennoe pravo*» (natural law), existing before the creation of the state and opposed to «*gosudarstvennoe pravo*» (state law), or «*grazhdanskie zakony*» (civic laws). In another work he writes about just and clear laws whose establishment is impeded by the presence of «*voennye dela*» (military

(A.P. Sumarokov, *Dramaticheskie sochineniia* (ed. Iu. Stennik) (Leningrad, 1990), pp. 49-50).

[62] In an ode written in 1761 in honour of Elizabeth Petrovna Lomonosov considers war as a sort of revitalizing force:
«Inescapable fate
Has made it so in all peoples
The martial trumpet awakens
The downcast to lively spirits»
(M.V. Lomonosov, *Polnoe sobranie sochinenii*, VIII (Moskva-Leningrad, 1950-1959), p. 746).

[63] See particularly V.P. Lystsov, 'M.V. Lomonosov o sokhranenii i uvelichenii narodonaseleniia', in *M.V. Lomonosov o sotsial'no-ekonomicheskom razvitii Rossii* (Voronezh, 1969), pp. 197-250.

[64] M.V. Lomonosov, *Polnoe sobranie sochinenii*, VI, p. 383.

[65] In the only finished part, giving an interpretation of the causes preventing the proliferation of the population, Soviet critics wanted to see also an anti-feudal spirit, especially when comparing this work with the almost contemporary project on the same subject composed by P.I. Shuvalov in 1754 *O raznykh gosudarstvennoi pol'zy sposobakh* (See B.B. Kafengauz, 'Nezavershennyi trud M.V. Lomonosova', *Doklady i soobshcheniia Instituta istorii AN SSSR*, no. 3 (1954)). On Lomonosov's «Western» formation and his models, see A.A. Morozov, 'M.V. Lomonosov i teleologiia Khristiana Vol'fa', in P.N. Berkov, I.Z. Serman, *Literaturnoe tvorchestvo M.V. Lomonosova* (Moskva-Leningrad, 1962).

affairs)[66]. It is against this background that the sporadic attestations in favour of peace expressed by Lomonosov should be seen. In his poetic work they are to be found mainly in two occasional compositions, two odes, one written in 1747 and the other in 1759, both in honour of Elizabeth Petrovna. The first celebrates the sixth anniversary of her ascension to the throne, under the repeated auspices of peace. To her are ascribed words of peace[67] and dedicated epithets such as «Angel mirnykh nashikh let»[68]. But it seems likely, as the Soviet scholars editing Lomonosov's complete works suggest, that the particular effectiveness of these perorations had its origin in an event of contemporary politics: Lomonosov wished to avert the expedition of the Russian army to the banks of the Rhine, against Prussia and France. He considered only *«oboronitel'nye»* (defensive) wars to be just. In the other *«pokhval'naia oda»*, written in 1759 and celebrating a victory by the Russian army, a picturesque invocation to the God of Peace promptly to put an end to the war can be found[69].

When we turn to the work of G. Derzhavin, we find preeminently the author of odes celebrating victories and military feats, the poet who paints grandiose pictures of war[70] and enthusiastic portraits of commanders, admirals and field-marshals of the Russian army, the singer of Suvorov's

---

[66] Referring to the legislative activity of Peter I, Lomonosov wrote: «The first calling of the rulers God has set on the lands is to govern the world (...) Although military affairs and other great enterprises, and especially the ending of his life significantly hindered the great sovereign in establishing constant and clear laws in everything, nevertheless he expended so much labour upon this, as the many decrees, statutes and regulations testify (...) But even though it was not perfectly consolidated by clear and ordered laws, justice was, however, inscribed in his heart». The passage is quoted in I.D. Martysevich, *Voprosy gosudarstva i prava v trudakh M.V. Lomonosova* (Moskva, 1961), p. 74.

[67] «I have had my fill of these victories, she said,
For which streams of blood pour forth.
I take pleasure in the happiness of Russian folk,
I would not exchange their tranquillity
For the whole of west and east».
And again:
«Here the peaceful expansion of sciences
Enjoyed the favour of Elizabeth».
(M.V. Lomonosov, *Polnoe sobranie sochinenii*, VIII, pp. 198, 199).

[68] *Ibid.*, p. 141.

[69] «O God! God of Peace, rise up
Pour out your universal love to us
In the name of Peter's Daughter
Seal shut the door of war».
(*Ibid.*, p. 656).

[70] For an analysis of the stylistic techniques used by Derzhavin in the treatment of the war theme, see A.I. Kuz'min, 'Batal'naia obraznost' u G.R. Derzhavina', in D.F. Markov (ed.), *Stranitsy istorii russkoi literatury* (Moskva, 1971), pp. 223-233.

victories, and, in addition, the great opponent par excellence of Napoleon[71]. But compared with the triumphal pathos of Lomonosov's odes, Derzhavin undeniably introduces into his «*pobednye ody*» (victory odes) realistic features. Together with enthusiastic descriptions of the victorious battles he describes the tiredness of the soldiers, the agony of the wounded, all elements detracting from the exaltation of war[72].

2.2.4. Malinovskii's contemporaries

The presence of thoughts on peace in Russian tracts and literature of the XVII and XVIII centuries is, as we have seen, restricted to a few sporadic, although vital, expressions. Under the influence of the Enlightenment, a new emphasis was placed on reflections on this theme[73]. It was particularly in the work of two thinkers of Malinovskii's time that the themes of war and peace were developed at length and in depth: S.E. Desnitskii[74] and Ia.P. Kozel'skii[75].

---

[71] The poet writes on this theme for seventeen years, from 1798 to 1814, and places Napoleon as a central hero in a cycle of satirical verses of popular inspiration, in which Derzhavin finds again the «soldatskii» lexicon of his early years. See I. Mess-Baher, '«Soldatskaia» satira i allegoriia v neizdannykh antinapoleonovskikh stikhakh Derzhavina', *Study Group on Eighteenth-Century Russia Newsletter*, no. 8 (1980), pp. 70-85.

[72] In one of the most highly esteemed of his patriotic odes, entitled *Na vziatie Izmaila*, of 1790, Derzhavin intones an effective hymn to peace:
«War, like the northern lights
Astonishes only the common folk;
Like the shining of a bright rainbow,
Every wise man loves quietness.
What has the most fragrant scent?
What is sweeter than honey, more beautiful than gold,
And more precious than porphyry?
It is not you, whose glances on all
pour forth an abundant coolness,
Fine and beneficial Peace?»
(*Sochineniia Derzhavina s ob"iasnitel'nymi primechaniiami Ia. Grota*, I (Spb., 1864), p. 359).

[73] See S.V. Paparigopulo, 'Progressivnye russkie mysliteli XVIII veka o mire i voine', *Voprosy filosofii*, no. 2 (1960), pp. 132-142. See also A.I. Kuz'min, 'Russkaia deistvitel'nost'' v khudozhestvennoi literature epokhi prosveshcheniia', in A.I. Kuz'min, *Geroicheskaia tema v russkoi literature* (Moskva, 1974), pp. 104-138. A discussion of the ideas on peace in the Russian Enlightenment can be found in A.O. Chubar'ian, *Evropeiskaia ideia v istorii. Problemy voiny i mira* (Moskva, 1987), pp. 124-145.

[74] On him see the present work, pp. 8-9. On his political views, see in particular P.S. Gratsianskii, *Desnitskii* (Moskva, 1978), S.A. Pokrovskii, *Politicheskie i pravovye vzgliady S. E. Desnitskogo* (Moskva, 1955).

[75] Iu.Ia. Kogan, *Prosvetitel' XVIII veka Ia.P. Kozel'skii* (Moskva, 1958).

The critique of war and of conquerors has an important part in
Desnitskii's thinking[76]. In his opinion, war was to be rejected because of its
being contradictory to general economic, scientific and artistic development.
He particularly highlighted the negative influence of war on trade, which he
considered the strongest unifying element in the establishment of good
relationships among European peoples. In this respect Desnitskii considered
the campaign against Turkey of 1768-1774 a just war, justified as it was by
the necessity to gain access to the sea for purposes of trade and to defend
other peoples from the Turkish empire. The Russian thinker believed that the
causes of war were to be detected in the nature of geographical and state
frontiers: he considered significant, for example, that England, being an
island, caused only a limited number of wars, if compared with other states.

Desnitskii did not ignore the ideas of the European thinkers who dealt
with the problems of peace and war. He attacked above all Grotius, whose
views were known in Russia[77]. He criticized his doctrine as destined mainly
for sovereigns and limited to the definition of the cases in which a war can be
considered a just war. Taking into account the work of Hobbes and
Pufendorf[78], Desnitskii stated that in these authors the law on peace and war
was wrongly deduced from the «natural» state of an abstract individual.

Kozel'skii's thinking on peace and war is expressed in his *Filosofskie
predlozheniia* (1768) and in his *Predislovie k 'Istorii datskoi' Gol'berta* [79]. In
these works he condemned the «voennoe pravo», defined as just an
opportunity to cause other people any possible evil, even death, without
fearing any punishment. Kozel'skii's ideal of a society prospering without
relevant differences among men is consistent with the ideas he developed on
peace: he attacked the *«zavoevatel'nye voiny»* as arising from the desire for
wealth of an insignificant part of a people, and not from the need of the entire
people. He saw with favour a future possible *«uravnenie prav narodov»*
(equalization of the rights of the peoples), which could go far beyond
civilized Europe and include all other peoples. An interesting point is

---

[76] His ideas on peace were developed particularly in his *Slovo o priamom i
blizhaishem sposobe k naucheniiu iurisprudentsii, Predstavlenie ob uchrezhdenii
zakonodatel'noi vlasti, Iuridicheskoe rassuzhdenie o sobstvennosti*. His works are
published in I.Ia. Shchipanov (ed.), *Izbrannye proizvedeniia russkikh myslitelei vtoroi
poloviny XVIII veka*, I (Moskva, 1952).

[77] See footnote no. 11.

[78] On the influence of this author on Russian thinking, see W. Gleason, 'Pufendorf
and Wolff in the Literature of Catherinian Russia', *Germano-Slavica*, II, 6 (1978), pp.
427-437.

[79] These two works are published in I.Ia. Shchipanov (ed.), *Izbrannye proizvedeniia
russkikh myslitelei vtoroi poloviny XVIII veka,* I (Moskva, 1952).

represented by Kozel'skii's position on armies: although he did not question the existence of national armies, which he considered necessary for defence purposes, he proposed to restrict their size in proportion to the size of the states they belonged to, and to organize them on a voluntary basis.

A harsh critique of aggressive war, combined with a critical depiction of the glory originating in conquests, can also be found in the work of A. Radishchev[80], while N. Novikov was the author of a *Rassuzhdenie o voine*, written in 1781, in which he distinguished between just and unjust wars[81]. Another Russian concerned with the idea of peace at the time when Malinovskii wrote was R.M. Tsebrikov[82]. His *Dnevnik* (1788) and his translation of Goudar's peace project (*Mir Evropy ili proekt vseobshchego zamireniia* [83], appeared in 1789) demonstrate his radical views on the elimination of war.

The approach of N. Karamzin to the problem of peace is quite controversial: he decidely rejected war at an early stage of his life (particularly in his poems *K D* and *Voennaia pesn'*, written in 1788) and was still a convinced defender of peace at the time of his English encounter with Malinovskii. During the first years following the French revolution his position on war changed in keeping with his general evolution in a conservative sense[84]: his opposition to radical political transformations led him to a different evaluation of the importance of warfare for the stability of the Russian empire[85].

---

[80] Criticism of war heroism is developed in his work *Zitie Fedora Vasil'evicha Ushakova* and in the section of his *Puteshestvie* entitled 'Khotilov'. On this subject see in particular, 'A.N. Radishchev i russkaia voennaia mysl' v XVIII v.', *Uchenye zapiski Tartuskogo universiteta*, no. 67, pp. 194-207.

[81] Novikov's work, published in *Moskovskoe ezhemesiachnoe izdanie*, contains an open call to enthusiastic acceptance of war in the cases he considers it is legitimate. He wrote: «Love for the fatherland, love for the common good oblige us to take satisfaction in devoting our property and lives to the reinforcement of the state and the well-being of fellow citizens» (quoted by G.P. Makogonenko, *Nikolai Novikov i russkoe prosveshchenie XVIII veka* (Moskva-Leningrad, 1952), pp. 438-441).

[82] On him and his relationship with Malinovskii see the present work, chapter 1.1.4..

[83] Chubar'ian (*op.cit.*, pp. 130-132) erroneously analyses this project as belonging to Tsebrikov himself.

[84] See Iu.M. Lotman, 'Politicheskoe myshlenie Radishcheva i Karamzina i opyt frantsuzskoi revoliutsii', in Fridlender, G.M. (ed.), *Velikaia frantsuzskaia revoliutsiia i russkaia literatura* (Leningrad, 1990), pp. 55-68.

[85] See J.L. Black, 'N.M. Karamzin, Napoleon and the Notion of Defensive War in Russian History', *Canadian Slavonic Papers,* XII, no. 1 (1970), pp. 30-46. See also M. Schippan, 'N.M. Karamzin und J.de Maistre über den Weg Russlands (1811)', *Zeitschrift für Slawistik,* 36 (1991), no. 4, pp. 535-543.

If ideas on peace began to appear more frequently in the works of Russian statesmen and historians, they were never integrated, nevertheless, in a single sustained treatment, nor did they develop a tradition of perpetual peace projects[86] comparable to that established in Western Europe.

2.3. Malinovskii's peace project and the European models

Whilst the weight of Russian autochthonous speculation on peace cannot be considered of decisive importance for the development of Malinovskii's thought, the question of the European influences requires a different evaluation. Europe could boast a solid tradition of reflections about the ways to achieve a warless world, which was extremely varied in its developments.

Malinovskii's decision to devote a significant part of his intellectual energies to the critique of war and the analysis of ways to achieve peace is certainly related to the period in which he lived, characterized by some of the most catastrophic wars in European history. Malinovskii's first work on peace dates from 1790, one year after the French revolution. His last published article appeared in 1813, just before the opening of the Conference of Vienna.

It should be noted that although war was the main political event of this age, speculation was not predominantly devoted to the elaboration of peace plans but rather to the justification of revolution or to the defence of the old European order from revolution. Malinovskii placed an emphasis on methods to achieve a peaceful society which substantially differentiates him from the overall climate of his age. His ideas appear more likely to have been influenced by the European literature previous to the French revolution than by that which appeared at the time when he was writing.

---

[86] It should be noted, however, that in 1767 the Baltic J.H. von Lilienfeld had written a project entitled *Neues Staats Gebäude*. On it see G.v. Rauch, 'Ein baltischer Friedens- und Europaplan von 1767', in *Turun Historiallinen Arkisto*, no. 31 (1976), pp. 221-233.

In the *Slovar' russkikh svetskikh pisatelei metropolita Evgeniia* (Moskva, 1845), a *Proekt traktata mezhdu Evropeiskimi Gosudariami dlia vechnogo istrebleniia v Evrope voiny* is mentioned among the unpublished works left by M. Chulkov (p. 245). This information is reported also in later sources. Regrettably, a work under this title has not been found. Another project of perpetual peace was apparently written at the end of the eighteenth century by Platon Zubov (see J. ter Meulen, *From Erasmus to Tolstoy. The Peace Literature of Four Centuries*, ed. P. van den Dungen (New York, Westport, London, 1990), p. 77). There is no trace of this project.

Despite the fact that Malinovskii's propositions show a remarkable degree of originality and do not seem to derive directly from any of the projects elaborated in Europe, they reveal a debt to Western speculation on peace with respect to a number of specific aspects. The problem of establishing precisely the various sources which the Russian thinker came to know directly and those which affected his thinking is made particularly difficult by Malinovskii's extreme reluctance to give indications of this sort. In the *Dissertation*, as in all his remaining works, he is not very generous in providing the names of authors who inspired him or provoked his objections. The most significant similarities with the ideas of other European peace thinkers will be highlighted here in an attempt to establish Malinovskii's originality against the background of the literature available in his age.

It is highly unlikely, on the other hand, that the Russian thinker exerted a direct influence on the subsequent European debate. As was pointed out in the introduction to this work, his general fortune was negligible. With regard to peace thinking, the fact that he wrote in Russian represented a peculiarity which hindered the circulation of his undoubtedly original ideas.

In the eighteenth century Western reflection on peace and war was dominated by two different traditions: the doctrine of the law of nations and the perpetual peace projects. Although these two traditions proceeded on parallel lines and were influenced by the same historical events, they seldom converged.

Since the creation of the European nation states, the main aim of the law of nations was to regulate the occurrence of war among sovereign states. Although it progressively came to cover also other aspects of the legal relations between states, such as diplomacy, the effectiveness of treatises, trade, etc., the core of the law of nations remained a body of norms aimed at regulating the legitimacy of warfare (*ius ad bellum*) and the legitimacy in warfare (*ius in bello*).

Malinovskii was certainly familiar with this tradition. Diplomats were usually trained on standard textbooks such as that of Grotius[87] and of his followers, and it is reasonable to assume that he, as a person attached to the Russian diplomatic mission in London and as Consul General in Moldavia

---

[87] For his work *De Jure Belli ac Pacis* (1625) Hugo Grotius (1583-1645) is generally considered «the Father of International Law» (See H. Vreeland, *Hugo Grotius, The Father of the Modern Science of International Law* (New York, 1917)). His work was translated into several languages. See the English translation by W. Whewell in *Hugonis Grotii, 'De jure belli ac pacis'* (Cambridge, 1853). To Grotius belongs in fact the first codification of the law of nations and the distinction between just and unjust wars.

and Wallachia later, was aware of the main aspects of the «international law» of his age. In Part III of the *Dissertation* Malinovskii devotes an entire section to the literature on the law of nations (section seven, 'Nauka narodnogo prava'). One of the few works cited by him is Emmerich de Vattel's treatise[88], the most popular text on the law of nations in the second half of the eighteenth century. The science of the law of nations is deeply criticized by Malinovskii, who clearly rejects the entire approach.

In this respect it is crucial to understand what Malinovskii meant by the notion of the law of nations. From the beginning of the seventeenth century the Latin expression «*ius gentium*», which was translated in French as «*loi des gens*», in German as «*Völkerrecht*» and in Russian as «*pravo narodov*», was used with a double meaning: it covered both the law between states and the law above the state[89]. By the outbreak of the French revolution, the «*ius gentium*» doctrine left much of its «natural law» legacy to concentrate on what, according to modern terminology, is positive international law.

As shown in the previous analysis[90], Malinovskii explains why the expression «*pravo narodov*» is misleading: «it is not the law of peoples, but the law of powers, for in it people are divided up according to power blocks and not according to their nationality»[91]. His dissatisfaction with this linguistic use could perhaps be due to his acquaintance with the English terminology. However, he was not the only thinker who criticized this term. A few years before him, Immanuel Kant had stressed in *The Metaphysics of Morals* (1797) that «it is not strictly correct to speak, as we usually do, of the right of nations [Völkerrecht]; it should rather be called the right of states - ius publicum civitatum»[92]. Therefore, when Malinovskii, like Kant, mentioned «pravo narodov» (or «Völkerrecht», or «*ius gentium*») he referred to inter-state law.

The first controversial issue concerns the status of the law of nations. Its theorists stated that it should be considered as natural law applied to the relations among nations. The lack of binding powers of the law of nations, they argued, did not allow comparison with domestic public law. Malinovskii

---

[88] Emmerich de Vattel, *Les droits des gens ou Principes de la loi naturelle appliqués à la conduite et aux affaires des nations et des souverains* (Neuchâtel, 1758).

[89] In English «ius gentium» was translated from the beginning of the seventeenth century as «law of nations»; the English expression was, in fact, much more pragmatic than any other, and much better suited to address the aspects of what is today called international law. It should also be mentioned that the expression «international law» was first introduced by Jeremy Bentham in his works of 1786-1789.

[90] See the present work, pp. 110-112.

[91] Part III (edited by Skowronek), p. 45.

[92] H. Reiss (ed.), *Kant. Political Writings* (Cambridge, 1991), p. 165.

considered this position unacceptable. There was no reason why law *within* a
nation should be considered more important than law *between* nations and,
although it was true that it lacked effectiveness, the theorists of the law of
nations are considered responsible for this: «They have accomodated
themselves to the present state of affairs. And instead of condemning it, they
have derived rules from it and based their science of the law of nations upon
them»[93].

As there was no attempt in the law of nations to ban all wars, but only to
distinguish them as «just» and «unjust», Malinovskii noted that all wars
appear, or pretend to be, «just» to the eyes of the party initiating war. The
idea of a *«ius ad bellum»* has not any effective meaning in a community
lacking a third and more authoritative institution, able to judge which party
was right and which party was wrong.

Even the idea that wars could be regulated by legal norms appeared
ridiculous to Malinovskii, who wrote:

> this philanthropy and moderation no more assist the cruelties of war than
> the philanthropy and mercy of an executioner (...) We should be ashamed
> to deceive ourselves with such considerations. We must completely
> abandon war[94].

This sharp critique of the law of nations has some similarities with what
Kant wrote a few years earlier in his philosophical project entitled *Zum
ewigen Frieden. Ein philosophischer Entwurf* (1795), where the three main
authors of the law of nations - Grotius, Pufendorf and Vattel - were called
«sorry comforters»[95].

Malinovskii was certainly acquainted with the *ius gentium* doctrine, but
this knowledge led him to reject its main principles as excluding peoples
from any effective decision. The existence of autocratic sovereigns
invalidated one of the premises of the law of nations approach, the idea that
states were societies of individuals joined to achieve welfare and security.

The perpetual peace projects were the other contemporary tradition
concerned with peace and war. They flourished in Europe from the beginning
of the seventeenth century[96] and were aimed at eliminating war by creating

---

[93] Part III, p. 45.

[94] *Ibid.*, p. 42.

[95] See the English translation *Towards Perpetual Peace. A Philosophical Project*, in
Reiss, *op.cit.*, p. 103.

[96] The peace projects have received considerable attention from historians: see A.
Lodyzhenskii, *Proekty vechnogo mira i ikh znachenie* (Moskva, 1880); S.J. Hemleben,
Plans for World Peace through Six Centuries (Chicago, 1942); C. Lange, A. Schou,

supra-national institutions empowered to arbitrate any possible conflict among nations. Rather than an attempt to regulate bilateral relations between states, as the *ius gentium*, peace projects seeked to address and possibly solve conflicts in a wider and global context.

Among the authors of perpetual peace projects we find celebrated philosophers: William Penn, Jean-Jacques Rousseau, Jeremy Bentham, Immanuel Kant, Johann Gottlieb Fichte, Claude-Henri de Saint-Simon. Other authors, such as Emeric Crucé, John Bellers, the Abbé de Saint-Pierre, Ange Goudar, Pierre-André Gargas, are remembered today only for their attempt to design peace projects.

The authors of perpetual peace projects were often criticized as utopians and visionaries. Malinovskii mentioned this phenomenon when he wrote:

> the good desire for perpetual peace and the unhappy policy of the necessity of war are two extremes, between which a judicious middle way must be chosen. God alone can secure general peace on earth, but meanwhile his appointed sovereigns, rulers of the peoples, have the duty and the means to anticipate strife and war by the decisive enactment of international laws and their firm observance[97].

Distancing himself from any «pious wish for a perpetual peace», Malinovskii consciously referred to the specific tradition of perpetual peace projects. But, even if critical of the most utopian aspects of this tradition, he shared with it the intention to use all possible methods to ban war:

> The preservation of general and stable peace in Europe is considered impossible and for that reason is not contemplated. People think that they cannot live without war, because wars have been from time immemorial; but the prolonged existence of evil does not prove its inevitability[98].

Histoire de l'Internationalisme, 3 vols. (Kristiana and Oslo, 1919, 1944, 1954); ter Meulen, J., *Der Gedanke der Internationalen Organisation in seiner Entwicklung*, 3 vols. (The Hague, 1921, 1929, 1940); K. von Raumer (ed.), *Ewiger Friede. Friedensrufe und Friedenspläne seit der Renaissance* (Freiburg, 1953); F.H. Hinsley, *Powers and the Pursuit of Peace. Theory and Practice in the History of Relations between States* (Cambridge, 1963); A. Dietze, W. Dietze (eds.) *Ewiger Friede? Dokumente einer deutschen Diskussion um 1800* (Leipzig, Weimar, 1989), D. Archibugi, F. Voltaggio (eds.), *Filosofi per la pace. I progetti per la pace perpetua* (Roma, 1991); D. Archibugi, 'Models of International Organization in Perpetual Peace Projects', *Review of International Studies* (1992), 18, pp. 295-317.

[97] *Izbrannye obshchestvenno-politicheskie sochineniia*, p. 81.

[98] Part III, p. 42.

Part I of the *Dissertation* was focused on a defence of peace which echoed traditional arguments and images[99]. The peace plan presented in Part II represents an attempt to transform the «pious wish for a perpetual peace» into a political project. As in the majority of perpetual peace projects, Malinovskii's solution for the elimination of war consists in the institution of a supra-national body to arbitrate and resolve conflicts, his «General Union and Council»:

> This council should preserve the general security and property and give advance warning of any disruption of the calm, and resolve the proposed arguments between peoples according to the established order (p. 77).

This specific institutional proposal shows that Malinovskii was not just one of the numerous peace lovers who, as seen in section 2.2., populated Russian culture. He was a legal pacifist and his plan represents the only Russian example of a perpetual peace project.

Other thinkers had proposed the creation of such a supra-national institution. In his *Nouveau Cynée* (1623)[100] the Parisian Emeric Crucé (1590?-1648), a contemporary of Grotius, had suggested creating an assembly of the Ambassadors of the world based in Venice. C.F.I. Castel Abbé de Saint-Pierre (1658-1743) elaborated numerous versions of his *Projet pour rendre la paix perpétuelle en Europe* (1713), which took shape after the Treaty of Utrecht of 1712[101]. His plan was characterized by a higher degree of legal elaboration. He proposed the creation of a *Union Européenne* in which the sovereigns were to be represented by their deputies in a Congress (or Senate) based in Utrecht. His works gained vast popularity and were

---

[99] Malinovskii's indignation against the insanity of war strongly recalls Erasmus' works in defence of peace. Generally recognized as the founder of the entire tradition of the plea for peace, Desiderius Erasmus (1466-1536) illustrated his views particularly in *Institutio principis christiani* (1515), *Querela pacis* (1516), *Dulce bellum inexpertis* (1517). Erasmus' ideas had a wide dissemination throughout Europe. Malinovskii certainly knew his *Enchiridion militis christiani* (1501), which was translated into Russian and published in Moscow in 1783 by Novikov under the title *Pamiatnik voina-khristianina*. The affinities between the two thinkers are not merely on a stylistic level. Malinovskii's debt to Erasmus is quite apparent in his attack on the Church's involvement in war and in the idea that fighting against an enemy contradicts the most essential teaching of the Christian doctrine.

[100] See M. Eliav-Feldon, 'Universal Peace for the Benefit of Trade: the Vision of Eméric Crucé', in H. Ben-Israel et al. (eds.), *Religion, Ideology and Nationalism in Europe and America* (Jerusalem, 1986).

[101] The ponderous *Projet pour rendre la paix perpétuelle en Europe* was republished recently (Paris, 1986). On his peace projects see H.H. Post, *La Société des Nations de l'abbé de Saint-Pierre* (Amsterdam, 1932).

discussed (frequently criticized as unrealistic and utopian) by Leibniz, Voltaire, Rousseau, D'Alembert, Kant and Saint-Simon.

According to Crucé and Saint-Pierre, decisions in the Union should be taken according to majority rule. All states, regardless of their size and power, should be given the same importance on the basis of the criterion «one state, one vote».

Saint-Pierre's plan was often considered the major source of inspiration for Malinovskii's proposal, on the basis of the judgement of a contemporary anonymous reviewer of the *Dissertation on Peace and War*, who wrote:

> the author of course had in mind the well-known project of perpetual peace (projet de paix perpetuelle) of the Abbé de Saint-Pierre. For some articles and the very means of bringing about this universal peace are the same[102].

Certainly the large circulation of Saint-Pierre's project could favour its knowledge on Malinovskii's part. The synthesis of Saint-Pierre's ideas written by Rousseau was translated in Russian by the poet I.F. Bogdanovich in 1771[103].

The points of contact between Crucé and Saint-Pierre's projects are numerous. Malinovskii follows them in the idea of creating a permanent union empowered with the use of force against states violating its decisions. He shares for example the idea that such a Union should have a permanent residence:

> Once a particular country has been appointed for this council to reside in, it is necessary to acknowledge it sacred and independent for the sake of the permanent and safe residence of the council's plenipotentiaries[104].

This notwithstanding, Malinovskii's plan fundamentally diverges from the ideological premises characterizing Crucé and Saint-Pierre's approach: in these projects the sovereigns and their ambassadors were the only bodies involved in the Union, while citizens and peoples were deliberately excluded from its functioning.

---

[102] *Severnyi vestnik*, no. 2 (1804), p. 322. This view is criticized as unfounded by Arab-Ogly (*Izbrannye obshchestvenno-politicheskie sochineniia*, p. 27). Before him another Soviet scholar had mentioned, on the other hand, the influence of Rousseau, Bentham and Kant on Malinovskii's treatise (F.I. Kozhevnikov, *Uchebnoe posobie po mezhdunarodnomu publichnomu pravu* (Moskva, 1947), p. 18).

[103] See the present work, pp. 22.

[104] *Izbrannye obshchestvenno-politicheskie sochineniia*, pp. 76-77.

In point of fact, one of the aims of the Union advocated by Crucé and Saint-Pierre was the defence of the sovereigns against any possible rebellion. The armed forces of the united sovereigns were to be used against sovereigns who jeopardized peace and security as well as against subjects willing to overthrow their kings. Malinovskii proposed the creation of an international army[105], but he never planned its use to quell rebellion by the subjects of a state.

Malinovskii's aim was not to create a league of sovereigns against their peoples. Jean-Jacques Rousseau criticized Saint-Pierre's project arguing that «it is not possible to protect princes against rebellion by their subjects without at the same time guaranteeing the subjects against the tyranny of the princes; otherwise the institution could not survive»[106]; it is legitimate to suppose that Malinovskii shared this opinion. The plenipotentiaries forming the General Council proposed by him were not to be ambassadors of the sovereigns but members elected by general consensus and revocable by the majority. That would represent a guarantee against autocratic regimes.

Unfortunately, Malinovskii is very far from being explicit about how these plenipotentiaries were to be appointed. He probably imagined a sort of International Court of Justice, since he wrote that its members were required to be «foremost in talents and virtues». This idea of a court of arbitration formed by representatives of the states had been previously advanced by the Czech Jan Amos Comenius (1592-1670) in his *Angelus pacis ad Legatos pacis Anglos et Belgas Bredam missus* (1667)[107]. We can suppose that Malinovskii was familiar with his work, since it appeared in a Slavic area[108].

---

[105] Malinovskii mentioned the use of an 'obshchaia sila' (*Izbrannye obshchestvenno-politicheskie sochineniia*, p. 77).

[106] After having summarised Saint-Pierre's thesis in the *Extrait du Projet de Paix Perpétuelle de Monsieur l'Abbé de Saint-Pierre*, which was written in 1756 and published in 1761, Rousseau wrote also a *Jugement sur le projet de paix perpétuelle* (1758) which contains his independent opinions on this subject. See *The Political Writings of Jean-Jacques Rousseau* (Oxford, 1962), p. 389. See J.L. Windenberger, *La République confédérative des petits Etats. Essay sur le système de politique étrangère de J.-J. Rousseau* (Paris, 1900); S. Hoffman, 'Rousseau on War and Peace', *American Political Science Review*, LVII (1962).

It should be recalled that in his fragment on peace Pushkin referred to Saint-Pierre's plan in Rousseau's version (see the present work, chapter 4.2.4.).

[107] See the English-Latin edition *The Angel of Peace* (New York, 1945). On Comenius see J. Popelova, *The Significance of Comenius for World Culture and the Peace Movement* (Prague, 1956).

[108] Specific features of Comenius' work anticipate positions Malinovskii adopted in the *Dissertation*: he proposed the elimination of secret diplomacy, the selection of the representatives of the states on the basis of their outstanding moral and intellectual qualities and the establishment of tolerance among all non-Catholic faiths. He was also

Another contemporary of Malinovskii, Pierre-André Gargas, proposed in 1797 the establishment of an International Tribunal formed by wise men aged above forty years[109]. The circulation of this text was however limited to Southern France, and it is unlikely that Malinovskii was acquainted with it.

An important feature of Malinovskii's Council is the fact that it is not attributed only a judicial power. The Russian thinker proposed to ascribe to that institution some of the typical functions of an executive power, including the power to use force against states violating legality. Despite the fact that he provides very few institutional details, it is possible to foresee in Malinovskii's proposal the features of a sort of elected European government.

The idea of a European Diet or Parliament formed by authoritative representatives rather than by the sovereigns' ambassadors had been supported by the English Quakers William Penn and John Bellers[110]. In *An Essay towards the Present and Future Peace of Europe* (1693) Penn (1644-1718) proposed the formation of a «Sovereign or Imperial Diet, Parliament or State of Europe», which should be concerned with the elaboration of rules for the establishment of peace and justice. Penn proposed to give a number of seats roughly proportional to the wealth of each country. This allowed the establishment of a criterion of representation which went beyond the principle «one state, one vote» held by Crucé and Saint-Pierre. Penn proposed that the European deputies should vote according to what they considered to be right, and not according to the interests of their fatherland. On very similar lines, in his *Some Reasons for an European State* (1710) John Bellers (1654-1725) proposed that Europe should be divided into one hundred provinces, and each province should appoint one representative to the European assembly.

Malinovskii's reference to the Quakers' attitude to peace in the chapter entitled 'Vospitanie i vera', and to his own Quaker experience in 'Rossiianin v Anglii' gives substance to the hypothesis that he was familiar with Quaker literature. These two plans were widely known in the Quaker community and they probably represented a source of inspiration for the design of Malinovskii's General Union[111].

---

one of the few thinkers who conceived a plan for the moral and political regeneration of European peoples as a necessary complement to the pursuit of peace.

109 See his essay *Contract Social surnomé Union Francmaçone* (Toulon, 1797).

110 See T. Terasaki, *William Penn et la paix* (Paris, 1926); E.C.O. Beatty, *William Penn as a Social Philosopher* (New York, 1939). See also M.E. Hirst, *The Quakers in Peace and War. An Account of their Peace Principles and Practice* (London, 1923).

111 In this respect it may be worth mentioning, on the other hand, a curious work appearing a few years before Malinovskii's treatise, in which an anonymous author illustrated his hope of the establishment of perpetual peace. This work was entitled

Although Penn and Bellers imagined a European Parliament which was not directly linked to the will of the sovereigns, they were not as explicit as Malinovskii in proposing an elective criterion for the appointment of the European deputies. Shortly after, in 1814, this was clearly proposed by Claude-Henri de Saint-Simon. In his essay entitled 'The Reorganization of the European Community', written in collaboration with A. Thierry, he recommended for the first time the election of a European Parliament on the basis of the principle «one man, one vote»[112].

Saint-Simon and Malinovskii shared, nevertheless, the idea that once such a European institution was achieved, it should have a hierarchical power over the conflicts occurring at a local level. Malinovskii argued that:

> If it happens (...) that these regions at their own assembly are unable to agree about something and are set to quarrel, they will propound it through their plenipotentiaries to the General European Assembly, and submit to its decision. The agreement of the general assembly of one language is not sufficient to justify any kind of hostile action, the decision of the general assembly of all languages is required, whose verdicts must be implemented[113].

Eleven years after, Saint-Simon supported the same view:

> If a particular part of the European population, under a particular government, wishes to form a separate union, or to come under another government, it is for the European parliament to decide the issue. It will decide, not in the interests of the governments, but of the peoples, bearing in mind always the best possible organization of the European Confederation[114].

Malinovskii and Saint-Simon conceived their European Union as a sort of Federal state rather than a Confederation of states. Certainly Saint-Simon

---

Lasting Peace to Europe: the Dream of an Ancient Cosmopolite and was published in London in 1781 (See A.G. Cross, *'Anglofiliia u trona'. Britantsy i russkie v vek Ekateriny II. Katalog vystavki* (London, 1992), p. 22). Dedicated to Catherine II, it was dictated by enthusiasm for her position on armed neutrality (See I. de Madariaga, *Britain, Russia and the Armed Neutrality of 1780* (London, 1962). In the literary dream the author, accompanied by a woman who embodied Humanity, undertakes an imaginary voyage to ancient Rome, Spain and France to enumerate the atrocities perpetrated by political and religious leaders of the past. He then witnesses a ceremony during which the European sovereigns abdicate in favour of peoples. Afterwards «the General Assembly, and States of Europe, composed a code of laws suitable to each nation, taken from the different advices of all the learned men of Europe (...) Those who had not entered in the general union, formed the only frontiers of all the others» (p. 40).

112 H. Saint-Simon, *Social Organization, the Science of Man and Other Writings,* ed. F. Markham (New York, 1964).

113 Part III, p. 36.

114 H. Saint-Simon, *op.cit.,* p. 48-49.

was influenced in this by the American experience, and it is very likely that Malinovskii, who translated a book by A. Hamilton on the manufacturing industry[115], was also aware of the political content of the *Federalist*, the book that Hamilton co-authored with J. Madison and J. Jay[116].

Malinovskii was also aware, on the other hand, of the fact that a constitutional form similar to that of the United States would not fit the variety of European culture: «For union the European peoples are all rather alike, but they are different as regards citizenship»[117]. Echoing Rousseau, he believed that self-determination worked better in small communities: «Small regions are much easier to run and it is not difficult to establish a good government for them»[118].

The creation of Malinovskii's General Council was to guarantee a greater participation of citizens in international policy, since diplomatic secrecy was to become superfluous. As shown above, he suggested publishing regular accounts of the main political decisions, in order to facilitate the participation of peoples in foreign policy issues.

The practice of diplomatic secrecy was not blamed only by Malinovskii. In his *Plan for an Universal and Perpetual Peace* Jeremy Bentham (1748-1832)[119] gave considerable prominence to a severe critique of secrecy characterizing the Foreign Affairs departments. This was seen as «repugnant to the interests of liberty and peace» and particularly intolerable in the activity of an assembly concerned with international relations: «The proceedings of such Congress or Diet should all be public»[120].

On a crucial point Malinovskii appears to be at odds with the majority of peace projects: the acceptance of the *status quo* as regards states' boundaries and controversies. Crucé, Penn, Bellers and Saint-Pierre agreed that sovereigns, as a preliminary condition for the achievement of a common union, should abandon forever any territorial and political claim over their partners.

Malinovskii, on the contrary, was against the maintenance of the *status quo* among European states, and wished to change entirely the political

---

[115] See the present work, chapter 3.4..

[116] A. Hamilton, J. Jay, J. Madison, *The Federalist* (1788) (Chicago, 1952).

[117] Part III, p. 32.

[118] Part III, p. 40.

[119] The Plan was written between 1786 and 1789, but published only later, in J. Bowring (ed.), *The Works of Jeremy Bentham* (Edinburgh, 1838-1843). The hypothesis of Malinovskii's familiarity with a manuscript copy of this work is not sustained by any evidence (see the present work, p. 31).

[120] J. Bentham *Plan for an Universal and Perpetual Peace* (London, 1927), pp. 31, 30.

configuration of the continent, as he believed that the existing frontiers were not representative of homogeneous cultural, social and political communities. In sections three and four of Part III of the *Dissertation*, which are some of the most powerful pages of his political works, he argued that European peoples would have been freed by undertaking major changes in European frontiers: «This division, however dear it would cost, will amply pay for itself by putting an end to conquests, henceforth returning the protection of each people to its own hands»[121].

Although the acceptance of the *status quo* was a distinctive feature of the vast majority of peace plans, there were two significant exceptions: the plans elaborated by the Duc of Sully and by Cardinal Alberoni. According to the Duc of Sully, peace could be achieved only as the result of a balance of powers among European states. His *Gran Dessin* which he presented as inspired by Henry IV[122], contained a complete redefinition of the political organization of Europe. This should be achieved by means of the very thing the plan was supposed to ban: war. Despite the influence that this plan exerted on peace thinkers (in particular Penn, Saint-Pierre and Rousseau), it is not entitled to belong to the tradition of perpetual peace projects.

The second exception is represented by Cardinal Alberoni[123], who proposed the establishment of a treaty among European states to fight the Turkish Empire and to acquire its territories. The peace among European states advocated by him was in fact an alliance against a common enemy. Because of the very «instrumental» origin of Sully and Alberoni's plans, they are to be considered at odds with proper peace thinking. They also show evident discrepancies with Malinovskii's project: the Russian thinker was far from thinking that his plan should be achieved by means of war. Moreover, the reorganization of Europe he advocated was not in the interest of sovereigns but rather in that of peoples.

As was argued, Malinovskii's critique of the *status quo* and his attempt to create a different form of organization in Europe are to be strictly related to the period in which he wrote. During the Napoleonic wars, there was no effective *status quo* to defend. Consolidated European states disappeared

---

[121] Part III, p. 40.

[122] Sully included his *Gran Dessin* in his *Œconomies royales*, published in 1638. See the English translation *The Gran Design of Henri IV from the Memoires of Maximilien de Béthune Duc of Sully* (London, 1921). See also A. Puharré, *Les Projets d'organization européenne d'après le Grand Dessin de Henri IV et de Sully* (Paris, 1954).

[123] Cardinale Alberoni, *Progetto di una Dieta perpetua per mantenere la pubblica tranquillità* (1735).

overnight, others were suddenly created. Virtually no state, with the notable exception of Great Britain, kept its frontiers unchanged.

The preservation of the *status quo* as a method to guarantee peace was not a viable political possibility in that context. The alternative was either to restore the geo-political organization dominating Europe before the French revolution or to create a European federation under French hegemony.

Malinovskii did not support either of these two views, which were not considered by him as able to respond to the real interests of European peoples. His plan to create common ethno-linguistic entities was a way to take advantage of the Napoleonic turmoil and to achieve more satisfactory political communities.

A society based on councils at local as well as at European levels[124] was not only a form of political organization which corresponded to the interests of peoples. It was also a system which would favour the establishment of peace. In fact, Malinovskii argued that «War is produced by the common forces of the people, and in so far as it demands their cooperation, also needs their agreement»[125]. He praised the experience of Sweden and Britain, since their Parliaments had at least some powers to counterbalance the willingness of sovereigns to wage war. He also criticized these countries for being partly inconsistent, since the power to wage war was still in the hands of the sovereigns.

If in all states the decision to wage war was under the control of peoples, it would be much easier to establish a common security system:

> The right of the people in declaration of war is a general concern to all Europe, for mutual security and the assurance of peace. Each power will be more certain of the obligations of the other, with the people to guarantee them, instead of the inconstant disposition of rulers, who can be distracted by a momentary passion or a gullible acceptance of another's suggestion or may even be bribed (...) But the whole people is exempt from these temptations and allurements and is not prone to such a rapid and sudden inflammation of the passions[126].

Malinovskii's argument that governments under popular control are less prone to make war than autocratic governments was also made in the project written by Immanuel Kant. The Prussian philosopher argued that all states

---

124 R. Picchio, in an unpublished paper presented at the Italian-Russian Peace Studies Conference (Napoli, 1990) has indicated that the expression used by Malinovskii recalls the modern institution of the Soviet of Soviets.

125 Part III, p. 52.

126 Part III, pp. 52-53.

should be republican in order to achieve perpetual peace[127], and gave the following explanation:

> If, as is inevitably the case under [the republican] constitution, the consent of the citizens is required to decide whether or not war is to be declared, it is very natural that they will have great hesitation in embarking on so dangerous an enterprise. For this would mean calling down on themselves all the miseries of war[128].

While Kant argued that democratic governments tend to favour war less than autocratic ones, Malinovskii made a more precise statement, namely that governments respectful of the popular will are trusted by neighbouring states, and therefore reduce the danger of war[129].

As was argued, the issues Malinovskii addressed during his lifetime were deeply connected to the existing peace literature and originally re-elaborated in accordance with his historical age.

Analyzing the different approaches to peace thinking, Norberto Bobbio proposed an interesting taxonomy: a peace plan is «instrumental» when it acts on means (such as disarmament), «finalistic» when it acts on humans (which includes non violence, education, religious beliefs), «social» when it acts on social structures (reforms or revolutions) and «legal» when it proposes the creation of appropriate institutions[130]. Malinovskii can be considered predominantly a «legal» peace thinker. The most relevant method he advocated to guarantee peace was in fact the creation of the General Union, characterized by both judiciary and executive powers.

Within the rich European tradition of perpetual peace projects, we can reasonably suppose that Malinovskii was aware of the works of Penn, Saint-Pierre (at least in Rousseau's *Extrait*), Goudar and Kant and probably had some knowledge of Bentham's unpublished plan.

---

[127] According to the language of Kant's age, a republican constitution meant a representative democracy. See, for example *The Federalist, op.cit.*, no. 14: «In a democracy the people meet and exercise the government in person; in a republic, they assemble and administer it by their representatives and agents.»

[128] Kant, *Perpetual Peace*, in *op.cit.*, p. 100.

[129] The hypothesis that democracies do not fight each other is currently at the frontbench of the debate of international relations (see, for example, the review of the issue of B. Russett, *Grasping the Democratic Peace* (Princeton, 1993)). Malinovskii appears as the first international theorist who advanced this hypothesis and provided an explanation for it.

[130] N. Bobbio, *Il problema della guerra e le vie della pace* (Bologna, 1984). See also Max Scheler, 'The Idea of Peace and Pacifism', *Journal of the British Society for Phenomenology,* VII (1976), no. 4, pp. 154-166, and VIII (1977), no. 1, pp. 36-50.

We argued that Malinovskii is by all means a member of the family of philosophers for perpetual peace. His main original feature consists in the proposal of a General Council connected to local councils. His idea of a reorganization of European states on the basis of linguistic and cultural homogeneous communities has no antecedents, and should be related to the historical period in which it was elaborated: it represented an original and significant attempt to re-shape the continent during the Napoleonic wars.

He was also the first peace thinker who proposed an elective international institution, despite the fact that he did not provide many details on this subject.

Malinovskii's search for peace was not limited to a mere institutional design. In the spirit of the Enlightenment, he believed that a peaceful society required a different civic community, and proposed a number of social reforms, which will be illustrated in chapters three and four. The social concern behind his peace plan represents another of its original features.

The comparison of the *Dissertation on Peace and War* with its European models indicates that Malinovskii's work deserves a place in the history of peace ideas greater than the one it has so far enjoyed.

CHAPTER 3: THE SOCIAL REFORMER

This chapter will explore Malinovskii's programme of social reforms as it appears in various works, published and unpublished, in which he treats themes of social interest.

Malinovskii's works on social issues were not widely circulated and thus the impact that his ideas might have had on contemporary debate on the most crucial issues was severely limited. A few considerations will thus be devoted to this problem.

The main subject of this chapter will be Malinovskii's attitude towards serfdom, respecting the importance attributed to this problem by the thinker himself and by many of his contemporaries. Attention will however also be given to themes such as the development of agriculture and the social impact of religious conflicts.

The four specific works in which Malinovskii's statements about the problem of serf emancipation were formulated will be analyzed to show the evolution of his position, from the substantially moralistic approach of the *povest' Pustynnik* (1799), to the realistically progressive proposals of the 'Zapiska o osvobozhdenii rabov' (1802) and of the 'Razmyshlenie o preobrazovanii gosudarstvennogo ustroistva Rossii' (1803), to the grandiose plan contained in Part III of his *Rassuzhdenie* (1801-1803).

3.1. Malinovskii as a social thinker

Malinovskii's intellectual activity in all fields was informed by a main preoccupation: to serve, as he declared at his debut on the «public» scene, «human happiness»[1], in keeping with the social commitment characterizing the ideals of the enlightened thinkers of his time. His *Rassuzhdenie*, which still remains the most paradigmatic expression of this «universal» attitude, gives the clearest evidence of his intention to embrace virtually all aspects of social and political life.

A few preliminary considerations cannot however be avoided, regarding a particular feature of his role as a social thinker and reformer: the attitude to secrecy. In the few cases in which Malinovskii chose publicity for his works, he rarely declared his authorship, when circulating them. It is a matter of fact that he wrote in years in which self-censorship was a measure adopted quite naturally by the man of letters, and in which in general the perception that the authors had of themselves was very far from the modern one[2]. It is nevertheless curious to observe how many important fragments of his vision of the world had to wait until the present before emerging from the mysterious initials or the anonymity behind which they were hidden.

The ambiguous attitude shown by Malinovskii towards «publicity» has been highlighted before, in the present work. It affected particularly deeply his works of a social character, strengthening a contradictory feature familiar to modern observers of that period: his proposals, like many other eighteenth-century reforming projects, remained in the area of utopian, purely theoretical speculation. If we take the case of his works on serfdom, that circumstance will be apparent: of the four which we consider relevant to illuminate his position on the question, *Pustynnik* appeared, partially, only in the Soviet epoch, the 'Zapiska o osvobozhdenii rabov' became known in 1888, several years after the peasant reform had been accomplished, the 'Razmyshlenie o preobrazovanii gosudarstvennogo ustroistva Rossii' escaped the status of private document only in 1915 and *Rassuzhdenie o mire i voine* Part III was never published in Russia.

---

[1] See p. 17 of the present work.

[2] On the variations in this perception, see W. Gareth Jones, 'The Image of the Eighteenth-Century Russian Author', in R. Bartlett, J. M. Hartley (eds.), *Russia in the Age of the Enlightenment* (Basingstoke, 1990), pp. 57-74, and in general I. Masanov, *V mire psevdonimov, anonimov i literaturnykh poddelok* (Moscow, 1963); V. Vinogradov, *Problema avtorstva i teoriia stilei* (Moscow, 1961).

These considerations lead us to face another problem already mentioned in this work: the impact that Malinovskii sought for his work and, in general, the enigma of the real circulation of his works during his lifetime. In this respect, we could embark upon a series of questions: in which forms, through which channels did Malinovskii intend to make his work influential on the contemporary scene, why did he not succeed, and to what degree was his reluctance to seek «publicity» intentional? Did he implicitly postpone to a more favourable time ideas which were considered too advanced? Did the apparent «secrecy» of these works ensure another, «internal» circulation among the few persons involved in the movement for reform in Russia?[3]

If all these questions still cannot be given a certain answer, they cannot, on the other hand, invalidate the value of the ideas Malinovskii expressed on social issues during his lifetime. These ideas are disseminated in various works. Malinovskii's claim to the status of social thinker is fundamentally based, nevertheless, on Part III of his *Rassuzhdenie o mire i voine*. Here the objects of his social concern receive the clearest integration with the rest of his projects. In the treatise, in fact, the vision of a world free from the menace of war is plausible for the author only in the perspective of a social life in which conflicts are reduced to an acceptable minimum and controlled by just laws. After proposing a redefinition of the shapes of states according to the principles of ethno-linguistic communities, and claiming a correct regulation of the relations among states, the author gives in fact an analysis of civil society constituting the basis for the state so identified.

Malinovskii's 'social' thought appears here as mainly structured into three sets of proposals, each of them treating one major cause of conflict: the ownership of the land; religious differences; the need for education. The first in importance is the one regarding the problem of the land: Malinovskii observed the abnormal presence of poverty, discrimination and unhappiness in society, and the most effective measures to eliminate them consisted, in his opinion, in the possession by everybody of a tract of land.

In chapter VI, entitled 'Vospitanie i vera', the author grouped together the two other important causes of tension. Malinovskii's fundamental

---

[3] At present there is evidence to assume that Malinovskii had a particularly prominent role in the work of the «Neglasnyi komitet» created during the first years of Alexander I's reign; the spirit of two of the works mentioned above ('Razmyshlenie' and 'Zapiska'), and the external circumstances in which they were written seem nevertheless to make this idea plausible.

concern for education (to which the last chapter of this study will be devoted) was rooted in the wish to give a solid basis to his egalitarian projects: in the purest spirit of the Enlightenment, he believed that a more widespread use of Reason would be a condition leading to a better world and he attributed overriding importance to the acquisition of a higher level of education for everybody.

For the conflicts originating in religious differences and in the division of peoples and ethnic groups within each people, the solution advanced by Malinovskii was synthesized in a policy of toleration, based on a heterodox sharing of the same universal ethical values, according to a more authentic interpretation of the Christian faith. The different dogmas and rituals followed by the European peoples made them forget also that the essence of the Christian doctrine was the rejection of war. The Russian thinker mentions with sympathy on two occasions, in this chapter, the example of the Quakers[4], as the only faith which deserved to be followed.

Malinovskii returned in many other works to religious matters and also translated a number of texts of a spiritual nature[5]. One of the issues on which he repeatedly focused his attention was the problem related to the presence of the Jews in Russia, which was also discussed by Malinovskii's contemporaries[6]. The Jewish question was introduced by the Russian thinker with a clear perception of its social and political aspects. In his

---

[4] For a discussion of this preference expressed by Malinovskii, see pp. 47-50 of the present work.

[5] Malinovskii's religious translations included: *Kniga Ekkleziasta, to est' propovednika Tsaria Solomona* (IRLI, Fond 244, op. 25, no. 309); *Kniga proroka Isaii (ibid.); Natural'naia kartina otnoshenii mezhdu Bogom, chelovekom i vselennykh sushchestvuiushchikh (ibid.,* no. 310); *Skazanie o prechistoi Marii (ibid.,* no. 324); *Nastavlenie dannoe mne velikoiu tsaritseiu nebesnoiu (ibid.,* nos. 330, 331); *Tainstvennyi grad Bozhii. Vtoraia chast', soderzhashchaia tainstva ot voploshcheniia slova v devstvennom chreve Marii do vozneseniia* (TSDIAU, Fond 2039, op.1, no. 63, ff. 1-20); *Nazidatel'nye nastavleniia na sorokodevnyi post Gospoda Iisusa Khrista v pustyni (ibid.,* no. 65, ff. 1-24, and no. 75, ff. 1-88). There are also various articles of religious character (IRLI, Fond 244, op. 25, nos. 313,314,315,316,324,326). Some of them are given titles: 'Sie tainstvo est' vostanovlenie slavnogo moego tsarstva'; 'D'avol nas nenavidit'; 'Volia - sie est' bozhestvennoe v cheloveke stremlenie ko blago'.

[6] G. Derzhavin, for example, devoted a *Mnenie* to the problem (see volume VII of *Sochineniia Derzhavina* (Spb., 1864-1883)). After the ambiguous policy toward the Jews pursued by Catherine II and Paul, in the early years of Alexander's reign the Jewish question was at the centre of an intense debate, culminating in the Statute of 1804. There are numerous studies on this subject, see particularly: N.N. Golitsyn, *Istoriia russkogo zakonodatel'stva o Evreiakh* (Spb., 1886); I.Iu. Gessen, *Evrei v Rossii* (Spb., 1906), and his *Istoriia evreiskogo naroda v Rossii* (Leningrad, 1925); J.D. Klier, *Russia Gathers Her Jews. The Origins of the 'Jewish Question' in Russia, 1772-1825* (Dekalb, Illinois, 1986), and his 'Muscovite Faces and Petersburg Masks: the Problem of Religious Judeophobia in Eighteenth-Century Russia', in R. Bartlett, A. Cross, K. Rasmussen (eds.), *Russia and the World of the Eighteenth Century* (Columbus, Ohio,1988), pp. 125-139.

'Zapiski o Moldavii' there is a section entitled 'Zhidy', in which Malinovskii investigates the reasons for the particular position of the Jews among European peoples:

> Cupidity, their common passion (...), evidently proceeds from the insecurity of their condition and other people's scorn for them. Wealth alone can gain them respect, and the more others despise them, the less they care about their methods (...) To begin with in Europe they were masters in commerce; they were the first to introduce banks and bills of exchange: when we had learnt about it, they lost control of commerce: they became obliged at that time to resort to other means, which are either base or entail harming others, and for this reason Jews have become hated and despised[7].

At this stage, Malinovskii's solution to the question raised is the full integration of the Jews in the states in which they live:

> If they were accepted as fellow citizens in the lands in which they live, they would make themselves purposeful citizens (...). It is better not to allow them to live in a land at all (as formerly in Russia) than to allow them, but make in their regard some exceptions in the rights of citizenship[8].

Malinovskii came later to elaborate a concrete and detailed proposal on this problem, which is illustrated in 'Uteshenie dshcheri iudeiskoi'[9]. This note, still in manuscript form, was brought to the attention of the Holy Synod in 1803 in order to obtain permission for it to be printed. It is presented in five sections: 'Izbranie Evreiskago naroda, otlozhenie ego i budushchee obrashchenie', 'Khristianskoe pouchenie o zhidakh', 'Sredstva k ispravleniiu Evreev', 'Sovet Evreiskomu narodu', 'Desiat' kolen Izrailevykh'. The first two sections provide an historical sketch of the reasons leading the Jews to their present state of disgrace. There is a constant attempt on Malinovskii's part to criticize the animosity towards the Jews which derives from consolidated prejudices, in particular the Catholic claim that the Jews had committed the crime of deicide. In this connection the Russian thinker recalls that God's will was behind that event.

The heart of the proposal is contained in the section entitled 'Sredstva k ispravleniiu Evreev'. Here Malinovskii identifies the dual nature of the problem: on the one hand there is the moral decadence characterizing the Jews at the time, which is mainly due to the fact that they are forced to

---

[7] *Priiatnoe i poleznoe preprovozhdenie vremeni*, XIII (1797), pp. 423-424.

[8] *Ibid.*, p. 425.

[9] RGIA, Fond 796, op. 84, no. 633, ff. 9-21.

practise shameful activities such as usury; they should therefore be encouraged to return to honest economic occupations, which could ensure a purification of their community. On the other hand, Malinovskii acknowledges the present poor state of the European Jewry, faced with a lack of freedom, nationality and land, menaced in its existence and identity. He illustrates his proposal: the fertile Crimean steppes between the Dniepr and the Sea of Azov are the ideal area where the Jews could settle and prosper, engaged in peaceful and innocuous activities[10]. Malinovskii emphasizes the central role of his country in this project of European import[11]: only the Russian land, vast and scarcely inhabited, can provide such an opportunity for the Jews; the Russian state would then protect their settlement allowing them to have freedom of belief, property of their land, right to the status of «*osobennyi narod*» (a special people) and to self-government. He shows a sympathetic understanding for the difficulties in facing such a change for this people and invites them to an apparently simple reflection: «in your poor position every good thing is a new one, and only through change can you make yourselves happier»[12]. He prophetically warns against their further persecution if a solution is not found[13].

The Jewish question is also mentioned in *Osennie vechera*. The fifth article, entitled 'Liubov' Rossii', represents an appeal for unity for Russia which should be informed, as Malinovskii explicitly states, by that sense of «veroterpenie» (religious tolerance, also meant as a capacity to transcend national boundaries) cited by him as a typical feature of the Russian people. The article ends with a passage evoking the spiritual resurrection of the Jews, on the one hand, and the rise of Russian interest in their cause on the other:

> Among the multitude of diverse inhabitants of Russia is the blessed tribe of Israel - crawling over the earth in damnation and humiliation. - The wail of the daughters of Israel awakens the attention of Russia - but why is the banished slave weeping! Your waters are growing scarce! Cry out to the

---

[10] In this respect particular emphasis is placed by Malinovskii on the advantages of stock-breeding.

[11] «Russia, who formerly was alone in not being able to tolerate you, and barred you from residence, can alone do you more good than all other kingdoms. She can change your fate» (RGIA, Fond 796, op. 84, no. 633, f.19).

[12] *Ibid.*, f. 18.

[13] «The war that is beginning threatens their gatherings in Holland and Germany with new misfortunes and destruction» (*ibid.*); «But cruel times are approaching us. Your plans and your wealth will come to nothing» (*ibid.*, f. 19).

Most High, for His succour. He will open your eyes and you will behold
the water of life - it is beside you - in your lips, in your heart -[14].

Malinovskii's proposal for the Jews as it appears in these works
represents further important evidence of the spirit of religious and political
toleration which informed a significant part of his views on social question.

3.2. The peasant question in Malinovskii's system of ideas and in the contemporary debate

We have already highlighted the reasons why Malinovskii's coherent
corpus of works devoted to the solution of urgent and crucial social
problems found apparently very little echo in the cultural life of the time.
Even more striking is the fact that his advocacy of emancipation failed to
attract the attention of subsequent generations of scholars. Unlike the
«political» Malinovskii, who was dealing in his most significant work with
an issue like peace, which is traditionally difficult to frame and treat, the
lack of adequate attention in a field in which there exists an impressive mass
of studies both in Russia and in other countries is hardly justified and at best
difficult to understand.

The recurrence of the idea of the abolition of serfdom in different
places and times in Malinovskii's work is an indication of his unflagging
interest in this specific problem. It must be seen, however, also as a
reflection of his age: Malinovskii was expressing his personal advanced
views on a problem which had been discussed and analysed in its various
aspects over decades and had seen many different phases.

A number of plans, proposals and recommendations devoted to the
problem appeared during the Petrine epoch. Initially the peasants'
question[15] did not involve the servile status of the peasants, but existed
essentially as a search for methods to increase the productivity of the
Russian lands, or to collect the revenues more efficiently[16]. Essentially

---

[14] *Osennie vechera* (Spb., 1803), p. 39. The passage was omitted in Arab-Ogly's
edition.

[15] See P.K. Alefirenko, *Krest'ianskoe dvizhenie i krest'ianskii vopros v Rossii v 30-
50 gg. XVIII v.* (Moskva, 1958).

[16] Several plans were focused on these problems. Peter the Great highly considered
the *Propozitsii* (1712) of Fedor Saltykov, which, aimed at embracing a large spectrum of
the social and state life, also treated questions like the improvement of the revenue system

reformist in nature, the plans which appeared in this period were aimed at developing and perfecting the organs and the functions of the absolutist state, without touching the roots of the servile system.

The views expressed by I. Pososhkov on the question of peasantry in his *Kniga o skudosti o bogatstve* represent a quite typical position in the Petrine epoch: his proposals were focused on the landowners and were aimed at showing the economic advantages of a better treatment of the peasants, not of their emancipation. Pososhkov did not consider the peasants' poverty as deriving from their permanent state of servitude, but from accidental, temporary, factors, and therefore devoted much space to show how to prevent natural disasters, fires or brigandage. Peasants' ownership of the land was far from being a feasible concern: the land could not belong to them, because they themselves were a possession of the Tsar[17].

In the second half of the eighteenth century the debate on serfdom began to develop in Russia according to new principles[18]. A certain emphasis was put on the moral aspects of the problem. In 1767 a governmental undertaking, the Free Economic Society's Essay Competition on peasant property[19], helped to disseminate the idea that the current system of rural relations needed to be fundamentally reformed.

In 1774 Pugachev's manifestos claimed outright freedom and land for the peasants and gave a particular urgency to the search for a solution.

---

or the necessity to oblige the Russian church to pay taxes. The same preoccupations appeared in the *Donoshenie* of Ivan Filippov, who was in favour of the introduction of a system based on the ownership of a passport in order to avoid disorders and rebellions and to limit the cruelty of the landowners.

[17] It is therefore the Tsar who is invited to be more zealous about the welfare of his «property»: «The landowners are not the age-old proprietors of the peasants, on account of which they do not particularly care for them; while the peasants' direct proprietor is the autocrat of All Russia, they are temporary proprietors. And on this account it is not proper for the landowners to ruin them, they must preserve them according to the tsar's decree, so that the peasants are upstanding peasants and not poverty-stricken, in so far as the peasant wealth is the tsar's wealth» (I.T. Pososhkov, *Kniga o skudosti i bogatstve*, ed. B.B. Kafengauz (Moscow, 1937), p. 254). See the English edition, *The Book of Poverty and Wealth*, eds. A.P. Vlasto, L.R. Lewitter (London, 1987). See also D. Beauvois, 'La question paysanne sous Pierre le Grand vue par Pososhkov', *Revue du Nord*, no. 52 (1970), pp. 217-227.

[18] See R. Bartlett, 'The Question of Serfdom: Catherine II, the Russian Debate and the View from the Baltic Periphery (J.G. Eisen and G.H. Merkel)', in R. Bartlett, J. M. Hartley (eds.), *Russia in the Age of the Enlightenment* (Basingstoke, 1990), pp.142-166.

[19] See R. Bartlett, 'The St Petersburg Free Economic Society and Europe: The Essay Competition of 1766', in *Study Group on Eighteenth-Century Russia Newsletter*, no. 20 (1992), pp. 34-43.

The system of serfdom could count nevertheless on various supporters even in the age of Enlightenment[20]. The idea of emancipation was met with particular hostility by M. Shcherbatov. In 1768 he submitted to the Free Economic Society a document written in French, signed as «a citizen of the world»[21], in which he depicted the possibility of liberating the Russian serfs as the most devastating perspective for Russian society.

The solution for the menace of hunger and «*dorogovizna*» had instead to be found in the technical improvement of agricultural labour or in a better distribution of workers and similar measures, while the peasants should be left in the condition in which they had long been. These ideas were reiterated in other works, particularly that entitled 'Razmyshlenie o neudobstvakh v Rossii dat' svobodu krest'ianam i sluzhiteliam, ili sdelat' sobstvennost' imenii'[22].

The movement advocating the abolition of serfdom gained new momentum with Alexander's accession to the throne. A few enlightened writers expressed their disapproval for the institution of serfdom and highlighted its incompatibility with natural law and the correct economic development of their country. They raised once again the question of moral responsibility on the part of Russian landowners. Appealing to the good disposition of the Tsar, I.P. Pnin in his 'Opyt o prosveshchenii otnositel'no k Rossii' (1804), V.V. Popugaev in 'O blagopoluchii narodnykh tel' (1801-1802), A.S. Kaisarov in the 'Dissertatio inauguralis philosophico-politica de manumittendis per russiam servis' fully endorsed the perspective of the elimination of serfdom in Russia[23].

It is possible to identify two specific features in Malinovskii's approach to the problem of serfdom. On the one hand the Russian thinker managed to insert it in the context of a larger scheme, as part of the vast task that he intended to undertake towards a reform of the entire Russian society; on the other hand he consistently related the question of emancipation to the other centre of gravity of his thought: the problem of the elimination of war[24].

---

[20] See P. Kolchin, 'In Defence of Servitude: American Proslavery and Russian Proserfdom Arguments, 1760-1860', *American Historical Review*, LXXXV (1980), pp. 809-827.

[21] Published as 'Zapiska po krest'ianskomu voprosu', in M.M. Shcherbatov, *Neizdannye sochineniia*, ed. N. Rubinshtein (Moskva, 1935), pp. 3-15.

[22] The text was first published in *Chteniia Moskovskogo Obshchestva istorii i drevnostei rossiiskikh*, III (1861).

[23] These works are gathered and discussed in I.Ia. Shchipanov (ed.), *Russkie prosvetiteli ot Radishcheva do Dekabristov*, I (Moskva, 1966).

[24] In his 'Dissertatio inauguralis philosophico-politica de manumittendis per russiam servis', which appeared in Göttingen in 1806, A. Kaisarov advocated the liberation of the

His *Rassuzhdenie* Part III is the work in which we find that integration with problems of a different nature which is generally lacking in other places. Here the author shows how, once the main obstacle to human happiness is removed from the world scene, the next objective, in terms of importance, is the status of the peasants. It is not surprising to see how, to his eyes, the servile system presented a number of affinities with war as a general phenomenon: they were both historically unjustified, ethically unacceptable and economically disastrous, they were kept alive by a series of prejudices in bad faith, which claimed them to be, in turn, a necessary evil, a stabilizing element, a condition assuring a sense of continuity with the past, and served, in reality, the interests of a very limited share of the population.

The theoretical treatment of these two evils of his time is somewhat similar, and it appears clear that also the effects expected from their elimination were equally important in shaping Malinovskii's model of an ideal society. Creating good Russian citizens in the political sense, active and dedicated members of a national[25] and supra-national community, was an aspiration to be achieved primarily by promoting a reform of rural relations and by making that half of the Russian population living in state of slavery (as he observed in the 'Zapiska') a free and responsible class of people, well-integrated with the rest of society.

Malinovskii's ideas on peace affected his response to the peasant question and deepened his disapproval of the state of subjection in which the peasants lived. The connection between the two problems had been clear to Malinovskii since 1782, the year in which he wrote his first condemnation of war. In the same fragment is contained in fact also his first deprecation of serfdom, in which he highlighted the cruelty of the serfowner and his lack of gratitude towards the person who is considered his «*brat*» [26].

Russian serfs in the name of humanity and reason. Dedicated to Alexander I, the dissertation never appeared in Russia (the text was recently published in Russian under the title 'Ob osvobozhdenii krepostnykh v Rossii', in Shchipanov, *op.cit.,* I). This is one of the few works in which the problem of war is mentioned in the treatment of the theme of abolition of serfdom (*ibid.*, p. 362). The impact of war on the existence and consolidation of serfdom is however considered much less central than in Malinovskii's work.

[25] The idea of personal freedom as a necessary premise to patriotism is one of Malinovskii's key ideas. It was developed also by other enlightened writers, particularly V.V. Popugaev in his 'O blagopoluchii narodnykh tel' (1801-1802) (in Shchipanov, *op. cit.*, I, p. 288).

[26] The importance of the manuscript (RGALI, Fond 312, op. 1, no. 1, f.1) with respect to the peasant question attracted the attention of Meilakh (*Pushkin i ego epokha* (Moskva, 1958), p. 34).

Malinovskii's ideas on serf emancipation as they appear in the four works which we are going to consider show a distinct and significant position, developed over the course of several years of reflection on the same theme. Their treatment varies in the four works, according to the different space-time context and to the nature of the documents, while the emphasis is put each time on different aspects of the same problem. The nucleus of thought remains nevertheless the same.

Isolating the corpus of ideas on the peasant question will inevitably imply a certain degree of abstraction from what is the general system of Malinovskii's ideas. Only one of these texts is specifically devoted to the problem, his 'Zapiska o osvobozhdenii rabov'. In *Pustynnik* his statements on the specific problem represent, if not digressions, only a single aspect of the contents of the *povest'*; in his 'Razmyshlenie' they are inseparably connected with his plan for a general reform of the Russian state. An attempt will nevertheless be made in order to give an idea of the original integration, in Malinovskii's thought, of the specific issue in the general scheme.

It is not superfluous to point out that as his position evolved Malinovskii could count on a number of advantages denied to most of his contemporaries: he was familiar with the economical situation at the periphery of the Empire and abroad; he had a theoretical knowledge of agriculture and manufactures; he was able to integrate his proposals into a global vision incorporating many other problems. He was also spiritually close to the peasants, and deeply sympathetic to their needs, as shown particularly in private documents[27].

3.3. An analysis of four works

3.3.1. Pustynnik

The *povest' Pustynnik*, written in 1799, represents Malinovskii's first contribution to the question of serfdom. It does not contain a concrete programme of reforms aimed at removing it once and for all from Russia,

---

[27] In one of the letters devoted to his «Ufa project» we find the following statement: «then also in the peasant we will find a colleague and interlocutor or a fellow member and assistant» (see p. 63 of the present work).

but only a series of moral prescriptions meant to modify the cultural and spiritual context making its existence legitimate.

In the years immediately preceding Alexander I's reign, the system of serf labour seemed still strongly rooted on Russian estates, and the idea of the serfs as human beings having the same rights as other members of Russian society was met with hostility. A long and difficult process seemed to be necessary to establish a new way of perceiving the relations between landowners and peasants. Malinovskii was one of the intellectuals who believed that that process would require the formation of a new generation of Russian noblemen, aware of their privileges and developing a sense of moral commitment towards society as a whole, for the common good. The need to proceed first to a deep reformation of the social conscience of the landowners was thus the impulse inspiring this work, which was also Malinovskii's first and apparently unique experiment in the field of pure fiction. The novel represents his attempt to reconcile two realities equally necessary to the economic life of Russia and to prepare the ground for decisive reforms, suggesting simultaneously the necessity of an immediate mitigation of the tragic conditions of the serfs.

Bearing in mind Malinovskii's subsequent, more radical works on the same subject elaborated during Alexander's reign, it is difficult to believe that the moralistic statements contained in *Pustynnik* described exhaustively the author's position, even at this early stage. Information on the circumstances in which the *povest'* was written, together with a consideration of the unfavourable historical time, can help to clarify the spirit in which it was conceived.

Its composition dates back to 1799, the same year in which Malinovskii had the idea of founding a periodical bearing the title of this *povest'*. That project was never realized, and it is difficult to say now to what extent the periodical issued later, *Osennie vechera*, followed the original plan. Certainly *Pustynnik* and *Osennie vechera* were initiatives oriented in the same direction: to educate a large public by illustrating the correct position to hold on many social and political problems affecting contemporary Russia.

The edifying prescriptions of Malinovskii's hermit never reached the Russian reader: the novel remained in manuscript for almost two centuries, and its first publication, in Arab-Ogly's edition, in 1958, was incomplete. The editor published only three chapters, those entitled 'Besplodnyi brak', 'Sel'skoe khoziaistvo', 'Prazdnost' i roskosh''. The other three chapters, still unpublished, bear the titles 'Vstuplenie v gorod' (I), 'Tserkov' i uchilishche'

(II), and 'Sonfrantsuzy' (VI)[28]. As shown by the titles, the six sections
intended to cover some of the most controversial aspects of Russian social
life of the time. Depicting scenes ranging from the church to the village and
the city, the author intended to construct the *povest'* as a series of
opportunities for the hermit to condemn or admonish his contemporaries,
initiating a fierce polemic with those responsible for the major evils of
Russian society.

The decision to recur to a fictional genre for this passionate appeal to
the best part of Russian aristocratic society led Malinovskii to adopt some of
the features of the «*sentimental'naia povest'*» in vogue at the time[29]. The
predominantly edifying, didactic character of this work, however, places it
at the boundaries with proper publicistic writing[30]. Malinovskii's decision to
choose the figure of the *pustynnik* as the moralizing voice of his novel
could hardly be seen as original. His use of the hermit, however, is not
without interest.

In Western literature this hero was frequently chosen to illustrate the
idea that the edification of the human soul was possible only in a life of
solitary contemplation, after a rejection of the vanity of the world. The
circumstances leading to this refusal varied significantly according to the
individual personality of the author or the literary age in which the work
was written[31]. Russian literature of the eighteenth century offered a number
of variations on this theme. Among them it may be worth mentioning two
examples.

In 1788 a short story entitled *Pustynnik* appeared on the pages of the
journal *Detskoe chtenie dlia serdtsa i razuma*. A close examination of this
novel, presented as a translation from French, led A.G. Cross in recent
years to conclude that its author is N. Karamzin[32]. As he points out,

---

[28] See the manuscript in IRLI, F. 244, op. 25, no. 307, ff. 25-55.

[29] The entire tale is focused on individual emotional reactions, frequently emphasized
by a strategic use of tears: they are quick to appear in the eyes of the repentant *pomeshchik*
and are shown as an evidence of his wife's unhappy and bored life.

[30] The use of sentimental devices combined in a particular way with civic
commitment in works such as *Puteshestvie iz Peterburga v Moskvu* or the less radical tale
Filon (1796) by I.I. Martynov. For a discussion of these problems, see P.A. Orlov,
Russkii sentimentalizm (Moskva, 1977), in particular the chapter 'Demokraticheskii
sentimentalizm'. See also N.D. Kochetkova, 'Geroi russkogo sentimentalizma', *XVIII
vek*, XIV (1983), pp. 121-142.

[31] For the treatment of this theme in European literature, see J. Fitzell, *The Hermit in
German Literature* (Chapel Hill, 1961), particularly chapter II, 'The Hermit and Society',
and R.D. Mayo, *The English Novel in the Magazines 1740-1815* (Evanstone, Ill., 1962).

[32] A.G. Cross, 'Karamzin's First Short Story?', in L.H. Legters (ed.), *Russia.
Essays in History and Literature* (Leiden, 1972).

Karamzin's 'Pustynnik' «is neither a hermit or an anchorite, but rather a 'country-dweller'», who decides to live in seclusion after unfortunate spiritual experiences[33]. Before Karamzin, A. Sumarokov had written a drama bearing the same title[34].

Malinovskii's tale, however, seems to stand apart from this European and Russian tradition: the setting of his life as a hermit is not described here, neither do we know anything about his previous life and the reasons behind his rejection of the world. This hermit does not act as an element isolated from the rest of society[35]; on the contrary, he firmly believes in the possibility of fighting successfully against the evils of society and appealing to the best part of the human soul. The relevant move, for Malinovskii's *pustynnik*, is thus from reclusion to action; his hero revitalizes the literary convention by embodying some of the most progressive ideas of his time on subjects like education, faith, economics and fashion.

The hermit, about whom we only know that he lived long «*v glubokom uedinenii*» (in deep solitude)[36], decides to visit a famous town: «withdrawal from the world had not diminished his love for his fellow humans, but rather increased his pity for their vices and misfortunes, the less he felt this twofold burden upon himself, the more he noticed how onerous it was to others»[37]. In the chapter entitled 'Besplodnyi brak' the hero of the *povest'* is introduced by a noblewoman into a magnificent house. At the beginning of the chapter the reader had been introduced to his speculations about the outcome of the abstract duel between luxury and poverty. In the noblewoman's house the hermit can face the more evident illustration of that juxtaposition between indigence and luxury[38]. He explains to his hosts how this opposition is strictly connected with another, that between industry and sloth: not knowing the real value of their wealth,

---

[33] *Ibid.*, p. 40.

[34] The one-act drama *Pustynnik*, centered on the figure of a Christian hermit, was written in 1757.

[35] The theme of isolation from society recurs frequently in Malinovskii's intellectual biography. See its appearance in the «Ufa project» and its last incarnation in the life at the Tsarskoe Selo Lycée.

[36] IRLI, Fond 244, op. 25, no. 307, f. 5.

[37] *Ibid.*. Seemingly, one of the reasons leading this figure to leave his life as a hermit was the danger represented for Europe by Napoleon: we read that «He was particularly alarmed by the general rumour of terrible calamities, which were spreading through the whole of Europe, and laying entire states and countries to waste: he wished to discover the reasons for it» (IRLI, Fond 244, op. 25, no. 307, ff. 5-6). The last chapter ('Sonfrantsuzy') also contains precise indications in this sense.

[38] About the centrality of this subject in Malinovskii's personal life, see the present work, pp. 61-62.

the Russian noblemen do not know with whom to share the advantages deriving from it and are constantly in search of vain occupations with the single aim of dissipating it.

The entire novel is imbued with a sense of sympathy for the weakest and poorest part of Russian society. The participation of the hermit in the fate of the Russian peasant reaches its climax in the chapter entitled 'Sel'skoe khoziaistvo', which is entirely devoted to this theme. Here the hermit compares the artificial grace and richness of the noblemen's garden and house with the scene of dirt and degradation which confronts him as soon as he sets foot in an *izba* of the village. A baby in dirty rags cries in his bed because the blind old woman who is supposed to look after him is not even able to give him the bottle of milk[39]. When the hermit asks why the mother of the baby is not with him, the old woman replies that she is *«out for the barshchina»* [40]. The sympathetic observer turns then his report into a passionate act of accusation, if not of the entire servile system, at least of the abuses allowed even by the noblest representatives of the landowning class:

> How can you, such gentle and kind masters, be indifferent to the so wretched, pitiful state of your peasants, your breadwinners, to whom you are obliged for all the plenty and wealth you have! (...) All your peasants are like your children, entrusted to your care (...) Having neither will, nor knowledge, in their obedience and ignorance, they are like real children, they do nothing for themselves (...) The fatherland itself, allowing you such limitless power, demands from you an attitude in keeping with it (pp. 141-142).

The theme of the necessary gratitude of the landowner towards the *«krest'ianin-kormilets»* (peasant-breadwinner) echoed reflections which were not new in the criticism of serfdom and which were destined to survive particularly strongly in the populist theories developed a few decades later. The vision of the peasant as deserving the particulare care of the landowner, being the most vital member of society, upon whom depends the state of the entire homeland, was particularly familiar to Malinovskii.

---

[39] See similar depictions of the Russian *izba* in Radishchev's *Puteshestvie iz Peterburga v Moskvu*, in the chapter entitled 'Peshki', and in 'Otryvok puteshestviia v *** I *** T ***', which appeared in *Zhivopisets* in 1772 (I, no. 5).

[40] V.F. Malinovskii, *Izbrannye obshchestvenno-politicheskie sochineniia*, p. 140. Further references are made by page number to this edition. The *barshchina* was the labour that the Russian serf was obliged to perform for his landowner.

With respect to the concrete prescriptions to mitigate the cruelty of the current situation, about which information is requested by the landowners, the hermit suggests:

> So live in the country and learn by experience! Find good neighbours and listen to them, books themselves[41] can help you, but best of all choose clever, hardworking and honest people from among your peasants and consult with them. Your labours will be rewarded by your own and your peasants' prosperity (p. 142).

Believing in the possibility of converting the two noblemen to the right cause, the hermit invites them to abandon any other vain concern: «allow yourself a rest from the various concerns of luxury and vanity» (p. 138). His sermon comprises attacks against superficiality, superstition, fashion, and depravation, but is something more than an attempt to put the noblemen at peace with their conscience. Malinovskii's hero has polemical words for the official religion that can only recommend prayer, and suggests instead being effectively closer to the peasants and the adoption of concrete measures to modify the conditions of the poor.

Quite typically, considering Malinovskii's intellectual biography, in the fourth chapter his criticism of Russian society turns into an exaltation of the English way of life, characterized by a healthy connection between the love for agriculture and correct social manners, in an ideal sequel to the analysis offered in his 'Rossiianin v Anglii' and in the first two parts of the *Rassuzhdenie*.

If compared with the *Rassuzhdenie* Part III and the other two works on the same subject, Malinovskii's condemnation of current rural relationships in Russia is characterized in *Pustynnik* by a stronger moralizing attitude and a less reasoned rigour; it represents, however, an interesting starting point, which leads quite soon to a more consistent and radical position.

3.3.2. 'Zapiska o osvobozhdenii rabov'

The 'Zapiska o osvobozhdenii rabov', written in 1802, assures Malinovskii of a special place in the history of the debate on the emancipation of Russian peasants. At the end of the nineteenth century V.I.

---

[41] The 'books' are probably the technical treatises dealing with practical agriculture, which had, as we have seen, so great a success in those years.

Semevskii first published fragments of this work[42]. In his fundamental study on the peasant problem the Russian scholar devoted only one page to Malinovskii's project; he managed nevertheless to highlight its importance and to integrate it into the history of the debate preceding the Emancipation.

In the evolution of Malinovskii's specific thought regarding this problem, the 'Zapiska' represents a transcending of the moralistic position he adopted in *Pustynnik* [43] and the most explicit expression of his anti-feudal ideas. It has to be seen in close relationship with his 'Razmyshlenie o preobrazovanii gosudarstvennogo ustroistva Rossii'[44], and with *Rassuzhdenie* Part III, with which it shares a vision of slavery as engendered by war.

The brief work, a sort of pamphlet entirely devoted to the theme of peasant freedom, was written in November 1802, during Malinovskii's stay in Jassy, and was addressed to the attention of Russian public opinion in the person of a particularly influential figure on the political scene of those years, Count V. Kochubei. This old friend since the time of the London mission was now the Minister of Home Affairs and was playing an important role in the work of the Secret Committee. Soon after Alexander's accession to the throne substantial reforms of a liberal character had been enacted, and constitutional projects had been taken up, in conformity with the progressive ideas[45] of the young Emperor. But a constitution could be enacted only after an administrative reorganization had been carried out. On 24 June 1801 Alexander secretly convened a committee of four persons, A.A. Czartoryski, N.N. Novosil'tsev, P.A. Stroganov and Kochubei, asking

---

[42] V.I. Semevskii, *Krest'ianskii vopros v Rossii v XVIII i pervoi polovine XIX veka* (Spb., 1888), p. 431.

[43] The passages referring to the suffering faces of the peasants re-echo nevertheless the touching strains of *Pustynnik*.

[44] The 'Zapiska' is written as a reply to a question Malinovskii asked himself about Russia: «in what lies her greatest deficiency?» (*Izbrannye obshchestvenno-politicheskie sochineniia*, p. 111). 'Razmyshlenie o preobrazovanii gosudarstvennogo ustroistva Rossii' is structured as a reply to the same question: it opens with the statement: «Russia lacks people, laws, enlightenment, old generals» (V. Semevskii, 'Razmyshlenie V.F. Malinovskogo o preobrazovanii gosudarstvennogo ustroistva Rossii', *Golos minuvshego*, no. 10 (1915), p. 115).

[45] Several studies have been devoted to the reforms during Alexander I's reign. See particularly A. Mc Connell,' Alexander I's Hundred Days: The Politics of a Paternalistic reformer', *Slavic Review*, no. 3 (1969), pp. 373-393; S.V. Mironenko, *Samoderzhavie i reformy. Politicheskaia bor'ba v Rossii v nachale XIX v.* (Moskva, 1989); M.M. Safonov, *Problema reform v pravitel'stvennoi politike Rossii na rubezhe XVIII i XIX vv.* (Leningrad, 1988).

them to draw up a report on conditions in Russia and to sketch an outline of urgently needed administrative reforms[46].

One of the problems on which the informal body was engaged was serfdom, with all its accompanying evils; its abolition or retention had to be discussed with caution, since so much for the future of the Empire was at stake. Malinovskii's contribution to the search for a solution is represented by his 'Zapiska' and by 'Razmyshlenie o preobrazovanii gosudarstvennogo ustroistva Rossii'.

The document, a pseudo-personal work with references to autobiographical details, was accompanied by a letter in which Malinovskii emphasized how favourable the historical conditions were, pointing out that his reflections had their indispensable premises in the «well-known philanthropic inclinations of the sovereign emperor»[47]. He believed that the time was ripe in Russia for a direct attack on the institution of serfdom. This consideration explains the character of urgency deeply affecting his presentation of the problem. Malinovskii hoped that his note would have an immediate effect upon the search for a solution to the peasant question.

Most of the rhetorical incisiveness of this article is anticipated in the title itself, in the formulation *«osvobozhdenie rabov»* (the liberation of the slaves), which is later reiterated in the text. Neither the use of the word *«osvobozhdenie»* or that of *«rab»* was particularly original in the context of the debate on serfdom: the reference to the Russian peasant as a slave had been in fact a topos in the criticism of the feudal order since the time of the Free Economic Society's essay of 1766 on peasant property[48]. It is, however, the juxtaposition of the two words[49] which makes Malinovskii's formulation particularly effective. He explained his definition, emphasizing the importance of freedom for the development of a national awareness:

> People, who are not glad of their existence, who drag through their lives
> against their will, in labour and want - that is the essence of a slave. Fellow

---

[46] The work of the Committee is examined in detail by Safonov also in his 'Protokoly Neglasnogo komiteta', *Vspomogatel'nye istoricheskie distsipliny*, VII (1976), pp. 191-209.

[47] *Izbrannye obshchestvenno-politicheskie sochineniia*, p. 161. Further references are made by page number to this edition.

[48] The application of this word to Russian peasants is typical, for example, of the proposal of A.Ia. Polenov, 'O krepostnom sostoianii krest'ian v Rossii', in I.Ia. Shchipanov (ed.), *Izbrannye proizvedeniia russkikh myslitelei vtoroi poloviny XVIII v.*, II (Moskva, 1952). The general point of reference was black slavery, a theme of great impact in European culture as early as the mid-century, which was reflected inevitably in the Russian debate on serfdom as well.

[49] It echoes another title in the *Rassuzhdenie* Part III, 'Osvobozhdenie narodov'.

> countrymen and Christian kindred are slaves, live like prisoners in our
> fatherland, alienated from all its rights and privileges and even from the
> protection and care of laws in respect of property and the very security of
> life (p. 111).

The need for the freedom of these people is thus seen by Malinovskii as the essence of the problem, which it is now possible to recognize and overcome, preparing the way for the solution of other major problems affecting Russia:

> Now, when the government is trying through all its measures to
> consolidate the prosperity of Russia, we must pose the question: in what
> lies her greatest deficiency? In inhabitants - to populate the many fertile
> lands that are lying empty. Various means have been tried to relieve this
> shortage, neither effort nor expense has been spared, but the one most
> important thing has been left, for which the present time has grown ripe.
> The liberation of the slaves! Freedom is the air essential to human
> existence, not only for its multiplication, but also for its preservation (p.
> 111).

In the analysis contained in this brief work, Malinovskii did not hide, first of all, his negative evaluation of what had been the state policy since that time:

> These institutions, commands and various orders for supervising the relief
> of the slavish condition by landowners are weak medicines, which
> temporarily soothe the pain (p. 112)[50].

This represents a considerable move away from his previous faith in the good will of the Russian *pomeshchiki*, as expressed in *Pustynnik*.

Partly shaping his rhetorical devices to meet the possible expectations of his authoritative interlocutor, Malinovskii produces the devastating perspective of a peasant rebellion similar to that which occurred in Russia in 1797, if adequate measures were not taken in time by the government. Repression was not the right way to to solve the problem:

> Settlements are destroyed by fire and sword, prayers and pleas are
> restrained by the whip and by exile. But have not sparks remained under
> the ashes, cannot the flame flare up? (p. 112) [51].

---

[50] He seems to refer here to a decree of 1797, promulgated by Paul I, according to which the compulsory work done by the peasants for the landowners should have been limited to three days a week and forbidden on Sundays.

[51] It should be noted that this affirmation bears an explicit anti-revolutionary meaning. The image of the spark symbolizing revolution was used elsewhere by Malinovskii: «(...) for every revolution weaves itself a nest in the hearts of people, who are deprived of a lawful way to demonstrate their sorrows and griefs, like a spark hiding itself in the cinders»

Malinovskii's discussion of the theme of serfdom is particularly interesting and original in its explicit connection with two other major problems affecting Russia: the bad population distribution and the evils of war. The necessity of *«razmnozhenie naroda»* (the multiplication of the people) was one of the main concerns of his time[52], and Malinovskii is persuaded that «the multiplication of the people goes hand in hand with its prosperity and the devastation of the land with the misfortunes of its inhabitants» (p. 111). The disgraceful state of slavery affecting more than half the Russian population appears thus as counterproductive also when searching to find a remedy for the illogical and unproductive settlement of people in Russia.

Malinovskii then sketches a brief historical excursus on the institution of serfdom in order to show how its appearance in Russia represents nothing but another negative effect of war: it was the necessity to escape conscription that limited the peasants' freedom of movement and let them become in this way a possession of the Russian landowners.

> The grandfathers and great grandfathers of the grandees and powerful nobles of the present (...) did not know of serfs (...) Influenced by war and the necessities of the times, the ordinance of the census made the peasant stay with one landowner, depriving him of the right to transfer freely to another, and in the same way the mutual agreements on lodging and labour came to an end (p. 112).

The depiction of serfdom as an anti-historical phenomenon for Russia, which could be almost entirely ascribed to war, leads Malinovskii to reflect on the measures which are to be taken parallel to the emancipation of the peasants. Therefore an important part of his project is devoted to illustrating the necessity of reorganizing recruitment in Russia according to new principles and taking advantage of the temporary state of peace after the Treaty of Amiens.

In Malinovskii's interpretation the reforms should not be undertaken in the name of mere economic reasons of immediate convenience, as had occurred in several projects in the previous decades, neither on the basis of a pious and paternalistic appeal to a moral obligation on the part of the

---

(letter quoted in G.S. Grosul, *Dunaiskie kniazhestva v politike Rossii. 1774-1806* (Kishinev, 1975), p. 203).

[52] We find the same observation in Kaisarov, who identifies the major obstacle to reproduction in the fact that the Russian peasants are «deprived of freedom and property» ('Ob osvobozhdenii krepostnykh v Rossii', in Shchipanov, *Russkie prosvetiteli ot Radishcheva do Dekabristov*, I, p. 370).

landowners. They must take place for the future general benefit of the entire Russian population, and will themselves provide the basis for that *«razmnozhenie naroda»*. Malinovskii sums up his project and the way to implement it. It should be a gradual process, to be carried out through a governmental *ukaz*, and it should take the needs of the peasants as well as the satisfaction of the landowners into account:

> A commission specially instituted for this great undertaking can manage its completion without any intervention. On the chosen day of this renewal of Russia (...) the destruction of slavery by the lawful power of government will be proclaimed throughout its expanse by appropriate officials in towns and villages. Due to the necessity to maintain order, serfs serving at their masters' homes must spend about a month in their former state of obedience under the protection of the government. The move from the land should not be allowed suddenly, but after several months (p. 113).

Certainly the liberation of serfs could have positive repercussions also on general economic development, promoting a higher productivity of the Russian land. In this respect, Malinovskii feels the need to criticize one of the «false causes» frequently proposed for the insufficient productivity of agricultural labour: the supposed idleness of Russian peasants[53].

> The Russian is not idle, neither does a warm climate change him, but slavery is the cause of his remissness. When there is no inner impulse to labour, only the stick can give it, and when it is used, no work is done without it (p. 114).

An interesting and controversial point is represented by Malinovskii's proposal to solve the specific problem of the bad population distribution in the country. He considers favourably the perspective of transferring people from one place to another in order to reshape the boundaries between inhabited and desert territories in Russia in a more productive way[54]. The problem is that

> Resettlements organized by landowners are rarely successful; they always have the aspect of an exile. With this thought everyone parts from his homeland and arrives at the new home without the inclination or impulse to work, and manages in some fashion or other the allotted portion of fields, considering himself foreign to them; but a free man is not like this;

---

[53] Stated almost a century earlier by Pososhkov («Peasant life is meagre from no other cause than their own idleness») (Kafengauz, *op. cit.*, p. 242), the idea had strongly survived in the arguments of some defenders of serfdom contemporary to Malinovskii.

[54] On the problem of population policy, see R. Bartlett, *Human Capital. The Settlement of Foreigners in Russia 1762-1804* (Cambridge, 1979), particularly chapter 6, 'Immigration and Colonies.1797-1804'.

> confident in his control and ownership of the land, he hurries to the new
> place full of curiosity, expecting greater benefits from his labours there (p.
> 114).

This is also one of the two passages of the 'Zapiska' in which
Malinovskii mentions a crucial point, that of peasants' land tenure. Here he
seems to favour the idea of a *«sobstvennost' zemli»* (ownership of the land).
In the other passage he says something different:

> By establishing a rule, that state lands, newly set aside for settlement,
> should belong to the landowner whose peasants settle it, the nobles will
> undergo no loss, nor damage, nor destruction (p. 113).

Semevskii rightly highlighted the contradiction between the two
statements quoted above, but assumed that with the claim to peasants' tenure
Malinovskii probably intended only the right to work the land[55]. This
reductive interpretation of Malinovskii's position about peasants' land
tenure, based on an assumption which is not supported by the evidence,
probably affected the subsequent undervaluation of the contribution made
by this thinker to the problem of serfdom.

It is certainly true that, as the title of the work stresses quite clearly,
priority is here given to the emancipation of the peasants, and that
Malinovskii maintains a certain degree of ambiguity about the other aspect.
But equally unquestionable is the fact that the assignment of land to
everybody is an idea which is particularly important in Malinovskii's
general vision of the problem, as can be seen from his position in the
Rassuzhdenie and in *Pustynnik*. It will remain a central notion later as well,
as his diaries show.

3.3.3. 'Razmyshlenie o preobrazovanii gosudarstvennogo ustroistva Rossii'

From May to October 1803, after his return from Moldavia, and in
the context of a wide-ranging interest in the fate of Russia, Malinovskii

---

[55] «Apparently, by the last words he intends only the right to unimpeded use of the
land on condition of meticulous fulfillment of the conditions, agreed with the landowner»
(V.I. Semevskii, *Krest'ianskii vopros v Rossii v XVIII i pervoi polovine XIX veka*, p.
431).

recorded in his *dnevnik* [56] his speculations about the reforms needed in his country. The fragmentary, non-homogeneous character of these pages, where some issues are given an elaborate treatment and others merely mentioned en passant, is one of their fascinating features: Malinovskii investigates once again the reasons for the Russian anomalies and in a few cases his thought takes the shape of a list of *«nedostatki»* (shortcomings) affecting his country.

The constitutional transformations of Russia are the aspect to which Malinovskii pays most attention. The idea of creating a representative government was shared by Alexander I himself and the group of refomers around him[57]. Malinovskii's position on the subject is stated here extremely clearly and is the typical stance of an enlightened liberal:

> It is necessary to assemble deputies who will consider the shortcomings and abuses of the whole empire, advise on their relief and draw up a reliable government, and the permanent laws appropriate for it. Otherwise Russia will be lost, ruling itself with temporary injunctions, each breaking another (...) The assembly of deputies (...) will establish a secure basis for general prosperity[58].

The attempt to plan a more democratic organization for the Russian state leads Malinovskii quite naturally to the treatment of the peasant question as one of the major obstacles to its realization. The part of the diary devoted to it is not long, but is nevertheless significant. Malinovskii complains about the poor state of agriculture in Russia and the desperate conditions of the peasants and again condemns the feudal system. As in the *Zapiska*, important stress is put here on the urgent character that the

---

[56] After Semevskii's and Arab-Ogly's publication, the diary was republished recently in I.Ia. Shchipanov (ed.), *Russkie prosvetiteli ot Radishcheva do Dekabristov*, I, pp. 249-270.

[57] Before his accession to the throne the young Alexander had confided to Czartoryski, La Harpe and Count Kochubei his dream of giving a constitution to his country (See A. Gielgud (ed.), *Memoirs of Prince Adam Czartoryski and His Correspondence with Alexander I*, 2 vols. (London, 1888)). The politics of his first years included the abolition of torture, the release of thousands of prisoners, the confirmation of the Charter to the Nobility. The project of giving a proper constitution was nevertheless not carried out. His interest in constitutional problems such as the separation of powers, the participation of educated members of society in the government, the election of officials and the establishment of forums for public opinions, were recurring features not only for the constitutions he fostered or installed abroad (in Finland, 1809, France, 1814, Switzerland and Poland, 1815, the Germanies, 1818-9), but also in the discussions of projects for Russia repeatedly promoted by him (with Rosenkampf in 1804, Speranskii in 1807-12 and Novosil'tsev in 1818-20).

[58] *Izbrannye obshchestvenno-politicheskie sochineniia*, p. 121. Further references are made by page number to this edition.

measures against serfdom must have: «It is necessary to think about liberation in good time: slavery is the instigator of uprising and mutinies» (p. 119).

Following Alexander I's *ukaz* of 1803 about the «volnye khlebopashtsy», whereby landowners were empowered to free their serfs, provided that certain conditions were fulfilled, the debate on serfdom had entered a delicate, though more advanced, phase. That measure is mentioned by Malinovskii to introduce his own proposal, where he highlights a particularly weak point in Alexander's *ukaz*:

> There is a decree about liberation through redemption with the agreement of the landowner. Enough rich peasants and extravagant landowners will be found. But it is necessary to avoid quarrels: some will ask a lot for discharge, others will be reluctant to give it. Would it not be better to fix in law the price of paying off and renting the land, and decisively legalize it so that anyone fulfilling the condition indicated may be liberated without deferring to the agreement of the landowner? (p. 119).

The most interesting aspect of Malinovskii's scheme is his idea that the landowner's consent for the emancipation of his peasants should not be obligatory. His deep knowledge of the transformations in rural relationships occurring in other European countries gives him the opportunity to highlight another point, which was to be a central theme in the debate of the subsequent decades: the emancipation of the peasants must take place with land:

> Legislation must be cautious, so as not to introduce into Russia, as has happened in other European countries, landless peasants, called small people in Germany and in England cottagers, because apart from their shacks and kitchen gardens they have nothing. This change occurred there due to the increase in land tax. Finding themselves unable to pay it they sold their lands and from masters they turned into agricultural workers or dispersed to the towns and furthered the development of factories and manufactures, which date from this time (p. 120).

Incidentally, this theme offers Malinovskii the opportunity to take part once again in the polemic about the mutual relationship of agriculture and industrial activities in a country like Russia:

> Russia, because of its expanse, not only benefits from but needs its lands worked, in preference to all other occupations, which, in common with commerce, must be kept at a moderate level in relation to the encouragement of agriculture, and have as their only object that of giving proprietors somewhere to market their products (p. 120).

When the text of the diary was published, in 1915, Semevskii failed to stress the advanced character of Malinovskii's proposals for emancipation, although he recognized that he was aware of the necessity of this measure[59]. Probably Malinovskii's being in favour of the assignation of the land to everybody (without the landowner's assent) did not catch Semevskii's attention partly because he did not have access to other works in which this theme was treated. Full confirmation of his progressive approach would have been available to the Russian historian if he had examined Part III of the *Rassuzhdenie*.

Emancipating the peasants with land would imply introducing a redemption fee *(otkup)*. Malinovskii enters into complicated estimations concerning this problem, not without considering other aspects of the question:

> Many landowners want to retain their seignorial lands: used to farming and being expert at it, they can retain their lands to society's benefit. Besides, others would have nothing to do in the country without farming (p. 120).

Another argument advanced by Malinovskii is the moral obligation towards emancipation:

> He who loves virtue and the fatherland must strive to end slavery. It spoils the disposition of the Russian (...). On the one hand, people become accustomed to unlimited will, on the other, to submission and a blind obedience. Licence and fear are the fruits of slavery. The difference in the higher orders' treatment of subordinate foreigners and Russians results from the latter being customarily seen as slaves (pp. 120-121).

Only emancipation can thus radically transform the nature of the relationships among all members of Russian society.

---

[59] He mentioned Malinovskii's «recognition of the inevitability of the liberation of serfs» (V. Semevskii, 'Razmyshlenie V.F. Malinovskogo o preobrazovanii gosudarstvennogo ustroistva Rossii', p. 246), but only to repeat the opinion he had expressed years before: referring to his own presentation of Malinovski's 'Zapiska o osvobozhdenii rabov' in the volume *Krest'ianskii vopros v Rossii,* he reiterated that «he proposes the destruction of serfdom and allows the movement of peasants, but without speaking of their endowment with land, only advising that the commission established for this great affair should try to forestall abuses», *ibid.*.

Malinovskii's unequivocally pro-peasant position in those years is also documented in the letters sent at that time to the Moldavian metropolit (V.A. Urechia, *Istoria rominilor*, XI, pp. 24-27).

3.3.4. 'Rassuzhdenie o mire i voine' Part III

Part III of the *Rassuzhdenie o mire i voine* is entirely devoted to the search for the concrete measures necessary to provide the condition of «*blagoustroistvo*» (good order) which can lead to the general «*blagodenstvie*» (prosperity) of peoples. One of the proposals on which the Russian thinker particularly focuses his attention is that regarding the problem of the land.

In the chapter specifically devoted to this subject are found Malinovskii's most articulate arguments in favour of emancipation. Unlike *Pustynnik*, where his appeal is addressed to the conscience, and the two other works, dictated by a contingent necessity to enter into practical details about the implementation of his projects in Russia, here we find a desire to give general directives, in keeping with the theoretical depth informing the entire treatise on peace.

It is not without significance that the title under which we find his proposal on the peasant question is 'Razdelenie zemel": Malinovskii echoes the title of the preceding chapter, 'Razdelenie iazykov' (devoted to the idea of regrouping the European peoples) to highlight the continuity of thought and intentional commitment to a global vision, in which these sorts of problems do not concern single countries, but large communities. Inserted in the context of a treatise on peace, Malinovskii's ideas on the land are presented as necessarily subordinate to those on war:

> A consideration of the apportionment of land to each family in a region is not a digression from the main subject of peace and war, but a consequence of it, in so far as the structure of the whole depends on the accord of its constituent parts. Peace is not well founded from without, when within rich and poor wage war throughout Europe[60].

The central idea on which the chapter is focused is thus «udel zemli kazhdomu semeistvu»: the assignation of land to every family, avoiding those conflicts deriving from social differences. A more egalitarian possession of the land could positively affect various aspects of the relationship between the citizen and the state, and make it more stable and effective. First of all, nobody would feel like a foreigner in his homeland, and would on the contrary take an active part in civic life:

---

[60] *Rassuzhdenie o mire i voine*, ed. J. Skowronek, in '«Rozwazania o pokoju i wojnie» Wasyla F. Malinowskiego', *Teki archiwalne*, no. 17 (1978), p. 43. Further references are made by page number to this edition.

> In order to make government a public concern, it is necessary to set up all
> its members, so that everything that affects their fatherland affects them,
> and this cannot be done in a better way than by assigning inheritance (p.
> 41).

The theoretical position from which Malinovskii derives his idea of the
«razdelenie zemel'»[61] is the vision of the land as a common, vital
possession, rooted in religious faith:

> It is our mother, the one who feeds us, the source of true plenty and the
> means of satisfying natural requirements, without which alone we cannot
> live (p. 40).

> The land is the Lord's, we are newcomers and wanderers upon it (p. 41).

The ideal form of possession seems therefore to him «to set aside for
each in inheritance a commensurate plot of land» (p. 40). An allotment will
be assigned, in inheritance, to a «pater familias» who will decide who,
among his sons, is to make his living out of the land. If the property is sold
or lost in other ways, its periodical redistribution should again provide a
correct division. Malinovskii conceives this measure as aiming to prevent
both the concentration of properties and indigence, and derives this idea
directly from an Old Testament teaching:

> So that inheritances do not degenerate through poverty or negligence in the
> course of time, the ancient statutes of a wise legislation, providing for the
> return to each person of his sold inheritance in a solemn fiftieth year,
> should be restored. Much is taken from the Old Testament in all the
> teachings of the Christian faith, how can this be offensive? Why have
> Christian priests taken over the Levites' right to collect a tithe? If this
> custom has proved pleasing to them, then the beneficial custom of
> returning inheritances in a solemn year of jubilee should be pleasing to the
> people (p. 41)

The main objective pursued by the distribution of land (for which
historical authority is claimed: «thus the Spartans and the Romans lived», p.
41) is «to make government a public concern». Such a measure would
produce a number of positive effects on the general welfare of society. One
of them could be represented by encouraging a return to the countryside,
thus helping to reverse the chaotic development of modern cities:

---

[61] This idea was rooted in an aspect of Russian life of the past, see on the subject
V.A. Aleksandrov, 'Land Re-allotment in the Peasant Communes of the Late Feudal
Russia', in R. Bartlett (ed.), *Land Commune and Peasant Community in Russia* (London,
1990).

> Besides it is time for Europeans to reduce their towns, where mankind
> becomes corrupt and lives in poverty. It is necessary to provide channels
> for superfluous inhabitants to be drawn away and be returned to natural
> simplicity (p. 41).

Malinovskii's proposal would also have positive repercussions on a fact
troubling the conscience of many Russians at that time: the corruption of
morals. As shown in other works, Malinovskii believed that dissoluteness
derived from the two extremes of excess and indigence:

> To correct behaviour and lead people toward conjugal life, it is necessary to
> secure the upkeep of the family through inheritance. To halt this
> burgeoning luxury, this voluptuousness and decadence, which weaken the
> rich, it is necessary to decrease their lands and assign them to the poor, to
> bring them to a most natural state of industriousness, and to distract them
> from the many vices, which spread on from them (p. 42).

Using a plain, almost bureaucratic style to express his position on the
problem of the land, Malinovskii managed in point of fact to say something
particularly revolutionary about one of the most crucial themes for Russia
at that time.

An interesting aspect of the ideas expressed here by Malinovskii on the
ownership of the land is that although his evident point of reference is
Russia, he does not consider his proposals as applying only or exclusively to
his fatherland. His knowledge of other European countries is sufficiently
deep to allow him to see that his radical proposal of land egalitarianism has
no precedents in Europe:

> There will be sufficient land in every region, when no-one has a
> superfluity. A limit to great estates should be fixed in every region. The
> lands of the rich have increased to the point where the poor have nowhere
> to live, the industrious have nothing to work on, in many European
> countries a significant portion of village dwellers have no fields (p. 41).

England does not escape his criticism:

> The English are celebrated for their charitable works; they warm and feed
> their poor. But let them rather assign them a plot of land from the spare
> capacity of their estates and thus give them the means to support
> themselves by their labours (p. 42).

Looking at the problem from a European perspective makes a peculiar
paradox possible: Malinovskii never pronounces the name of his fatherland,

in this section, although the unbearable condition of the peasants in Russia was probably the main concern of his social thought.

3.4. Agriculture or manufactures? Malinovskii's translation of Hamilton's 'Report'.

Malinovskii's approach to the peasant question was characterized by a particularly deep knowledge of two phenomena whose consideration inevitably impinged on the debate on serfdom: the advance of agriculture and the process of industrialization.

The Russian thinker ascribed a prominent role to agriculture. The first years of his intellectual development were characterized by a deep interest in rural relations, which derived from his closeness to a figure particularly concerned with agricultural problems, A.A. Samborskii. The emphasis on the central role of agriculture for the Russian economy had been a feature characteristic of the cultural atmosphere in the 1760s and 1770s, which was influenced by the new interest in agriculture and estate management developed in Europe in the mid-century. A consistent theoretical reinforcement of this stream of thought had come from the physiocratic theories. In Russia the foundation of the Free Economic Society[62] in 1764 had been achieved with the precise intention of giving new «social» relevance to studies on agriculture.

The general demand for a higher standard in organizing the functioning of estates was to be the basis of one of the most fertile connections between Russia and other European countries. Scientific expeditions were organized to learn the principles and practical rules of agriculture abroad, with the intention of sowing in Russia the seeds of that science. In particular, the prosperous state of agriculture in England and the laudable enterprises of British farmers were a hardly avoidable topos in the Russian cultural life of that time. The names of A. Young and J. Arbuthnot were pronounced with respect and admiration in Russia[63].

---

[62] On 15 June 1794 Malinovskii had become a member of the Free Economic Society. On this institution see V.V. Oreshkin, *Vol'noe ekonomicheskoe obshchestvo v Rossii 1765-1917. Istoriko-ekonomicheskii ocherk* (Moskva, 1963).

[63] For a detailed discussion of the introduction of English agriculture into Russia, see A.G. Cross, *«By the Banks of the Thames»: Russians in Eighteenth-Century Britain* (Newtonville, Mass., 1980), particularly chapter 3, 'To speed the plough'.

One of the Russian intellectuals who was most involved, over the course of almost three decades, with the idea of transferring the achievements of British agriculture to his own country was Samborskii. His books on agriculture gave an important contribution to the development of that science in Russia; his interest in agriculture, nevertheless, was not merely theoretical; it had an important practical side, as witnessed by his numerous attempts to implement a project, blessed by Catherine, to set up a school of practical agriculture in Russia, and by the zealous instruction of the group of young men sent to study agriculture in England and consigned to his care. The detailed studies made in recent years on his sojourn in England, his personal contacts and his general intellectual work[64] enable us to identify him as one of the specific sources of Malinovskii's own attention to agriculture.

Vasilii Fedorovich had come to know well the role of agriculture in the British economy and the progress made in that country thanks to the application of new knowledge. He certainly shared with Russian agriculturalists their enthusiasm for the new agriculture, but he did not share their confidence in the possibility that that science would guarantee a higher level of prosperity. Observing the state of agrarian relationships in Russia, Malinovskii had no doubts about the fact that the servile status of the peasants heavily compromised the model of an ideally managed Russian countryside. He did not consider the peasant's freedom as a minor detail in the process of improving productivity. On the contrary, the advantages of free labour in the agriculture of other countries had already been clearly identified by him[65].

Malinovskii elaborated his views on the role of agriculture in economic life mindful, however, of the achievements of contemporary thought on industrialization[66], mainly based on European sources[67]. In 1807

---

[64] *Ibid.*, pp. 39-44, 60-73.

[65] In his *Zapiski o Moldavii* he wrote: «The land here either properly belongs to the peasants or is rented from the landowners. They can leave it when they want to, and so the boyars cherish them and are afraid to oppress them, for otherwise their land would be left without workers and they themselves without income. The peasants, being free, do not saunter idly about and are not reluctant to work» (*Priiatnoe i poleznoe preprovozhdenie vremeni*, XIII (1797), p. 423).

[66] Among the studies devoted to the development of manufactures in Russia, see F.Ia. Polianskii, *Gorodskoe remeslo i manufaktura v Rossii XVIII v.* (Moskva, 1960).

[67] Original elaboration on the development of manufactures appeared a few years later in Russia. In 1815 N.S. Mordvinov wrote *Nekotorye soobrazheniia po predmetu manufaktur v Rossii i o tarife*. Mordvinov (1754-1845), a naval officer, in 1774-77 was on English ships in America and sympathized with liberal ideas. Close to Speranskii, he

his translation of A. Hamilton's *Report on the Subject of Manufactures* appeared in St Petersburg under the title *Otchet general-kaznacheia Aleksandra Gamil'tona, uchinennyi Amerikanskim shtatam 1791 g. o pol'ze manufaktur, v otnoshenii onykh k torgovle i zemledeliiu.*

It would probably be a mistake to imply a total agreement with Hamilton on Malinovskii's part, especially considering the preference he frequently expressed for a rural-oriented society as opposed to an urban one[68]. It should not be overlooked, however, that the work was meant to abolish a series of prejudices against manufactures, including the idea of a strong opposition between manufacturing and agricultural interests.

There is little doubt, then, that Malinovskii considered legitimate the author's preoccupation with showing the social importance of his interest in manufactures. Hamilton had declared:

> Not only the wealth; but the independence and security of a Country, appear to be materially connected with prosperity of manufactures. Every nation, with a view to those great objects, ought to endeavour to possess within itself all the essentials on national supply[69].

Malinovskii considered knowledge of the American experience as particularly valuable for Russian society. As stated in his preface to the translation, he found a number of similarities between the American United Provinces and Russia,

> as in respect of the extent of the lands, the climate and natural products, so also in respect of the disproportionate spread of the population and the state of infancy, in which various generally beneficial institutions are; for this reason all the principles, remarks and methods proposed here are extremely apposite to our fatherland too[70].

Similar views were shared by some of his Russian contemporaries, who developed the idea of a particular affinity between the two «new»

---

became Minister for Naval Affairs and in 1823-1840 president of the Free Economic Society.

[68] In *Rassuzhdenie* Part III Malinovskii identifies in the general ownership of land a condition sufficient to avoid the evils of industrialization: «so that the inhabitants are not like tools or machines for manufacture, nor idly lounging about, ready to fill the ranks of hired workers» (*Rassuzhdenie o mire i voine*, ed. J. Skowronek, in '«Rozwazania o pokoju i wojnie» Wasyla F. Malinowskiego', p. 43).

[69] H.C. Syrett, J.E. Cook (eds.), *The Papers of Alexander Hamilton* (New York and London, 1966), X, p. 291.

[70] *Otchet general-kaznacheia Aleksandra Gamil'tona, uchinennyi Amerikanskim shtatam 1791 g. o pol'ze manufaktur i otnoshenii onykh k torgovle i zemledeliiu* (Spb., 1807), p. I.

countries[71]. In point of fact, the policy of establishing and consolidating manufactures was recommended by Hamilton not only for the United States, but also for other countries suffering from the European monopoly.

In his preface Malinovskii also explained the reasons which had led him to choose to translate that particular work instead of a number of purely theoretical treatments of the problem:

> The book proposed is about the usefulness of manufactures, with a demonstration of means for its encouragement; it is not one of the other numerous works, which contain theoretic expressions of reasons, but is a product of the experience of a man of the State, known throughout the world for his particular talents and skill in management.

In point of fact, after the American Revolution the growing interest in the establishment of manufactures, in contrast with the pre-Revolutionary hostility to it, was reflected in a number of works[72]. Hamilton's report, aimed at meeting all the objections directed against manufactures, was written with close reference to the ideas expressed by Adam Smith in his *The Wealth of Nations* and shared the same criticism of the Physiocratic approach to the problem.

The general importance of Malinovskii's translation with respect to his position on the peasant question is evident: it combined with his agricultural knowledge to shape a picture of economic development in conditions of freedom, or at least in forms alien to the system of serf labour institutionalized in Russia. It is more difficult to supply evidence of Malinovskii's stance on a series of particular questions treated in Hamilton's report. A careful comparison of the Russian text with the original shows that the translation is a close one[73]. Malinovskii confines himself to the role of faithful and respectful translator, to an extent rare in Russian adapter-translators of the eighteenth century. His excellent knowledge of the English language enables him to follow Hamilton even in the most difficult passages. His only interventions are structural. For the benefit of the Russian reader,

---

[71] For a study of the subject, see N.N. Bolkhovitinov, *The Beginnings of Russian-American Relations 1775-1815* (Cambridge, Massachusetts, and London, 1975) (first published in Moscow in 1966). See also N. Marcialis (ed.), *E i russi scoprirono l'America* (Roma, 1989).

[72] A survey of the works with which Hamilton was familiar is provided in H.C. Syrett, J.E. Cook (eds.), *The Papers of Alexander Hamilton*, p. 231.

[73] With reference to this work, the hypothesis of a pseudo-translation, concealing an original work, had been suggested. The practice of the time and Malinovskii's personal reticence about disclosing his authorship fully authorized this hypothesis, suggested by N.B. Malinovskaia. Our comparison was made using the text of the final version published in Syrett, *op. cit.*, pp. 230-341.

he divides Hamilton's report into two parts: the first is a discussion of the current objections to the encouragement of manufactures and an investigation, on the other hand, of its utility; the second is devoted to a study of the specific objects requiring encouragement and of the subsequent necessary measures. Always following the letter of the text, Malinovskii introduces useful subtitles for each section.

There are very few cases in which Malinovskii summarizes the views of Hamilton, and he apparently cuts passages only when the discussion becomes excessively technical or involves concepts absolutely alien to Russian society[74]. In other cases Malinovskii's changes seem to follow a different criterion: he omits a passage mentioning the American revolution and its positive effect on the pecuniary resources of the States[75]. In another place the sentence «before the revolution» is rendered in Russian as «before the separation of America»[76]. Malinovskii also avoided translating a short passage referring to a slave revolt on the plantations in Haiti (occurring in 1791), whose effect on the prices of grain was shown by Hamilton[77].

If we consider the official nature of the translation[78], Malinovskii's extremely cautious approach to those delicate subjects is, however, not at all surprising.

---

[74] This is the case, for example, of a detailed discussion of problems related to the property of the land and modalities of cultivation of the soil, involving figures, like the American farmer, not existing in Russia (pp. 243-245 of the *Report's* edition quoted above); of a complicated explanation of the effect of funded debt on the economy of the country (pp. 278-282); of a passage involving American legislation on taxes (pp. 302-304).

[75] *Ibid.*, p. 290.

[76] *Ibid.*, p. 315. P. 107 in Malinovskii's translation.

[77] P. 323 in Hamilton's *Report*, p.125 in Malinovskii's translation. One of the first writers who used the theme of slavery in America as an allusion to serfdom in Russia was probably Radishchev in his *Puteshestvie iz Moskvy v Peterburg*. On this subject see in particular V. Orlov, *Russkie prosvetiteli 1790-1800 godov* (Moskva, 1953).

[78] It was commissioned by the Minister of Finance D.A. Gur'ev, see the present work, pp. 51-52.

CHAPTER 4: THE PEDAGOGUE

This chapter is an investigation of Malinovskii's contribution to the birth and life of the Tsarskoe Selo Lycée, the school which was to gain the reputation of the most «revolutionary» institution in nineteenth-century Russia. The fruits of the Lycée's progressive education were to go beyond the boundaries of the Lycée and become part of the Russian history of freedom, thanks to the Decembrist experience.

For the first time in Russian history, an educated elite took up arms against Russian autocracy. A few former pupils of the Lycée were involved. The Tsarskoe Selo Lycée, founded with the aim of training a bureaucratic elite for the Russian state, came thus to nurture an opposition undermining the basis of the existing system. This study will attempt to evaluate Malinovskii's role in this evolution. It covers almost exclusively the first years of the Lycée's existence, those directly affected by Malinovskii, although his influence was to last longer than the mere three years he was Director.

Part I analyzes the history of the Lycée with reference to Malinovskii's general contribution to its creation and subsequent development. The abundance of secondary sources on the Lycée, revealing a great diversity in interpretation, does not, however, provide a just assessment of the role of its first Director. A gallery of the professors and of the subjects they taught can provide a necessary first insight into the orientation of the Lycée, and this will be followed by an examination of the students' life.

Part II reestablishes Malinovskii's specific contribution to the life of the Lycée. It is divided into a survey of Malinovskii's ideas on education and an analysis of how they were embodied in the life of the Lycée. It also

deals with a particularly controversial subject: Malinovskii's influence on
Russia's greatest poet, A.S. Pushkin.

4.1. The Tsarskoe Selo Lycée

4.1.1. The original plan and the 1811 charter

The Russian Lycée which opened in 1811 at Tsarskoe Selo acquired
legendary features almost from the beginning. The circumstances in which
the school was founded and the projects behind it are part of this legend.

The site to which the Tsarskoe Selo Lycée owed its name until 1843,
when it was moved to St Petersburg and renamed the Alexander Lycée[1],
was not the result of a casual choice. According to numerous sources, the
original idea behind it had been to give an *«obshchestvennoe»* (civic)
education to the Grand Dukes Nikolai and Mikhail Pavlovichi[2]. No other
location could thus have been more suitable and «natural» than a wing of
the imperial palace at Tsarskoe Selo. The denomination *«litsei»*, preferred
to other words such as *gimnaziia*, or *universitet*, which were more usual for
the Russian educational system, was supposed to contain an element of
originality: it was to define a new type of institution combining different
aspects of those two models[3].

---

[1] The Alexander Lycée was closed in 1917.

[2] See S.V. Pavlova, '«Vy pomnite, kogda voznik litsei...»', in S.M. Nekrasov (ed.),
'...I v prosveshchenii stat' s vekom naravne'. Sbornik nauchnykh trudov (Spb., 1992), pp.
6-20, and I.Ia. Seleznev, *Istoricheskii ocherk Imperatorskogo byvshego Tsarskosel'skogo,
nyne Aleksandrovskogo Litseia za pervoe ego piatidesiatiletie, s 1811 po 1861 god* (Spb.,
1861), p. 16. According to Seleznev, who was one of its librarians and the author of one of
the first and most «official» studies on the Lycée, that original intention also explains why
Alexander I took so active a part in the elaboration of the plan. Ties with the imperial
families were also to be kept later, in various forms. The extensive work by M.
Rudenskaia, S. Rudenskaia, *'Nastavnikam ... za blago vozdadim'* (Leningrad, 1986)
integrates the history of the Lycée with information about its present life, particularly about
the Memorial Museum of the Lycée founded at Tsarskoe Selo in 1949.

[3] It should be remembered that M.N. Murav'ev used this word in his proposal for a
reorganization of Moscow University in 1804-1806 (see Seleznev, *op. cit.*, p. 4). This
formula took concrete shape in other cases in Russia: during the first two decades of the
nineteenth century appeared the Demidovskii Litsei in Iaroslavl', Kremenetskii Litsei,
Rishel'evskii Litsei in Odessa, Nezhinskii Litsei (see Pavlova, *op. cit.*, p. 12).

According to D. Kobeko, the preference for this word had to be seen in connection
with Martynov's journal Litsei (*Imperatorskii tsarskosel'skii litsei. Nastavniki i pitomtsy.
1811-1843* (Spb., 1911), p. 21).

While the initial idea about the Lycée was soon abandoned, the decision about its location remained valid. The elaboration of the plan concerning its structure, status and functioning was undertaken by the State Secretary M.M. Speranskii, and was particularly complex. It should be seen in the context of the reforms involving the educational system which took place during the first years of Alexander I's reign. Among the Tsar's advisers on educational affairs were F. La Harpe (one of his former tutors), M.N. Murav'ev and V.N. Karazin. The question of reforming education in Russia was taken up by the Secret Committee in 1801. Its work led to a general plan which included the creation of new universities and the foundation, in 1802, of the Ministry of Public Education (*Ministerstvo Narodnogo Prosveshcheniia)*[4].

The 'Obshchie pravila narodnogo prosveshcheniia', which were meant to regulate the functioning of the existing institutions and the creation of new universities and schools in Russia, appeared the following year. Despite the new autonomy and opportunities given to universities with the *Ustav* issued in 1804, the Russian aristocracy, which was the primary target of these reforms, continued not to be particularly attracted by the governmental institutions: during the first decades of the century the noble families rejected the idea of a «mixed» education, continuing to prefer a domestic, private upbringing, preferably under the supervision of foreign tutors[5].

On 11 December 1808 Speranskii submitted to Alexander I a document called 'Ob usovershenii obshchego narodnogo vospitaniia', which pointed to the lack of concern of young Russian aristocrats for their education and proposed a number of measures to increase their literacy[6]. He simultaneously elaborated a specific project called 'Pervonachaln'noe nachertanie osobennogo Litseia'[7]. The new scholastic institution he had in mind was to be destined for brilliant pupils coming from different social classes and groomed to become high-level bureaucrats in the Russian state. Besides this brief project submitted to Alexander I there exists also its

---

[4] See S.V. Rozhdenstvenskii, *Istoricheskii obzor deiatel'nosti Ministerstva narodnogo prosveshcheniia. 1802-1902* (Spb., 1902).

[5] On this see also F.A. Walker, 'Popular Response to Public Education in the Reign of Alexander I (1801-1825)', *History of Education Quarterly* (Winter, 1984), pp. 527-543.

[6] 'Ob usovershenii obshchego narodnogo vospitaniia', in *Antologiia pedagogicheskoi mysli Rossii pervoi poloviny XIX veka* (Moskva, 1987).

[7] M.M. Speranskii, 'Pervonachal'noe nachertanie osobennogo Litseia', *Litseiskii zhurnal*, IV (1906-1907), no. 3.

rough draft[8], called 'Proekt obrazovaniia Tsarskosel'skogo litseia', in which all of its fundamental principles are illustrated in detail. It was first analyzed by Meilakh, who suggested that it was written «with the closest participation of the future leaders of the Lycée Malinovskii and Kunitsyn»[9]. This document is deeply inspired by the spirit of the Enlightenment: it stresses the need for teaching moral and philosophical sciences to regenerate the sense of duty in the individual and in society; it locates the educators' primary aim in helping pupils to develop their personal ability to think and make judgments, avoiding empty rhetorical exercises. Despite our difficulty in establishing the extent of Malinovskii's original contribution to this document, it is nevertheless possible to highlight a few points where his thoughts might have been particularly relevant: the idea that the education of the pupils should be informed by a sense of national awareness made possible by a deep knowledge of Russian history; the persuasion that among the subjects predominance should be given to the study of Law, and particularly the Law of Nations[10]; the emphasis on «civic» implications in the teaching of moral sciences.

Speranskii's plan for a Russian Lycée met a need generally recognized in Russia, even by the less progressive part of society: namely more qualified personnel for important civil service posts[11]. These posts were usually occupied by aristocrats who had served in the military service, without any knowledge of the functioning of the civil service. The backwardness of the Russian high level bureaucracy[12] amply justified the birth of a new institution primarily devoted to the training of its officials. The conflicts were to be rather about the methods and principles to apply in their education. For Speranskii, Malinovskii and the people of enlightened ideas involved in the Lycée project, it became quite clear that its effects would not be limited to the merely practical aim prescribed by the Russian government: to form a class of high-level bureaucrats for administrative,

---

[8] Speranskii's rough draft is held in RGIA, Fond 1251, op. 2, no. 4, ff. 12-19.

[9] B.S. Meilakh, *Pushkin i ego epokha* (Moskva, 1958), p. 24.

[10] *Ibid.*, p. 25.

[11] The school managed to be faithful to this aim, revolutionary episodes notwithstanding: it was calculated that «in its 106-year history, the Lyceum produced twenty-four ministers or their equivalent, thirty-five appointed and eleven elected members of the State Council, and seventy-three senators» (quoted by A.A. Sinel, 'The Socialization of the Russian Bureaucratic Elite, 1811-1917: Life at Tsarskoe Selo Lyceum and the School of Jurisprudence', *Russian History*, III (1976), no. 1, p. 2).

[12] See J.A. Armstrong, *The European Administrative Elite* (Princeton, 1973); see also his 'Tsarist and Soviet Elite Administrators', *Slavic Review*, XXXI, (1972), no. 1, pp. 1-28.

diplomatic and judicial appointments. If correctly directed, it was to offer a unique opportunity to create a category of «new people», able to contribute substantially to the constitutional transformation of Russian society. The debate about the foundation of the Lycée thus carried strong political implications from the beginning.

The task of revising Speranskii's project for the Lycée was given to Minister A.K. Razumovskii[13] and to the Minister of Home Affairs V.P. Kochubei. In matters of education Razumovskii (Minister from 1810 to 1816) was at that time under the influence of Joseph de Maistre[14], who was ambassador in Russia from 1803 to 1817. In his letters to Razumovskii[15] the envoy of the Kingdom of Sardinia warned against the negative consequences of a liberal education, inspired by the philosophy of the Enlightenment, and pointed out the ruinous effect it had had in France. De Maistre considered the sciences in general not suitable for Russians, and the teaching of Psychology and Law proposed for Tsarskoe Selo particularly dangerous. Razumovskii reported to the Tsar some of his remarks, particularly those concerning the need for strict control over the students' life and readings.

Another personality was closely involved in the project's final revision: the Director of the Department of the Ministry of Education I.I. Martynov. A man of moderately liberal views, he managed to be quite faithful to the principles inspiring the original project, although he ignored a number of points, particularly Speranskii's idea of admitting students «iz raznykh sostoianii» and the need for the study of philosophy.

After a discussion about the future charter which lasted almost two years, the decree on the establishment of the Lycée was signed on 12 August 1810. The *Ustav*, also known as 'Postanovlenie o Litsee'[16], is the most relevant document for our understanding of the features that the new

---

[13] While Soviet and contemporary research tended to highlight the role of Speranskii in the preliminary phase of the creation of the Lycée, during the nineteenth century the Lycée's hagiographers put a special emphasis on Razumovskii's role. Seleznev was particularly zealous in this: he mentioned only en passant Speranskii and virtually ignored Malinovskii.

[14] See M. Schippan, 'N.M. Karamzin und J.de Maistre über den Weg Russlands (1811)', *Zeitschrift für Slawistik*, 36 (1991), no. 4, pp. 535-543; D.W. Edwards, 'Count Joseph Marie de Maistre and Russian Educational Policy, 1803-1828', *Slavic Review*, no. 36 (1977), pp. 54-75.

[15] See R.de Maistre (ed.), 'Cinq lettres sur l'éducation publique en Russie, à M. le comte Razumowsky', *Lettres et opuscules inédits du comte Joseph de Maistre* (Paris, 1851) II. See also M. Stepanov, 'Zhosef De Mestr v Rossii', *Literaturnoe nasledstvo*, XXIX-XXX (1937), pp. 577-726.

[16] *Gramota, pozhalovannaia Imperatorskomu Litseiu imperatorom Aleksandrom I 22 sentiabria 1811 goda* (Petrograd, 1916). See on it the article by Pavlova, *op. cit.*.

institution was expected to have. In its preface the primary aim of the Lycée was clearly stated: «We wished to earmark especially for important sectors of the State service a certain number of young people who are particularly distinguished in talents and moral qualities». It specified a number of other aspects concerning the life of the Lycée. According to this document, teaching would have been divided into two courses, *nachaln'yi* (initial) and *okonchatel'nyi* (final), each lasting three years. The first course would have covered topics usually studied at the gymnasium, the second course concentrated on university subjects.

The special concern of the Lycée would have been to give the students a broad and non-specialized education. In keeping with the imperatives of the time, a particular emphasis was also put on the moral training of the lyceists. The age of the pupils admitted to the Lycée had to be between ten and twelve: quite an early age to begin a regular course of this type. They had to spend the entire six years of their education within the Lycée, without having the possibility of leaving it, even on holidays.

It is worth noting that among the other subjects a prominent place was given to the study of Russian language and history, not something to be taken for granted in the contemporary Russian institutions where the cult of foreign cultures and languages was predominant. In the chapter of the *Ustav* entitled 'Sposob ucheniia' precise directions were given about the way in which knowledge had to be imparted: the teachers were supposed to help the pupils in developing their individual abilities in thinking actively and critically, escaping from scholastic learning.

Another innovative feature stated in a number of secondary sources on the Lycée was the abolition of corporal punishments. The *Ustav* did not specify this point, it only enumerated all the possible sanctions reserved for the students[17]; among these none included the physical humiliation so typical at that time almost everywhere in Europe. In point of fact, corporal punishment had already been abolished in Russia, but this directive was virtually ignored, to the extent that Count Razumovskii believed it necessary to confirm it with a circular issued on 18 March 1811 and aimed to ensure its faithful application[18].

---

[17] According to the *Ustav* (paragraph 110), they could be of four types, or degrees: «A) Separation within the class at a special table. B) The names of the idle pupils will be exhibited in the class in white letters on the blackboard. C) Exclusion from the common table. The pupil will receive bread and water. This punishment cannot continue beyond two days. D) Solitary confinement in the course of which the Director is to visit and give suitable admonitions. Such punishment cannot conceivably last longer than three days».

[18] See Kobeko, *op.cit.*, p. 342.

4.1.2. Subjects and Teachers

The institution founded at Tsarskoe Selo offered from the beginning a quite exceptional educational experience. Put at the same level with universities and given a number of liberties and privileges, it became quite soon the object of great expectations in Russian society.

It was conceived as an «ideal» institution aimed to provide a truly «Russian» education: the student finishing the Lycée was meant to be prepared to serve the Russian state faithfully , having a solid knowledge of its cultural features and a deep awareness of the common weal. The selection of the teaching staff and the organization and distribution of the subjects played a decisive role in establishing the orientation of the Lycée. When the special section of the *Ustav* devoted to the «*sposob ucheniia*» (method of teaching) had to be translated into the practice of a concrete programme, the role of the Director was obviously of particular importance[19].

It would be a mistake to identify in the Lycée a compact and harmonious experience alien from any conflict. In point of fact, the positions within its walls were extremely diverse. Nevertheless, Malinovskii doubtless managed to create around him a group of «enlightened» professors, characterized by the same or similar orientation, reflecting different aspects of the Russian Enlightenment. An important part of the teaching was thus directed to the idea that the pupil had to penetrate the world using his reason, in the truest spirit of the Enlightenment. The recurrence of certain ideas in different courses tended to give the students a solid political and ideological formation (with a strong emphasis on «morality»), a fact with no precedent in the Russian educational system.

The future public servants educated at Tsarskoe Selo had to have a broad cultural education. The unusual number of outstanding poets who were formed in its first course frequently invites the suggestion that the Lycée was a distinctly «literary» experience. In point of fact, its educational programme was not predominantly oriented towards the humanities. It was characterized by a balanced combination of humanities, exact disciplines and natural sciences; these latter had an important practical side: the school

---

[19] On 10 October he wrote: «I met with the professors to consult about the children's activities» ('Pamiatnaia kniga Litseia').

was provided with one of the most modern cabinets of mathematics and physics of the time. In keeping with the prescriptions of the *Ustav*, during their first course the students were taught: 1) Russian, Latin, French, German; 2) Moral Sciences: Divinity, Moral Philosophy, Logic; 3) Mathematical and Physical Sciences: Arithmetics, Linear Trigonometry, Physics; 4) Historical Sciences: Russian and Foreign History, Geography and Chronology; 5) Fundamentals of Belles Lettres: study of selected passages from literary works and Rhetoric; 6) Fine Arts: Calligraphy, Drawing, 7) Gymnastics[20]. The second course included fundamentally the same topics taught at a more complex level.

A survey of the personal and professional features of the teaching staff[21] is of primary importance in understanding the way the courses were held and consequently in acquiring a picture of the general orientation of the Lycée. In this respect particularly valuable is the accurate record of many courses held in the Lycée kept by its most studious pupil, A.M. Gorchakov, future Chancellor and Minister of Foreign Affairs[22]. One of the most outstanding figures among the professors was A.P. Kunitsyn[23]. Particular attention has been traditionally devoted to him, as the teacher who made the major contribution to establishing the «*litseiskii dukh*» (the spirit of the Lycée). Born into a family of modest origin, he had been educated in the St Petersburg Pedagogical Institute and spent a period in Göttingen[24]. Seemingly he was one of the first to be recruited by Malinovskii to take part in the Lycée's teaching, in which he was involved from 1811 to 1820. His speech on the occasion of the opening of the Lycée in October 1811[25] was the most remarkable event of that day and gained him the reputation of a man of radical views. In this speech Kunitsyn, using a strikingly audacious intonation, introduced the students to the ideas which were to inform his teaching programme: the importance of law in society,

---

[20] See Seleznev, *op.cit.*, pp. 11-12.

[21] For a detailed review of the teaching staff, see in particular Seleznev, pp. 112-136, and M. Rudenskaia, S. Rudenskaia, *'Nastavnikam ... za blago vozdadim'*, pp. 42-90.

[22] See B.S. Meilakh, 'Litseiskie lektsii', *Krasnyi arkhiv*, no. 1 (1937), pp. 75-206.

[23] About him see O.A. Iatsenko, '«Kunitsynu dan' serdtsa i vina...»', in Nekrasov (ed.), *op. cit.*, pp. 45-56; B. Hollingsworth, 'A.P. Kunitsyn and the Social Movement under Alexander I', *Slavonic and East European Review*, XLIII (1964), pp. 115-129; F.N. Smirnov, 'A.P. Kunitsyn i dekabristy', *Vestnik moskovskoi universitety*, no. 5 (1961), pp. 60-69.

[24] On the importance of this experience in the formation of Russian students, see M. Wischnitzer, *Die Universität Göttingen und die Entwicklung der Liberalen Ideen in Russland in erstern Viertel des 19 Jahrhunderts* (Berlin, 1907).

[25] 'Nastavlenie, chitannoe vospitannikam pri otkrytii imperatorskogo Tsarskosel'skogo litseia'.

the sense of civic responsibility as a primary characteristic of future public servants and the attention they had to have for the needs of the Russian people. His course of moral and political sciences consisted of twelve cycles, which had to be distributed during the six-year course as follows: 1.*Logika* (Logic) 2.*Psikhologiia* (Psychology) 3.*Nravstvennost'* (Morality) 4.*Pravo estestvennoe chastnoe* (Private Natural Law) 5.*Pravo estestvennoe publichnoe* (Public Natural Law) 6.*Pravo narodnoe* (Law of the Nations) 7.*Pravo grazhdanskoe russkoe* (Russian Civic Law) 8.*Pravo publichnoe russkoe* (Russian Public Law) 9.*Pravo ugolovnoe russkoe* (Russian Penal Law) 10.*Pravo rimskoe* (Roman Law) 11.*Politicheskaia ekonomiia* (Political Economy) 12.*Finansy* (Finances).

The fact that Tsarskoe Selo's students could become legislators of their country was assigned a particular importance by the Director himself. In numerous writings he pointed out the importance of just laws in every field of human activity. It is significant that to teach such major topics Malinovskii called on a man to whose views on many problems of Russian society he could fully subscribe: in his lectures on Natural Law Kunitsyn taught the students the need to restore a connection between law and the notions of «*obshchee blago*» (general good) and «*obshchaia svoboda*» (general freedom) and illustrated the idea of sovereignty of the people; he condemned the state of slavery of the Russian peasants and attacked tyranny and the abuse of law by the rich and powerful, showing at the same time his awareness of the constitutional projects elaborated in Russia in those years[26]. He was an authentic man of the Enlightenment, deeply influenced by the Rousseauian idea of the social contract. In Kunitsyn Malinovskii found his most reliable and courageous colleague[27]; his less important position in the Lycée authorized him to act as a sort of more radical alterego for the Director's own ideas of reform. Malinovskii's presence could on the other hand represent a guarantee for Kunitsyn's lectures, which were apparently the most popular among the *litseisty* [28], to be regularly held.

During his appointment in the Lycée, Kunitsyn wrote several articles published in *Syn otechestva* ('Poslanie k russkim', 'Zamechaniia na nyneshniuiu voinu', 'Rech' skifskogo posla Aleksandru Makedonskomu').

---

[26] See the analysis of his lectures made by Meilakh, *Pushkin i ego epokha*, pp. 66-84.

[27] In a letter to his brother Pavel he wrote: «the children of A.L. are housed with Kunitsyn, you know he is clever, and consequently they will benefit» (RGALI, Fond 312, op. 1, no. 6, f. 5).

[28] His influence on Pushkin, who repeatedly expressed his indebtedness to his teaching, has been much studied.

His book *Estestvennoe pravo*, published in St Petersburg between 1818 and 1820, was the first original work on the subject to appear in Russia. It was harshly criticized as instilling «in the hearts of inexperienced youth the spirit of disobedience, self-will and free thought»[29] and the censorship did not allow the newly published book to be circulated. The teaching of Natural Law was forbidden in Russia from 1820 to 1827. Kunitsyn was no longer allowed to teach in the Lycée and had to leave Tsarskoe Selo.

Another professor who manifested clear ideological affinities with Malinovskii but was less radical than Kunitsyn was the historian I.K. Kaidanov, who taught in the Lycée for thirty years. He came from the Kiev Spiritual Academy, received further education in the St Petersburg Pedagogical Institute, like Kunitsyn and another professor, Kartsov, and spent three years at Göttingen University. In 1814 he published the first part of his *Osnovaniia vseobshchei politicheskoi istorii*, devoted to ancient history, which became one of the textbooks of the Lycée. He was the author of many other publications of historical and philosophical character.

His lectures included a particular subject, statistics, which meant something quite different from the modern subject: it was concerned with the nature, political and social condition of the various European states. Kaidanov criticized the despotic forms of autocracy and paid great attention to the problem of legitimacy of imperial power and to that of the welfare of peoples. A prominent place in his survey of European states was given to the examination of England; that country was seen by Kaidanov as having a political system which was fundamentally admirable, but characterized nevertheless by a number of controversial aspects: social differences, a colonial policy marked by lack of respect for other peoples, and slavery[30]. The state of France before and after the Revolution was another recurrent subject; analyzing it, Kaidanov made a distinction between its initial beneficial impulse and its bloody development, and ended with a harsh condemnation of Napoleon as an usurper and liar, reflecting the typical interpretation of progressive Russians at that time.

---

[29] 'Otnoshenie ministra dukhovnykh del i narodnogo prosveshcheniia' quoted by Seleznev, *op.cit.*, p. 126.

[30] We may imagine intense discussions between the students and Malinovskii, and suppose a particular solidarity between Kaidanov and the Director, one of the privileged Russians who actually visited that country and toward which he was still affectionate and critical at the same time. In this respect Professor Koshanskii wrote about Malinovskii: «The spirit and enlightenment of the English People attracted his attention and made a particular impression on him, which was noticeable to the end of his life» (TSDIAU, Fond 2039, op. 1, no. 54, f. 4).

Given the poor state of historical studies on Russia at that time (a fact particularly highlighted by Malinovskii himself in a number of writings), the survey of the political systems of European states was accompanied by an analysis of the Russian empire, informed by love for the fatherland and respect for the autochthonous tradition and favourably highlighting the contribution of Peter I to the development of Russia. One of the main obstacles to the positive development of the Russian economy was seen by Kaidanov as serfdom. In this professor the students therefore had another fervent opponent of slavery.

The Tsarskoe Selo Lycée's programme was centred on modern languages (incidentally, Malinovskii mastered all the European languages taught there), reflecting the practical approach in education characterizing the training of future public servants. The students were not supposed to receive a classical education, therefore they did not study Greek, but had to have a good knowledge of Latin. N.F. Koshanskii, an expert on classic literatures, was appointed the first Professor of Latin and Russian. His *Latinskaia grammatika* and the anthology *Tsvety grecheskoi poezii* appeared in Russia the same year he was appointed professor at Tsarskoe Selo. Koshanskii was also the author of *Nachal'nye pravila rossiiskoi grammatiki* (1806). He was responsible not only for the first serious introduction of the students to the classical world[31], but also for their understanding of ancient political systems, in which the civic qualities of republican heroes were highlighted in the spirit of the Enlightenment. Teaching rhetoric, for example, Koshanskii illustrated its historical importance as a means by which political decisions could be democratically taken; the knowledge of this art was not to be, on the other hand, an arid exercise, but had to be filled with practical meaning, being conceived as a necessary professional instrument for future Russian orators.

Koshanskii also had an important role in organizing the literary activities autonomously undertaken by the students. He temporarily replaced Malinovskii when he died[32] and was the author of an obituary of the first

---

[31] Koshanskii's lectures were republished in N. Petrunina (ed.), 'Iz materialov pushkinskogo litseia', *Pushkin. Issledovaniia i materialy*, XIII (1989), pp. 306-345. On Koshanskii as a teacher at Tsarskoe Selo see also A.D. Pudova, '«Glubokoe uchenie drevnostei...»' (Pushkin i Koshanskii)', in Nekrasov (ed.), *op. cit.*, pp. 57-69. Koshanskii was in all probability a Mason, a member of the Lodge «Izbrannyi Mikhail» (see Meilakh, *op. cit.*, p. 101).

[32] Gauenshil'd was appointed as second temporary Director.

Director[33], in which he positively evaluated his political views and his personal qualities[34]. In May 1814 Koshanskii's physical condition became so bad that he had to give up teaching for a period of time; he was replaced for one year by A.I. Galich, a «*filosof-shellingianets*» [35], and then he was given an assistant, P.E. Georgievskii.

The Swiss D.I. De Boudry was appointed to teach French, and remained in the Lycée until his death in 1821. He was the oldest teacher. The brother of Jean Paul Marat[36] (with whom he regularly corresponded), he had left Geneva after participating in the revolt of the early 1780s; he had arrived in Russia in 1784 and had taken charge of the education of the children of V.P. Saltykov. In his lessons the students of Tsarskoe Selo could hear echoes of the speeches of the French Revolution.

Ia.I. Kartsov, the mathematician, taught until 1831; because of the predominant interest in humanities shown by the students, his lessons were not particularly popular[37]. Kartsov was «*iz dukhovnogo zvaniia*» (of religious rank), had been educated in the St Petersburg Pedagogical Institute and travelled in Germany and France. He was called to teach in the Lycée in August 1811, together with Kunitsyn and Kaidanov. He was responsible for organizing the physics room.

If the teaching of professors like Kunitsyn, Kaidanov and Koshanskii had the same direction and was intended to create independent young men of enlightened ideas, significant variations from this model could be observed in the other teachers.

German was taught by the Transylvanian Professor F.L. Gauenschild, a member of the Vienna Academy. His appointment at Tsarskoe Selo was supported by S.S. Uvarov, who was curator (*popechitel'*) of the St

[33] N.F. Koshanskii, 'Izvestie o zhizni Malinovskogo', *Syn otechestva*, XVIII (1814) no. 13, pp. 220-223. The manuscript version of the article (RGADA, Fond 188, op. 1, no. 216, ff. 1-5) is different, less official. It contains a *titul'nyi list* (title page) (f. 4) referring to the book of tales *Zolotoe zerkalo*, published in St Petersburg in 1809; although Malinovskii was not its author, it is included in the list of books published by the Director alongside his *Rassuzhdenie* and *Otchet Gamil'tona* (f. 5). A copy of the manuscript version of the obituary is held in TSDIAU, Fond 2039, op. 1, no. 54, ff. 2-5.

[34] «His character was distinguished by two chief traits: good nature and sensitivity; the former was so extensive that he did not intentionally offend anyone, and to the latter every unfortunate had a right» (*Ibid.*, f. 5).

[35] M. Rudenskaia, S. Rudenskaia, *'Nastavnikam ... za blago vozdadim*, p. 73.

[36] He assumed a different name, after the city of Boudry, in which he was born.

[37] In his memoirs I.I. Pushchin refers to the scarce interest shown by the students in Kartsov's lectures. Once Pushkin was called to the board to solve a problem of algebra, and having failed, he was sent back to his place by Kartsov, who told him: «Sit down in your place and write verses» (I.I. Pushchin, *Zapiski o Pushkine. Pis'ma*, eds. M.P. Mironenko, S.V. Mironenko (Moskva, 1988), p. 48.

Petersburg Educational District (*uchebnyi okrug*) and son-in-law of Razumovskii. Barely familiar with the Russian language[38], he taught German via French. An assistant was appointed for him in the person of the Livonian Baron A.Ia Rennenkampf. Gauenschild was dismissed in 1822. His role in the Lycée has still to be clarified, as his pedagogical abilities were seemingly not the main reason why he had been called to Tsarskoe Selo. He was suspected to be a diplomatic agent of the Austrian government sent there for espionage[39]. Particularly hated by students, he had a tense relationship with Malinovskii, Koshanskii and Kunitsyn, and later with Engel'gardt.

Archpriest Muzovskoi regularly taught divinity until 1816, when the second Director, E.A. Engel'gardt, felt it necessary to ask the Metropolitan to appoint an ecclesiastic especially for the Lycée, who was found in the person of I.S. Kochetov.

Apart from professors and adjuncts, there were the ordinary teachers: calligraphy was taught until 1851 by the «grandiloquent» F.P. Kalinich, a former chorister at Court; S.G. Chirikov taught drawing at Tsarskoe Selo for three decades. Great importance was given to this discipline in the Lycée: alongside the reproduction of classical models, the students were encouraged to express their ability in free drawing[40]. Teachers were also appointed for the additional activities the students were involved in during the recreation hours: apart from the official teaching, they were taught privately music, singing, fencing, dancing (from 1814), riding (from 1816) and swimming (from 1817)[41].

---

[38] He managed nevertheless to translate into German the first three volumes of Karamzin's *Istoriia gosudarstva Rossiiskogo*. He won Karamzin's friendship and was able to read his work before it was published.

[39] See Meilakh, *op. cit.*, pp. 132-133, M. Rudenskaia, S. Rudenskaia, *'Nastavnikam ... za blago vozdadim*, pp. 293-297.

[40] The propensity of the *litseisty* for caricatures is well-known. Chirikov had an important role in developing this ability (see O.A. Iatsenko, 'Beri svoi bystryi karandash', in Nekrasov (ed.), *op. cit.*, pp. 70-80). Malinovskii actively supported Chirikov in pursuing his method, particularly with respect to the need for particular technical materials (*ibid.*, pp. 73-74).

[41] It is interesting to note that the teaching of «*voennye iskusstva*» (military arts) to the oldest students was introduced only in 1816. (See Seleznev, *op. cit.*, p. 132). In 1815 Kartsov requested to be exonerated from the further teaching of war sciences. From 1816 a specialist was appointed to teach it, *polkovnik* F.B. El'sner.

A general characteristic of the teaching programme was a certain flexibility in the distribution of the subjects, as well as in the number of hours they were taught, which could vary[42].

The professors formed the Lycée's Conference, a collective organ in which they could discuss didactic and administrative questions, students' achievements and similar issues. It was presided over by the Director and by a Secretary. Ordinary meetings were to be held monthly, extraordinary meetings whenever necessary. The Conference was responsible directly to the Minister, to whom a copy of the minutes of the meetings had to be regularly sent. Each six months the Conference examined the students, and at the end of the year regulated their passage from one class to the next. The Conference was in close contact with other Russian universities of the time, with which it exchanged information and publications.

4.1.3. The Students and their life

In accordance with paragraph 31 of the *Ustav*, the pupils' entire day in the Lycée had to be strictly structured. Their daily regime was as follows: they woke up at six in the morning and spent their first two hours getting dressed, saying their prayers and repeating their lessons; worked in their classrooms for two hours; at ten had breakfast and a walk; after an hour of class they had another walk and repeated their lessons; at one had lunch, at two calligraphy and drawing, from three to five had class, then rested, walked and did gymnastics; at eight had dinner, walked and repeated their lessons before going to bed at ten. They slept in individual small cells located in a common dormitory on the fourth floor of the building.

---

[42] To illustrate how the different subjects and hours were distributed in the Lycée, it is useful, if not rigorously representative, to reproduce the time-table referring to the last months of 1812 (in Seleznev, *op.cit.*, pp. 60-61):

Latin	6 hours	Koshanskii, Kunitsyn
French	10 hours	De Boudry, Kunitsyn, Rennenkampf
German	10 hours	Gauenschild, Kartsov, Rennenkampf
Russian	3 hours	Koshanskii
Law of God	1 hour	Muzovskoi
Logic	2 hours	Kunitsyn
Maths	4 hours	Kartsov
Geography	3 hours	Kaidanov
History	3 hours	Kaidanov
Calligraphy	3 hours	Kalinich
Drawing	2 hours	Chirikov

The class hours were therefore not concentrated in the morning or in the afternoon but distributed during the entire day, alternated with recreational activities and preparation for class. This strict regimentation enabled the pedagogues to have control of a large part of their students' lives in the Lycée[43].

Another main feature of the Lycée was the rule according to which the students could not leave Tsarskoe Selo and its environs during the entire six years of their course. This restriction included the fact that the students could not go back to their homes even during the holidays, which took place in July. They could have private visitors only occasionally. The pupils were thus to enter Tsarskoe Selo at the age of ten-twelve years and to leave it as adults, whose formation took place quite independently from the outside world. They were nevertheless better informed about events in their country and abroad than the majority of their contemporaries: in the Lycée's reading room Russian and foreign newspapers were provided in abundance and were probably discussed with relative freedom. They had access to the Lycée's rich library, which as early as 1812 contained more than eight hundred volumes[44]. Representing a unique educational experiment, the Lycée was visited by a number of men of letters and personalities involved in contemporary Russian and European politics[45], including, in 1812, Prince Alexandru Ipsilanti, future leader of a movement for the emancipation of Greece, and his brother Dimitriu[46].

---

[43] In Sinel, *op. cit.*, an analysis of the Lycée as a «total institution» aimed to inculcate its own culture is provided; the socialization process, the role of the family as a rival institution and the role of the peer group are described in this light.

[44] Figure given by Seleznev, *op. cit.*, p. 44. Only later strict control was introduced over the students' reading: they had to get the inspector's permission to borrow books.

[45] Meilakh enumerates among them F. Glinka, P. Chadaaev, P. Pestel' (*Pushkin i ego epokha*, p. 143). In the report entitled 'Nechto o Tsarskosel'skom litsee i dukhe onogo', it was said that «it was then fashionable to visit the young people at the Lycée; they even on the quiet (that is without permission, but overtly) went out to parties in private houses, travelled to Petersburg, hob-nobbed with officers and visited many people who played significant roles in Petersburg... In the Lycée they began to read all the prohibited books, there was an archive there of all the manuscripts which passed secretly from hand to hand, and finally it reached the point that if something forbidden needed seeking out, they applied directly to the Lycée» (quoted by Meilakh, p. 144). In May 1816 Karamzin settled at Tsarskoe Selo with his family, close to the house of the Director (see M. Rudenskaia, S. Rudenskaia, *'Nastavnikam ... za blago vozdadim'*, p. 123, pp. 251-253).

[46] They were the sons of the Moldavian sovereign Constantin Ipsilanti, with whom Malinovskii dealt when he was in Jassy. Seemingly Pushkin was in close contact with A. Ipsilanti when he was in Kishinev (Meilakh, *Pushkin i ego epokha*, p. 143). It is interesting to note that in Kishinev Pushkin became a member of the Masonic lodge «Ovidii», which was in contact with the «Soiuz blagodenstviia»; this latter exercized an influence on the lodge «Izbrannyi Mikhail» to which Koshanskii belonged (M. Rudenskaia, S. Rudenskaia, *'Nastavnikam ... za blago vozdadim*, p. 141).

Seclusion was a feature inspiring a considerable part of the pedagogical thought of eighteenth-century Russia. It dated back to the Rousseauian notion about the negative role of the environment in the educational process. The idea that isolating the pupils enabled their tutors to protect them from the vices of society had been advocated with particular fervour by Catherine II's adviser Ivan Betskoi in his activity as school reformer during the 1760s and 1770s[47]. Obligatory isolation was never previously realized to the extent it was at Tsarskoe Selo. It reinforced in the Lycée's students the sense of being part of a select community and helped to develop a particularly strong corporate spirit, which lasted for many years. Even after leaving Tsarskoe Selo, the former students would keep in touch with each other, and commemorate the Lycée every year on 19 October with meetings and poems[48].

As in the majority of Russian institutions of the time, the students wore a school uniform. This consisted of a single-breasted caftan made of blue cloth; the red standing collar and the cuffs of the same colour were embroidered in silver for the younger pupils and in gold for the elder; the lining was light blue and the buttons golden, the camisole and lower part were in white cloth[49]. Wearing a uniform, a quite typical habit, also strengthened the sense of egalitarianism which was one of the main features inspiring the existence of Tsarskoe Selo. Egalitarianism was encouraged not exclusively among the pupils but also in their relations with the people of different social conditions with whom they came in contact. The pupils were assisted in their practical needs by the Lycée's «*diad'ki*». Five for each course, they provided help with changing linen, repairing uniforms, replacing the necessary items for personal hygiene and study, and surveilling the dormitory during the night[50]. The students were forbidden to have an arrogant attitude towards them and were invited to show them respect, «although they were their serfs»[51].

A supervisory system was organized to watch over the students: a *nadziratel'* (an inspector), assisted by *gubernery*, had to be responsible for

---

[47] See D.L. Ransel, 'Ivan Betskoi and the Institutionalization of the Enlightenment in Russia', *Canadian-American Slavic Studies*, XIV, 3 (1980), pp. 327-338.

[48] On their political character see Meilakh, *Pushkin i ego epokha*, p. 159.

[49] Seleznev, p. 10.

[50] Each room was not entirely separated from the next two, they could communicate from above.

[51] It was stated in the section of the rules for the students entitled 'Ob obrashchenii vospitannikov s nizshimi' (see M. Rudenskaia, S. Rudenskaia, *'Nastavnikam ... za blago vozdadim*, p. 97).

their moral conduct. Inspector «po uchebnoi i nravstvennoi chasti» from 1811 to 1813 was M.S. Piletskii-Urbanovich[52]. His attempts to introduce a police system of surveillance made him a figure detested both by teachers and students of the first course. The students themselves managed to obtain his dismissal after their protests about the system of control favoured by him, which was not particularly suitable to the general Lycée orientation[53].

An important side of the students' life was represented by their «extra-curricular» activities. Starting from the very beginning, they were involved in occupations mainly of a literary character[54]. Partly under the supervision of Professor Koshanskii, partly independently, they formed literary societies and issued a number of manuscript journals, written in prose and verse and containing translations, some of them illustrated with drawings and caricatures. Students' magazines were a quite typical phenomenon in Russian «closed» educational institutions. At Tsarskoe Selo they represented simultaneously a form of internal communication which enabled an unusually bright generation of students to express their literary interests and political enthusiasms, and to criticize the inner life as well as the outside world. But the predominant mood was not serious. In the pages of these journals the education they received was reflected through a satirical mirror, the events and teaching of the Lycée ironically commented on[55]. The students signed their contributions with initials and referred to each other using nicknames (each had their own). Modelled on «important» journals of those years, these magazines often parodied them. Some of them had a very short life or fell victim to the 1813 directive forbidding the publication of journals in the Lycée, officially because they «distracted their attention from studying». Others were to be continued by later generations of students. Taken altogether, they present a faithful picture of the unusually lively atmosphere within the Lycée. In 1811 appeared the

---

[52] Some of the directives signed by him are in TSDIAU, Fond 2039, op.1, no. 28, ff.1-2; no. 29, ff. 1-2.

[53] Pushkin was primarily involved in this, together with I. Malinovskii and Kiuchel'becker (see Meilakh, *Pushkin i ego epokha*, p. 134). Piletskii was replaced by V.V. Chachkov and then by S.S. Frolov.

[54] K.Ia. Grot, *Pushkinskii Litsei (1811-1817). Bumagi pervogo kursa, sobrannye akademikom Ia.K. Grotom* (Spb., 1911). See also V.P. Gaevskii, 'Pushkin v Litsee i litseiskie ego stikhotvoreniia', *Sovremennik*, no.8 (1863).

[55] Just to give a short example: they invented the humorous sentence:
«Vera, Nadezhda i Liubov',
Svekla, Kapusta i Morkov'»
(Faith, Hope and Love/ Beetroots, Cabbages and Carrots). The childish *prigovorka*, which appeared in the first issue of the *Vestnik* (published by K.Ia. Grot, *op. cit.*, p. 250), dismissed all the meaning of those key-words in the contemporary culture.

Tsarsko-Sel'skie litseiskie gazety and the *Vestnik*, in 1812 *Dlia udovol'stvia i pol'zy* and *Neopytnoe pero*, in 1813 *Iunye plovtsy* and *Litseiskii mudrets*. Although only fragments of these periodicals have survived, they are for us a valuable source of information about the students' mutual relations and their attitude towards their educators, inspectors and the Minister of Education.

It is necessary to specify that not all Tsarskoe Selo's students were involved in these voluntary initiatives. The school policy, as we have seen, was oriented towards encouraging the highest conformity in all possible ways. Notwithstanding this, within the first course different groups were soon formed. As in the case of the teachers, the students' outlooks were far from being identical, there were conflicts and different positions, defenders of conservative values and supporters of the new Russia.

The involvement in school magazines reflected quite faithfully the students' belonging to the group more receptive to the «spirit of the Lycée». In point of fact, if expressions frequently mentioned with reference to Tsarskoe Selo (such as *«litseiskaia respublika»*, *«litseiskii soiuz»*, *«sviatoe bratstvo»*) were established and used by a large number of students in their letters or papers[56], not all the students were affected to the same extent by the Lycée's liberal orientation.

The students were exposed to the same atmosphere, which reflected the complexity of the Russian intellectual climate of those years, and in which men of progressive ideas such as Malinovskii, Kunitsyn, Kaidanov, Koshanskii (with significant internal differences) were predominant. The fruits of Tsarskoe Selo's education, nevertheless, were not distributed impartially among the twenty-nine[57] *«litseisty»*.

The Lycée's historiographers (particularly Soviet) tended frequently to simplify the grouping into two fields, identified according to the pupils' proximity to the most celebrated Russian poet, A.S. Pushkin. The first group was thus formed by the poet's friends: I. Pushchin, A. Del'vig, V. Kiukhel'beker, F. Matiushkin, M. Iakovlev, I. Malinovskii, V. Vol'khovskii, A. Gorchakov, N. Korsakov, A. Illichevskii, K. Danzas. In point of fact, their names are the most recurrent in all the literary activities of the Lycée.

The second group was formed by the «others»: A. Bakunin, S. Broglio, P. Grevenits, S. Esakov, S. Komovskii, A. Kornilov, M. Korf, K.

---

[56] Kiukhel'beker was one of the first to introduce its use, in 1814.

[57] In 1813 the thirtieth student originally selected, K. Gur'ev, was excluded from the Lycée due to his bad behaviour.

Kostenskii, S. Lomonosov, A. Martynov, D. Maslov, P. Miasoedov, N. Rzhevskii, P. Savrasov, F. Steven, A. Tyrkov, P. Iudin[58].

The place that the Tsarskoe Selo's alumni were to occupy in Russian society also reflected their grouping during their Lycée years. For many of them it just opened the way to a quiet life in the Russian civic or military service. If Kiukhel'beker, Vol'khovskii and Pushchin were to be involved in the Decembrist revolt, Pushkin and Del'vig pursued the career of poets; as did Illichevskii, although with less success, and Kiukhel'beker.

Others followed a completely different path: Gorchakov became Chancellor and Minister of Foreign Affairs, Korf also attained a high post, Kostenskii became an ordinary bureaucrat and Steven governor in Vyborg. The composer and poet Korsakov died in Italy after converting to the Catholic faith, Matiushkin became a famous seafarer and Iakovlev a composer. Broglio, the son of a Sardinian aristocrat, was involved in the revolutionary movement in Piedmont. Korf wrote a reactionary book on Decembrists and a few reminiscences on the Lycée which are far from objective[59]. His close friend Komovskii also left a quite critical diary about the Lycée[60].

The range and variety in the students' destinies can be seen as more than mere chance; it can also be interpreted as an effect of the different, sometimes contradictory experiences offered by the Lycée. The most modern and progressive educational ideals were embodied in an institution which was conceived as the «Imperatorskii» Tsarskosel'skii Litsei and was characterized by firm ties with the Imperial family, whose presence punctuated the solemn ceremonies marking the most important events of the students' life. Side by side with men of enlightened ideas, or even radicals, the Lycée was ruled by reactionary officials and frightening inspectors. The students had to face a rigid daily schedule but were left completely free to satirize every aspect of that life in the journals they created and directed.

[58] On this classification into «druz'ia» (friends) and simple «soucheniki» (fellow-pupils) is based the work by M. Rudenskaia, S. Rudenskaia, Oni uchilis' s Pushkinym, op. cit..

[59] M.A. Korf, Zhizn' grafa Speranskogo (Spb, 1861); 'Zapiska grafa M.A. Korfa', in Grot, Ia.K., Pushkin, ego litseiskie tovarishchi i nastavniki (Spb, 1887).

[60] Published in K.Ia. Grot, Pushkinskii Litsei (1811-1817). Bumagi pervogo kursa, sobrannye akademikom Ia.K. Grotom (Spb., 1911).

4.2. Malinovskii at Tsarskoe Selo

4.2.1. A major inspirer of the Lycée's atmosphere

In the historiography of the Tsarskoe Selo Lycée there is general agreement about the importance of the moral and ideological atmosphere established there from the outset. During the first decades of the Lycée's existence this opinion was shared with particular fervour by the opponents of reforming processes in Russia. The idea of a *«litseiskii dukh»* responsible for disseminating the seeds of «love of freedom» in Russian society and closely connected with the events of 14 December 1825 established itself quite solidly immediately after the failed revolt. In point of fact, the spirit of eighteenth-century rationalism and the emphasis on republican principles with which teaching at Tsarskoe Selo was imbued inspired a considerable part of the Decembrist movement[61].

In 1826 in an official report entitled 'Nechto o Tsarskosel'skom litsee i dukhe onogo', prepared by the writer Faddei Bulgarin for the Third Department, the Lycée was identified as a revolutionary centre par excellence[62]. The expression «the spirit of the Lycée», which was to become particularly widespread, was used there to synthesize an atmosphere characterized by familiarity with forbidden revolutionary literature, disregard of discipline and opposition to authority.

The first nineteenth-century historiographers of the Lycée were all «internal», being former students, like N. Gastfreind, D. Kobeko, K.Ia Grot, or former librarians, like I.Seleznev; as authors of official reports, they sought to depict its life in an idyllic light, in which the legend about the school was intentionally deprived of any «political» colouring.

A significant part of the Soviet historical tradition overstated, on the other hand, the revolutionary impact of the Lycée and filled the legend

---

[61] On Decembrists see particularly V.I. Semevskii, *Politicheskie i obshchestvennye idei dekabristov* (Spb, 1909); M.P. Alekseev, B.S. Meilakh (eds.), *Dekabristy i ikh vremia. Materialy i soobshcheniia* (Moskva-Leningrad, 1951); A.G. Mazour, *The First Russian Revolution, 1825* (Stanford, California, 1961); M. Raeff, *The Decembrist Movement* (Englewood Cliffs, N.J., 1966).

[62] A part of the foreign press commented in similar terms on the revolt of 1825. In 1826 Metternich sent a dispatch to the Austrian ambassador in St Petersburg mentioning his request for news about the Lycée. He wrote that he had asked Gauenshil'd to give him the necessary information in order to understand how the legitimate sons of Alexander I came to organize a revolt against him (quoted by M. Rudenskaia, S. Rudenskaia, *'Nastavnikam ... za blago vozdadim*, p. 143).

about it with rhetoric. The transformation of the educational experiment initiated in 1811 into something which changed Russian history was pointed out in a number of studies devoted to the Lycée and to Pushkin's years at Tsarskoe Selo. The specific contribution to the establishment of the *«litseiskii dukh»* given by its first Director was nevertheless insufficiently studied[63].

The period spent by Malinovskii as educator of the Tsarskoe Selo's *litseisty* is one of the less obscure episodes in the biography of the Russian thinker. In both Russian and Soviet studies on the Lycée, nevertheless, the name of the first Director was mentioned in a rather misleading way. We are faced either with the peaceful, overly weak figure of the pre-revolutionary legend about the ideal Lycée, or with the one-sided *prosvetitel'-demokrat* of the Soviet interpretation. Both traditions pay too little attention to the way he specifically influenced the education of the young *litseisty*.

There were a number of factors which hindered a proper evaluation of Malinovskii's role: the short period covered by his directorship; his discreet personal style, enemy of any attempt at public recognition; the acknowledgement of the important role of the second Director, E.A. Engel'gardt, obscuring in many ways his own; ignorance of Malinovskii's previous activity as thinker and writer.

Malinovskii was first seen as a figure directly and strongly influencing the Lycée by Iu. Tynianov, who wrote: «the future Decembrists developed at the Lycée under his influence»[64]. A few decades later Meilakh reinforced this opinion by providing the first proper study based on the idea that «the basis of the ideo-educative work and the very direction of the Lycée's upbringing derived from the views of Malinovskii»[65].

Our opinion is that the Tsarskoe Selo Lycée must be identified to a much greater extent than hitherto as Malinovskii's creation. His spiritual paternity of the Lycée can be traced at various levels. The importance of gathering around himself a number of professors sharing his views has been

---

[63] In 1958 Meilakh outlined the persistence of the idea that «Pushkin's Lycée was some sort of 'happy chance'. It is further unclear who directed the Lycée's freedom of thought, how and in what the turbulent political life of Russia in those years was reflected at the Lycée» (Meilakh, *Pushkin i ego epokha*, pp. 16-17). Before him, Tynianov suggested the need to investigate in this direction (See Iu. Tynianov, 'Pushkin i Kiukhel'beker', *Literaturnoe nasledstvo*, no. 16-18 (1934), p. 320-378). Despite the numerous studies on the Lycée, a satisfactory and thorough interpretation of its spirit is still awaited.

[64] Iu. Tynianov, *V.K. Kiukhel'beker. Lirika i poemy*, I (Leningrad, 1939), p. VIII.

[65] Meilakh, *Pushkin i ego epokha*, p. 36.

shown above. The promising Lycée regulations collected in the *Ustav* might have remained as mere empty schemes; Malinovskii's role in allowing professors like Kunitsyn, Koshanskii and Kaidanov to do their work without excessive interference was decisive. Together with them he conscientiously pursued the aim of developing among the students the capacity for political and social criticism. «Political commitment» was a feature destined to become characteristic of the Russian student[66]. Malinovskii disseminated in the Lycée the ideas of «*obshchii dukh*» and «*obshchaia pol'za*» which had inspired his entire life; they were to recur in the work of many of the students educated at Tsarskoe Selo[67]. The motto «*Dlia obshchei pol'zy*» was inscribed on the medals given by the Lycée to the best students.

Malinovskii's directorship lasted only three years, being cut short by his premature death, but the students were affected by his practical example in their initial, highly receptive years in the Lycée, the most crucial in their formation. In this respect it is important to make the following distinction about Malinovskii's educative significance. His originality and depth as a theoretical pedagogue certainly may not have been exceptional, especially if compared with his corpus of ideas on peace; when it came to organizing the life at Tsarskoe Selo, he managed, however, to establish a system which was to leave an enduring trace in the history of the Lycée. He created the image of a Director particularly close to his students, a model which was successfully followed by his successors, above all Engel'gardt.

E.A. Engel'gardt was appointed Director in 1816, after a transitional phase. Although a man of moderate views, he did not attempt, especially during the first two years[68], to change substantially the Lycée tradition established by his predecessor. He highly appreciated Kunitsyn's teaching, was involved in conflicts with the Minister of Public Education Prince A.N. Golitsyn about the liberal orientation of the Lycée, and was very close to the students[69]. He was obliged to leave his post in 1823, after the Lycée was

[66] On the Russian student movement during the period 1855-1914, see the chapter 'Confronting Student Activism', in J.C. McClelland, *Autocrats and Academicians* (Chicago and London, 1979).

[67] See Meilakh, *Pushkin i ego epokha*, p. 37. See also the re-publication of Illichevskii's letters in L.B. Mikhailova, 'Vospominaniia litseistov', *Mir cheloveka*, no. 1 (1994), pp. 65-89.

[68] In a note for the Tsar, Engel'gardt even claimed more freedom and autonomy from the Ministry for the work he was to undertake as Director (*zapiska* published in *Russkii arkhiv*, no. 7-8 (1872), pp. 1474-1476).

[69] It is interesting to note how one of the points on which Engel'gardt was to be criticized was the close relation with the students inherited from Malinovskii. In a letter

moved from the Ministry of Public Education to the Military School (*Upravlenie voenno-uchebnykh zavedenii*)[70]. He remained in correspondence with many former lyceists and Decembrists, while the Lycée turned into a completely different institution. After him the third Director was Gol'tgoer, an Arakcheev man, and in 1829 Nicholas I could express the hope that «no more pupils, like those who graduated to Engel'gardt's taste, will come out of the Lycée»[71].

In this connection, it is worthy of note that Malinovskii's primary role in establishing the Lycée's ethos was evident to his students:

> E.A. Engel'gardt stands before us as an exceptional and progressive pedagogue, who has striven to the limit of his powers and possibilities to preserve the best traditions of the Lycée, those introduced by its first director, V.F. Malinovskii[72].

4.2.2. Malinovskii's ideas on education

Malinovskii expressed his views on education long before he was appointed Director of the new Lycée. The analysis of the official acts concerning his activity in the Lycée must therefore be integrated with consideration of other sources of a private and literary nature, and extending over a longer period of time. Moreover, it is legitimate to suggest that his previous credentials as a pedagogue were a decisive factor in his appointment.

Although he was the son of a pedagogue, Malinovskii owed his concern for education to the century in which he was born rather than to his personal history. The age of the Enlightenment put a particular stress on the question of education, and there was hardly a writer or a publicist who

---

dated 1810 the second Director wrote: «I have been informed that the close and friendly tie between me and the pupils does not do at all» (Quoted by Meilakh, *Pushkin i ego epokha*, p. 47)

[70] This was to be a decisive change in the Lycée's life. It was transformed into an institution which did not have anything in common with its glorious beginnings: admission policy became more restrictive, the selection of the teaching body followed different criteria and the scholastic programmes were revised. Any echo of freedom was definitely eliminated after the Decembrist revolt, when it was found that among the young men arrested in St Petersburg eight were former lyceists (only two of them were nevertheless condemned). A new, «tiuremnyi» order was established.

[71] Meilakh, *Pushkin i ego epokha*, p. 49.

[72] Note by Gorchakov, published in B.S. Meilakh, 'Kharakteristiki vospitannikov litseia v zapisiakh E.A. Engel'gardta', in *Pushkin. Issledovaniia i materialy*, III (Moskva-Leningrad, 1960), p. 348.

did not feel the compulsion to contribute to this theme during the last four decades of the eighteenth century[73]. Catherine II's serious attempts at reforming the Russian school system[74] were based on a belief which was shared by many of her contemporaries: the power of education to model new citizens. Novikov was one of the most prolific authors on this theme[75]. His writing 'O vospitanii i nastavlenii detei' (1783)[76] is central in illustrating his ideas on «raising children to be happy people and useful citizens». Important statements about the character and nature of instruction can be found in Karamzin's[77] and Shcherbatov's[78] work.

The beginning of the nineteenth century saw a new impulse towards the question of education with the reforms undertaken during the first years of Alexander I's reign. Authors like A.F. Bestuzhev[79], I.P. Pnin[80], V.V. Popugaev[81] and a number of others expressed their pedagogical views in

---

[73] Literature on Russian pedagogical thought is vast. In Russian see in particular M.I. Demkov, *Istoriia russkoi pedagogiki*, I-II (Revel', Spb., 1895,1898); P.F. Kapterev, *Istoriia russkoi pedagogiki* (Petrograd, 1915); M.F. Shabaeva (ed.), *Ocherki istorii shkoly i pedagogicheskoi mysli narodov SSSR: XVIII v. - pervaia polovina XIX v.* (Moskva, 1973). One of the main works in English is J.L. Black, *Citizens for the Fatherland. Education, Educators, and Pedagogical Ideals in Eighteenth-Century Russia* (New York, 1979).

[74] The Empress's efforts on behalf of education contributed fundamentally to the establishment of her reputation as an enlightened monarch in Europe. See in particular I.de Madariaga, 'The Foundation of the Russian Educational System by Catherine II', *Slavonic and East European Review*, XXXVI (1979), pp. 369-395.

[75] See N.I. Novikov, *Izbrannye pedagogicheskie sochineniia*, ed. N.A. Trushin (Moscow, 1959). Novikov's theoretical statements were illustrated in practice in some of his editorial initiatives. See on this W.G. Jones, 'Russia's First Magazine for Children: Novikov's «Detskoe Chtenie dlia Serdtsa i Razuma» (1785-89)', in R. Bartlett, A. Cross, K. Rasmussen (eds.), *Russia and the World of the Eighteenth Century* (Columbus, Ohio, 1988), pp. 177-187.

[76] Published in 1783 in *Pribavlenie k Moskovskim vedomostiam*. See the English translation by V. Snow, 'On the Upbringing and Instruction of Children', in M. Raeff, *Russian Intellectual History: An Anthology* (New York, 1966), pp. 68-86.

[77] Statements on education appear in 'Nechto o naukakh, iskusstvakh i prosveshchenii' (in *Aglaia*, 1794) and in the *Panteon inostrannoi slovesnosti*.

[78] See his 'Proekt o narodnom obrazovanii', in M.M. Shcherbatov, *Sochineniia*, eds. I.P. Krushchov, A.G. Voronov (Spb., 1896-1898). On the subject see also A. Lentin, 'Prince M.M. Shcherbatov as a Champion of Scientific Education', *Irish Slavonic Studies*, no. 11 (1990), pp. 73-78. The article is focused on Shcherbatov's writing entitled 'O sposobakh prepodavaniia raznye nauki', conceived as a sort of textbook for the scientific education, strictly private, of young noblemen.

[79] 'O vospitanii', in I.Ia. Shchipanov (ed.), *Russkie prosvetiteli ot Radishcheva do Dekabristov* (Moskva, 1966), I.

[80] 'Opyt i prosveshchenii otnositel'no k Rossii', in Shchipanov, *op.cit.* Pnin was an editor of the *Sankt-Peterburgskii zhurnal*, which was actively involved in the debate on education. See on this A.G. Cross, 'Pnin and the Sanktpeterburgskii zhurnal (1798)', *Canadian-American Slavic Studies*, VII, no. 1 (1973), pp.78-84.

[81] 'O blagopoluchii narodnykh tel', in Shchipanov, *op.cit.*

those years. Apart from the substantial agreement about the dependence of a well-ordered, functioning state on education, their ideas varied significantly about its various aspects: methods and purposes of instruction, range of subjects, the need for a predominantly moral or scientific upbringing, the question of the education of women, the interest in physical education. Their views were strongly influenced by the body of principles elaborated by Western thinkers: echoes of the educational thought of Erasmus, Fénelon, Comenius, Montaigne, Locke, and Voltaire were an essential part of the Russian debate[82].

To establish Malinovskii's thought on pedagogy is not easy, spread as it is through the various writings in which he touched upon the question of education. In them we can find his general theoretical position before he was practically involved in the organization of the Lycée. It is significant that more than twenty years before the founding of the first Russian Lycée, Malinovskii devoted one of the letters of his 'Rossiianin v Anglii' to the detailed description of its English prototype:

> In the London neighbourhood there are a number of boarding schools for children, they are called Academies, and for the most part they are in villages not too far from the town, which is also very worthy imitating, both because of the clean air and because the children do not have so many things that distract their attention[83].

From this letter we gain an idea of the extent to which Malinovskii was intellectually and emotionally involved in this enterprise. The direct knowledge of these institutions certainly put him in a privileged position when the features of the Russian Lycée had to be elaborated. Analogies between the model observed in England and the institution realized at Tsarskoe Selo can be found on various levels:

> The children live in these Academies and return home only during the vacations. They are sent off early to these Academies, where they learn to read, write, do Mathematics, Geography, Latin, Greek and French, drawing, dance and music. Their keep is simple. An hour before lessons they breakfast on hot milk and bread. For lunch they are given pudding and roast beef, or another type of meat with greens and potatoes. For supper they are fed on bread, butter and cheese. This simple but satisfying food, and in addition their playfulness in the open air, however bad the weather, makes them strong and healthy.

---

82 For a description of the West European writings translated in Russian during the second half of the eighteenth century, see M.J. Okenfuss, 'Popular Educational Tracts in Enlightenment Russia: A Preliminary Survey', *Canadian-American Slavic Studies*, XIV, 3 (1980), pp. 307-326.

83 *Priiatnoe i poleznoe preprovozhdenie vremeni*, XII (1796), p. 409.

The only relevant difference between the two types of institution is to be seen in the private status of the English one[84]:

> These Academies are maintained by private individuals. Keep and tuition cost around three hundred roubles a year at the usual Academies. But there are other much dearer and much cheaper.

The absence of a work treating separately the theme of education is not a sign of Malinovskii's only occasional concern for it, but is evidence of the connection of education with other more general problems in Russian society. This is particularly apparent in his major work, *Dissertation on Peace and War*, in which education is seen as a primary element to reinforce national awareness and self-identity. In this respect he particularly stressed the necessity for each state to have its own universities and to pursue the education of its citizens in their own language:

> every society should take care over education; not only in academic study, but in the instillation from infancy of good habits of moderation and love of the fatherland (...) As not every region has the means to teach all sciences, in each language's state there must be universities, to which those who wish to can go to study, so that attachment to one's own language is established from youth (...) All the teachers should also share one language[85].

The social importance of education is emphasized in Malinovskii's idea that every person living in a country should have access to a certain level of education[86]:

> The ability to read and count is the inalterable need of every condition, likewise everything we need to know and to understand the state of our own society and its relations to all others in their union; everyone should know these things[87].

Despite the development of schooling for girls favoured by Catherine II, this issue was still controversial at the time when Malinovskii was

---

[84] The Lycée was entirely financed by the Russian state. The annual sum assigned to the Lycée was 96,545 rubles (Seleznev, *op. cit.*, p.14).

[85] *Rassuzhdenie o mire i voine*, ed. J. Skowronek, in '«Rozwazania o pokoju i wojnie» Wasyla F. Malinowskiego', *Teki archiwalne*, no. 17 (1978), p. 43.

[86] It is worth noting that especially after the French Revolution advocating universal education was not particularly common in Russia.

[87] *Rassuzhdenie o mire i voine*, ed. J. Skowronek, p. 43.

writing[88]. His opinion is well illustrated in his praise for educated women in 'Rossiianin v Anglii' and in his contempt for illiterate Moldavians. Furthermore, he saw in women potentially ideal instructors for children[89].

In the last issue of *Osennie vechera* he introduced the subject of education in close connection with his considerations on love for the fatherland:

> the institution of the universities is an important factor in the unification of inhabitants distinct in language and customs, all the more as all the impressions gained in youth remain ineradicable throughout life (...) teaching must apply its efforts to arousing a social spirit, to bringing closer through this all fellow countrymen and to giving them a worthy and useful training[90].

In 'Rossiianin v Anglii' Malinovskii mentioned the importance of Rousseau's *Emile* [91] in his formation. In the 'Zapiski o Moldavii' he reiterated his reference to this text as one of the most important sources of his pedagogical views:

> I recalled Rousseau's *Emile* and I think that everyone should without fail learn some sort of trade. Such a person will be above all the vicissitudes of fortune; wherever he is, he will always be able to earn his living[92].

Malinovskii's attention to educational matters included every level of the Russian school system. He was particularly concerned with promoting an improvement in the conditions in which school teachers did their work, which was vitally important for society. In *Pustynnik*, in the chapter entitled 'Tserkov' i uchilishche', the hermit visits a primary school in which he meets a teacher living in conditions of extreme indigence. Struck by this, he blames the society around him:

> Surely your citizens are not as hard-hearted as the stones in which they are confined? Surely there is someone who enters into your condition and rewards you for your labours? How is that none of the parents of your pupils help you? And why is your salary so low? How can it be that when

---

[88] On this see in particular 'Educating Women in Eighteenth-Century Russia', in J.L. Black, *Citizens for the Fatherland*, *op.cit.*

[89] See the present work, p. 61.

[90] *Osennie vechera*, p. 60.

[91] Published in 1762, it was translated into Russian in 1779 (in an abridged version). Despite Catherine II's official disapproval, the book acquired a certain popularity.

[92] *Priiatnoe i poleznoe preprovozhdenie vremeni*, XIV (1797), p. 36. The instrumental approach to education was to be one of the main features of the Tsarskoe Selo Lycée, conceived as the place where the bureaucratic elite had to be instructed.

this was arranged, they did not consider how much better behaved and
more reliable married teachers would be than unmarried?[93]

In this respect it is also important to remember that Malinovskii gave
an important role to charitable institutions in society[94].

In 1811 Malinovskii's involvement in education passed from a general
concern for the need to disseminate knowledge and promote science to the
very specific task of drafting new rules for a new institution. The corpus of
extant documents relating to his pedagogical activity at the Lycée is not
particularly rich: a number of administrative acts; a succinct
correspondence with Razumovskii[95]; a few brief references in his private
diaries of the time. His series of lectures is lost[96]. The problem of these
lectures deserves a few words. The Director, obliged by the Lycée *Ustav* to
replace teachers when they were absent, probably prepared a number of
lectures[97]. Nevertheless, at the moment they seem to be the only documents
which remained untraced.

In the period preceding the opening of the Lycée, Malinovskii wrote a
series of notes which, together with his administrative communications to
the Ministry, present the pedagogical principles he thought necessary to
apply at the Lycée. The document is called 'Pamiatnaia kniga litseia' and is
dated 20 August 1811. Here his ideas are organized in points. Particularly
relevant are the following:

> 2. It is necessary to disclose children's intellectual faculties, immediately
> revealing a subject as if there - Le coeur qui s'apuie sur un sage conseil est
> come une muraille bien crepie avec enduit de chaux et de sable. (...) During
> walks conversation is allowed.
> 3. After comparison, another important thing in developing the mind is
> noting degrees of change, from a blade of grass to an oak, from an insect to
> cattle (...).

[93] Dated 28 June 1799, IRLI, F. 244, op. 25, no. 307, ll. 21-22.

[94] Malinovskii expressed admiration for the English charitable institutions in
'Rossiianin v Anglii' and in *Osennie vechera*. In his concern for their existence he showed
another element of affinity with Novikov and his initiatives. See on this W.G. Jones, 'The
«Morning Light» Charity Schools, 1777-80', *The Slavonic and East European Review*,
LVI, 1 (1978), pp. 47-67.

[95] TSDIAU, Fond 2039, op.1, no. 30; no. 32, ff. 1-10 (Perepiska ministra
Prosveshcheniia Razumovskogo s direktorom litseia).

[96] The only document we found which could possibly be identified as a fragment of
these series of lectures is a brief manuscript entitled 'Urok o chislakh' and dated 14 January
1813, Tsarskoe Selo (IRLI, Fond 244, op. 25, no. 325).

[97] Their existence is mentioned in various studies on Malinovskii. Arab-Ogly even
specified that they were «on international and natural law» (*op. cit.*, p. 36).

> 4. Having disclosed intellectual faculties, to teach the distinction of good
> from evil, and how not to act or speak or think without reasoning, in so far
> as every thought is converted into a desire and further into action[98].

The problem of «*dobro i zlo*» (good and evil), to which an entire page of this text is devoted, all in French, was particularly full of «civic» implications at that time. The emphasis on the development of reason is also explicit. The physical development of the pupils was no less important than the cultivation of the mind. Malinovskii had stressed this point particularly in his *Dissertation on Peace and War*: «the gymnastic exercises of the young people should be the favourite spectacle of the whole society»[99]. As we have seen, walking was an important part of the day of the *litseisty*, being regularly alternated with class hours. Walking in the magnificent grounds of Tsarskoe Selo was conceived by Malinovskii as a pedagogical principle no less than an esthetic pleasure. The observation of nature[100] played a significant role in the learning process. Malinovskii's motto in this respect could indeed be «*progulki vazhnee chem lektsii*» (walks are more important then lectures), as suggested by Tynianov[101]. In the 'Pamiatnaia kniga litseia' he wrote:

> During walks, conversation is allowed; to impress something in the
> memory, it is better to explain it, while indicating a subject which is from
> time to time renewed. To say as clearly that the stroll itself is pleasant as
> repose after labour[102].

The Director was also deeply concerned about the importance of creating ideal hygienic and healthy conditions for the students. Later, in one of his reports to the Minister, he had the opportunity to highlight the positive effects of this treatment:

> The health of the pupils is maintained in supreme conditions, the hospital is
> almost always empty: walks, baths and good food protect them from
> debility and attacks. In the house cleanliness and order are observed in all
> areas: warmth is kept to a prescribed temperature, the sleeping corridor,

---

[98] IRLI, Fond 244, op. 25, no. 290. Fragments were published in Meilakh, *Pushkin i ego epokha*, pp. 41-42, and in P.G. Tichini, O.I. Bilets'kii (eds.), *O.S. Pushkin (statti ta materiali)* (Kiev, 1938), p. 181.

[99] *Rassuzhdenie o mire i voine*, Part III, Skowronek's edition, p. 43.

[100] He wrote: «Nature is like a book from which we take the representation of our thoughts» (TSDIAU, Fond 2039, op. 1, no. 83, f. 3).

[101] The formula is adopted by Tynianov to characterize the innovative position of Malinovskii (*Pushkin* (Moskva, 1937), p. 292).

[102] IRLI, Fond 244, op. 25, no. 290, f.1.

through adjustments introduced by the architect, is heated to an agreed
level[103].

The speech prepared by Malinovskii for the inauguration of the Lycée
is an important document of his educational principles[104]: it stressed the
primacy of reason and the importance of instilling proper moral notions; it
was characterized by the sense of fatherhood and the preference for non-
repressive education which informed his task as a pedagogue.

Malinovskii's role as Director of the Lycée was limited by Minister
Razumovskii's interferences. The *Ustav* of 1811 (paragraph 15) stated that
the Director could be confirmed or dismissed only by the Emperor, upon
the recommendation of the Minister of Public Education. While universities
had been given a certain degree of autonomy in 1804, the Lycée had been
put under the direct supervision of the Minister, who personally supervised
various aspects of its activity. Malinovskii had to send a weekly report, a
«vedomost' o sostoianii Litseia» informing him about the life in the Lycée.

As shown by the episode of the inauguration, the conflict with
Razumovskii acquired from the beginning the features of a fight between
two different ideological positions, in which Malinovskii embodied the need
for non-conventional, progressive education, and Razumovskii the recourse
to power and repressive methods. This conflict was played out in the very
practical, daily life of the Lycée. Malinovskii's official correspondence with
Razumovskii is quite illuminating of their positions concerning several
concrete problems.

On 12 December 1811 the Director arranged an official event at
Tsarskoe Selo at which professors and students gathered to select the best
students, whose names were written in golden letters on a white board in
the central hall. Razumovskii criticized this system of acknowledging
success introduced by Malinovskii as unnecessary and ordered him to
eliminate it[105].

Another occasion of conflict concerned the system of internal control.
We have already mentioned the case of Piletskii-Urbanovich. Malinovskii
actively supported the teachers and the students in their request for the
inspector to be removed. He wrote to the Minister:

> The inspector of the moral side assists me very eagerly, but unfortunately
> he is not tolerated by many of the tutors, and if this resulted only from his

---

[103] IRLI, Fond 244, op.25, no.8 , ll. 5-5a. Dated 26 November 1812, *«sekretno»*.
[104] The discourse is described in chapter 1.4.2. of the present work.
[105] See M. Rudenskaia, S. Rudenskaia, *'Nastavnikam ... za blago vozdadim*, p. 38.

indelicacy, I would have hoped to change his manner and actions, through his evident obedience, but I notice a certain antipathy between them based on the opposition of their principles[106].

On 13 March 1812 Razumovskii wrote to the Director to convince him about the «instructive» necessity to «allocate places to the pupils in the classes in accordance with their progress in learning and behaviour»[107]. The introduction of such a formal discrimination was not supported by Malinovskii, who nevertheless had finally to give in[108].

Occasion of conflict was also the institution of a pension attached to the Lycée. Malinovskii was particularly involved in it and managed to see its inauguration just two months before his death. His son Iosif was to attend it. The «Blagorodnyi Litseiskii Pansion»[109] was opened on 27 January 1814. Located in a different part of Tsarskoe Selo but close to the Lycée[110], it was designed to supply new students for it. Razumovskii, ignoring the regulation about the Pension according to which its Director had to be a Russian, appointed Professor Gauenschild, who did not even receive Russian citizenship[111]. Malinovskii, who did not favour the idea of having foreign teachers of French and German (he thought it was necessary to «make do without foreigners»[112]), supported another candidate, Koshanskii. On 12 November 1813 Razumovskii wrote to Malinovskii:

> Professor Koshanskii gave me his petition regarding his appointment as director of the Pension set up in Tsarskoe Selo; but as I have already appointed another official to this position, I entrust you to inform Koshanskii of this[113].

The reply from Malinovskii came the day after. It was immediate and harsh, pointing out the break of rules by the omnipotent Minister:

> I announced to Professor Koshanskii that another official has already been appointed as director of the Pension set up in Tsarskoe Selo, as regards

---

[106] IRLI, Fond 244, op. 25, no. 8, ll. 5a-6.

[107] *Ibid.*, no. 32, f. 8.

[108] *Ibid.*, no. 30, f. 1.

[109] See N. Golitsyn, *Blagorodnyi pansion imperatorskogo tsarskosel'skogo litseia 1814-1829* (Spb., 1869). See also Seleznev, *op.cit.*, pp. 34-35, 36-41, 104-110.

[110] It was built by the architect V.P. Stasov (see M. Rudenskaia, S. Rudenskaia, *'Nastavnikam ... za blago vozdadim*, p. 253).

[111] Seleznev, *op. cit.*, p. 103.

[112] IRLI, Fond 244, op. 25, no. 8 , l. 6.

[113] TSDIAU, Fond 2039, op. 1, no. 32, f. 10.

which I also have the honour to report that until now I have no information
about his application[114].

4.2.3. A Director and a father

As shown before, isolation from the outside world was one of the
features characterizing education at Tsarskoe Selo. Malinovskii noted from
the beginning how difficult it was for the pupils to accept the prohibition on
leaving the Lycée. On 20 October 1811, the day after the inauguration, he
wrote: «Some children received the fact that they would never, even in any
vacation, be allowed home, with deep feelings»[115]. This condition gave
Malinovskii, in his capacity as Director, the opportunity to create a sort of
privileged world, isolated from the rest of society, in which to establish
new rules and behaviour inspired by the ideals he believed in.

Education was conceived by him not only as a constant advance of
knowledge, but also as the instilling of just moral and religious principles:
the evening prayers of the students were an important part of their day. The
way he treated the young students was informed by the most egalitarian
principles. He took particular care of pupils coming from non-noble
families[116]. He was also quite aware of the fact that there was a cultural
clash between the students, mainly young aristocrats[117], and the teachers,
who, quite typically for Russian gymnasiums and universities of that time,
were former seminarists, «*popovichi*», or «*raznochintsy*». Holding solid
opinions on the role of education in reforming society[118], he discouraged
discriminatory attitudes originating in social differences and attempted to
reconcile the inevitable conflicts.

Malinovskii also tended to establish a system which abolished coercion
and sanctions. In a page of his diary for 21 March 1812 we read:

> A person must constrain himself to do good and speak the truth (...) there
> is some freedom in any coercion to do good (...) But there is a difference

---

[114] Rough draft, *ibid.*, f. 1a.

[115] IRLI, Fond 244, op. 25, no. 290, f. 5.

[116] Contrarily to Razumovskii, he saw favourably the idea of promotion in social
class through education. See the case of Vol'khovskii mentioned above (p. 100).

[117] For a survey of the social background of the *litseisty*, see N.Ia. Eidel'man, *Tvoi
vosemnadtsatyi vek. Prekrasen nash soiuz...* (Moskva, 1991), pp. 227-228.

[118] «(slavery) spoils the disposition of the Russian. This arrogance, quick temper and
mercenary baseness and servility are from upbringing, life and dealing with slaves»
('Razmyshlenie o preobrazovanii gosudarstvennogo ustroistva Rossii', in *Izbrannye
obshchestvenno-politicheskie sochineniia*, p. 121).

between a person constraining himself and being constrained, for no good can result when a man is constrained by another to do good[119].

When Korf was caught reading a forbidden book (*Voyage de Platon en Italie*) instead of attending the drawing class, the Director merely suggested that he should join the other pupils in the class[120].

As shown above, one of the effects of the condition of isolation at Tsarskoe Selo was to reinforce the collective feeling among the students. It engendered, on the other hand, the need to replace their geographically distant homes with familiar figures. This was particularly important considering the relatively «intimate» dimensions of this institution compared with the majority of contemporary Russian gymnasiums and universities. The pupils of the only class working at Tsarskoe Selo during the first three years could see in Vasilii Fedorovich a particularly familiar and intimate figure. Close contacts and informal conversations with him were quite frequent[121]. In addition, evening gatherings in the two-storey house in front of the Lycée[122] in which the Director lived with his family were not an unusual event. His personal qualities and his educational approach made his relationship with the students unusually positive[123]. As witnessed by published and unpublished sources, Malinovskii came to act as a substitute for their natural family. One of the students wrote:

> Granting to the children a certain freedom in manner, he never surrounded them with fear, and before resorting to severe measures, he tried to win over the young heart by gentleness, patience and a friendly manner. The custom, which later turned into a rule for the pupils, of spending leisure hours in the director's family (...) Malinovskii's family replaced their own families for them[124].

---

[119] TSDIAU, Fond 2039, op. 1, no. 83, ff. 28,32.

[120] 'Starina Tsarskosel'skogo litseia', *Russkii archiv*, I (1876), p. 481.

[121] Some of the statements and considerations contained in his private diaries of those years offer an insight into the probable themes of those conversations: Malinovskii wrote about «dobro i zlo», «vremia i vechnost'», the knowledge of God (RGALI, Fond 312, op.1, no. 3, ff. 47-54), or prepared reflections for the evening prayer (f. 50).

[122] It was more modest than it appears nowadays, being substantially restructured by Engel'gardt (see M. Rudenskaia, S. Rudenskaia, 'Nastavnikam ... za blago vozdadim, p. 245).

[123] Regrettably, Malinovskii did not write a «personal» report on his students comparable to that left by the second director Engel'gardt. On it see B. Meilakh, 'Kharakteristiki vospitannikov litseia v zapisiakh E.A. Engel'gardta', in N.V. Izmailov (ed.), *Pushkin. Issledovaniia i materialy*, III (1960), pp. 347-361. We have therefore only official reports to deal with (See the draft of his 'vedomost' ob uspekhakh litseistov', IRLI, Fond 244, op. 25, no. 291).

[124] TSDIAU, Fond 2039, op.1, no. 62, f. 2. The document is signed «pervogo kursa litseist».

Malinovskii's habit of receiving the *litseisty* of the first course in his home[125] was certainly also due to the fact that among them was his own son Ivan[126]. But he did not discriminate against other students, as Gorchakov remarked:

> Je ne connais point d'expression pour louer m. Malinoffsky (*sic*); quel excellent, quel digne homme; il se comporte avec nous comme avec ses enfants et il ne fait de différence entre nous et son fils[127].

Ivan Malinovskii (1796-1873) was already sixteen when the school opened, but he was admitted to the Lycée thanks to an innocent bureaucratic stratagem: in the official documents his age was reduced by two years. His nickname among the students was «*kazak*», alluding to his particularly lively and impulsive character. A letter written by Malinovskii to Ivan survives, in which his paternal concern for the intemperance of his son overlaps quite significantly with the educative principles he had adopted as Director of the Lycée. Replying to a letter from Ivan, Malinovskii wrote:

> Your letter, gentle son, is good because it declares that love of your fatherland, which you have in your heart: not only your age, but also the circumstances in Russia, quiet and calm until now, have restrained these feelings, just as now the cold is restraining the trees from adorning themselves with leaves: you will find much more still in your soul, unknown before, feelings develop with age and it is there that the business of upbringing lies: to direct these feelings to the good, and just as exortation and concern are required from our side for this, so attentiveness and submission are required from yours. Some things will seem not right to you, but that is a shortcoming of age, which makes it impossible to understand all things as one should, and for that reason it behoves you to believe first, and then later to allow your mind to assess the advantages of

---

[125] The students started to gather in the Director's house before the beginning of the courses, for practical reasons connected with the arrangement of their future life in the Lycée. Referring to his first meeting with Pushkin, Pushchin wrote: «I found out about his admission at the first meeting at our director's, V.F.Malinovskii's, where we were called together more than once at the start to be measured and then to be fitted with dress, linen, jack-boots, boots, hats and so on. At these gatherings we all more or less got acquainted. On these occasions the director's son Ivan was already something like a host to us». (*op.cit.*, p. 33).

[126] His other son Andrei Malinovskii finished the Lycée in 1823 (receiving a golden medal), became an officer of the Guard, was involved in the events of 1825 and was arrested; was then sent to the Caucasian army and was under police control until his death. In TSDIAU there are two letters signed by André Malinovsky, written in French and without addressee (Fond 2053, op.1, nos. 1291,1292).

[127] Letter dated 26 November 1811, quoted by M. Rudenskaia, S. Rudenskaia, *'Nastavnikam ... za blago vozdadim*, p. 47.

the judgement of your elders (...) on this power is based, it is the guardian
of the well-being of its subordinates[128].

Ivan Vasil'evich was always to be faithful to the ideals of the Lycée
and to his father's teaching. He was to remember in his diary the
importance that the example and advice of his father had on his life[129]. He
corresponded with other *litseisty* and jealously kept most of his father's
papers[130].

4.2.4. Malinovskii and A.S. Pushkin

The question of Malinovskii's influence on the intellectual and spiritual
formation of the young Pushkin is a challenging and inspiring theme. The
idea that the teaching and the personality of the first Director left an
important echo in the mind of the young poet is quite fascinating, and
appears entirely authorized in the context of the life at the Tsarskoe Selo
Lycée. This idea certainly deserves to be pursued in depth, on the basis of a
comparative analysis of the ideas expressed by the two Russian intellectuals.
It could add new elements to the picture of Pushkin's ideological sources
and show on the other hand the persistence of Malinovskii's legacy in
Russian culture.

Such an analysis goes beyond the scope of the present work. It is
nevertheless possible to highlight a few elements which corroborate the
hypothesis of a certain closeness between the Director and his pupil,
although at present we cannot ascertain whether this closeness developed
into a particular affinity[131].

---

[128] Dated 14 February 1813, RGALI, Fond 312, op. 1, no. 5, ff. 3-4.

[129] See N. Petrunina (ed.), 'Iz materialov pushkinskogo litseia', *Pushkin. Issledovaniia i materialy*, XIII (1989), p. 339. The diary of I.V. Malinovskii published there refers to the years 1816-1817.

[130] In 1825 he retired from service in the Russian army (where he was *polkovnik*) and moved to the village of Kamenka, located in the Iziumskii district, which he had inherited from his grandfather Samborskii. There he undertook various measures to relieve the conditions of the local peasantry. He was deeply upset when his younger brother Andrei Vasil'evich and his brother-in-law Rozen were arrested for their involvement with the Decembrist revolt. In 1845 he married E.F. Vol'khovskaia. For more detailed information about him, see M.P. Rudenskaia, S.D. Rudenskaia, *Oni uchilis' s Pushkinym* (Leningrad, 1976), pp. 127-141; and by the same author, *S litseiskogo poroga* (Leningrad, 1984), pp. 118-129.

[131] It is significant that the two Russians had particularly warm and inspiring encounters in the pages of Tynianov's novel *Pushkin* (Moskva, 1937).

The close friendship between Ivan Malinovskii and the young Pushkin represents one of these elements. It was to play a fundamental role in the personal life of the poet even after his years at Tsarskoe Selo. Significantly, on his death-bed Pushkin said: «What a shame that neither Pushchin or Malinovskii are here; it would be easier for me to die»[132]. Although this friendship became particularly close after the Director's death[133], the hypothesis of Vasilii Fedorovich's role in it is entirely plausible.

A second fact to be considered is the existence of well-rooted connections between the Malinovskii and the Pushkin families[134] going back to the years preceding the founding of the Tsarskoe Selo Lycée (which can perhaps explain the decision to include Aleksandr Sergeevich among the students examined for admission). Another circumstance indicates the personal contacts between Malinovskii and Pushkin beyond the official relations characterizing life at the Tsarskoe Selo Lycée[135]: in 1813 the pupil presented the Director with one of his drawings, entitled «Prodavets kvasa»[136].

The idea that the figure of Malinovskii was particularly significant in Pushkin's early years is supported by other evidence as well, which can be found in the poet's papers: two references to Vasilii Fedorovich in his 'Plan avtobiograficheskikh zapisok'. Pushkin's notes referring to his early Lycée period are not available today: at the end of 1825, in an excess of precaution, he burnt his *litseiskie zapiski* containing his first impressions. The reaction to the Decembrist revolt came in fact to affect considerably the record of the Lycée's events and life: Pushchin also destroyed his diary

[132] See 'Starina Tsarskosel'skogo litseia', *Russkii arkhiv*, I (1875), p. 479.

[133] In her memoirs his daughter Sof'ia Ivanovna Shtakenshneider wrote that on the day of the funeral of the Director Pushkin was the first to console Ivan Vasil'evich, and that on that occasion they swore their perpetual friendship.

[134] See pp. 13-14 of the present work.

[135] See in particular V.V. Veresaev, *Pushkin v zhizni* (Moskva 1936), and M.A. Tsiavlovskii, *Letopis' zhizni i tvorchestva A.S. Pushkina* (Moskva, 1951).

[136] See L.B. Modzalevskii, B. Tomashevskii (eds.), *Rukopisi Pushkina khraniashchiesiia v Pushkinskom dome* (Leningrad, 1935), p. 281. The drawing is reproduced and described in S.M. Asnash, A.N. Iakhontov, *Opisanie Pushkinskogo Muzeia imperatorskogo Aleksandrovskogo Litseia* (Spb, 1899), pp. 40-41. Another fact to consider in this respect is that in 1889 Ja. Grot wrote to Malinovskii's daughter Mariia to thank her for two letters by Pushkin she sent to him, promising that he was going to make use of them for a biography of Pushkin (TSDIAU, Fond 2039, op. 1, no. 54, f. 8).

and other materials before being arrested[137], and Kiukhel'beker probably did the same with his early diary[138].

Pushkin was to return later to the idea of writing an extensive autobiography. The document known as 'Plan avtobiograficheskikh zapisok' (or 'Programma avtobiografii')[139], written probably in 1830, contains his project in this sense. These autobiographical notes were never followed by any extensive work, they remained only a fragment. Under the year 1811 we read nevertheless: «*The Lycée*. Opening. The Tsar. Malinovskii. Kunitsyn. Arakcheev». We do not know the treatment which Pushkin intended to reserve for the figure of his first Director. It must be considered quite significant, at all events, that he felt the compulsion to include the Director among the remarkable events characterizing the day of the inauguration of the Lycée. His name is mentioned again for the year 1814, to record his death («Death of Malinovskii»).

On Malinovskii's part, on the other hand, references to the Lycée's pupils taken individually are extremely scanty. Nothing suggests that the Director saw in the eleven-year boy the poetic genius he was to become. In Malinovskii's unofficial papers there is no record of his relationship with the young Pushkin. The only documents in which Aleksandr Sergeevich is mentioned are those of an official nature. From them we gain the idea that the Director's picture of Pushkin was that of a substantially mediocre student. After the first impression given on the occasion of the admission exam[140], Malinovskii came to elaborate a not particularly complimentary opinion on Pushkin: «empty-headed and frivolous, skilled in French and drawing, in arithmetic he is lazy and lagging behind»[141]. In the draft of his 'vedomost' ob uspekhakh litseistov', he recorded his judgement on Pushkin's success in all the subjects. In Russian he showed «more insight and taste than application, but there is emulation. Fairly good progress»; in French he «has become more diligent and progress is steady»; in German he was «extremely intelligent, ingenious and witty, but not at all industrious and progress is insignificant»; in Mathematics showed «wit, but for idle chat, very lazy and not modest in the class, mediocre progress»; in History

---

[137] He later published his reminiscences: I.I. Pushchin, *Zapiski o Pushkine. Pis'ma*, ed. S.Ia. Shtraikh (Moskva, 1956).

[138] V.N. Orlov, S.I. Khmel'nitskii (eds.), *Dnevnik V.K. Kiukhel'bekera* (Leningrad, 1929).

[139] P.V. Annenkov, *Materialy dlia biografii A.S. Pushkina* (Moskva, 1984).

[140] See pp. 84 of the present work.

[141] IRLI, Fond 244, op. 25, no. 290.

had «more talent than application, distracted, progress quite good»; on his behaviour, Malinovskii wrote: «frivolous, a rake»[142].

The hypothesis of the Director's influence on Pushkin is not invalidated by these judgments on the young pupil: apparently Malinovskii's opinion did not diverge markedly from that of other teachers attending to his education. During his early Lycée period talent and potential were in fact recognized in Pushkin, but the superficiality and inconsistency of his personality were equally noted, especially by Kunitsyn and Kartsov[143].

The question of Malinovskii's influence on Pushkin can more fruitfully be seen in the wider context of a circumstance universally recognized: the fact that the education achieved by Pushkin at Tsarskoe Selo played a crucial role in the formation of his social and political ideas[144]. As we argued, the establishment of the «litseiskii dukh» and the creation of the liberal atmosphere characterizing that institution was primarily due to the contribution of the first Director.

The recurrence of the Lycée theme at various stages in Pushkin's work struck generations of *pushkinisty* [145]. In particular the verses from *Evgenii Onegin* (part VIII) gave immortality to the meaning the poet gave to the years he spent at Tsarskoe Selo:

In those days, when in the Lycée gardens
I flourished serenely... [146]

[142] *Ibid.*, no. 291.

[143] V.V. Veresaev, *Pushkin v zhizni* (Moskva, Leningrad, 1932), pp. 41-42.

[144] Pushkin's interpretation of the major social problems characterizing Russia during the first part of the nineteenth century has been investigated in a number of studies: see S.L. Abramovich, 'Krest'ianskii vopros v stat'e Pushkina «Puteshestvie iz Moskvy v Peterburg»', *Pushkin. Issledovaniia i materialy*, IV (1962), pp. 208-236; P. Drews, 'Puskin als politischer Dichter', *Zeitschrift für slawische Philologie*, no. 43 (1983), pp. 38-54; G.M. Fridlender, 'Vol'nost' i zakon (Pushkin i Velikaia frantsuzskaia revoliutsiia)', in G.M. Fridlender (ed.), *Velikaia frantsuzskaia revoliutsiia i russkaia literatura* (Leningrad, 1990); I.V. Nemirovskii, 'Stat'ia A.S. Pushkina «Aleksandr Radishchev» i obshchestvennaia bor'ba 1801-1802 godov', in A.M. Panchenko (ed.), *XVIII vek*, XVII (1991), pp. 123-134; S. Driver, *Pushkin. Literature and Social Ideas* (New York-Oxford, 1989).

[145] V. Gaevskii, 'Pushkin v Litsee i litseiskie ego stikhotvoreniia', *Sovremennik*, no. 7 (1863). The influence of his early years in the Lycée has been recently highlighted in P. Volokhonskaia, '«V sadakh litseia ia bezmiatezhno rastsvetal»', in Nekrasov (ed.), pp. 81-90.

[146] (V te dni, kogda v sadakh Litseia/ Ia bezmiatezhno rastsvetal...). A part of the pre-revolutionary *pushkinovedenie* tended to interpret Pushkin's affection for his Lycée period as a pure manifestation of nostalgic feelings about youth, a quite common phenomenon. In point of fact, the «political» Pushkin, the author of odes and poems written immediately after he finished Lycée, like 'Vol'nost'', 'Skazki' (Noël), 'K Chaadaevu' and

Equally universally quoted are Pushkin's 'Vospominaniia v Tsarskom Sele', the poem he wrote for his final examination at the Lycée. Echoes of the importance of his education at Tsarskoe Selo can be traced in a number of writings of various natures[147].

The specific role of Malinovskii in the formation of the young Pushkin was not given particular attention as a phenomenon distinct from the general influence of the Tsarskoe Selo Lycée. This can be easily explained as a consequence of the general underevaluation of Malinovskii's contribution to the life in the Lycée which was illustrated above.

The fact that Pushkin reserved for Kunitsyn, and not for Malinovskii, the role of being the primary ideological figure orienting his Lycée's years[148] contributed to consolidate the tradition which tended to exclude an influential role on Malinovskii's part.

Pushkin's disaffection for the second Director Engel'gardt, on the other hand, is a well-established fact: the relation between the two men was punctuated by mutual incomprehension and a number of incidents[149]. The real reasons behind this antipathy on Pushkin's part still remain obscure[150]; it is legitimate, nevertheless, to suppose that it originated in Pushkin's preference for the figure and the ideals of his first Director. In this respect it is interesting to consider the opinion which A.E. Rozen was to express later. According to him, Malinovskii's death affected negatively Pushkin's poetic development, compromising his moral integrity:

---

others, gave a major contribution to the understanding of the Lycée as informed by the legendary «litseiskii dukh».

[147] In 1826 Pushkin wrote a 'Zapiska o narodnom vospitanii' (1826), commissioned by Nicholas I in order to test his political loyalty. In it he managed nevertheless to be fundamentally faithful to the educational ideals according to which he was brought up at Tsarskoe Selo. He expressed his preference for non-private education and criticized the militarization of the educational institutions.

[148] About him Pushkin wrote: «He created us, he cherished our ardour...», and frequently referred to his influence. See O.A. Iatsenko, '«Kunitsynu dan' serdtsa i vina...»', in Nekrasov (ed.), op. cit., pp. 45-56. An analysis of Kunitsyn's influence on Pushkins' views on law is provided in V. Val'denberg, 'Pushkin i Kunitsyn', Slavia, XIV, no. 3 (1937), pp. 321-328.

[149] The episode in which Engel'gardt discovered a caricature of him made by Pushkin immediately after an apparent «reconciliation» between them is frequently quoted in the literature about the Lycée, as well as the love letter sent by Pushkin to a young French widow living in Engel'gardt's house.

[150] Pushkin was probably annoyed by the restrictions exercised by the Director over his life at the Lycée. Engel'gardt had nevertheless a high opinion of Pushkin's talent and later even intervened in his favour, on the occasion of his prosecution in 1820.

> We are convinced that, had he taken the first intake through to graduation, the standard of those educated there would have been yet higher and more moral, and in particular Pushkin would have been more moral, and a more sensible, and above all more moral character would have shone forth in his poetry[151].

Echoes of Malinovskii's contribution to the intellectual development of Pushkin were not studied. In one significant, though limited field, his name was nevertheless associated with that of the poet: the ideas on peace.

Among the poet's manuscripts there is a short fragment written in French and devoted to perpetual peace[152]. After recording his considerations on this subject, Pushkin mentioned Saint-Pierre's peace project in Rousseau's version[153]. Some work has been devoted to the analysis of Pushkin's critique of war and his ideas on peace[154]. Particularly interesting in this respect is the study by M. Alekseev[155]. In his research on the European and Russian sources of Pushkin's considerations on peace, he attributed an important role to Malinovskii. He excluded that the *litseisty* could ignore the fact that their Director was the author of a treatise on peace and war, and explored the possibility that the young Pushkin was exposed in his early years to the ideas which he was to develop later. Alekseev particularly highlighted the influence of Malinovskii's negative judgment on the heroism and glory associated with war events, which was echoed by Pushkin in a passage of his fragment on perpetual peace. He also pointed out the fact that Pushkin's reflections on peace took place in Kishinev, where the echoes of Malinovskii's activity in his capacity of consul general of Moldavia and Wallachia were still alive. He did not exclude the possibility that Pushkin's reflections were made in connection

---

[151] Quoted by Tynianov, in 'Pushkin i Kiukhel'beker', *Literaturnoe nasledstvo*, p. 327.

[152] A.S. Pushkin, *Polnoe sobranie sochinenii* (Moskva-Leningrad, 1931), V, p. 411. B. Tomashevskii discovered the text and was the editor of the first publication of the fragment included in this edition.

[153] *Extrait du Projet de Paix Perpétuelle de Monsieur l'Abbé de Saint-Pierre* (1758-59).

[154] B.M. Eikhenbaum, 'Problema «vechnogo mira»', *Russkaia mysl'*, no. 8-9 (1914), pp. 116-119; B. Tomashevskii, 'Pushkin i vechnyi mir', *Zvezda*, no. 7 (1930), pp. 227-231.

[155] M.P. Alekseev, 'Pushkin i problema «Vechnogo mira»', in *Pushkin i sravnitel'no-istoricheskie issledovaniia* (Leningrad, 1972), pp. 160-207.

with the contemporary elaboration of the Decembrists' ideas on war and on the reform of the Russian army[156].

A further study of the echoes of the Director's thought in Pushkin's outlook, extended to a wider range of themes and based on consideration of the entire body of Malinovskii's works, will certainly shed light on the subject of the intellectual relation between two of the most interesting figures of the Russia of the time.

---

[156] See E.A. Prokof'ev, *Bor'ba dekabristov za peredovoe russkoe voennoe iskusstvo* (Moskva, 1953), and *Voennye vzgliady dekabristov* (Moskva, 1953). See also N.Ia. Eidel'man, *Pushkin i dekabristy* (Moskva, 1979).

CONCLUSIONS

The many-sided figure of Vasilii Malinovskii reflects to a significant degree the striving for universality typical of the eighteenth century. During the three decades in which he developed his activity, he consistently attempted to cover a number of crucial problems engaging conservative and progressive forces in Russia and Europe. In his work criticism of warfare and of imperialistic policies in Europe, attacks on absolutism and feudal institutions in Russia and pleas for the elimination of national, class, religious, and gender prejudices were significantly combined. His work fully deserves the attention of students of Russian cultural history, particularly when considered in the context of a period characterized by a relative scarcity of equally representative figures.

As information about the Russian thinker was gathered, a fact became quite apparent: in his intellectual life elements of continuity were more significant than turning points. His evolution never represented a significant change of views. Through different historical phases and personal vicissitudes, Malinovskii displayed a capacity to be faithful to the ideals of his youth, which were also those of the culture of the Enlightenment.

Moving from Moscow University to the College of Foreign Affairs, from London to Jassy and from St Petersburg to Tsarskoe Selo, his unflagging love for humanity and wish to be manifestly engaged on the just side of society never receded. In his dealings with Russian functionaries, Moldavian peasants or European theorists of war he had on various occasions to face incredulity, abuse of power, disregard and scorn towards his ideas. He continued to pursue them, never sceptical about the potentialities of the human mind for good and the resources of Russian society to reform itself.

His acute observation of distant cultures in his two travel accounts, 'Rossiianin v Anglii' and 'Zapiski o Moldavii', was particularly important for explaining the origins of his unusually wide political and social horizon. Malinovskii was never a casual or uninterested traveller. In his travels, always resulting from an explicit request by him to the Russian administration, he pursued an exploration of different cultural realities which contributed substantially to the formation of his own identity.

Analysis of Malinovskii's travel letters also provided an insight into an underexplored field: evaluation of the Russian thinker as a man of letters. The author of those lively and picturesque reports from Great Britain and Moldavia, as well as letters of a strictly private nature, never showed an interest in literature for its own sake, but only in its capacity to convey messages of political and social relevance. This notwithstanding, Malinovskii did not neglect the achievement of subtle and refined effects in his prose, facilitated by his unusual linguistic sensibility. Particularly in his travel accounts and in his only work of a purely fictional nature, the tale *Pustynnik*, he developed an interesting style, imbued with archaic echoes and singularly influenced by non-Russian sentence structures.

The study of Malinovskii's life also attempted to restore the picture of his considerable personality in its various aspects. Consideration of his character was generally restricted to the image of a weak, harmless figure, mainly established by the Lycée's historiography. From the reconstruction based on documents of a private nature there emerged the portrait of a man experiencing deep dissatisfactions and spiritual conflicts as well as profound passions engendering ambitious projects. Malinovskii's revolt against contemporary society resulted especially in the elaboration of his 'Ufa project'. As was argued, its failure determined the transferral of that dream to the ideal travel undertaken by the hero of his tale *Pustynnik* in contemporary Russia, and subsequently to the numerous ways to change existing society which Malinovskii pursued.

The exploration of the views of the peace thinker showed a nearness of the plan elaborated by the Russian to the European tradition on war and peace. His *Dissertation on Peace and War* (1803) did not share much with the diplomatic approach typical of the law of nations, mostly involved in lengthy discussions of cases of legitimacy of, and in, warfare. Being aimed at definitively abolishing war, and not at regulating it, the plan conceived by Malinovskii appeared as entirely belonging to the tradition of perpetual peace projects which had its origin in Emeric Crucé and its major exponents in William Penn, the Abbé de Saint-Pierre, Rousseau, Bentham and Kant. Within this tradition, Malinovskii elaborated some original insights which represent an important contribution to it: the idea of self-determination of peoples and his particular notion of the rights of peoples; the principle of electivity for the plenipotentiaries of the European General Union; the distinction of three separate levels in political organization (national, regional, European).

As was argued, the most interesting aspect of the proposal contained in the *Dissertation* remains nevertheless the idea fully to re-design the boundaries of Europe in order to re-create homogeneous regions based upon common language, ethnic and cultural origins. While the majority of perpetual peace projects, including those of Crucé, Penn and Saint-Pierre, had stressed that a peace treaty among European powers could be achieved only if all the parties involved would accept the *status quo* in terms of boundaries and territories, Malinovskii did not fear utopian ambitions, and imagined European monarchs voluntarily abandoning their sovereignity over parts of their territories. His design was made possible by the dramatic changes introduced by the Napoleonic wars in the geo-political map of Europe. Far from advocating a restoration of the situation previous to the French revolution, the Russian thinker believed that the general peace of Europe was to be found in a new equilibrium based on reason rather than on power, and secured by just laws.

The role of law in shaping and directing changes emerged also in Malinovskii's views on social reforms. At a certain point in his evolution, the thinker became aware of the necessity of reforming in particular one aspect of Russian society which was undermining the very basis of the expectations of welfare and happiness of his country: the status of servitude of the peasants. Unlike most of his contemporaries, he could very clearly discern the historical arguability of serfdom and its centrality in a project of social and administrative reform.

From an examination of the group of works, published and unpublished, devoted to the peasant question, Malinovskii's proposal to emancipate the Russian serfs and to assign to every citizen a tract of land emerged clearly. Thanks to this idea, which was undoubtedly radical and innovative for his times, the figure of Malinovskii as a social reformer acquires credibility and significance.

His high estimation of the human factor in rural economy distinguished his approach from that of contemporary literature on agriculture, and found an echo in his attacks against exploitation in a developing industrial economy which were mainly directed to advanced countries, and particularly to England. Abolition of serfdom was not his only concern of a social nature. His consideration of the repercussions on society of religious and ethnic conflicts led him to elaborate other projects informed by tolerance and an authentic Christian morality. Imbued with a philanthropic spirit and optimistic faith in the good will of human beings, Malinovskii's strategy as a social reformer did not exclude, however, the art of seizing political opportunities: his concrete proposals coincided with the brief period of ferment for institutional change allowed by Alexander I soon after his accession to the throne.

Unpublished or rare materials also provided the basis for a more correct reassessment of Malinovskii's ultimate effort at reform: his activity as the first Director of the Tsarskoe Selo Lycée. Its analysis was focused on the recognition of an explicit link between Malinovskii's intellectual stance and the establishment of a fruitful liberal atmosphere in the first Russian Lycée. The limited circulation of his works, including those containing his theoretical credentials as a pedagogue, had compromised a correct evaluation of his real role in the foundation and organization of that institution. While official nineteenth-century historiography of the Lycée tended to minimize his importance, the first Director did not substantially benefit from subsequent reconsiderations.

As we argued, he in fact modelled that unusually bright group of students in conformity with his lifelong principles: he propounded among them the primacy of reason and law in a well-ordered society, disseminated a sort of patriotism which was deeply imbued with civic virtues, and highlighted the inescapability of moral imperatives. The *litseisty* were actively encouraged to develop egalitarianism within their group and the perception of their special status in Russian society. Those young men embodied Malinovskii's hopes of a better future. Taking part in the failed revolt of 14 December 1825, some of them contributed to the history of Russia far beyond their first Director's most extreme expectations.

Substantially neglected during his lifetime, Malinovskii remained an unheard voice for long years. Recognition of the lasting value of his ideal of peace in a well-ordered society re-appeared however in contemporary Russia, in the country involved in the process of major and dramatic reforms inaugurated by *Perestroika*. Vasilii Fedorovich was the only thinker mentioned by Mikhail Sergeevich Gorbachev in his Nobel lecture in

Oslo, on 5 June 1991[1]. It is significant that the modernity of Malinovskii's call for peace as a premise for prosperity and justice and in the spirit of a genuine co-operation among different countries was highlighted by the figure most representative of reform in the Russia of our time.

Perspectives for future research. This work, which is the first extensive study on Malinovskii, does not pretend to exhaustiveness. Even without considering the possibility (entirely plausible) of discovering further writings belonging to the Russian thinker in the anonymous production of the eighteenth and early nineteenth centuries, the extant body of work is sufficiently rich to offer a number of elements for future research. One of these is the exploration of the abundant material of a religious nature left by Malinovskii, which includes translations, re-workings and original works. Not only his attention to Hebrew literature, but in general his incessant speculation on spiritual and religious matters, which represented a characteristic feature of the Russian Enlightenment, deserves to be thoroughly studied. To ascertain Malinovskii's religious sources and preferences would help to complete the picture of his ideological points of reference, and to define also in this field the extent of his original elaboration.

Another fascinating perspective, which went beyond the boundaries of the present book, is represented by the exploration of the influence possibly exerted by Malinovskii on one of the major Russian writers, Lev Tolstoi. Although the title of the great writer's novel, *War and Peace*, immediately invites one to suppose a deliberate reference to Malinovskii's treatise, the *Dissertation on Peace and War* does not figure among the sources for Tolstoi's masterpiece which are generally listed[2]. A few substantial facts suggest nevertheless a possible filiation of ideas: in Russian cultural history Tolstoi's pacifism is as unique as Malinovskii's project for a universal peace; in both authors the ideal of peace combines fundamentally with

---

[1] "Peace 'propagates wealth and justice, which constitute the prosperity of nations', a peace which is 'just a respite from wars is not worthy of the name', peace implies 'general counsel'. This is written almost 200 years ago by Vasili Fedorovich Malinovski - the Dean of the Tsarskoye Selo Lyceum in which the great Pushkin was educated" (*Soviet Weekly*, June 13, 1991, p. 8).

[2] Malinovskii's work is never mentioned among the sources indicated as those used by Tolstoi for his *War and Peace*. He certainly used the book of a former student of the Tsarskoe Selo Lycée, M. Korf's *Zhizn' grafa Speranskogo* (Spb., 1861), in particular for the portrayal of Speranskii (see V.B. Shklovskii, *Mater'ial i stil' v romane L'va Tolstova 'Voina i mir'* (Moskva, 1928), pp. 248-249, pp. 57-58). For Tolstoy's sources, see also B.M. Eikhenbaum, *Lev Tolstoi* (Leningrad, 1928).

recognition of the Christian teaching in its full meaning; the quest for social reforms aimed at achieving emancipation and civic rights indispensably completes the picture of a world at peace imagined by the two thinkers. Their philosophical approach to war was characterized by a number of common features, including the question of limitation of war by means of laws, the critique of the concept of the just war, and the arguments against the role of Great Men in history, which in both authors was particularly personified by one military leader: Napoleon.

Malinovskii's influence on Aleksandr Pushkin, on the other hand, was outlined in the present work with a particular reference to the transmission of the ideal of peace from the first Director to the most successful student of the Tsarskoe Selo Lycée. A more extensive analysis of the survival in Pushkin's work (and in the Decembrist movement) of themes and ideas disseminated by Malinovskii would certainly bring its surprises and shed a new and unexpected light on the poet's sources of inspiration.

Further investigation should also involve an important aspect of Malinovskii's intellectual biography which was given only an hypothetical importance in the present book: his membership of the Russian Freemasonry. Possibly acquiring more factual information (not available at the time when this study was completed), it would be useful to confirm all arguments suggesting such an hypothesis and consistently insert this element into the interpretation of his thought. Also the purely "bureaucratic" side of Malinovskii's life was somewhat neglected: a more detailed consideration of the official documents concerning his activity during the long years he spent at the College of Foreign Affairs would be illuminating for the comprehension of his figure as a state servant, and could explain the reasons for his deep dissatisfation.

Another area to which it was impossible to give adequate treatment in the present work and which could reveal itself as quite stimulating, is the specifically linguistic one. Throughout Malinovskii's work there is a corpus of recurring expressions which contribute quite essentially to delineating his thought. In some cases these expressions correspond to a deliberate effort to create new linguistic forms to identify new concepts; in other cases they are not original but their use is significant in connecting Malinovskii to specific ideological fields marked by their appearance. A study of Malinovskii's key-words would thus in an important way sustain and corroborate the analysis of his thought.

BIBLIOGRAPHY

1. Primary sources on V.F. Malinovskii

1.1. Archival sources:

Malinovskii's manuscripts and documents are held in

IRLI (Institut russkoi literatury), Fond 244, op. 25, nos. 4, 7, 8, 110, 119, 120, 290, 291, 301, 307-336, 350. Fond 312, op. 1, nos. 7, 8; op. 2, nos. 3. R. III, op. 2, nos. 2179, 2180, 2182-2184, 2185-2194.

RGIA (Russkii gosudarstvennyi istoricheskii arkhiv), Fond 796, op. 84, no. 633.

RGIA (Russkii gosudarstvennyi istoricheskii arkhiv) in St Petersburg, Fond 379, op. 1, no. 13939 (arkhiv no. 82).

RGALI (Russkii gosudarstvennyi arkhiv literatury i iskusstva), Fond 312, op. 1, nos. 3, 7; op. 2, nos. 3.

RGADA (Russkii gosudarstvennyi arkhiv drevnikh aktov), Fond 180, op. 1, nos. 57, 58, 60. Fond 188, op. 1, no. 216. Fond 1261, op. 2822. Fond 1261, op. 3, no. 723.

AVPR (Arkhiv vneshnei politiki rossii), Fond Kantseliariia, op. 7869, ff. 3-32.

TSDIAU (Tsentral'nii derzhavnii istorichnii arkhiv Ukraini), Fond 2039, op. 1, nos. 30-33, 54, 62, 63, 65, 68, 75, 77, 78, 83, 88, 103, 104, 2179; Fond 2053, op. 1, nos. 134, 190, 426, 540, 626, 808, 982.

1.2. Editions of Malinovskii's work:

'Rossiianin v Anglii', *Priiatnoe i poleznoe preprovozhdenie vremeni*, IX
    (1796), pp. 56-63, pp. 65-71, pp. 97-107; XI (1796), pp. 11-14, pp. 61-
    75, pp. 97-101, pp. 145-148, pp. 209-219, pp. 257-264, pp. 321-332,
    XII (1796), pp. 356-367, pp. 381-395, pp. 403-410.
'Zapiski o Moldavii', *Priiatnoe i poleznoe preprovozhdenie vremeni*, XIII
    (1797), pp. 417-425; XIV (1797), pp. 10-15, pp. 26-37.
Rassuzhdenie o mire i voine (Spb., 1803).
Osennie vechera (Spb., 1803).
*Otchet general-kaznacheia Aleksandra Gamil'tona, uchinennyi
    Amerikanskim shtatam 1791 g. o pol'ze manufaktur v otnoshenii onykh
    k torgovle i zemledeliiu* (Spb., 1807), translated and with a preface by
    Malinovskii.
'Obshchii mir', *Syn otechestva*, LI (1813), no. 10, pp. 235-244.
Sochineniia Derzhavina c ob"iasnitel'nymi primechaniami Ia. Grota, VI
    (Spb., 1871), p. 239 (publication of a letter of Malinovskii).
Semevskii, V., 'Razmyshlenie V.F. Malinovskogo o preobrazovanii
    gosudarstvennogo ustroistva Rossii', *Golos minuvshego*, no. 10 (1915),
    pp. 239-264 (publication of extracts from one of Malinovskii's diaries).
Izbrannye obshchestvenno-politicheskie sochineniia, ed. E.A. Arab-Ogly
    (Moskva, 1958).
Narochnitskii, A.L. (ed.), *Vneshniaia politika Rossii XIX i nachala XX veka.
    Dokumenty rossiiskogo Ministerstva inostrannykh del*, I, no. 1,
    (Moskva, 1960), pp. 144-145, p. 172, pp. 237-238 (publication of three
    letters of Malinovskii from Jassy).
Rassuzhdenie o mire i voine, Part I and II, in Andreeva, I.S., Gulyga, A.V.
    (eds.), *Traktaty o vechnom mire* (Moskva, 1963).
'Iz dnevnika', in Shchipanov, I.Ia. (ed.), *Russkie prosvetiteli ot Radishcheva
    do Dekabristov*, I (Moskva, 1966), pp. 249-270.
Jeu, B.(ed.), *Le pensée des Lumières en Russie* (Paris, 1973) (translation into
    French of Part I of *Rassuzhdenie o mire i voine* and other writings).
Rassuzhdenie o mire i voine, ed. J. Skowronek, in '"Rozwazania o pokoju i
    wojnie" Wasyla F. Malinowskiego', *Teki archiwalne*, no. 17 (1978),
    pp. 30-57 (publication of Part III).
Ragionamento sulla pace e sulla guerra, ed. P. Ferretti (Napoli, 1990)
    (translation into Italian of Part I, II, III of *Rassuzhdenie o mire i voine*
    and other writings).

2. Secondary sources on Malinovskii's work and activity:

Arab-Ogly, E.A., 'Vydaiushchiisia russkii prosvetitel'-demokrat'.(K 150-letiiu vykhoda v svet "Rassuzhdeniia o mire i voine"), *Voprosy filosofii*, no. 2 (1954), pp. 181-197.

Arab-Ogly, E.A., 'Vydaiushchiisia russkii prosvetitel'', in Malinovskii, V.F., *Izbrannye obshchestvenno-politicheskie sochineniia*, ed. E.A. Arab-Ogly (Moskva, 1958), pp. 3-38.

Besprozvannyi, V., 'Kto byl avtorom "Rossiianina v Anglii"?', *V chest' 70-letiiu professora Iu.M. Lotmana* (Tartu, 1992), pp. 49-56.

Bogach, G., *Alte pazhin' de istoriografie literare* (Kishinev, 1984), pp. 87-106.

Butler, W.E., 'Law and Peace in Prerevolutionary Russia: the Case of V.F. Malinovskii', in Witte, J., Alexander, F.S. (eds.), *The Weightier Matters of the Law* (Atlanta, 1988), pp.163-175.

Cross, A.G., *"By the Banks of the Thames": Russians in Eighteenth-Century Britain* (Newtonville, Mass.,1980), pp. 32-33.

Cross, A.G., 'Russian Perceptions of England and Russian National Awareness at the End of the Eighteenth and the Beginning of the Nineteenth Centuries', *The Slavonic and East European Review*, LXI (1983), pp. 89-106.

Cross, A.G., 'Whose Initials? Unidentified Persons in Karamzin's Letters from England', *Study Group on Eighteenth-Century Russia Newsletter*, no. 6 (1978), pp. 26-36.

Cross, A.G., *'Anglofiliia u trona'. Britantsy i russkie v vek Ekateriny II. Katalog vystavki* (London, 1992), p. 102.

Chubar'ian, A.O., *Evropeiskaia ideia v istorii. Problemy voiny i mira* (Moskva, 1987).

Dolgova, S.R., 'O pervom direktore Tsarskosel'skogo litseia', *Sovetskie arkhivy*, no. 6 (1974), pp. 100-106.

Dolgova, S.R., 'Aleksei Fedorovich Malinovskii', in A.F. Malinovskii, *Obozrenie Moskvy*, ed. S.R. Dolgova (Moskva, 1992), pp. 202-203.

Dostian, I. S., '"Evropeiskaia utopiia" V. F. Malinovskogo', *Voprosy istorii*, no. 6 (1979), pp. 32-46.

Dostian, I.S., 'Dunaiskie kniazhestva v russkoi publitsistike kontsa XVIII i nachala XIX veka', *Revue Roumaine d'Histoire*, XX, no. 1 (1981), p. 33.

Ferretti, P., Archibugi, D., *Vasilij Malinovskij. Un pensatore russo tra la Rivoluzione Francese e la Restaurazione*, in V.F. Malinovskij, *Ragionamento sulla pace e sulla guerra*, (Napoli, 1990), pp. 11-33.

Ferretti, P., 'V.F. Malinovskii and his "Rassuzhdenie o mire i voine"', *Study Group on Eighteenth-Century Russia. Newsletter*, no. 21 (1993), pp. 7-9.

Ferretti, P., 'A "Rossijanin v Anglii" in 1789-1791: V.F. Malinovskij', *Russica Romana*, no. 2 (1995), pp. 83-109.

Ferretti, P., 'L'ultima povest' del Settecento russo: "Pustynnik", di Vasilij Malinovskij, *Europa Orientalis*, no.1 (1996), pp. 165-179.

Ferretti, P., '"Razdelenie zemel'": A Proposal against the Servile System by V.F. Malinovskii', in M. di Salvo, L. Hughes (eds.), *A Window on Russia: Papers from the V International Conference of the Study Group on Eighteenth-Century Russia. Gargnano 1994* (Rome, 1996), pp. 107-113.

Grosul, G., 'Rol' V.F. Malinovskogo v razvitii druzhestvennykh russko-moldavskikh politicheskikh sviazei', *Materialy nauchnoi konferentsii profes.-prepod. sostava KGU, posviashchennoi 300-letiiu D. Kantemira* (Kishinev, 1974).

Kachenovskii, D.I., 'Dissertation on War and Peace by Basil Mahnofsky (*sic*), St. Petersburgh, 1803', *The Herald of Peace* (1 June 1858), pp. 71-72.

Kamenskii, Z.A., *Filosofskie idei russkogo Prosveshcheniia* (Moskva, 1971), pp. 63-66.

Kobeko, D., *Imperatorskii tsarskosel'skii litsei. Nastavniki i pitomtsy. 1811-1843* (Spb., 1911).

Kobeko, D., 'Pervyi direktor tsarskosel'skogo litseia', *Zhurnal Ministerstva narodnogo prosveshcheniia*, no. 7 (1915), pp. 3-17.

Koshanskii, N.F., 'Izvestie o zhizni Malinovskogo', *Syn otechestva*, XVIII (1814) no. 13, pp. 220-223.

Lotman, Iu.M., *Sotvorenie Karamzina* (Moskva, 1987), pp. 190-192.

Maksimov, A.G., '"Osennie vechera" 1803 g. Ezhenedel'noe izdanie V.F. Malinovskogo', *Literaturnyi vestnik*, V (1903), pp. 445-450.

Meilakh, B., *Pushkin i ego epokha* (Moskva, 1958), pp. 29-42.

Meshkova-Malinovskaia, N.B., *O novoi rabote V.F. Malinovskogo* (Moskva, unpublished).

Meshkova-Malinovskaia, N.B., *O pervom direktore Litseia V.F. Malinovskom* (Moskva, unpublished).

Mikhailova, L.B., 'Neproiznesennaia rech' direktora litseia', *Vechernii Leningrad*, no. 68 (1989), p. 3.

Mikhailova, L.B., Lebedeva, E.S., 'V nachale zhizni pomniu ia', in S.M. Nekrasov (ed.), *'...I v prosveshchenii stat' s vekom naravne'*. Sbornik nauchnykh trudov (Spb., 1992), pp. 35-45.

Rubets, A.A., *'Nastavnikam, khranivshim iunost' nashu'. Pamiatnaia knizhka chinov imperatorskogo Aleksandrovskogo, byvshego tsarskosel'skogo, litseia. S 1811 po 1911 god* (Spb., 1911), pp. 194-204.

Rudenskaia, M., 'Vasilii Fedorovich Malinovskii', *Kodry*, no. 10 (1970), pp.143-149.

Rudenskaia, M., Rudenskaia, S., *'Nastavnikam...za blago vozdadim'* (Leningrad, 1986), pp. 42-52.

Schippan, M., 'Die Französische Revolution von 1789 und Friedenvorstellungen in Russland bis 1825', *Zeitschrift für Slawistik*, no. 34 (1989), pp. 353-361.

Seleznev, I. Ia., *Istoricheskii ocherk Imperatorskogo byvshego Tsarskosel'skogo, nyne Aleksandrovskogo Litseia za pervoe ego piatidesiatiletie, s 1811 po 1861 god* (Spb., 1861).

Skowronek, J., 'Memorial Wasilija Fiodorowicza Malinowskiego o narodowym samokresleniu, jako podstawie niezawislego bytu politicznego narodow, pod tytulem 'Rozwazania o pokoju i wojnie', czesc III Jassy 1801-S.Peterburg 1803', in Adam Jerzy Czartoryski, *Pamietniki i memorialy polityczne 1776-1809*, ed. J. Skowronek (Warszawa, 1986), pp. 567-597.

Skowronek, J., '"Rozwazania o pokoju i wojnie" Wasyla F. Malinowskiego', *Teki archiwalne*, no. 17 (1978), pp. 23-30.

Vianu, A., 'Iluministul rus V.F. Malinovski in principatele Dunarene', *Studii. Revista de istorie*, no. 2 (1960), pp.165-181.

3. Malinovskii's work and his epoch

Berkov, P.N., *Istoriia russkoi zhurnalistiki XVIII veka* (Moskva-Leningrad, 1952).

Cross, A.G., 'Karamzin's First Short Story?', in L.H. Legters (ed.), *Russia. Essays in History and Literature* (Leiden, 1972).

Cross, A.G., 'N.M. Karamzin's "Messenger of Europe" (*Vestnik Evropy*), 1802-3', *Forum for Modern Language Studies*, V, no.1 (1969), pp. 1-25.

Cross, A.G., *N.M. Karamzin. A Study of his Literary Career. 1783-1803* (London and Amsterdam, 1971).

Cross, A.G., *Anglo-Russica. Aspects of Cultural Relations between Great Britain and Russia in the Eighteenth and Early Nineteenth Centuries* (Oxford/Providence 1993).

Gruzdev, A., *Zhanrovoe novatorstvo russkoi literatury kontsa XVIII-XIX vv.* (Leningrad, 1974).

Hartley, J.M., *Alexander I* (London and New York, 1994).

Juttner, S., Schlobach, J. (eds.), *Europäische Aufklärung(en). Einheit und nationale Vielfalt* (Hamburg, 1992).

Kamenskii, A.B., *Pod seniiu Ekateriny - Vtoraia polovina XVIII veka* (Spb., 1992).

Komarov, A.I., 'Zhurnalistika i kritika 1800-1810-kh godov', in *Ocherki po istorii russkoi zhurnalistiki i kritiki*, I (Leningrad, 1950), pp. 155-176.

Kubacheva, B.N., '"Vostochnaia" povest' v russkoi literature XVIII - nachala XIX veka', *XVIII vek*, V (1962), pp. 295-315.

Lang, D.M., 'Some Forerunners of the Decembrists', *Cambridge Journal*, I, no. 10 (1948), pp. 623-634.

Lentin, A., 'Shcherbatov, Constitutionalism and the 'Despotism' of Sweden's Gustav III', in R. Bartlett, A. Cross, K. Rasmussen (eds.), *Russia and the World of the Eighteenth Century* (Columbus, Ohio,1988), pp. 36-57.

Lentin, A., 'Shcherbatov, Inoculation and Dr Dimsdale', *Study Group on Eighteenth-Century Russia Newsletter*, no. 17 (1989), pp. 8-11.

Levin, Iu.D., 'Angliiskaia prosvetitel'skaia zhurnalistika v russkoi literature XVIII veka', in Alekseev, M.P. (ed.), *Epokha prosveshcheniia. Iz istorii mezhdunarodnykh sviazei russkoi literatury* (Leningrad, 1967), pp. 3-79.

Lisovskii, N.M., *Bibliografiia russkoi periodicheskoi pechati 1703-1900 gg. Materialy dlia istorii russkoi zhurnalistiki* (Spb., 1895-1913).

Lotman, Iu.M., 'Politicheskoe myshlenie Radishcheva i Karamzina i opyt frantsuzskoi revoliutsii', in Fridlender, G.M. (ed.), *Velikaia frantsuzskaia revoliutsiia i russkaia literatura* (Leningrad, 1990), pp. 55-68.

Lotman, Iu.M., 'Puti razvitiia russkoi prosvetitel'skoi prozy XVIII veka', in *Problemy russkogo prosveshcheniia v literature XVIII veka* (Moskva-Leningrad, 1961), pp. 79-106.

Makogonenko, G.P. (ed.), *A.N. Radishchev i literatura ego vremeni, XVIII vek*, XII (1977).

Makogonenko, G.P., *Nikolai Novikov i russkoe prosveshchenie XVIII veka* (Moskva-Leningrad, 1952).

Makogonenko, G.P., *Radishchev i ego vremia* (Moskva, 1956).

Omel'chenko, O.A., *'Zakonnaia monarkhiia' Ekateriny II: Prosveshchennyi absoliutizm v Rossii* (Moskva, 1993).

Orlov, V.N., *Russkie prosvetiteli 1790-1800-kh godov* (Moskva, 1956).

Raeff, M., 'Filling the Gap between Radishchev and the Decembrists', *Slavic Review*, XXVI, no. 3 (1967), pp. 395-413.

Shchipanov, I.Ia. (ed.), *Izbrannye proizvedeniia russkikh myslitelei vtoroi poloviny XVIII veka*, I (Moskva, 1952).

Shchipanov, I.Ia. (ed.), *Russkie prosvetiteli ot Radishcheva do Dekabristov* (Moskva, 1966).

Shchipanov, I.Ia., *Filosofiia russkogo prosveshcheniia* (Moskva, 1971).

Shtrange, M.M., *Russkoe obshchestvo i frantsuzskaia revoliutsiia 1789-1794* (Moskva, 1956).

Sipovskii, V.V., *N.M. Karamzin, avtor 'Pisem russkogo puteshestvennika'* (Spb., 1899).

Sivkov, K.V., *Puteshestviia russkikh liudei za granitsu v XVIII veke* (Spb., 1914).

Skowronek, J., *Antynapoleonskie koncepcje Czartoryskiego* (Warszawa, 1969).

Sobolev, V., *Periodicheskaia pechat' v Rossii v nachale XIX veka i zhurnalistika dekabristov* (Moskva, 1952).

Stennik, Iu.V., 'Tema Velikoi frantsuzskoi revoliutsii v konservativnoi literature i publitsistike 1790-kh godov', in Fridlender, G.M. (ed.), *Velikaia frantsuzskaia revoliutsiia i russkaia literatura* (Leningrad, 1990), pp. 69-90.

Tartakovskii, A.G., *Russkaia memuaristika XVIII-pervoi poloviny XIX v. Ot rukopisi k knige* (Moskva, 1991).

Tatarina, L., *Istoriia russkoi literatury i zhurnalistiki XVIII v.* (Moskva, 1979).

Utkina, N.F., Nichik, V.M., Shkurinov, P.S., *Russkaia mysl' v vek Prosveshcheniia* (Moskva, 1991).

Walicki, A., *A History of Russian Thought: From the Enlightenment to Marxism* (Stanford, 1979).

Zhivov, V.M., *Kul'turnye konflikty v istorii russkogo literaturnogo iazyka XVIII - nachala XIX veka* (Moskva, 1990).

Chapter 2: The Peace Thinker

a) War and peace in the Russian tradition

Benson, S., 'The Role of Western Political Thought in Petrine Russia', *Canadian-American Slavic Studies*, VIII, 2 (1974), pp. 254-274.

Butler, W., 'P. P. Shafirov and the Law of Nations', in P.P. Shafirov, *A Discourse Concerning the Just War between Sweden and Russia: 1700-1721*, ed. W. Butler (Dobbs Ferry, 1973).

Butler, W., *Russian Law: Historical and Political Perspectives* (Leyden, 1977).

Bychkov, A.F. (ed.), 'Vokrug Ochakova. 1788 (Dnevnik ochevidtsa)', *Russkaia starina*, IX, no. 84 (1895), pp. 147-212.

Chubar'ian, A.O., *Evropeiskaia ideia v istorii. Problemy voiny i mira* (Moskva, 1987).

Eleonskaia, A.S., '"Obed dushevnyi" i "Vecheria dushevnaia" Simeona Polotskogo v istoriko-literaturnom protsesse', in Robinson, A. (ed.), *Razvitie barokko i zarozhdenie klassitsisma v Rossii. XVII- nachala XVIII v.* (Moskva, 1989), pp. 170-188.

Gleason, W., 'Pufendorf and Wolff in the Literature of Catherinian Russia', *Germano-Slavica*, II, no. 6 (1978), pp. 427-437.

Gordon, L.S., 'Ange Goudars "Projet de pacification générale" und sein russischer Übersetzer', in L.S. Gordon, *Studien zur plebejisch-demokratischen Tradition in der französischen Aufklärung* (Berlin, 1972), pp. 207-210.

Grabar, V.E., 'Pervaia russkaia kniga po mezhdunarodnomu pravu ("Rassuzhdenie" P.P. Shafirova)', *Vestnik Moskovskogo universiteta*, no. 7 (1950) pp.101-110.

Grabar, V.E., *Materialy k istorii literatury mezhdunarodnogo prava v Rossii (1647-1917)*, Moskva, 1958. (Translated in Grabar, V.E., *The History of International Law in Russia, 1647-1917*, ed. W. Butler (Oxford, 1990).

Gratsianskii, P.S., *Desnitskii* (Moskva, 1978).

Gratsianskii, P.S., *Politicheskaia i pravovaia mysl' Rossii vtoroi poloviny XVIII veka* (Moskva, 1984).

Jones, R.E., 'The Nobility and Russian Foreign Policy 1560-1811', *Cahiers du Monde russe et soviétique*, XXXIV, 1-2 (1993), pp. 159-170.

Kogan, Iu.Ia., *Ocherki po istorii russkoi ateisticheskoi mysli XVIII* (Moskva, 1962).

Kogan, Iu.Ia., *Prosvetitel' XVIII veka Ia. P. Kozel'skii* (Moskva, 1958).

Kozhevnikov, F.I. *Uchebnoe posobie po mezhdunarodnomu publichnomu pravu* (Moskva, 1947), p. 18.

Kozhevnikov, F.I., *Russkoe gosudarstvo i mezhdunarodnoe pravo* (Moskva, 1947).

Kozhevnikov, F.I., *Uchebnoe posobie po mezhdunarodnomu publichnomu pravu* (Moskva, 1947).

Kuz'min, A.I., 'Batal'naia obraznost' u G.R. Derzhavina', in Markov, D. (ed.), *Stranitsy istorii russkoi literatury* (Moskva, 1971), pp. 223-233.

Kuz'min, A.I., 'Literatura i voina v petrovskuiu epokhu', in Kuz'min, A. I., *Geroicheskaia tema v russkoi literature* (Moskva, 1974), pp. 48-103.

Kuz'min, A.I., 'R.M. Tsebrikov - literator XVIII veka', in *Problemy teorii i istorii literatury* (Moskva, 1971), pp. 106-111.

Kuz'min, A.I., 'Russkaia deistvitel'nost' v khudozhestvennoi literature epokhi prosveshcheniia', in Kuz'min, A. I., *Geroicheskaia tema v russkoi literature* (Moskva, 1974), pp. 104-138.

Kuz'min, A.I., 'Voennaia tema v literature petrovskogo vremeni', *XVIII vek*, IX (1974), pp.168-183.

Lodyzhenskii, A., *Proekty vechnogo mira i ikh znachenie* (Moskva, 1880).

Paparigopulo, S.V., 'Progressivnye russkie mysliteli XVIII veka o mire i voine', *Voprosy filosofii*, no. 2 (1960), pp. 132-142.

Pavlov-Sil'vanskii, N., 'Proekty reform v zapiskakh sovremennikov Petra Velikogo', *Zapiski istoriko-filologicheskogo fakul'teta Imperatorskogo S-Peterburgskogo universiteta*, no. 42 (1897).

Pokrovskii, S.A., *Politicheskie i pravovye vzgliady S. E. Desnitskogo* (Moskva, 1955).

Pushkarev, L.N., 'Problema voiny i mira v tvorchestve pridvornykh obshchestvenno-politicheskikh deiatelei Rossii. Vtoraia polovina XVII v.', in Pushkarev, L.N., *Obshchestvenno-politicheskaia mysl' Rossii. Vtoraia polovina XVII veka* (Moskva, 1982), pp. 202-218.

Schippan, M., 'Die Französische Revolution von 1789 und Friedenvorstellungen in Russland bis 1825', *Zeitschrift für Slawistik*, no. 34 (1989), pp. 353-361.

b) The European models:

Archibugi, D., 'Models of international organization in perpetual peace projects', *Review of International Studies*, XVIII (1992), no. 4, pp. 295-317.

Archibugi, D. 'Immanuel Kant, peace, and cosmopolitan law', *European Journal of International Relations*, no. 4 (1995), pp. 429-456.

Archibugi, D., Voltaggio, F. (eds.), *Filosofi per la pace* (Roma, 1991).

Dietze A., W.(eds.), *Ewiger Friede? Dokumente einer deutschen Diskussion um 1800* (Leipzig, Weimar, 1989).

Eliav-Feldon, M., 'Grand Designs. The Peace Plans of the Late Renaissance', *Vivarium*, XXVII (1989), no. 1, pp. 51-76.

Gallie, W.B., *Philosophers of Peace and War. Kant, Clausewitz, Marx, Engels and Tolstoi* (Cambridge, 1978).

Hemleben, S.J., *Plans for World Peace through Six Centuries* (Chicago, 1942).

Hinsley, F.H., *Powers and the Pursuit of Peace. Theory and Practice in the History of Relations between States* (Cambridge, 1963).

Kende, I., 'The History of Peace: Concept and Organizations from the Late Middle Ages to the 1870s', *Journal of Peace Research*, XXVI, no. 3 (1988), pp. 233-247.

Lange, C., Schou A., *Histoire de l'Internationalisme*, 3 vols. (Kristiana and Oslo, 1919, 1944, 1954).

Puharré, A., *Les Projets d'organization européenne d'après le Grand Dessin de Henri IV et de Sully* (Paris, 1954).

Raumer von K. (ed.), *Ewiger Friede. Friedensrufe und Friedenspläne seit der Renaissance* (Freiburg, 1953).

ter Meulen, J., *Der Gedanke der Internationalen Organisation in seiner Entwicklung*, 3 vols. (The Hague, 1921, 1929, 1940).

ter Meulen, J., *From Erasmus to Tolstoy. The Peace Literature of Four Centuries*, ed. P. van den Dungen (New York, Westport, London, 1990).

Chapter 3: The Social Reformer

Babkin, D.S., 'Russkaia potaennaia sotsial'naia utopiia XVIII veka', *Russkaia literatura*, no. 4 (1968), pp. 92-106.

Bartlett, R., 'Russia's First Abolitionist: The Political Philosophy of J.G. Eisen', *Jahrbücher für Geschichte Osteuropas*, no. 39 (1991).

Bartlett, R., 'The Question of Serfdom: Catherine II, the Russian Debate and the View from the Baltic Periphery (J.G. Eisen and G.H. Merkel)', in

R. Bartlett, J. M. Hartley (eds.), *Russia in the Age of the Enlightenment* (Basingstoke, 1990), pp.142-166.

Breuillard, J., 'Fragments d'utopies dans la littérature russe du XVIIIe siècle. Levsin et Xeraskov', *Revue des études slaves*, LVI, f. 1 (1984), pp. 17-32.

Chechulin, N.D., *Russkii sotsial'nyi roman XVIII veka* (Spb., 1900).

Chistov, K.V., *Russkie narodnye sotsial'no-utopicheskie legendy XVII-XIX vv.* (Moskva, 1967).

Klibanov, A.I., *Narodnaia sotsial'naia utopiia v Rossii. Period feodalizma* (Moskva, 1977).

Klier, J.D., *Russia Gathers Her Jews. The Origins of the 'Jewish Question' in Russia, 1772-1825* (Dekalb, Illinois, 1986).

Kolchin, P., 'In Defence of Servitude: American Proslavery and Russian Proserfdom Arguments, 1760-1860', *American Historical Review*, LXXXV (1980), pp. 809-827.

Mironenko, S.V., *Samoderzhavie i reformy. Politicheskaia bor'ba v Rossii v nachale XIX v.* (Moskva, 1989).

Nicolai G.M., *Russia bifronte. Da Pietro I a Caterina II attraverso la Corruzione dei costumi in Russia di Scerbatov e il Viaggio da Pietroburgo a Mosca di Radiscev* (Roma, 1990).

Pushkarev, L.N., *Obshchestvenno-politicheskaia mysl' Rossii. Vtoraia polovina XVII v. Ocherki istorii* (Moskva, 1982).

Rossi Varese, M. (ed.), *Utopisti russi del primo Ottocento* (Napoli, 1982).

Safonov, M.M., *Problema reform v pravitel'stvennoi politike Rossii na rubezhe XVIII i XIX vv.* (Leningrad, 1988).

Semevskii, V.I., *Krest'ianskii vopros v Rossii v XVIII i pervoi polovine XIX veka* (Spb., 1888).

Serman, I., 'Istoriia i utopiia v russkoi obshchestvennoi mysli i literature XVIII veka', *Slavica Hierosolymitana*, V-VI (1981), pp. 81-98.

Sviatlovskii, V.V., *Russkii utopicheskii roman* (Petrograd, 1922).

Venturi, F., *Il populismo russo* (Torino, 1952).

Chapter 4: The Pedagogue

Abramovich, S.L., 'Krest'ianskii vopros v stat'e Pushkina "Puteshestvie iz Moskvy v Peterburg"', *Pushkin. Issledovaniia i materialy,* IV (1962), pp. 208-236.

Alekseev, M.P, Meilakh, B.S.(eds.), *Dekabristy i ikh vremia. Materialy i soobshcheniia* (Moskva-Leningrad, 1951).

Alekseev, M.P., 'Pushkin i problema "Vechnogo mira"', in *Pushkin i sravnitel'no-istoricheskie issledovaniia* (Leningrad, 1972), pp. 160-207.

Annenkov, P.V., *Materialy dlia biografii A.S. Pushkina* (Moskva, 1984).

Black, J.L., *Citizens for the Fatherland. Education, Educators, and Pedagogical Ideals in Eighteenth-Century Russia* (New York, 1979).

Brower, D.R., *Training the Nihilists. Education and Radicalism in Tsarist Russia* (Ithaca-London, 1975).

Demkov, M.I., *Istoriia russkoi pedagogiki,* I-II (Revel', Spb., 1895,1898).

Drews, P., 'Puskin als politischer Dichter', *Zeitschrift für slawische Philologie,* no. 43 (1983), pp. 38-54.

Eidel'man, N.Ia., *Pushkin i dekabristy* (Moskva, 1979).

Eidel'man, N.Ia., *Tvoi vosemnadtsatyi vek. Prekrasen nash soiuz...* (Moskva, 1991).

Eikhenbaum, B.M., 'Problema "vechnogo mira"', *Russkaia mysl',* no. 8-9 (1914), pp. 116-119.

Flynn, J.T., *The University Reform of Tsar Alexander I. 1802-1835* (Washington, D.C.,1988).

Fridlender, G.M., 'Vol'nost' i zakon (Pushkin i Velikaia frantsuzskaia revoliutsiia)', in Fridlender, G.M. (ed.), *Velikaia frantsuzskaia revoliutsiia i russkaia literatura* (Leningrad, 1990).

Gaevskii, V., 'Pushkin v Litsee i litseiskie ego stikhotvoreniia', *Sovremennik,* no. 8 (1863).

Gastfreind, N., *Tovarishchi Pushkina po Imperatorskomu Tsarskosel'skomu litseiu. Materialy dlia slovaria litseistov pervogo kursa 1811-1817 godov, I-III* (Spb., 1912-1913).

Gorodetskii, B.M., '"Puteshestvie iz Moskvy v Peterburg" A.S. Pushkina', *Pushkin. Issledovaniia i materialy,* III (1960), pp. 218-267.

Grot, Ia.K., *Pushkin, ego litseiskie tovarishchi i nastavniki* (Spb., 1899).

Grot, K.Ia., *Pushkinskii Litsei (1811-1817). Bumagi pervogo kursa, sobrannye akademikom Ia.K. Grotom* (Spb., 1911).

Iakhontov, A.N., *Istoricheskii ocherk Imperatorskogo aleksandrovskogo (b. Tsarskosel'skogo) litseia* (Paris, 1936).

Jones, W.G., 'Russia's First Magazine for Children: Novikov's "Detskoe Chtenie dlia Serdtsa i Razuma" (1785-89)', in R. Bartlett, A. Cross, K. Rasmussen (eds.), *Russia and the World of the Eighteenth Century* (Columbus, Ohio,1988), pp. 177-187.

Jones, W.G., 'The "Morning Light" Charity Schools, 1777-80', *The Slavonic and East European Review,* LVI, 1 (1978), pp. 47-67.

Kapterev, P.F., *Istoriia russkoi pedagogiki* (Petrograd, 1915).

Korf, M.A., *Zizn' grafa Speranskogo* (Spb., 1861).

Kuz'min, A.I., 'A.S. Pushkin: istoricheskaia pravda i poeticheskii vymysel', in Kuz'min, A.I., *Geroicheskaia tema v russkoi literature* (Moskva, 1974).

Lentin, A., 'Prince M.M. Shcherbatov as a Champion of Scientific Education', *Irish Slavonic Studies,* no. 11 (1990), pp. 73-78.

Madariaga, I.de, 'The Foundation of the Russian Educational System by Catherine II', *Slavonic and East European Review,* XXXVI (1979), pp. 369-395.

Masal'skii, K.S. (ed.), *Druzheskie pis'ma grafa M.M. Speranskogo k P.G. Masal'skomu* (Spb., 1862).

Mazour, A.G., *The First Russian Revolution, 1825* (Stanford, California, 1961).

McArthur, G.H., 'Freemasonry and Enlightenment in Russia: the Views of N.I. Novikov', *Canadian-American Slavic Studies*, XIV, 3 (1980), pp.361-375.

McClelland, J.C., *Autocrats and Academicians* (Chicago and London, 1979).

Meilakh, B.S., 'Kharakteristiki vospitannikov litseia v zapisiakh E.A. Engel'gardta', in N. V. Izmailov (ed.), *Pushkin. Issledovaniia i materialy*, III (1960), pp. 347-361.

Meilakh, B.S., 'Litseiskie lektsii', *Krasnyi arkhiv*, no. 1 (1937), pp. 75-206.

Meilakh, B.S., 'Pushkin i ego epokha', *Zvezda*, nn. 1-2-3 (1949).

Meilakh, B.S., *Pushkin i ego epokha* (Moskva, 1958).

Mikhailova, L.B., 'Vospominaniia litseistov', *Mir cheloveka*, no. 1 (1994), pp. 65-89.

Men'e, A., 'Russkii vosemnadtsatyi vek i formirovanie Pushkina', *XVIII vek*, VII (1966), pp. 339-344.

Nechkina, M.V., *Dvizhenie dekabristov* (Moskva, 1955), I, pp. 91-107.

Novikov, N.I., *Izbrannye pedagogicheskie sochineniia*, ed. N.A. Trushin (Moscow, 1959).

Okenfuss, M.J., 'Popular Educational Tracts in Enlightenment Russia: A Preliminary Survey', *Canadian-American Slavic Studies*, XIV, 3 (1980), pp. 307-326.

Petrunina, N. (ed.), 'Iz materialov pushkinskogo litseia', *Pushkin. Issledovaniia i materialy*, XIII (1989), pp. 306-345.

Pushchin, I.I., *Zapiski o Pushkine. Pis'ma*, ed. S.Ia. Shtraikh (Moskva, 1956). 2 edition: M.P. Mironenko, S.V. Mironenko (eds.) (Moskva, 1988).

Raeff, M., *The Decembrist Movement* (Englewood Cliffs, N.J., 1966).

Ransel, D.L., 'Ivan Betskoi and the Insitutionalization of the Enlightenment in Russia', *Canadian-American Slavic Studies*, XIV, 3 (1980), pp.327-338.

Rozhdenstvenskii, S.V., *Istoricheskii obzor deiatel'nosti Ministerstva narodnogo prosveshcheniia. 1802-1902* (Spb., 1902).

Rudenskaia, M., Rudenskaia, S., *'Nastavnikam ... za blago vozdadim'*(Leningrad, 1986).

Rudenskaia, S.D., *Oni uchilis' s Pushkinym* (Leningrad, 1976).

Rudenskaia, S.D., *S litseiskogo poroga* (Leningrad, 1984).

Semevskii, V.I., *Politicheskie i obshchestvennye idei dekabristov* (Spb., 1909).

Shabaeva, M.F.(ed.), *Ocherki istorii shkoly i pedagogicheskoi mysli narodov SSSR: XVIII v. - pervaia polovina XIX v.* (Moskva, 1973).

Sinel, A.A., 'The Socialization of the Russian Bureaucratic Elite, 1811-1917: Life at Tsarskoe Selo Lyceum and the School of Jurisprudence', *Russian History*, III, 1 (1976), pp. 1-32.

Tomashevskii, B., 'Pushkin i vechnyi mir', *Zvezda*, no. 7 (1930), pp. 227-231.

Tynianov, Iu., 'Pushkin i Kiukhel'beker', *Literaturnoe nasledstvo*, no. 16-18 (1934), pp. 320-378.

Tynianov, Iu., *Pushkin* (Moskva, 1937).

Voronov, A.S., *Istoriko-statisticheskoe obozrenie uchebnykh zavedenii S.Peterburgskogo uchebnogo okruga s 1715 po 1828 g. vkliuchitel'no* (Spb., 1849).

Vyrubov, G.N., *Zapiska ob ustroistve imperatorskogo Aleksandrovskogo litseia i programmakh prepodovaniia v nem* (Spb., 1901).

Walker, F.A., 'Popular Response to Public Education in the Reign of Alexander I (1801-1825)', *History of Education Quarterly* (Winter, 1984), pp. 527-543.

INDEX

ARCHIVES INTERNATIONALES D'HISTOIRE DES IDÉES
*
INTERNATIONAL ARCHIVES OF THE HISTORY OF IDEAS

43. P. Dibon: *Inventaire de la correspondance (1595-1650) d'André Rivet (1572-1651)*. 1971 ISBN 90-247-5112-8
44. K.A. Kottman: *Law and Apocalypse*. The Moral Thought of Luis de Leon (1527?-1591). 1972 ISBN 90-247-1183-5
45. F.G. Nauen: *Revolution, Idealism and Human Freedom*. Schelling, Hölderlin and Hegel, and the Crisis of Early German Idealism. 1971 ISBN 90-247-5117-9
46. H. Jensen: *Motivation and the Moral Sense in Francis Hutcheson's* [1694-1746] *Ethical Theory*. 1971 ISBN 90-247-1187-8
47. A. Rosenberg: *[Simon] Tyssot de Patot and His Work (1655–1738)*. 1972
ISBN 90-247-1199-1
48. C. Walton: *De la recherche du bien*. A study of [Nicolas de] Malebranche's [1638-1715] Science of Ethics. 1972
ISBN 90-247-1205-X
49. P.J.S. Whitmore (ed.): *A 17th-Century Exposure of Superstition*. Select Text of Claude Pithoys (1587-1676). 1972 ISBN 90-247-1298-X
50. A. Sauvy: *Livres saisis à Paris entre 1678 et 1701*. D'après une étude préliminaire de Motoko Ninomiya. 1972 ISBN 90-247-1347-1
51. W.R. Redmond: *Bibliography of the Philosophy in the Iberian Colonies of America*. 1972 ISBN 90-247-1190-8
52. C.B. Schmitt: *Cicero Scepticus*. A Study of the Influence of the *Academica* in the Renaissance. 1972 ISBN 90-247-1299-8
53. J. Hoyles: *The Edges of Augustanism*. The Aesthetics of Spirituality in Thomas Ken, John Byrom and William Law. 1972 ISBN 90-247-1317-X
54. J. Bruggeman and A.J. van de Ven (éds.): *Inventaire* des pièces d'Archives françaises se rapportant à l'Abbaye de Port-Royal des Champs et son cercle et à la Résistance contre la Bulle *Unigenitus* et à l'Appel. 1972 ISBN 90-247-5122-5
55. J.W. Montgomery: *Cross and Crucible*. Johann Valentin Andreae (1586–1654), Phoenix of the Theologians. Volume I: Andreae's Life, World-View, and Relations with Rosicrucianism and Alchemy; Volume II: The *Chymische Hochzeit* with Notes and Commentary. 1973 Set ISBN 90-247-5054-7
56. O. Lutaud: *Des révolutions d'Angleterre à la Révolution française*. Le tyrannicide & *Killing No Murder* (Cromwell, *Athalie*, Bonaparte). 1973 ISBN 90-247-1509-1
57. F. Duchesneau: *L'Empirisme de Locke*. 1973 ISBN 90-247-1349-8
58. R. Simon (éd.): *Henry de Boulainviller* - Œuvres Philosophiques, Tome I. 1973
ISBN 90-247-1332-3
For Œvres Philosophiques, Tome II *see below under Volume 70*.
59. E.E. Harris: *Salvation from Despair*. A Reappraisal of Spinoza's Philosophy. 1973
ISBN 90-247-5158-6
60. J.-F. Battail: *L'Avocat philosophe Géraud de Cordemoy (1626-1684)*. 1973
ISBN 90-247-1542-3
61. T. Liu: *Discord in Zion*. The Puritan Divines and the Puritan Revolution (1640-1660). 1973 ISBN 90-247-5156-X
62. A. Strugnell: *Diderot's Politics*. A Study of the Evolution of Diderot's Political Thought after the *Encyclopédie*. 1973 ISBN 90-247-1540-7

ARCHIVES INTERNATIONALES D'HISTOIRE DES IDÉES
*
INTERNATIONAL ARCHIVES OF THE HISTORY OF IDEAS

63. G. Defaux: *Pantagruel et les Sophistes*. Contribution à l'histoire de l'humanisme chrétien au 16e siècle. 1973   ISBN 90-247-1566-0
64. G. Planty-Bonjour: *Hegel et la pensée philosophique en Russie (1830-1917)*. 1974   ISBN 90-247-1576-8
65. R.J. Brook: *[George] Berkeley's Philosophy of Science*. 1973   ISBN 90-247-1555-5
66. T.E. Jessop: *A Bibliography of George Berkeley*. With: *Inventory of Berkeley's Manuscript Remains* by A.A. Luce. 2nd revised and enlarged ed. 1973   ISBN 90-247-1577-6
67. E.I. Perry: *From Theology to History*. French Religious Controversy and the Revocation of the Edict of Nantes. 1973   ISBN 90-247-1578-4
68. P. Dibbon, H. Bots et E. Bots-Estourgie: *Inventaire de la correspondance (1631–1671) de Johannes Fredericus Gronovius* [1611–1671]. 1974   ISBN 90-247-1600-4
69. A.B. Collins: *The Secular is Sacred*. Platonism and Thomism in Marsilio Ficino's *Platonic Theology*. 1974   ISBN 90-247-1588-1
70. R. Simon (éd.): *Henry de Boulainviller*. Œuvres Philosophiques, Tome II. 1975   ISBN 90-247-1633-0
   For Œvres Philosophiques, Tome I *see under Volume 58.*
71. J.A.G. Tans et H. Schmitz du Moulin: *Pasquier Quesnel devant la Congrégation de l'Index*. Correspondance avec Francesco Barberini et mémoires sur la mise à l'Index de son édition des Œuvres de Saint Léon, publiés avec introduction et annotations. 1974   ISBN 90-247-1661-6
72. J.W. Carven: *Napoleon and the Lazarists (1804–1809)*. 1974   ISBN 90-247-1667-5
73. G. Symcox: *The Crisis of French Sea Power (1688–1697)*. From the *Guerre d'Escadre* to the *Guerre de Course*. 1974   ISBN 90-247-1645-4
74. R. MacGillivray: *Restoration Historians and the English Civil War*. 1974   ISBN 90-247-1678-0
75. A. Soman (ed.): *The Massacre of St. Bartholomew*. Reappraisals and Documents. 1974   ISBN 90-247-1652-7
76. R.E. Wanner: *Claude Fleury (1640-1723) as an Educational Historiographer and Thinker*. With an Introduction by W.W. Brickman. 1975   ISBN 90-247-1684-5
77. R.T. Carroll: *The Common-Sense Philosophy of Religion of Bishop Edward Stillingfleet (1635-1699)*. 1975   ISBN 90-247-1647-0
78. J. Macary: *Masque et lumières au 18e [siècle]*. André-François Deslandes, Citoyen et philosophe (1689-1757). 1975   ISBN 90-247-1698-5
79. S.M. Mason: *Montesquieu's Idea of Justice*. 1975   ISBN 90-247-1670-5
80. D.J.H. van Elden: *Esprits fins et esprits géométriques dans les portraits de Saint-Simon*. Contributions à l'étude du vocabulaire et du style. 1975   ISBN 90-247-1726-4
81. I. Primer (ed.): *Mandeville Studies*. New Explorations in the Art and Thought of Dr Bernard Mandeville (1670-1733). 1975   ISBN 90-247-1686-1
82. C.G. Noreña: *Studies in Spanish Renaissance Thought*. 1975   ISBN 90-247-1727-2
83. G. Wilson: *A Medievalist in the 18th Century*. Le Grand d'Aussy and the Fabliaux ou Contes. 1975   ISBN 90-247-1782-5
84. J.-R. Armogathe: *Theologia Cartesiana*. L'explication physique de l'Eucharistie chez Descartes et Dom Robert Desgabets. 1977   ISBN 90-247-1869-4

ARCHIVES INTERNATIONALES D'HISTOIRE DES IDÉES
*
INTERNATIONAL ARCHIVES OF THE HISTORY OF IDEAS

85. Bérault Stuart, Seigneur d'Aubigny: *Traité sur l'art de la guerre*. Introduction et édition par Élie de Comminges. 1976   ISBN 90-247-1871-6
86. S.L. Kaplan: *Bread, Politics and Political Economy in the Reign of Louis XV*. 2 vols., 1976   Set ISBN 90-247-1873-2
87. M. Lienhard (ed.): *The Origins and Characteristics of Anabaptism / Les débuts et les caractéristiques de l'Anabaptisme*. With an Extensive Bibliography / Avec une bibliographie détaillée. 1977   ISBN 90-247-1896-1
88. R. Descartes: *Règles utiles et claires pour la direction de l'esprit en la recherche de la vérité*. Traduction selon le lexique cartésien, et annotation conceptuelle par J.-L. Marion. Avec des notes mathématiques de P. Costabel. 1977   ISBN 90-247-1907-0
89. K. Hardesty: *The 'Supplément' to the 'Encyclopédie'*. [Diderot et d'Alembert]. 1977   ISBN 90-247-1965-8
90. H.B. White: *Antiquity Forgot*. Essays on Shakespeare, [Francis] Bacon, and Rembrandt. 1978   ISBN 90-247-1971-2
91. P.B.M. Blaas: *Continuity and Anachronism*. Parliamentary and Constitutional Development in Whig Historiography and in the Anti-Whig Reaction between 1890 and 1930. 1978   ISBN 90-247-2063-X
92. S.L. Kaplan (ed.): *La Bagarre*. Ferdinando Galiani's (1728-1787) 'Lost' Parody. With an Introduction by the Editor. 1979   ISBN 90-247-2125-3
93. E. McNiven Hine: *A Critical Study of [Étienne Bonnot de] Condillac's* [1714-1780] *'Traité des Systèmes'*. 1979   ISBN 90-247-2120-2
94. M.R.G. Spiller: *Concerning Natural Experimental Philosphy*. Meric Casaubon [1599-1671] and the Royal Society. 1980   ISBN 90-247-2414-7
95. F. Duchesneau: *La physiologie des Lumières*. Empirisme, modèles et théories. 1982   ISBN 90-247-2500-3
96. M. Heyd: *Between Orthodoxy and the Enlightenment*. Jean-Robert Chouet [1642-1731] and the Introduction of Cartesian Science in the Academy of Geneva. 1982   ISBN 90-247-2508-9
97. James O'Higgins: *Yves de Vallone* [1666/7-1705]: *The Making of an Esprit Fort*. 1982   ISBN 90-247-2520-8
98. M.L. Kuntz: *Guillaume Postel* [1510-1581]. Prophet of the Restitution of All Things. His Life and Thought. 1981   ISBN 90-247-2523-2
99. A. Rosenberg: *Nicolas Gueudeville and His Work (1652-172?)*. 1982   ISBN 90-247-2533-X
100. S.L. Jaki: *Uneasy Genius: The Life and Work of Pierre Duhem* [1861-1916]. 1984   ISBN 90-247-2897-5; Pb (1987) 90-247-3532-7
101. Anne Conway [1631-1679]: *The Principles of the Most Ancient Modern Philosophy*. Edited and with an Introduction by P. Loptson. 1982   ISBN 90-247-2671-9
102. E.C. Patterson: *[Mrs.] Mary [Fairfax Greig] Sommerville* [1780-1872] *and the Cultivation of Science (1815-1840)*. 1983   ISBN 90-247-2823-1
103. C.J. Berry: *Hume, Hegel and Human Nature*. 1982   ISBN 90-247-2682-4
104. C.J. Betts: *Early Deism in France*. From the so-called 'déistes' of Lyon (1564) to Voltaire's 'Lettres philosophiques' (1734). 1984   ISBN 90-247-2923-8

ARCHIVES INTERNATIONALES D'HISTOIRE DES IDÉES
*
INTERNATIONAL ARCHIVES OF THE HISTORY OF IDEAS

105. R. Gascoigne: *Religion, Rationality and Community.* Sacred and Secular in the Thought of Hegel and His Critics. 1985   ISBN 90-247-2992-0

106. S. Tweyman: *Scepticism and Belief in Hume's 'Dialogues Concerning Natural Religion'.* 1986   ISBN 90-247-3090-2

107. G. Cerny: *Theology, Politics and Letters at the Crossroads of European Civilization.* Jacques Basnage [1653-1723] and the Baylean Huguenot Refugees in the Dutch Republic. 1987   ISBN 90-247-3150-X

108. Spinoza's *Algebraic Calculation of the Rainbow* & *Calculation of Changes.* Edited and Translated from Dutch, with an Introduction, Explanatory Notes and an Appendix by M.J. Petry. 1985   ISBN 90-247-3149-6

109. R.G. McRae: *Philosophy and the Absolute.* The Modes of Hegel's Speculation. 1985   ISBN 90-247-3151-8

110. J.D. North and J.J. Roche (eds.): *The Light of Nature.* Essays in the History and Philosophy of Science presented to A.C. Crombie. 1985   ISBN 90-247-3165-8

111. C. Walton and P.J. Johnson (eds.): *[Thomas] Hobbes's 'Science of Natural Justice'.* 1987   ISBN 90-247-3226-3

112. B.W. Head: *Ideology and Social Science.* Destutt de Tracy and French Liberalism. 1985   ISBN 90-247-3228-X

113. A.Th. Peperzak: *Philosophy and Politics.* A Commentary on the Preface to Hegel's *Philosophy of Right.* 1987   ISBN Hb 90-247-3337-5; Pb ISBN 90-247-3338-3

114. S. Pines and Y. Yovel (eds.): *Maimonides* [1135-1204] *and Philosophy.* Papers Presented at the 6th Jerusalem Philosophical Encounter (May 1985). 1986   ISBN 90-247-3439-8

115. T.J. Saxby: *The Quest for the New Jerusalem, Jean de Labadie* [1610-1674] *and the Labadists (1610-1744).* 1987   ISBN 90-247-3485-1

116. C.E. Harline: *Pamphlets, Printing, and Political Culture in the Early Dutch Republic.* 1987   ISBN 90-247-3511-4

117. R.A. Watson and J.E. Force (eds.): *The Sceptical Mode in Modern Philosophy.* Essays in Honor of Richard H. Popkin. 1988   ISBN 90-247-3584-X

118. R.T. Bienvenu and M. Feingold (eds.): *In the Presence of the Past.* Essays in Honor of Frank Manuel. 1991   ISBN 0-7923-1008-X

119. J. van den Berg and E.G.E. van der Wall (eds.): *Jewish-Christian Relations in the 17th Century.* Studies and Documents. 1988   ISBN 90-247-3617-X

120. N. Waszek: *The Scottish Enlightenment and Hegel's Account of 'Civil Society'.* 1988   ISBN 90-247-3596-3

121. J. Walker (ed.): *Thought and Faith in the Philosophy of Hegel.* 1991   ISBN 0-7923-1234-1

122. Henry More [1614-1687]: *The Immortality of the Soul.* Edited with Introduction and Notes by A. Jacob. 1987   ISBN 90-247-3512-2

123. P.B. Scheurer and G. Debrock (eds.): *Newton's Scientific and Philosophical Legacy.* 1988   ISBN 90-247-3723-0

124. D.R. Kelley and R.H. Popkin (eds.): *The Shapes of Knowledge from the Renaissance to the Enlightenment.* 1991   ISBN 0-7923-1259-7

ARCHIVES INTERNATIONALES D'HISTOIRE DES IDÉES
*
INTERNATIONAL ARCHIVES OF THE HISTORY OF IDEAS

ARCHIVES INTERNATIONALES D'HISTOIRE DES IDÉES
*
INTERNATIONAL ARCHIVES OF THE HISTORY OF IDEAS

146. M. de Baar, M. Löwensteyn, M. Monteiro and A.A. Sneller (eds.): *Choosing the Better Part. Anna Maria van Schurman (1607–1678)*. 1995   ISBN 0-7923-3799-9

147. M. Degenaar: *Molyneux's Problem*. Three Centuries of Discussion on the Perception of Forms. 1996   ISBN 0-7923-3934-7

148. S. Berti, F. Charles-Daubert and R.H. Popkin (eds.): *Heterodoxy, Spinozism, and Free Thought in Early-Eighteenth-Century Europe*. Studies on the *Traité des trois imposteurs*. 1996   ISBN 0-7923-4192-9

149. G.K. Browning (ed.): *Hegel's* Phenomenology of Spirit: *A Reappraisal*. 1997
    ISBN 0-7923-4480-4

150. G.A.J. Rogers, J.M. Vienne and Y.C. Zarka (eds.): *The Cambridge Platonists in Philosophical Context*. Politics, Metaphysics and Religion. 1997 ISBN 0-7923-4530-4

151. R.L. Williams: *The Letters of Dominique Chaix, Botanist-Curé*. 1997
    ISBN 0-7923-4615-7

152. R.H. Popkin, E. de Olaso and G. Tonelli (eds.): *Scepticism in the Enlightenment*. 1997
    ISBN 0-7923-4643-2

153. L. de la Forge. Translated and edited by D.M. Clarke: *Treatise on the Human Mind (1664)*. 1997   ISBN 0-7923-4778-1

154. S.P. Foster: *Melancholy Duty*. The Hume-Gibbon Attack on Christianity. 1997
    ISBN 0-7923-4785-4

155. P. Ferretti: *A Russian Advocate of Peace: Vasilii Malinovskii (1765–1814)*. 1998
    ISBN 0-7923-4848-6

KLUWER ACADEMIC PUBLISHERS – DORDRECHT / BOSTON / LONDON